## ONE YEAR DEVOTIONAL

*Bread for the Journey*

## SELWYN HUGHES

**Further Study Trevor J Partridge**

# Foreword

This is now the fifth edition in the *Every Day with Jesus One Year Devotional* series.

A strong conviction of mine is that the devotional life cannot adequately and properly be developed on isolated portions of spiritual truth read each day. It must be a developed whole. Hence the delineation of a continuous theme over a period of two months. Our research has shown that dealing with a theme over one month is too short and three months too long. For the majority of readers it seems two months is just right.

Another strong conviction of mine is that the devotional life cannot be developed unless the mind is developed. "That which does not hold the mind", says one writer, "will soon not hold the emotion and the will". I agree. Ever since I began writing devotional material close on 40 years ago I have tried not only to fire the spirit but also to instruct the mind.

Maintaining that balance has not been easy but it has always been my goal. Our mental understanding of spiritual things and our devotional life must grow together. What we assimilate with our mind must get down to the shrine of our devotional life and give it purpose and direction.

The six themes in this edition have once again been selected from the long running *Every Day with Jesus* bi-monthly series – now in its thirty-seventh year. Readers responded that the editions entitled *The Pursuit of Excellence* and *The Wondrous Cross* were a great source of blessing and encouragement. Moreover, the exposition of 1 Corinthians 13, *The More Excellent Way*, was another theme that brought positive responses from readers around the world.

My prayer once again is that the six themes presented in this fifth edition will help feed and sustain your soul as you continue on life's journey.

*Selwyn Hughes*

# How to use the Bible

A question I am often asked, especially by young Christians, is this: why do I need to read the Bible?

We need to read the Bible in order to know not only God's mind for the future but how to develop a daily walk with Him. God uses His Word to change people's lives and bring those lives into a deeper relationship with Himself and a greater conformity to His will. For over five decades now I have spent hours every week reading and studying the Scriptures. God has used this book to transform my life and to give me a sense of security in a shifting and insecure world.

How do we read the Bible? Do we just start at Genesis and make our way through to the book of Revelation? There are many ways to go about reading the Scriptures; let me mention the three most popular approaches.

One is to follow a reading plan such as is included in the *Every Day with Jesus Devotional Bible* or *Through the Bible in One Year*. The great advantage of following a reading plan is that your reading is arranged for you; in a sense you are being supervised. You are not left to the vagaries of uncertainty: what shall I read today, where shall I begin, at what point shall I end?

A second approach is to thread your way through the Scriptures by following a specific theme. It is quite staggering how many themes can be found in Scripture and what great spiritual rewards can be had by acquainting yourself with them. When I started writing *Every Day with Jesus* in 1965 I decided to follow the thematic approach and I wondered how long I would be able to keep it up. Now, over thirty-six years later, I am still writing and expounding on different themes of the Bible, and the truth is that I have more biblical themes and subjects than it is possible to deal with in one lifetime!

A third approach is by reading through a book of the Bible. This enables you to get into the mind of the writer and understand his message. Every book of the Bible has something unique and special to convey and, as with any book, this can only be understood when you read it from start to finish.

# How to use the Bible

It is important to remember that all reading of the Bible ought to be preceded by prayer. This puts you in a spiritually receptive frame of mind to receive what God has to say to you through His Word. The Bible can be read by anyone but it can only be understood by those whose hearts are in tune with God – those who have come into a personal relationship with Him and who maintain that relationship through daily or regular prayer. This is how the Bible puts it: "The man without the Spirit does not accept the things that come from the Spirit of God, for they are foolishness to him, and he cannot understand them, because they are spiritually discerned" (1 Cor. 2:14).

Praying before you open your Bible should not be a mere formality. It is not the *act* that will make the Bible come alive but the *attitude*. Prayer enables us to approach the Scriptures with a humble mind. The scientist who does not sit down before the facts of the universe with an open mind, is not prepared to give up every preconceived idea and is not willing to follow wherever nature will lead him, will discover little or nothing. It is the same with the reading of the Scriptures; we must come to it with a humble and receptive mind or we too will get nowhere. Prayer enables us to have the attitude that says, "Speak, for your servant is listening" (1 Sam. 3:10).

If we are to grow in the Christian life then we must do more than just *read* the Bible – we must *study* it. This means that we must give time to poring over it, considering it, thinking about what it is saying to us and assimilating into our hearts and minds its doctrines and its ideas.

I have already pointed out that one of the ways of reading the Bible is by taking a theme and tracing it through the various books of the Bible. The pleasure this brings can be greatly enhanced by using this as a regular means of Bible study. When we study the Bible with the aid of concordances, lexicons and so on, we feed our minds, but when we study the Bible devotionally, we apply the Word of God to our hearts. Both exercises are necessary if we are to be completely rounded people but we must see that it is at the place of the devotional that we open up our hearts and expose ourselves to God's resources.

Let me encourage you also to take advantage of a reading plan as a further basis of study. Following this will enable you to cover the whole of the Bible in a set period. Those who have used this method tell of the most amazing spiritual benefits. One person who had read through the whole of the Bible in a year said to me, "It demanded more discipline than I thought I was capable of, but the rewards have been enormous." When I asked her what these rewards were, she said, "I used to have a partial view of God's purposes because I dipped into my Bible just here and there as it suited me. Now, however, I feel as if I have been looking over God's shoulder as He laid out the universe, and I feel so secure in the knowledge that He found a place for me in that marvellous plan." There can be no doubt that reading through the entire Bible in a set period enables one to gain a perspective that has tremendous positive spiritual consequences.

The third form of study – reading through a book of the Bible at a time – has the advantage of helping you understand the unity and diversity of the Bible. It is quite incredible how so many writers sharing their thoughts at different times of history combine to say similar things and give a consistent emphasis. Reading and pondering on this gives you such an appreciation of the wisdom of God in putting together this marvellous volume that it fires your soul and quickly brings praise and adoration to your lips.

I have found the best way to study a book of the Bible is to read it through once for a sense of the whole, and then to read it again, making a note of anything that strikes me, such as a principle to be applied, an insight to be stored away in my heart, or a thought to be shared with someone who is struggling.

One thing is sure, time spent with the Bible is not wasted. The more one loves God the more one will love the Bible. And the more one loves the Bible the more one will love God. Always remember this unique volume – God's one and only published work – yields its treasures only to those who read it, study it and obey it.

*Selwyn Hughes*

# The More Excellent Way

# When we make Christ a stranger

*"But the greatest of these is love." (v.13)*
**For reading & meditation – 1 Corinthians 13:1–13**

We begin today an exposition of one of the most marvellous passages to be found anywhere in the Scriptures – 1 Corinthians 13. All my life I have longed to write on this particular section of Paul's writings, but until now I have never felt ready or adequate to do it. From time to time, I have commented in *Every Day with Jesus* on various phrases from this sublime passage, but I have never before attempted a full exposition. Recently, the Spirit seemed to nudge me and say as He did to the apostle John in the Revelation: "Now write what you see" (1:19, RSV).

We begin with the thought that perhaps at no time in history has it been more important to focus our attention on this pregnant passage than now, for today's Church, generally speaking, is becoming more preoccupied with power than it is with love. It is eager for miracles and manifestations, often with wrong motives. Not that a longing to see God work in mighty power is wrong; it becomes wrong when the desire for power overtakes the desire for love.

David Wilkerson, author of *The Cross and the Switchblade*, makes this solemn observation: "I say to you, it is possible to gather Spirit-filled people in one place, praising and lifting up their hands, and still have Christ walking among them as a stranger. We make Christ a stranger when we give the Holy Spirit pre-eminence over Him." Let's make it our prayer on this very first day of our meditations together that the greatest of all our spiritual pursuits will be the pursuit of love.

**FURTHER STUDY**

Psa. 146;
Deut. 7:8;
Jer. 31:3

1. What motivates God?
2. What is the quality of God's love?

## Prayer

O God, can it be that our longing for miracles and manifestations of power has become stronger than our longing for love? If it has, then forgive us, we pray. Help us to re-establish our priorities and make love our greatest aim. Amen.

# The supremacy of love

*"Eagerly pursue … this love – make it your aim,*
*your great quest …" (v.1, Amp. Bible)*

**For reading & meditation – 1 Corinthians 14:1–15**

If some sections of today's Church are in danger of putting power before love, ought we to withdraw from seeking after spiritual gifts and concentrate only on love? The answer is "No". Some have interpreted 1 Corinthians 13 as Paul's attempt to turn the attention of the Corinthian converts away from the exercise of spiritual gifts to focus exclusively on love. But Paul is not saying that love should be our *exclusive* focus; he is saying (so I believe) that love should be our *initial* focus.

Reference to 1 Corinthians 13 shows what Paul is really saying. He is not suggesting that the Corinthian converts should abandon the exercise of spiritual gifts, but rather that they should bring them under the control of love. In fact, he ends the twelfth chapter with: "But earnestly desire and zealously cultivate the greatest and best – the higher gifts and the choicest graces. And yet I will show you a still more excellent way – one that is better by far and the highest of them all, love" (12:31, Amp. Bible).

When I encourage you to make love your aim, don't hear me deriding spiritual gifts. I value them and I am glad of them. I am simply seeking to do here, in the midst of a power-conscious church age, what Paul did in the midst of the power-conscious Corinthians – hold aloft the supremacy of love. The real power chapter in 1 Corinthians is not 1 Corinthians 12 or even 1 Corinthians 14 – it is the love chapter in 1 Corinthians 13. For all else fades and fails. Love alone abides and holds the field.

**FURTHER STUDY**

Eph. Ch. 3; 4:16;
Gal. 5:6

1. What was Paul's desire for the Ephesians?
2. How is our faith to work?

## Prayer

O Father, help me grasp the point that whatever else comes and goes – love remains. Give me this persisting love so that all my values may be held intact – preserved by love. For I live in vain if I do not love. Amen.

# Love – vital as well as verbal

*"My command is this: Love each other
as I have loved you." (v.12)*

**For reading & meditation – John 15:1–17**

We know from our reading of the New Testament (especially the text before us today) that love was central to the life of our Lord Jesus Christ, and He insisted that love must be central to our own lives also. Was this emphasis lost as the Early Church developed? Decidedly not. Every one of the New Testament writers lays down this emphasis, particularly the apostles Peter and John. But nowhere is the emphasis on love more clearly seen than in the writings of the great apostle Paul.

Prior to his conversion, however, love was not Paul's strongest point. In his own way he loved God and professed allegiance to Him but, at the same time, he was ready to kill those who turned from the Jewish observances to trust instead the atoning sacrifice of Christ. Then came the amazing change. On the Damascus Road he was conquered by the love of Christ – conquered in outlook, in thought, in act, in character. As Henry Drummond points out: "The observing student of Scripture can detect a beautiful tenderness growing and ripening all through Paul's character as he gets older, but it ought not to be forgotten that the hand that wrote 'the greatest of these is love', when we meet it first, was stained with blood."

Paul was not only converted to love but became one of the greatest exhibitors of it. How could he have written so eloquently of love in 1 Corinthians 13 had it not gripped and mastered his life? Like his Master, he lived by love. And it was not just verbal – it was vital.

**FURTHER STUDY**

Acts 9:1–31;
26:1–23;
2 Cor. 5:14

1. How did Paul describe love's motivating power?
2. Can you echo Paul's testimony?

## Prayer

O Father, I am so grateful that Your Spirit, working through Paul, enabled him to hold aloft the torch of love. Help us, as Your Church in the twenty-first century, to make it our highest emphasis also. Amen.

# Depravity in the dictionary

*"This is how we know what love is: Jesus Christ laid down his life for us." (v.16)*

**For reading & meditation – 1 John 3:11–24**

Today we look at the word "love". What particular word is Paul using and what does it mean? No doubt many of you are aware that in the Greek language, there are several words for love; unfortunately, in English, we have just one. The English word "love" has a medley of meanings, ranging from the highest to the lowest. A dictionary definition of love runs like this: "A feeling of deep regard, fondness, devotion or deep affection, usually accompanied by a yearning or desire for a person of the opposite sex."

This definition reflects very much the ideas of contemporary society and as such, it is sub-Christian. Someone has said: "If you want to see the depravity of man, look in the dictionary, for words associated with man soon become depraved by that association." We can see that in the way the word "gay" has been eased out of everyday conversation, for nowadays it invariably means just one thing – a homosexual relationship. Freud defined love as sex love, or, to be fair, as almost entirely sex love. Adultery these days is described by some as "making love".

**FURTHER STUDY**

Deut. 10:12–22;
6:5;
Psa. 31:23

1. Write out your own definition of Christian love.
2. What does the Lord require of us?

How desperately our language needs to be redeemed. We will not be able to understand what Paul is talking about when he uses the word "love", nor dedicate ourselves to pursuing it, until we know the precise Greek word he is using and the meaning that lies behind that word. For if we go wrong as to the meaning of love, we will go wrong all down the line. Our first step will determine our last.

## Prayer

Father, I see that I cannot look to the world for the real meaning of love, for the world's thinking has been depraved. I would turn from the smog that overhangs our civilisation to breathe the fresh air of the Spirit. Teach me its true meaning. In Jesus' Name. Amen.

# Agape – the highest form of love

*"…God has poured out his love into our hearts …"* (v.5)

**For reading & meditation – Romans 5:1–11**

We said yesterday that if we are to understand the meaning of the word "love" as used by Paul in 1 Corinthians 13, then we must look further than a dictionary, which will not reflect the views of heaven.

Although, in English, we have just the one word "love", the original language of the New Testament has several words. There is *Eros* – the powerful sexual attraction between people of opposite sexes. Then there is *Philia* – the love displayed in the intimate bond that develops between parents and children, brothers and sisters, friends, business partners and so on. The most powerful word for love and the one used consistently by Paul in 1 Corinthians is *Agape*, which refers to divine love – unconditional, undeserved and unquenchable.

The Greeks of Paul's day tended to use the word "Eros" to express the idea of love for God and man, but the Christians adopted the word "Agape". The meaning that the Christians put into the word, however, did not reflect its Greek source. They adopted the word because it was the most suitable one, but they added to it a distinctly Christian emphasis. As Anders Nygren, a Greek scholar, puts it: "Eros is a man's way to God; Agape is God's way to man. Eros seeks to gain its life, a life divine, immortalised; Agape lives the life of God, therefore dares to lose it." Christians put into the word the idea of a love that arises, not on earth but in heaven – a spontaneous love, eager, rushing, overflowing. How beautiful. To be exposed to it is to be transformed by it.

---

**FURTHER STUDY**

Col. 3:1–14; 1:7–8;
1 Tim. 6:11

1. What did Paul exhort the Colossians to do?
2. What was Paul's word to Timothy?

---

## Prayer

O Father, help me not to come under any dominance other than the dominance of Your love. Show me how I can absorb more of Your love, so that more of Your love absorbs me. Amen.

<table>
<tr><td>

**Day**

**6**
</td><td>

# The difference of two words
</td></tr>
</table>

*"And this is my prayer: that your love may abound more and more ..." (v.9)*

**For reading & meditation – Philippians 1:1–11**

Nygren said that "in ancient times two men commented about God: Plato said, 'God is Eros'; John the apostle said, 'God is Agape'. Just the difference of two words, and yet there was a difference of two worlds." Two worlds of different meaning went into those two words. And this difference runs straight through all our ethics and all our religions. It divides them decisively.

All systems range themselves unconsciously on one side or the other, according as they embody Eros or Agape. Eros love will love for what it can get out of it. It turns everything – even God – into a means to an end. With Eros love, we love people for what they give us in return. If there is no return, then love dies. We love others because we see in them something that brings satisfaction to us – their beauty, their physical attractiveness, their sensuality. They meet a need in us, therefore we would like to acquire them. We can love God in this way too – by making Him serve our ends. It looks and sounds religious, but it is pure egocentricity.

*The cults are rooted in Eros.* They would not admit to it, of course, but the attitude underlying them is: "If I serve God, repeat certain slogans and obey certain rules, I will have peace of mind and inner serenity." Everything they do comes back to them. The centre of their universe is "me". They do not love God for Himself, they love Him for what they can get out of Him. There is a better way – "a more excellent way" – Agape love.

**FURTHER STUDY**

1 John 4:1–16;
3:16;
Eph. 5:1–2

*1. How does John define love?*
*2. How does he define God?*

## Prayer

O God, help me lay hold on this truth before I go deeper and show me how to organise my life, not around myself but around You. Take my Eros love and convert it into Your Agape. In Jesus' Name I pray. Amen.

# Is the Church sub-Christian?

*"… May you be rooted deep in love and founded securely on love." (v.17, Amp. Bible)*

**For reading & meditation – Ephesians 3:14–21**

Eros love is acquisitive – it loves in order to experience pleasurable feelings. With Eros love, if there is no return, then love soon dies or fades. How much of the love that we see in our churches, I ask myself, is Eros love and how much of it is Agape? If we expect to get something out of loving God, then that is Eros.

If we go to church, pray, tithe and attend to our Christian duties in order to put God under an obligation to us – to shield us from harm, ward off sickness, provide us with plenty of material goods – then that is Eros. In a conference of young people where the speaker gave a talk on the difference between Eros and Agape love, he asked the audience to raise their hands to indicate which of the two loves controlled and dominated their lives. Two-thirds said "Eros". He complimented them on their honesty and then asked them what they intended to do about it. At once several hundred young people dropped to their knees and began to pray. The speaker said: "I have never known a prayer meeting start so spontaneously and end up so powerfully, for many of those young people came through to a thrilling new understanding of Agape love."

I ask again: how much of our modern-day church life is built around Eros rather than Agape? Two-thirds? Perhaps one of the greatest dangers we face as the people of God is not that we have become anti-Christian but that we will become sub-Christian – disciples who are content to live on a lesser love.

**FURTHER STUDY**

John 15:1–13; 13:1; Rev. 1:5–6

1. What was the quality of Christ's love?
2. How did He demonstrate it?

## Prayer

O Father, forgive us that we pervert the Agape love You pour into us and make it into something else – something in our own image. Again we ask: take our Eros love and change it to Your Agape. In Jesus' Name. Amen.

# The judgment of love

*"By this all men will know that you are my disciples, if you love one another." (v.35)*

**For reading & meditation – John 13:31–38**

Now we begin our examination of Agape love verse by verse in 1 Corinthians 13. The chapter divides easily into three parts: love is contrasted (vv.1–3); analysed (vv.4–7); and defended (vv.8–13).

Paul begins by contrasting love with the things that people thought much of in those days – learning, religion and power. These three things were symbolised in the three nations and people that dominated the world at that time – the Greeks, the Hebrews and the Romans. The Greeks were the emphasisers of the power of speech and oratory; the Hebrews were the emphasisers of prophetic wisdom; the Romans the emphasisers of conquest and power. Paul stepped into the midst of them and said: "If I can speak in the tongues of men and even of angels [the Greeks], but have not love, I am only a noisy gong or a clanging cymbal. And if I have prophetic powers – that is, the gift of interpreting the divine will and purpose [the Hebrews] … and if I have sufficient faith so that I can remove mountains [the Romans], but have not love [God's love in me] I am nothing – a useless nobody" (Amp. Bible, vv.1,2).

**FURTHER STUDY**

Rom. 8:28–39;
Gal. 2:20;
Eph. 5:2

1. What was Paul's persuasion?
2. What was his conviction?

Can you see what he is saying? He is making the point that though we can speak with eloquence, interpret divine mysteries and wield tremendous power, but have not love, then we say nothing, know nothing and accomplish nothing. In all the annals of history, has ever a more devastating judgment fallen upon the systems of learning, religion and power than this? But it is, I hasten to add, a judgment that love is entitled to make.

## Prayer

Father, make the point even clearer to me as I go about my life day by day – unless I love, I say nothing, know nothing and do nothing. Help me love as You love, dear Lord, for I do not want to live in vain. Amen.

# The arterial highway of life

*"… that the love you have for me may be in them and
that I myself may be in them." (v.26)*

**For reading & meditation – John 17:13–26**

We ended yesterday with the thought that never before had a
more devastating judgment fallen upon the systems of
learning, religion and human accomplishment than is to be found in
the opening words of 1 Corinthians 13. The world was weighed and
found wanting. Paul showed that a more excellent way had arisen,
and apart from the way of love, the lesser ways led nowhere. It was
not that learning, religion and human accomplishment were
unimportant, but unless these areas of life are undergirded by love,
they amount to nothing.

It is interesting to note that throughout time, other civilisations
have searched for the meaning of life along similar lines to the world
of Paul's day. Take India, for example. The late E.S. Jones, a
missionary to India, said: "In her search to realise God, India
emphasises three main ways: the way of knowledge (Gyana Marga),
the way of devotion (Bhakti Marga) and the way of works (Karma
Marga)." It would seem the Hindu's search is along the three ways in
which the Mediterranean world searched. Here Paul's judgment of
love is just as devastating: "If I have all knowledge
(Gyana), all devotion (Bhakti), all deeds (Karma),
but have no love, then I know nothing, am
devoted to nothing and accomplish nothing."

Life founded on half-truths perishes for want
of inner sustaining power. I say again, the
qualities of knowledge, devotion and action are
not to be discounted or ignored. But the point is
that unless they are energised by love, they are
destined to fail. And why? Because the universe
was made for love – and only love abides.

**FURTHER STUDY**

John 14:1–23;
15:9; 16:27

1. How do we
demonstrate love
for Christ?
2. What was Christ's
injunction to His
disciples?

## Prayer

Father, I see that all my ways are ways of futility unless I can go the way of love.
Love is the arterial highway of life – help me walk along it this day and every day.
In Jesus' Name I ask it. Amen.

# Controlled by love

*"Love the Lord your God with all your heart and with all your soul ... mind ... strength ..." (v.30)*

**For reading & meditation – Mark 12:28–34**

Mankind seems to move along the three paths of knowledge, devotion and achievement in search of meaning and fulfilment. However, without God's love flowing in to direct and control these areas of life, they amount to nothing.

Let's apply the judgment of love to the modern world of psychology – a world I have explored to some depth. Modern psychology divides man into three areas: intellect, feeling and will. Some teachers lay emphasis upon the intellect and say that thinking is everything. Others lay emphasis upon emotion and say that emotion is everything. Still others lay emphasis upon the will and say that the will is everything. Each has its devotees, but unless the mind, the emotions and the will are controlled by Agape love, then the judgment of love says – we are nothing. For if we think everything, feel everything, do everything but have no love, then we think nothing, feel nothing and do nothing.

You see, nothing works out right unless it is controlled by love. Our text for today shows that we are required to love God with our

**FURTHER STUDY**

2 Thess. 3:1–5;
Jude 21;
Matt. 22:37

1. What does the Bible mean by the term "heart"?
2. What is to be the anchor for the heart?

total being. In other words, the mind, feelings and will are to be attached to God, who is love. Then, animated by love, we will feel right feelings, think right thoughts, will right actions and become the right kind of person. Love (Agape love) is the bond that holds the personality intact. If only the non-Christian psychologists and psychiatrists could see this, I have no doubt that their sincere and well-intentioned efforts would meet with much greater success.

## Prayer

O God my Father, it is clear that the world has missed the way – the way of love. Our confusions and clashes, our personality disorders, all testify to the fact that life is off centre. Bring us back to Your centre – the centre of love. For Jesus' sake. Amen.

# "Pain set to music"

*"… He will bring to light what is hidden in darkness and will expose the motives of men's hearts …" (v.5)*

**For reading & meditation – 1 Corinthians 4:1–17**

The whole of Paul's first letter to the Corinthians was written out of pain – the pain of a divided church, one group going with Apollos, another with Cephas and another with Paul. In addition to this, there was the pain of Christians turning to pagan practices and attitudes, the pain of Christians becoming selfish and self-centred, and the pain of Christians misunderstanding the spiritual gifts.

Against that background of pain, Paul picks up his pen and writes out of love. You simply cannot write at such depth unless it is out of a heart of pain – pain which has been turned to redemption. Someone has described this chapter as "pain set to music". The heartstrings are drawn so tight by pain that they are thus tuned to the higher notes of love. But before love can sing, it has to cut. This is why, in the first three verses of chapter 13, Paul cuts away at wrong motives and wrong attitudes, cuts away at speaking in tongues, miraculous powers, faith that removes mountains, personal sacrifice or even martyrdom – cuts these all away *unless their basis is love.*

I don't know about you, but I find these opening words of 1 Corinthians 13 the most challenging I know. They force me to look at my own motives as I teach, preach and write. A Christian magazine article in Britain wrote about me once under the title, "Preacher with the world's biggest daily congregation". I trembled as I read it, for I realised that unless my ministry was under the control of love, it would count for nothing.

FURTHER STUDY

James 1:1–12;
Psa. 17:3;
Zech. 13:9

1. What could the psalmist testify?
2. Can you echo the psalmist's words?

## Prayer

O Father, help me as I face the challenge of this day, for I see that You draw a cancelling line through everything which has no love in it. I stand before You for inspection. Try me and then make me whole. In Jesus' Name I ask it. Amen.

# To whom do we draw attention?

*"Keep yourselves in God's love ..."* (v.21)

**For reading & meditation – Jude 14–25**

What would happen, I wonder, if every Christian community (especially those where the charismatic gifts are in evidence) were to stop and examine how much of their ministry was motivated by love? Assuming that the self-examination was real and honest, I think I know what would happen. Firstly, we would be shocked to discover how much of what we describe as ministry is really manipulation – a veiled attempt to draw attention to ourselves.

In the days when I pastored churches, I can remember many occasions when I would have to sit down with people who had misused a spiritual gift and gently and lovingly correct them. I would say to them: "why do you think you allowed yourself to be carried to excess in the way you did?" Time and time again I would hear them say: "Because it made me feel good to be the centre of attention." But the basis of ministry in the Christian Church is not drawing attention to ourselves but drawing attention to Christ. The Church is designed by God to be Christocentric, not egocentric.

**FURTHER STUDY**

Psa. 139:15–24;
51:6;
1 Cor. 8:3

1. What was the psalmist's prayer?
2. What does God desire to see in us?

When we draw attention to ourselves, we are failing to draw attention to Him, and, as David Wilkerson said: "He becomes a stranger in our midst."

The second thing that would happen if we examined how much of our ministry is motivated by love is that the Spirit would come to our aid in a way that would produce even greater power than we are presently seeing. There is nothing God loves more than openness, honesty and reality. Where truth is, love cannot keep out.

## Prayer

O God, help us not to shrink from the moments of self-examination out of fear that we might find something we do not like. Give us courage to be real and honest and open. Then we know we are on line for real revival. Amen.

# "The spectrum of love"

*"Having loved his own who were in the world,
he loved them to the last." (v.1, margin)*

**For reading & meditation – John 13:1–17**

Henry Drummond likens Paul's analysis of love to light passing through a prism. He says: "As you have seen a man of science take a beam of light and pass it through a prism, as you have seen it come out on the other side of the prism broken up into its component colours – red and blue and yellow, and violet and orange and all the colours of the rainbow – so Paul passes this thing called love through the magnificent prism of his inspired intellect and it comes out on the other side, broken up into its elements. It is what we might call 'the spectrum of love'."

The spectrum of love, like the fruit of the Spirit, has nine ingredients: patience, kindness, generosity, humility, courtesy, unselfishness, good temper, guilelessness, sincerity. These exact words do not appear in 1 Corinthians 13, but the truth they represent most certainly is. The first thing that Paul says about love is that it is *patient* (v.4). The dictionary definition of patience is: suffering afflictions, pain, toil, calamity, provocation or other evils with a calm, unruffled temper.

The first emphasis, then, is that love can suffer, can take it. Love is outgoing, and by its very nature involves itself in the pain and suffering of its loved ones. To understand this aspect of love, we have only to look at the cross, where love showed its capacity to take on itself everything that would fall upon the objects of that love. So if love can go to a cross, it can go anywhere. It meets the supreme test and thereby passes all other tests.

FURTHER STUDY
Luke 21:10–19;
Eccl. 7:8;
Heb. 10:36

1. What do we need to have?
2. What did Jesus say to His disciples?

## Prayer

Lord Jesus, You who showed Your ability to meet the supreme test of the cross, pour into me the same kind of love – the love that is not just tender-hearted but tough-minded, with the capacity to take it and take it cheerfully. Amen.

# Trusting, trusting, trusting

*"… count it all joy when you fall into various trials …*
*the testing of your faith produces patience." (vv.2–3, NKJ)*

**For reading & meditation – James 1:1–12**

A young girl said: "It's been a habit of mine to respond negatively to sorrow. For the life of me I can't react to problems with a positive attitude. Why?" Her youth leader said: "You respond negatively to sorrow because the roots of life are in yourself. You are saying, 'Though I try I can't.' You are trying, trying, trying, instead of trusting, trusting, trusting. You are trying to bring forth fruit without the root."

Other than Agape love, there is no love strong enough to enable us to move out of self-centredness. If we do not possess Agape love (God's love in us), then we have a limited framework of reference in which to operate. We do not have the resources we need to cope with everything that comes.

In a crisis, the three greatest personalities of the New Testament, Jesus, Stephen and Paul, all prayed for their enemies. Jesus said on the cross: "Father, forgive them; for they know not what they do." Stephen prayed amid a shower of stones: "Lord, do not hold this sin against them." Paul said: "For I am already on the point of being sacrificed; the time of my departure has come … At my first defence no one took my part; all deserted me. May it not be charged against them!" It was the crowning act in the life of all three.

Why can love be patient? Because it knows that the universe is behind it; that in spite of what the present says, the future belongs to God. Nothing right can come out wrong and nothing wrong can come out right.

**FURTHER STUDY**

2 Tim. 4:6–17;
Luke 23:32–34;
Acts 7:54–60;
Rom. 5:3

1. What did Paul receive during his trial of patience?
2. What does patience produce?

## Prayer

My Father, yet again I would ask – fill me so full of Agape love that I will have an infinite capacity to take whatever comes. Help me to see that Your word is always the last word and therefore I can wait for it with joy. Amen.

# Another distinctive of love

*"Be kind and compassionate to one another, forgiving each other, just as in Christ God forgave you." (v.32)*

**For reading & meditation – Ephesians 4:17–32**

The second capacity of Agape love is that of being *kind*: "Love is kind", says the inspired apostle (1 Cor. 13:4).

Human love can be patient without being kind. I have met many patient people who did not leave a good impression because their patience was not gracious or kindly. But the love that flows out of God's heart into ours will not have this deficiency. Agape love will put up with irritating situations and go on being kind. A Christian who was becoming irritated while in a department store said to the assistant: "How much longer do I have to wait to be served in this place?" The assistant apologised and explained the reason for the delay, whereupon the man said: "All right, I will put up with it, but don't expect me to enjoy it." The Christian was functioning at that moment, not on Agape love, but on human love, which soon runs out of energy.

The exciting thing about God's love in us is that it has the capacity to enable us not only to hang on, but to be kind to those who keep us hanging on. Don't think, however, that this capacity of kindness makes a person a pushover. A young Christian once said to me: "I am afraid if I am kind, someone will take advantage of me." The love that is kind will not hesitate to confront any issue that needs confronting, but it will do it in a way that differentiates between the person and the problem. It shows respect for the person while seeking to overcome the problem.

**FURTHER STUDY**

Col. 3:12–17;
Rom. 12:10;
1 Pet. 3:8

1. What is to be the pattern for our kindness?
2. How can we "put on" kindness?

## Prayer

O Father, help me to understand that when I get irritated and frustrated by life, it is a silent witness to the fact I am running on my resources and not Yours. Help me to open my being to Your invading love – then I can cope with anything that comes. And cope with it kindly. Amen.

# Love – not sentimentality

*"Be kindly affectionate to one another ... in honour
giving preference to one another." (v.10, NKJ)*

**For reading & meditation – Romans 12:9–21**

We spend another day meditating on the thought that Agape love is not only patient, but kind. The hard-lipped patience you see in some Christian people may enable them to get through the day, but it does not enhance their Christian testimony. Those who are patient, but not kind in their patience, show something less than Agape love. The kindness that divine love brings with it into our personalities enables us to give back kindness when life is not kind to us. It means we are not just negatively patient but positively kind in the midst of the patience. A well-known hymn puts it this way:

> *Able to suffer without complaining*
> *To be misunderstood without explaining*
> *Able to give without receiving*
> *To be ignored without grieving*
> *Able to ask without commanding*
> *To love despite misunderstanding*
> *Able to turn to the Lord for guarding*
> *Able to wait for his own rewarding.*

**FURTHER STUDY**

2 Pet. 1:1–9;
1 Thess. 4:9–10;
Jer. 31:3

*1. How does God
draw us to Himself?
2. What are the steps
in the development of
our faith?*

This kind of love, it must be noted, is not maudlin sentimentality; it is tough as well as tender, strong as well as sensitive. People who do not know better may think of it as a clinging vine, but actually it is a sturdy oak, gnarled but not bowed under the storms of life. I tell you, a love that is patient and kind is the most formidable thing on our planet.

## Prayer

O Father, as the violet leaves its perfume on the heel that crushes it, so let me leave the perfume of divine kindness on all who may hurt me this day. In Jesus' Name I ask it. Amen.

# The purpose of Paul's negatives

*"Whoever does not love does not know God,*
*because God is love." (v.8)*

**For reading & meditation – 1 John 4:1–11**

We now look at four statements that show what love is not. Why does Paul use these four negatives to describe love? Is it just for effect? I cannot be sure, of course, but I think he is seeking to show that love has to be able to say "No" as well as "Yes". Just being positive in life is not enough. You may be positive with the wrong positive and with the wrong spirit behind the positive. You have to be negative to many things in order to be positive to the highest things. A great philosopher once said: "No one can say 'Yes' who hasn't said 'No'."

Some of the characteristics of love that Paul lines up in 1 Corinthians 13 are: "Love is patient … kind … always protects … trusts … hopes … perseveres" (vv.4, 7). These things could not stand out unless they had a negative backdrop to them: not jealous, not boastful, not arrogant or rude and so on. The very negatives imply a positive. Maturity means that we come to a position in life where we know how to reject as well as accept. To paraphrase the above statement from the philosopher: "No man is capable of accepting, who is not capable of rejecting."

Negativism is bad if it stops at positivism. Behind positivism must be a positive negativism that has said a positive "No" in order to say a positive "Yes". I am not just playing with words. When we are positive in relation to the loving thing, we are negative to the unloving thing.

**FURTHER STUDY**

2 Cor. 1:13–24;
Josh. 24:15;
Matt. 5:37

1. What were
Joshua's words to
the people?
2. How did Jesus
put it?

## Prayer

Gracious and loving Father, make me into a person who knows how to say both "Yes" and "No". Yes to the things that are loving and No to the things that are unloving. In Jesus' Name I pray. Amen.

# Living on an even keel

*"... Do not think of yourself more highly than you ought, but rather think of yourself with sober judgment ..." (v.3)*

**For reading & meditation – Romans 12:1–8**

Paul says: "Love is not jealous or boastful" (1 Cor. 13:4, RSV). Both jealousy and boastfulness show one thing – a deep sense of inferiority and worthlessness. If you are jealous of someone, you most probably (among other things) have feelings of inferiority in relation to that person.

Boastfulness is the obverse side of inferiority and worthlessness – you boast to cover things up. J.S. Bonell says: "If a man is blatant about his atheism, we may expect to find a desire for a belief in God. If he is constantly protesting his ideas, we may look for an inclination to doubt. If he is suffering from impulses to suicide, we may expect to find deep within him a marked desire to live and accomplish something in which he has been thwarted. If he induces conceit, we may expect to find inferiority. If he is distressed by a feeling of humiliation, we may be sure that pride is present also."

Agape love (God's love in us) has no inferiority complex – jealousy; nor has it a superiority complex – boastfulness. It is natural, normal and even. An inferiority complex keeps you down in the dumps and a superiority complex brings you into the same condition. A superiority complex is an attempt to lift oneself out of inferiority by a loud assertion of superiority, by boastfulness. But the boastfulness soon gives way and leaves you down in the dumps again. Divine love, or Agape love as we are calling it, will not lift you up to false heights nor drop you down into the despairing depths. It is neither up nor down – it is even.

**FURTHER STUDY**

Gal. 5:22–26;
Prov. 6:34;
1 Cor. 3:3

1. What are the marks of a worldly Christian?
2. If we live in the Spirit, what attitudes will we avoid?

## Prayer

O God, save me from the depths of false inferiority and also from the heights of false superiority. Give me the balanced, even-tempered heart that is so sure, serene and unruffled. Amen.

# Not "above" or "below" but "with"

*"… you are all one in Christ Jesus."*
(3:28)

**For reading & meditation – Galatians 3:26–4:7**

W̲e saw yesterday that Agape love saves us from inferiorities and superiorities. Kahlil Gibran puts it this way:

*Only those beneath me can envy or hate me.*
*I have never been envied or hated*
*I am above no one.*
*Only those above me can belittle me.*
*I have never been belittled*
*I am below no one.*

A Christian group I was once with started up a song I had never heard before. They looked around the room at each other, joined hands and sang: "Not *above* you, nor *below* you, but *with* you." I could sense that the group meant every word they sang to each other and I tell you, the fellowship and love I experienced among them the one evening I was with them made a deep and lasting impression on me.

Agape love delivers us from being "above" or "below" and enables us to take the position of "with". The person who is filled with divine love cannot, by the nature of things, be jealous of another. If there is jealousy, then it is obvious that Agape love is not flowing and the heart is under the constraint of a lesser love. For whoever loves his neighbour as himself can neither despise himself nor his neighbour. The dynamic thing about Agape love is this – once it invades a heart, it gives a person such a sense of worth that jealousy and boastfulness simply cannot take root.

> **FURTHER STUDY**
>
> James 4:10–17;
> Psa. 10:3;
> Prov. 25:14; 27:1
>
> 1. How does James describe our life?
> 2. What is the folly of boasting?

## Prayer

My Father and my God, I see so clearly that without Agape love, I do not really live – I simply exist. Let this love be illustrated in me this day in all my thoughts and relationships. In Jesus' Name I ask it. Amen.

# The basis of true humility

*"… Your gentleness has made me great."*
*(v.35, NKJ)*

**For reading & meditation – Psalm 18:16–36**

Paul says: "Love … is not arrogant or rude" (v.5, RSV). The Amplified Bible has: "It is not conceited – arrogant and inflated with pride; it is not rude (unmannerly) and does not act unbecomingly." The word "arrogant" seems at first to be so close to "boastful" that one wonders whether Paul is just being repetitive. Think of it this way – boastfulness is outward and verbal; arrogance is inward and comes across, not so much in our words as in our attitudes.

The rude and arrogant act the way they do because they are unsure of themselves. Only the humble are sure of themselves, and only those who are sure of themselves are humble. One of my favourite passages of Scripture is John 13, which says: "Jesus, knowing that the Father had given all things into his hands, and that he had come from God and was going to God … girded himself with a towel … and began to wash the disciples' feet" (vv.3–5, RSV).

What was the secret of Christ's humility? In my opinion, it was the consciousness of His greatness. Listen to it again: "Knowing that the Father had given all things into his hands … that he had come from God and was going to God … girded himself with a towel … and began to wash the disciples' feet." Only the great are humble; they have to be in order to be great. Believe me, you will never know greatness until you know humility, and you will never know humility until you know greatness – the greatness of who you are in God.

**FURTHER STUDY**

1 John 2:1–16;
Prov. 11:2;
Psa. 138:6

1. What is "the pride of life"?
2. What accompanies pride?

## Prayer

Father, pour Your love into me in greater measure than ever before, so that I may know the lowly heart and the kindly attitude. Make me so inwardly great that I can afford to be humble – in speech and in act. In Christ's Name I ask it. Amen.

# The true way to be humble

Day
**21**

*"I served the Lord with great humility and with
tears ... severely tested ..." (v.19)*

**For reading & meditation – Acts 20:17–38**

If we turn "Love is not arrogant or rude" from its negative form to
a positive one, the thought we come out with is – *humility*. I have
often reflected on the words of Phillip Brooks: "The true way to be
humble is not to stoop until you are smaller than yourself, but to
stand at your real height against some higher nature that will show
you what the real smallness of your greatest greatness is."

If this is true, then we must stand at our very highest. Look at
Christ and then be for ever humble. When we lose sight of Christ,
then self looms large. A man said to an evangelist: "I used to believe
in God, but now I don't believe in anything except myself. In fact
I am coming to believe that I myself am God." He gave up believing
in the true God and focused his attention on an idol – himself.
When we lose sight of God, we lose our source of humility.

Agape love enables us to be truly humble. A lot of what we call
humility in the Christian Church is really self-belittlement. True
humility flows out of a consciousness of greatness. Those who do
not see their greatness in God may act in humble ways, but their
humility flows out of wrong motives. They work
at being humble in the hope that it will provide
them with a sense of greatness. But the humility
of Jesus flowed out of His sense of greatness. All
things had been given into His hands, so He chose
to use those hands to wash the disciples' feet.

**FURTHER STUDY**

Luke 14:1–11;
Prov. 16:19;
Rom. 12:3

1. How did Jesus
illustrate humility?
2. How does Paul
say we should
view ourselves?

## Prayer

O God, help me never to lose sight of You and my greatness in You, for when I
do I lose the source of true humility. You stooped to serve me – now I shall
stoop to serve others. Amen.

# Love – the law of our being

*"Love does no harm to its neighbour. Therefore love is the fulfilment of the law." (v.10)*

**For reading & meditation – Romans 13:8–14**

"Love does not insist on its own way" (1 Cor. 13:5, RSV). So deeply entrenched in human nature is the desire to get our own way that only Agape love can give us victory over it.

One writer points out that outside of the help given to us through Jesus Christ, there are just two ways we can take in order to get the victory over wanting our own way. One is to retreat into empty silence, where we become a nonentity, everybody's doormat; the other is to sink into silent, sullen resentment. Many take the first way and become household drudges; they accept it as a kind of self-punishment for wanting their own way, a kind of masochism. Those who take the way of sullen resentment are painful to live with because they are like a time bomb just waiting to explode. Either way is a disaster to the personality and a threat to good relationships.

The best way of not wanting your own way is to allow God's love to penetrate your heart, for then you are caught up in something beyond yourself – a higher purpose. You find yourself wanting God's way more than your own way, for your inner being recognises that His way is always best. You don't care what happens so long as His purposes are furthered. This saves the self both from insistence on its own way and from disintegrating. You see, love is the law of our being, and when divine love flows in and through us, our personalities feel complete. Our inner being says: "This is what I was made for." And how!

**FURTHER STUDY**

1 Cor. 10:1–24;
Rom. 14:21;
2 Cor. 10:12;
Phil. 2:4

*1. What are we not to seek?*
*2. What are we to look for?*

## Prayer

My Father and my God, I see that only Your love flowing through me can break the tyranny of self-preoccupation and give me the outgoing heart that will find itself released, happy and fulfilled. Flow in, dear Lord – still more. Amen.

# Giving up our rights

*"Each of you should look not only to your own interests, but also to the interests of others." (v.4)*

**For reading & meditation – Philippians 2:1–13**

The Amplified Bible says in verse 4 of 1 Corinthians 13: "Love does not insist on its own rights or its own way, for it is not self-seeking." British children are taught the importance of personal rights. "An Englishman's home is his castle", we say, and I learned as a boy that even the King or Queen of England, if they came to the door of my home, would have to knock and wait to be admitted. Royal status does not give the right to enter into anyone's home uninvited. British people cling tightly to rights, but there comes a time when the law of love compels us to acknowledge a higher right – the right to give up our rights.

Henry Drummond argues that Paul's statement, "Love does not insist on its own rights" means being willing to recognise that we have no rights at all. He says: "It is not hard to give up our rights. They are often external. The hard thing is to give up ourselves. The more difficult thing still is not to seek things for ourselves at all. After we have sought them, bought them, won them, deserved them, we have taken the cream off them for ourselves already. Little difficulty, then, to give them up." If it is more difficult, as Henry Drummond has said, not to seek something for ourselves than, having sought it, to give it up, then we are faced with a hard and difficult challenge. Hard and difficult? Not really, for if we truly understand it, the way of God's love in us is an easier way than any other.

**FURTHER STUDY**

Matt. 26:36–39;
1 Cor. 10:31–33;
2 Cor. 8:1–9

1. How did Jesus demonstrate this submission?
2. What was Paul's motivation?

## Prayer

My Father and my God, quietly my ideas and opinions are being overturned – overturned by love. Help me understand the truth that happiness comes, not through getting, but through giving. In Christ's Name I ask it. Amen.

# "I don't get ulcers – I give them"

*"… you have purified yourselves … so that you have sincere love … love one another deeply …" (v.22)*

**For reading & meditation – 1 Peter 1:13–25**

"Love … is not irritable or resentful" (1 Cor. 13:5, RSV). The Amplified Bible has: "Love … is not touchy or fretful or resentful." Countless people in counselling sessions have said to me: "How can I get rid of touchiness?" I have come to regard irritation and resentment as two of the biggest evils that can take root in the human heart.

A businessman sat in his office and bellowed at a man on the other end of the line. A friend of the businessman, sitting with him in the office, said: "If you keep that up, you will get a stomach ulcer." The businessman said: "I don't get ulcers, I give them." He said it with an air of finality – but was it final? Was he only giving ulcers and not getting any? Perhaps his stomach had a tough lining that resisted ulceration, but if I know anything about human functioning, his spirit was certainly becoming ulcerated. And that, to my way of thinking, is a far worse condition than an ulcerated stomach. That which did not show up in the physical would inevitably show up in the spirit. Irritation toward others would produce increased irritation toward himself. Like Haman in the Bible, he would be hanged on the gallows he had prepared for others.

What is the root cause of irritation and resentment? I believe it to be an unsurrendered self. Once the self – the centre of irritation and resentment – is fully surrendered to Christ and Agape love is allowed to invade the whole of the personality, then irritability and resentment dissolve as quickly as sugar in hot tea.

FURTHER STUDY

Heb. 12:1–15;
Eph. 4:30–31;
Prov. 14:10

1. What results from not drawing on God's grace?
2. How can we grieve the Holy Spirit?

## Prayer

O Father, You who are truly Love, invade me this day with Love's strong and mighty power so that my ugly, touchy, resentful self shall be changed and become the beautiful self You purpose for me to be. In Jesus' Name I ask it. Amen.

# Fill up and feel the difference!

*"May the Lord direct your hearts into God's love ..."*
(v.5)

**For reading & meditation – 2 Thessalonians 3:1–18**

A farmer got up in a testimony meeting and said: "If you know how to surrender to God and let the power of His love take hold of you, then you won't short-change yourself." He meant, of course, that to live any other way than the way of love is to miss getting the best out of life – short-changing yourself. The irritable and resentful are always short-changing themselves, for life was not made to work that way.

The universe was designed by what J.B. Phillips calls "an Aggressive Lover". But God is more than just a person who acts lovingly; the Bible puts it in this way: "God is love" (1 John 4:8). Not just loving, or has love, or does loving things – He is love. This means that He cannot act against love and still be God; if He did the stars would tumble from the sky and the whole universe disintegrate, for the creation was made for love and can only function effectively when it is sustained by love.

The same applies to you and me; we too were designed to run on Agape love. If divine love does not permeate and penetrate our beings, we chug along the road of life like a car that is functioning on an inferior grade of petrol. It goes, but it does not go in the way it was designed. Our Creator never intended for us to function on resentment, so let's allow our heavenly Mechanic to flush out the inferior grade of love that may be within us and fill us up with Agape love. Then – feel the difference!

FURTHER STUDY
1 John 2:1–11;
2 John 6;
Psa. 107:8; 118:1

*1. How is God's love made complete in us?*
*2. What is His command?*

## Prayer

O God, how foolish I am to splutter and sputter along the road of life, tolerating the intolerable, when I can come to You and fill up with a different grade of love. Help me, dear Lord. Amen.

# Right – and yet wrong

*"… pursue righteousness, godliness, faith, love …"*
(v.11)

### For reading & meditation – 1 Timothy 6:3–21

We come to yet another step in the unfolding of love: "Love … does not rejoice at wrong, but rejoices in the right" (1 Cor. 13:6, RSV). It is surprising how easy it is for us to rejoice at wrong. We don't do it consciously, of course, because then we would recognise it and be compelled to do something about it. It goes on unconsciously beneath the surface of our thinking, but it is none the less devastating for all that.

One of the things I am grateful for is that over the years, I have had the privilege of sitting in hundreds of counselling sessions with people and have heard and seen them when they have come to a moment of self-awareness. Time and time again, when people have come to recognise some of the hidden underlying motives that motivated them to act and behave the way they did, I have heard them say: "I could never believe that I was capable of that." Consciously they would not be capable of it, but unconsciously they were.

A Christian worker I talked to some years ago was deeply critical of his fellow workers. Consciously he told himself: "These people are not living the life they should, and ought to be exposed." He came to recognise, however, that unconsciously he was saying to himself: "Their wrongness boosts my rightness." However correct his criticism, he was being driven by another law than the law of love.

**FURTHER STUDY**

Phil. 1:1–11;
Hos. 10:12;
Matt. 5:20

1. What are we to break up?
2. What are we to be filled with?

## Prayer

O Father, let Your love so invade my personality that it will penetrate, not only my conscious but my unconscious also. I would be inwardly unified and united – united by love. In Jesus' Name I ask it. Amen.

# "I wouldn't do that"

*"It has given me great joy to find some of your children walking in the truth …" (v.4)*

**For reading & meditation – 2 John 1–13**

I once talked to a young man who had become involved with a group who were concerned about the many obscene and pornographic books and magazines that were appearing on some of the newsagents bookshelves in his town. (The anti-pornography stand, by the way, is something that has my wholehearted support.) However, after a while he began to experience some deep inner conflicts and after many hours of talking and praying together, he came to see that the roots of his problem lay in the fact that he unconsciously delighted in the discovery of pornographic literature, for it satisfied his curiosity concerning sex and at the same time boosted his own estimate of himself: "I wouldn't do that." Once he came to recognise this and dealt with it, he was set free from the unconscious conflict and involved himself in a new way with the work he felt called to do.

What is the unconscious motive behind criticism, mote-picking or wanting to expose the wrongs of others? It is this – if I can find wrong in others, it will help to boost my superiority – their wrongness boosts my rightness. And what is the test of whether we are acting by love or by a desire to boost ourselves? It is simple: in pointing out wrong, do I become a more loving person in the process? If so, then love is the basis of my actions. If I become a less loving person, then it suggests I am operating from a motive that is not based on love.

FURTHER STUDY
Matt. 7:1–5;
Prov. 30:12;
Rom. 2:1

1. What human tendency did Jesus point out?
2. What was His remedy?

## Prayer

O Father, save me from secretly rejoicing when others show weakness or fall into sin. Help me to rejoice in nothing but good. Then I shall become what I rejoice in. Fill me with love. In Jesus' Name. Amen.

# Love uses all things

*"… they will lay hands on you and persecute you … This will result in your being witnesses to them." (vv.12–13)*

### For reading & meditation – Luke 21:5–19

Having looked at what love is not, Paul now turns to focus on four positive aspects of love: "Love bears all things, believes all things, hopes all things, endures all things" (1 Cor. 13:7, RSV). The first and the last are similar: "bears … endures". The two central ones are also similar: "believes … hopes". The two at the centre save the first and the last from just bearing and enduring. They therefore become *believing* and *hopeful* bearing and *believing* and *hopeful* enduring.

It is not a sad, morose, despairing kind of bearing; it is bearing with a smile of belief and hope. Bearing and enduring has a pulse at its centre, the beats of which are alternately belief and hope. This saves the bearing and enduring from being stoical and makes it Christian. The Stoics are the people who are committed to facing life's problems with the grim determination that nothing will get them down. This attitude produces brittleness in the personality, and you know what happens to things that are brittle – they easily break.

**FURTHER STUDY**

Eph. 4:1–8;
Col. 3:13

1. What did Paul urge the Ephesians and Colossians to do?
2. How does it apply to us?

The Christian in whom Agape love flows does not break – he bends. When, many years ago, I first came across the verse that is before us today in the Amplified Bible: "They will lay their hands on you and persecute you … This will be a time (an opportunity) for you to bear testimony", an entirely new world opened up before me. Before that I had concentrated on trying to analyse problems and explain them, but since then, I have seen that my task is not to explain them, but to use them.

## Prayer

Gracious and loving heavenly Father, drive this truth so deeply into my spirit this day that it will become one of the turning points of my life and experience. Help me see that Your Agape love enables me to bear all things – because I can use all things. Amen.

# "Cosmic optimism"

*"... we know that in all things God works for the good of those who love him ..." (v.28)*

**For reading & meditation – Romans 8:28–39**

God's love in us bears all things because it can use all things. Love is so creative that it can wrest from the worst situations something that is positive and good. Evil put Jesus on a cross but Jesus, being love, made that cross redemptive. When God's Agape love flows in us and through us, there is nothing, no matter how hurtful or evil it is, that cannot be caught up and transformed into good.

Tolstoy, in his book *My Confessions and My Religion*, says in substance: "There are those who say: (1) Life is all bad, so get drunk and forget it. (2) Life is bad, but struggle hard against it. (3) Life is bad, so do the logical thing and end it. (4) Life is bad, but live on and accept things as they come." How sad if that was the full statement on life. The Christian view of life is this: life may at times be hard and difficult, but no matter what comes, we have within us a redemptive energy called love that lifts us above every negative situation and turns every setback into a springboard.

There are limitations, of course. Even Jesus recognised that He was thwarted in His own community: "Only in his home town ... is a prophet without honour" (Mark 6:4). He was thwarted there, but that very limitation became a contribution and spilled over in love, healing and blessing to other parts of Palestine. Christianity has been described as "cosmic optimism". It is, for love uses everything that comes – good, bad and indifferent.

**FURTHER STUDY**

2 Cor. Ch. 4;
Psa. 34:19; 41:3;
Isa. 43:2

1. What was Paul's perspective on difficult times?
2. In what four ways did he express it?

## Prayer

Lord Jesus Christ, draw closer to me today and let Your love flow so deeply into me and through me that together we will turn every bad or evil thing that comes into glorious good. In Your dear Name I Ask it. Amen.

# Seeing with double vision

*"... 'You are Simon son of John. You shall be called Cephas' (that is, Peter, the Rock)." (v.42, NEB)*

**For reading & meditation – John 1:29–42**

What is it about Agape love that enables us to "believe the best of every person" (1 Cor 13:7, Amp. Bible)? I think it is because love sees with a double vision – seeing things, not merely as they are, but as they can be.

When He looked at Simon as he was, Jesus said: "You are Simon son of John." What was Simon like before love changed him? He was bluff, impulsive, loud-mouthed (and, on one occasion, foul-mouthed), a braggart, inconsiderate ... But what was Simon as he could be? Jesus says: "You shall be ... Cephas" (rock). What a change! The unstable becoming a rock. The impulsive blusterer could be clear in judgment and firm in will. The man who could curse and swear and deny all knowledge of his Lord to save his own skin would become a powerful spiritual leader with the privilege of opening the gates of the Kingdom to the first converts after Pentecost.

Can this be the same man that we read about in the Gospels? Simon's friends would not have seen it, but Jesus did. Why? Because Christ sees with double vision. His love always looks beyond what is to what can be. He looked on the unstable Simon and saw a Rock. He looked on Saul and saw Paul. He looked on Augustine the roué and saw Augustine the saint. And that is what will happen to us when we allow our hearts to be invaded by Agape love. We will take on the same perspective as our Lord and see people, not merely as they are, but as they can be.

**FURTHER STUDY**

John 21:1–22;
Eph. 6:24;
1 Pet. 1:8–9

1. What was Jesus' question to Peter?
2. What was Peter's response?

## Prayer

O Jesus, Lord and Master, help me to stand at Your elbow and get the double vision. Fill me so full of Agape love that I will become transformed in the way I look at people, and see them not as they are, but as they can be. For Your own Name's sake. Amen.

# The influence of Agape love

*"Then Peter stood up ... and addressed the crowd ..."*
*(v.14)*

**For reading & meditation – Acts 2:14–36**

Our Lord saw both Simon as he was, and the Simon he could become. The two were so different that they required different names. Agape love flowing through the heart of Christ toward Simon Peter took a while to bring about the change that Christ predicted (in fact, about three years), but, as we can see from the passage before us today, Peter became the fearless and unshakeable champion of a spiritual movement that shook the world.

In the same, but of course a lesser way, we too can come alongside men and women, as did our Lord, and look upon them as they can become. You may meet someone today who, at first glance, seems ineffective, inferior, frustrated, beaten by beastliness. Ask God to help you see them as they can become – saved, dependent, confident, effective, sanctified. I came across an interesting, though imperfect definition: "Democracy is the madness that believes about people that which isn't true, and yet without that belief they will never become what we believe them to be".

A positive attitude tends to create the very thing it believes in. If this is true of democracy, then how much truer it is of love. Of course, it is important to recognise that simply believing the best of a person will not by itself bring that person into the Kingdom of God. Everyone needs to make their own personal commitment to Christ in order to be saved. Believing the best of a person, however – a function of Agape love – gives added influence to all the other ways God uses in bringing people to Himself.

FURTHER STUDY

2 Cor. 8:1–9;
Rom. 12:10;
Phil. 2:4;
1 Cor. 10:32–33

1. What did Christ
demonstrate?
2. How did Paul's life
echo this?

## Prayer

Jesus, my loving Lord and Master, help me also to see with a double vision – to view people, not just as they are but what they can become in You. For I know that the attitude of love adds untold strength and power to my words. In Your Name. Amen.

# Hope – a powerful working force

*"… In his great mercy he has given us new birth into a living hope …"* (v.3)

**For reading & meditation – 1 Peter 1:3–13**

Agape love has at its heart a deathless hope. Love not only bears all things and believes all things but hopes all things (1 Cor. 13:7, RSV). The only faith that uses hope as a working force is the Christian faith.

There is a famous picture by G.F. Watts called "Hope", which shows a blindfolded woman sitting with bowed head on a sphere and holding a lyre in her hand. Only one string of the instrument remains unbroken, only one star shines in the sky. The artist, reaching out for some meaning that those who do not think in symbols find difficult to grasp, called the picture "Hope". Two charwomen were overheard talking about the picture; one said to the other: "'Hope'? Why is it called 'Hope'?" The other charlady, gazing at the figure perched precariously on the sphere, replied: "I suppose because she hopes she won't fall off."

Many people think of hope as a poor, precarious thing, an illusion, a vanity, a disease of the mind. The cynic has said: "He who lives on hope will die starving." Cowley said: "Hope is the most hopeless thing of all." Schopenhauer, the distinguished German philosopher, looked upon hope as "the bait by which nature gets her hook in our nose and makes us serve her interests rather than our own". That is the common assessment of hope in our world. But hope is not so thought of in the New Testament. It is seen there for the buoyant thing that it is – a conviction that, no matter what, Agape love will ultimately bring all things to a glorious end.

**FURTHER STUDY**

Rom. 15:1–4; 5:5; 1 Pet. 3:15

1. Where does our conviction spring from?
2. What should we always be ready to do?

## Prayer

My Father and my God, let my heart be so filled with Your love that the things around me which seem hopeless may come alive with hope. For I sense that when I am alive with hope, everything around me will become alive with it. Thank You, dear Father. Amen.

# Anchored to eternity

*"… a hope that reaches farther and enters into the …
certainty of the Presence within the veil." (v.19, Amp. Bible)*

**For reading & meditation – Hebrews 6:9–20**

Yesterday we saw that the world views hope as something illusory
and vain, while the New Testament looks upon it as a positive
virtue. How did this sharp contrast arise? An illusion: a steadfast
reality. A dream: a fact. Hope cannot be both. Which is right: the
world, or the New Testament? The answer is not difficult, for they
are talking of different things. There is a worldly and there is a
spiritual hope. There is gold and there is gilt.

The world's view of hope is more easily understood if we call
it by its rightful name – optimism. We cannot deny the value of
optimism, of course – it is not the full cream but there is something
to be said for skimmed milk. Optimism, we all know, is better than
pessimism, but really it does not have a strong foundation to stand
on. There are people facing problems today for which even the
greatest optimism will prove inadequate. A man whose wife was
gravely ill said to their minister: "It's all right. She is bound to get
better. I'm an optimist, you know. I always look on the bright side of
things." The minister buried the woman before the week was out.

Boisterous confidence which has no solid
foundation in fact looks pitifully ludicrous when
crushing disappointment comes. How different
from the New Testament's description of hope
which, in our text for today, is pictured as an
anchor that is fixed in eternity. Optimism drops
its anchor into the depths of trouble but cannot
find the bottom. Hope drops its anchor into the
depths of trouble and finds eternity.

**FURTHER STUDY**

1 Pet. 1:1–9;
Prov. 14:32;
Acts 24:15

1. How does Peter
describe this hope?
2. What effect does
hope have on
heaviness?

## Prayer

O Father, what deep reassurance it gives me to know that whatever I am called
upon to face today, my life is securely anchored to eternity. I have a hope that
may be disturbed but cannot be destroyed. I am so deeply, deeply thankful.
Amen.

<table>
<tr><td>**Day**<br>**34**</td><td colspan="2"><h1>God does not work our way</h1></td></tr>
</table>

*"… 'Your throne, O God, will last for ever and
ever …'" (v.8)*

**For reading & meditation – Hebrews 1:1–14**

What makes the Christian hope unique? Two powerful things –
the indestructibility of truth and the permanence of God's
eternal throne. However, "Truth", we are often told, "is the very first
casualty in war." But truth is mighty. It may be nailed to a cross,
taken down, hidden in a sepulchre and sealed with a great stone.
But it rises again! The life principle in it cannot be killed. Truth
partakes of the life of God and therefore of God's eternity. Its
triumph is always sure.

The second ground of our confident hope is that God
is on the throne. It may be difficult for many to believe that,
especially when God appears to allow so much injustice. The
problem is a very old one; it puzzled the psalmists and perplexed
the prophets. It even baffled Simon Peter as he stood and watched
Christ being taken captive by the soldiers. The question must have
hammered in his brain: "Why? Why? Why?"

However simplistic it may sound to those who want answers
they can clearly understand – *God does not work our way.* He allows

**FURTHER STUDY**

Psa. 24:1–10;
Isa. 9:1–7;
Matt. 8:27;
Eph. 1:22

*1. What is the
assurance of the
believer?*
*2. What did the
disciples marvel at?*

things to happen that make it appear that He is
unconcerned. But that can never be, for His very
nature is love. One thing is certain – even though
we cannot understand why He allows us to go
through many difficult experiences, He will never
forsake us in them. The cross is the pledge of that.
Our Lord will never forsake the world of His
incarnation. Hallelujah! God is on the throne!
This is why, when all the shallow hopes of the
world are dead – we can hope on.

## Prayer

O Father, let me abound in love, for I see that when I do, I abound in hope.
Help me to lay hold of these two facts – that truth is indestructible and that no
one will ever unseat You from Your throne. Father, my hope is eternally in You.
Amen.

# The loss of meaning

*"Let us fix our eyes on Jesus ... who for the joy set before
him endured the cross, scorning its shame ..."* (v.2)

**For reading & meditation – Hebrews 12:1–13**

The last of Paul's positives concerning love is: "Love *endures* all
things." Although the word "endures" is similar to the earlier
expression, "bears", there is a slight difference. To "bear" has more
to do with behaviour; to "endure" has more to do with the attitude
that underlies behaviour.

Paul said: "I endure everything for the sake of the elect [God's
chosen], that they too may obtain the salvation that is in Christ
Jesus" (2 Tim. 2:10). He was ready to "endure" everything because
he saw that his endurance was *"for the sake of the elect"*. God's love in
us fortifies us to carry on right to the very end of everything God
allows to come our way. Why? Because love would never let us go
through what we have to go through unless there was a purpose to
it. Convinced of this, we are able to face anything.

Creath Davies, in his book *How to Win in a Crisis*, says: "The
loss of meaning is perhaps the most devastating crisis we can
experience." He goes on to tell of the experience of Victor
Frankl, who was interned by Hitler in a concentration camp.
Frankl, a famous psychiatrist, observed that
those who survived the horror of the Nazi
concentration camps did so because they saw a
purpose for them being there. In other words, the
concentration camps came to have some *meaning*
for them. Without meaning, life becomes drained
of its colour and bleached of all interest. Love,
however, gives meaning to life. Believe me, it
would never expose us to life's hardships unless
there was a purpose in doing so.

**FURTHER STUDY**

Acts 20:17–24;
James 5:11;
Gal. 6:9

1. What did Paul
declare to the
Ephesian elders?
2. What does love
bring about in
due season?

## Prayer

O Father, I see how much I need not only to hear this truth, but to absorb it
into my being. Impress it so deeply within my spirit that I will never forget You
love me too much to let me go through difficult situations unless they have
meaning. Amen.

# "He who has a *why*"

*"Endure hardship with us like a good soldier
of Christ Jesus." (v.3)*

**For reading & meditation – 2 Timothy 2:1–13**

Let Victor Frankl put what he discovered in the Nazi concentration camps in his own words: "Any attempt to restore a man's inner strength in the camp had first to succeed in showing him some future goal. 'He who has a *why* to live for can bear with almost any *how*.' Whenever there was an opportunity for it, one had to give them a *why* – an aim for their lives – in order to strengthen them to bear the terrible *how* of their existence. Woe to him who saw no more sense in his life, no aim, no purpose, and therefore no point in carrying on. He was soon lost."

One of the components lying beneath non-organic depression is a sense of meaninglessness. Such despair often leads to suicide. Today, as you read these lines, many will bring their life to an end simply because they do not have a *why* for living. The loss of meaning can be much less dramatic than the experience in the concentration camps. There is a type of depression called "Sunday Depression", where people who have been active all the week in their work suddenly find themselves with nothing to do or no one to impress or please, whereupon the inner emptiness that is inside them becomes more apparent. The Christian whose heart is filled with Agape love will sense a meaning and a purpose in everything he or she is called to face. They can endure the *how* because they have a *why* – the *why* of eternal purpose and eternal meaning.

**FURTHER STUDY**

Eph. 1:1–12;
3:10–11;
Isa. 14:26–27

1. What is the purpose of God revealed in Ephesians?
2. What did Isaiah prophesy?

## Prayer

Gracious and loving Father, thank You for opening my eyes to see that endurance is not a chore, but a challenge. Love lets me go through things because love is at work giving meaning to all things. I am so deeply grateful. Amen.

# Eros fails – Agape never fails

*"… I have loved you with an everlasting love …" (v.3)*

**For reading & meditation – Jeremiah 31:1–14**

Paul now begins the section which Henry Drummond describes as the "defence of love" with the words: "Love never fails" (1 Cor. 13:8). The Amplified Bible has: "Love never fails – never fades out or becomes obsolete or comes to an end." How beautiful.

When Paul says: "Love never fails", he is referring to Agape love, which is the highest form of love in the universe. Every other kind of love is prone to failure. At the centre of Eros love are the seeds of its own failure, for Eros love is self-seeking love. If you love people for what you can get out of them, then they give you back in kind – they love you for what they can get out of you. That is self-defeating. Each suspects the motive of the other, and in such an atmosphere – love dies.

A wealthy businessman who was an alcoholic one day met a Christian who stopped and prayed for him and then just walked away. The man, all alone, suddenly felt God's healing presence in mind, soul and body. His nerves became calmed and now, years later, he says that miraculously the craving for alcohol dropped away and has never returned. He is now on fire with the love of God.

Not all conversions are as dramatic as this, but here is my point – suppose someone had said to the man: "Try to love God and you will be free of all craving for alcohol" – would that have helped? No, because in his own strength he could only have loved with Eros love. Eros love fails but Agape love never fails.

**FURTHER STUDY**

1 John 4:7–21;
2 Cor. 4:18;
Heb. 12:27

1. Where does Agape love start?
2. What important statement does John repeat twice?

## Prayer

O Father, I am so grateful that Your Agape love reached down to me and has lifted me to the highest heaven. It not only fills me with wonder and awe, but also with a passion to share it. May I share it liberally with all whom I meet this day. Amen.

# "Either way we win"

*"If the home is deserving, let your peace rest on it; if ... not, let your peace return to you." (vv.12–13)*

**For reading & meditation – Matthew 10:1–16**

Agape love never fails. Eros has a hook in it – a hook of self-interest; Agape wants nothing – except to give itself. There are times, of course, when it may seem that Agape love does fail. It may be that you have been loving someone with true Agape, but up to this moment your love has not evoked a response in them. You must realise that I am not talking now about a romantic relationship, but a situation in which you may be continuing to express Agape love to someone who fails to respond and continues to show resentment and hostility.

Does this mean that Agape is failing? No, for the statement, "Love never fails", does not mean that love will always succeed in gaining its object. So what does it mean? It means (so I believe) that even though you may not succeed in a situation where you have expressed Agape love, nevertheless you have not failed, for you yourself are all the better for loving.

Look again at our text for today – Jesus is saying that if the people of a house to whom you give peace do not receive it, then let your peace return to you. So you see, you are more peaceful for having given the peace. Either way you win. If they take it, good; if they don't take it, then it is still good. The loving and peaceful person always wins, for he becomes more loving in the giving out of love, even if the other person doesn't receive that love. There is no failure in the lives of those who express Agape love.

**FURTHER STUDY**

Luke 6:27–38;
Matt. 10:8;
Acts 20:35

1. What was Jesus'
instruction to His
disciples?
2. What was His
promise?

## Prayer

O Father, how exciting and releasing is this thought – that because love is so victorious, I simply cannot fail when I love. For I become more loving in the giving of love. Continue to love in and through me this day and every day. Amen.

# "Love makes the world go round"

*"For by him all things were created ... all things were created by him and for him." (v.16)*

**For reading & meditation – Colossians 1:13–23**

If it is true that "love never fails" (for it never fails to enrich the giver of love), is it also true that those who are unloving cannot succeed? Yes, I believe it is. Those who carry through an unloving deed do not really succeed, for the unloving action registers itself in them in a way that brings about an inner loss. The pay-off is in the person – they are demeaned by their unlovingness.

So outer success can be an inner failure. If "love never fails", then "unlove" never succeeds. It can't, by its very nature. I am persuaded that to love is the only way to live effectively. To act in any other way than in love is to inject into any situation a disruptive tendency which will sooner or later complicate the situation and tie it up in knots. The world was made to work in love's way and in no other way. If we try to make it work in any other way than love, we work our own ruin.

A business organisation I know runs a seminar entitled "Putting People First", in which business people are taught how to put others before themselves. This seminar is making a big impact even though it has a secular approach, for it is making the point that the loving attitude is the only thing that really works. Wouldn't it be wonderful if those who see this would go on to the next step and open up their beings to the Source of all love? Then they would find, not just an answer to living but *the* answer to living.

**FURTHER STUDY**

John 1:1–13;
1 John 3:1–2;
4:7–8; Eph. 5:2

1. What are we called?
2. What should our lifestyle reflect?

## Prayer

My Father, help me to love this day with Your love. Then all ugliness will be turned to beauty, all littleness into greatness and all pettiness into significance. In Jesus' Name I pray. Amen.

# "Transformed already"

*"… we, who … reflect the Lord's glory, are being transformed into his likeness with ever-increasing glory …" (v.18)*

**For reading & meditation – 2 Corinthians 3:1–18**

We have been saying that even when love does not succeed in changing the object of one's love, it never fails to bring about changes in the one who expresses love. This thought, however, must not be allowed to turn our gaze away from the fact that love does have a powerful influence in bringing about changes in others.

A woman who was bent on changing people but continually kept failing wrote (not to me): "The last morning of the conference I knew I was His, and knew that I had to stop trying to change everyone. You didn't know it, but everything you said was a confirmation of what God had previously been trying to say to me. Suddenly I began to see people through the eyes of Jesus, and when I looked at them through His eyes they all looked so wonderful, so transformed *already*. I am not capable of transforming anyone. But to love them and help them find Him is the answer. Thank you for showing me that."

The woman who had been trying to transform everyone was herself transformed by the love of Jesus within. Love does transform things, not into gold as did the touch of Midas, but into love, more precious than gold. If you are someone who likes changing people, then give it up now before you have a breakdown. It just won't work. Give out love and only love. For in the giving out of love, you not only transform yourself but there is a high chance that you will transform others. Hence – a double cure.

**FURTHER STUDY**

Luke 10:25–37;
Matt. 22:39;
1 Thess. 3:12

1. How did Jesus illustrate practical love?
2. What was His conclusion?

## Prayer

Father, help me to do just that – to give out love and only love. Show me that my task is not to transform people, but to love them. I fail only as I fail to love. Help me love as You love. In Jesus' Name I ask it. Amen.

# Love – a conquering force

*"… live a life of love, just as Christ loved us and gave himself up for us …" (v.2)*

**For reading & meditation – Ephesians 5:1–16**

What we have been saying about the power of love to transform is not something intangible and vague but real and powerful.

When the Communist portion of Chiang Kai-shek's army took over Nanking (now Nanjing), they began to loot the city, and entered homes to seize whatever they could find. A Chinese Christian, a professor of theology, decided that whatever happened, he would respond in love. When a soldier struck him on one side of the chest with the butt of his rifle, the professor pointed to his other side and said: "This too, please." The soldier dropped his gun in astonishment. The professor then found that some of the local people, who had followed the soldiers, were trying to get his brass bed down the stairs in order to take it away to their own home when it got stuck. The professor said: "Here, let me help you", whereupon they blushed to the roots of their hair and fled.

At last the Communists decided to take him off and shoot him, but as he was being led away, he put his arm through the arm of the ringleader and said: "You are my friend; I expect you to protect me." Then he marched along arm in arm to his execution. When they got to the place where they intended to execute him, they let him go, saying: "What can you do with a person like this?" Love may not always overcome evil in this way and save a person from death, but whether it does or not, you can be sure of this – it always has the last word.

**FURTHER STUDY**

Matt. 5:33–42;
1 Pet. 3:9

1. What 4 practical demonstrations of love did Jesus mention?
2. What will result when we take these steps?

## Prayer

Gracious Father, help me understand more deeply the truth that has been touched on today – that love always has the last word. It may sometimes seem that it has failed, but whether in death or in life, its power is always supreme. Thank You, Father. Amen.

# More of Paul's lists

*"Do everything in love." (v.14)*

**For reading & meditation – 1 Corinthians 16:1–14**

Following the statement, "Love never fails", Paul gives us yet another of his marvellous lists in order to remind us of the supremacy of love. He tells us that prophecy, tongues and knowledge would eventually pass away, but love and love alone would remain for ever.

We are told by Josephus and other first-century writers that it was almost every Jewish mother's ambition for her son to become a prophet. Prior to the coming of Christ, it had been nearly four hundred years since God had spoken to Israel through a prophet, and the whole nation waited wistfully for another messenger to come. Undoubtedly, had one appeared, they would have hung upon his every word and given him their undivided attention. Of course, Paul was probably thinking more of the gift of prophecy which he had commented on earlier in the letter, but whether we think in terms of the role of a prophet as referred to in Ephesians 4:11 or the gift of prophecy mentioned in 1 Corinthians 12:10, the issue is still the same – one day prophecy will pass away and will have no further purpose. Not so with love – love goes on for ever.

**FURTHER STUDY**

Mark 12:28–34;
James 2:8;
Gal. 5:6;
Matt. 24:35

1. What is the royal law?
2. In what way is love a law?

It must be noted, of course, that Paul is not denouncing or denigrating prophecy and saying it is of no value. He is simply saying it is a temporary thing – a valuable gift but one that will eventually pass away. The message Paul wants us to get is that the Church must not stop desiring the best gifts; it must be careful, however, that it does not covet them more than love.

## Prayer

O God my Father, I am so thankful that You inspired Paul to hold to his line – the line of this supremacy of love. Help us in this, the Church of the 21st century, to sound that same note without hesitation or fear. In Jesus' Name we pray. Amen.

# Love – the consistent motif

*"... do you love me? ..." (v.17)*

**For reading & meditation – John 21:15–25**

Today we see the supremacy of love over tongues. Here again, whether Paul had in mind the supernatural gift of tongues referred to in 1 Corinthians 12 or simply languages in general, they are all stamped with impermanence.

Many languages are dying. Experts say that unless great efforts are made to revive it, the Welsh language is in serious danger of lasting for only a few more generations. The same applies to the Irish language and the language of the Scottish Highlands (Gaelic). Take the Greek in which the New Testament was written – it is now just a language for study. The same applies to Latin. Love, however, will never die – it is guaranteed to last throughout all eternity.

Paul is putting things in this way, not simply to emphasise the impermanence of these things, but to show by contrast the supremacy of love. The great apostle has already told us that prophecy and tongues are nothing unless they are operated through love; now he is telling us that love will outlast them. In all other faiths, love is something that is touched on here and there – a chance note sounded among more dominant notes. Read the history of the world's religions, such as Islam, Buddhism, and so on, and you will see what I mean. In Christianity, however, love is not something that is put in and then cancelled out by other emphases. It is the whole motif – the supreme note.

**FURTHER STUDY**

Acts 2:1–13;
10:46–47;
1 Cor. 12:10

1. What happened on the Day of Pentecost?
2. How did Peter explain it?

## Prayer

O Father, thank You for striking one note as the supreme note – the note of love. Help me to decide right now that as love is the consistent motif of the gospel, it shall be the consistent motif of my life also. In Jesus' Name I ask it. Amen.

# The transience of knowledge

*"The world and its desires pass away, but the man who does the will of God lives for ever." (v.17)*

**For reading & meditation – 1 John 2:15–29**

Having told us that love will outlast prophecy and tongues, Paul goes farther and with even greater boldness adds: "where there is knowledge, it will pass away" (1 Cor. 13:8). Much of the knowledge of the ancients – where is it? It is largely gone. A schoolboy today knows more than Sir Isaac Newton knew. His knowledge has vanished away.

Some years ago, one of the faculty in the University of Edinburgh was asked by the university librarian to go to the library and pick out the books on his subject that were no longer needed. The faculty member replied: "This is something you can do yourself – just take every textbook that is more than ten years old and put it down the cellar." Yesterday's knowledge is no good for today, and tomorrow's knowledge may change the following day. This is the kind of world we live in – a world where knowledge passes away.

Can you tell me anything that is going to last? I can think of things Paul did not condescend to mention, but they are facts nevertheless – money, fortune, fame and so on. I feel it necessary to remind you once again that Paul is not condemning these things and saying they are worthless. They are good things and some are great things, but they are not the supreme thing. Love is the supreme thing. There is a great deal in the world that is beautiful and good, but it will not last. An immortal soul must give itself to the thing that is immortal. And the only immortal thing is – love.

**FURTHER STUDY**

Gal. 6:1–10; 5:13;
2 Cor. 9:6

*1. What is the divine principle?*
*2. How will you sow some love today?*

## Prayer

Father, help me to appreciate what is good and beautiful about the present, but help me to give myself only to that which is permanent. Just as You kept Paul's insight clear, keep mine clear too, I pray. In Jesus' Name. Amen.

# "Great – but not the greatest"

*"... The only thing that counts is faith expressing itself through love." (v.6)*

**For reading & meditation – Galatians 5:1–14**

We spend one more day meditating on Paul's statement: "As for prophecy ... it will pass away; as for tongues, they will ... cease; as for knowledge, it will pass away. For our knowledge ... and our prophecy is fragmentary (incomplete and imperfect)" (1 Cor. 13:8–9, Amp. Bible).

I am convinced that if the people of today's Church took these words to heart, it would revolutionise our approach to both our individual and corporate Christian living. Some Christians (thankfully, not all) are more interested in spectacular displays of prophecy, tongues and knowledge than they are in the demonstration of love. I am grateful to be alive to witness the miracles of great power that are in evidence, especially in the Third World, and here in the West, the gifts of the Spirit are seen operating in fellowships that once taught these things died out with the Early Church.

I am not against the operation of the power gifts in the Church; I am one hundred per cent for it. I feel it necessary, however, to put this caution – that these things ought not to be allowed to occupy our attention to such a degree that we lose sight of the fact that they will all one day disappear and vanish. The thing that survives is – love. The greatest thing in the world is not exciting meetings, powerful conferences or informative seminars. They are great, but they are not the greatest thing. Let it never be forgotten: the greatest thing is – love.

**FURTHER STUDY**

1 John 3:14–24;
5:2–4;
Eph. 5:1–2

1. How do we know we have passed from death to life?
2. How can we show the reality of our love?

## Prayer

My Father and my God, help me keep my perspective clear so that my initial focus is on the eternal and not the temporal. Continually keep before me, dear Lord, the fact that the only thing that will survive into eternity is love. In Jesus' Name I pray. Amen.

# "When the perfect comes"

*"Not that I have already obtained all this, or have already been made perfect, but I press on ..." (v.12)*

**For reading & meditation – Philippians 3:7–21**

Paul, having made the point that tongues, prophecy and knowledge will pass away but that love remains for ever, completes the thought: "But when the complete and perfect (total) comes, the incomplete and imperfect will vanish away – become antiquated, void and superseded" (1 Cor. 13:10, Amp. Bible).

Some think that the phrase "when the perfect comes" refers to the fact that when the Early Church had passed through its infancy and come to maturity, then the gifts of tongues and so on would no longer be needed and disappear. This is a view that held great sway in the Church until the late 1960s. The interesting thing is that many of those who taught this interpretation have themselves experienced a deep encounter with the Spirit that has caused them to view things differently. "When the perfect comes" does not have reference to the beginnings of the Church and its passage through infancy to maturity; it has to do with the completion of the Church when it arrives in eternity and is joined to Christ in perfect oneness.

One of the great Bible expositors of the twentieth century, Dr Martyn Lloyd-Jones, through his writings was responsible, perhaps more than anyone else, for showing thousands that the work of the Spirit in the Early Church was intended to continue until Christ comes. The reason why the things that took place in the Early Church have not been seen in other centuries is not because God withdrew them, but because the Church came not to expect them. In the Church, both individually and corporately, we tend to get what we expect.

**FURTHER STUDY**

Isa. 26:1–9;
Psa. 73:25;
Matt. 7:7;
1 Cor. 12:7

1. What did the psalmist express?
2. What did Jesus promise?

## Prayer

Father, I am grateful for this emphasis today, for I see that in seeking love I am not to neglect this other aspect also. Teach me to be a balanced Christian and to get my priorities in the right order. In Jesus' Name. Amen.

# "For God's sake – grow up!"

*"… speaking the truth in love, we will in all things grow up into him who is the Head, that is, Christ." (v.15)*

**For reading & meditation – Ephesians 4:1–16**

We come now to the statement made by Paul which is probably one of the best-known of all his sayings, both inside and outside the Church: "When I was a child, I talked like a child, I thought like a child, I reasoned like a child; now that I have become a man, I am done with childish ways and have put them aside" (1 Cor. 13:11, Amp. Bible). The verb used in the phrase "done with childish ways" is a very strong one in the original Greek: *katargeo*, which means "to put away in a decisive act".

I once heard a preacher preach on this text under the title: "For God's sake – grow up". When I heard him announce the title, I thought his choice of words to be insensitive, but when he started speaking, it all made sense. He pointed out that if we are to become mature sons and daughters of God, then we must make a conscious decision to put behind us all childish behaviour and decide to grow up. And we must do it, not just for our own sake, but for His sake: "For God's sake – grow up."

Are you still a "baby" Christian – even though you have been on the way for a good number of years? Do you regard the gifts of the Spirit as being more important than love? Do you hanker after supernatural manifestations more than the pursuit of holiness? You don't have to give up one in order to get the other – you just have to be mature enough to know which are the priorities.

**FURTHER STUDY**

2 Peter 1:1–11;
3:18;
Eph. 1:17;
1 Cor. 3:1

1. What did Paul say of the Corinthian church?
2. How can we grow up into maturity?

## Prayer

Father, I see that maturity begins with a decision. So I make it today. I choose the way of love over every other way. Help me to let love be the arbiter of everything. In Jesus' Name I ask it. Amen.

# Unsatisfied now – but then?

*"… in righteousness I shall see your face; when I awake,
I shall be satisfied with seeing your likeness." (v.15)*

**For reading & meditation – Psalm 17:1–15**

Even the most casual reader of 1 Corinthians 13 will be impressed with the fact that every verse is tightly packed with truth, beauty and inspiration. Verse 12 is no exception: "For now we are looking in a mirror that gives only a dim reflection … but then [when perfection comes] we shall see in reality and face to face" (Amp. Bible). If there was any doubt that the "perfection" talked about in verse 10 had to do with seeing Christ at His coming, then the matter is settled here.

Many commentators believe that Paul's reference to a mirror comes from the fact that Corinth was famous for its mirrors of polished metal. A "Corinthian mirror" was a prized possession, yet at best it reflected a somewhat blurred image. The word "dimly" (RSV) means it appears as an enigma, and Moffatt translates it as "baffling reflections". What Paul is saying is: our knowledge, which is just fragmentary, and our reasoning, which is often faulty, produce only a distorted image of divine reality.

At Christ's coming however, we shall know with a knowledge which we do not now have, and through that knowledge will come the full revelation of love. As long as our spirits are confined by our human condition, our true comprehension of the greatness of God's love will be only a dim perception, blurred by our partial blindness. But when the opaque veil of our humanity is torn away and the encroaching cataracts of our partial blindness are removed, we shall love in the same degree with which we are loved. Then imperfection will have put on perfection.

**FURTHER STUDY**

John Ch. 17;
Isa. 33:17;
1 John 3:2

1. What did Jesus say about His relationship with the Father?
2. What was John's conviction?

## Prayer

O God my Father, when I sense the prospect that lies before me, my heart cries out: "Even so, come, Lord Jesus." Help me live in the light of this expectation, not only today but every day. Amen.

# "Fully known, fully loved"

*"How precious to me are your thoughts, O God!
How vast is the sum of them!" (v.17)*

**For reading & meditation – Psalm 139:1–24**

What we know and experience of love is at best just a small part of what awaits us when we see our Lord face to face. The truth that we must hold on to, however, is this – although at this stage of our pilgrimage we do not fully know Him, He fully knows us. I will never fully comprehend the divine love while in this earthly frame, and due to this limitation, I shall not be able fully to love God, but that does not stop God loving me.

Time and time again, when I lament the fact that my love for God is not as strong as I know it ought to be, I reflect on the wonder of His love for me – and invariably my heart becomes strangely warmed. Why should this be? I think it is because the greatest truth in the universe is not that I love God, but that He loves me. Follow me into this thought as I try to unfold it as best I can.

I am sure you will remember the story of Dietrich Bonhoeffer, the German pastor who was imprisoned by Hitler and later executed. He left us a number of writings, one of which was a short poem entitled, "Who am I?" The poem begins with the question: "Who am I?" and ends thus: "Whoever I am, thou knowest, O God, *I am thine*" (italics mine). When he could not take solace in the fact that he knew God, the crucial thing that cut through his confusion and despair was that God *knew* him and loved him.

**FURTHER STUDY**

Isa. 43:1–2;
Matt. 28:11–20;
Ex. 33:14

1. What did God declare through Isaiah?
2. What was Jesus' promise to His disciples?

## Prayer

O my Father, help me to drop my anchor in the depths of this reassuring and encouraging revelation – that no matter how limited I am in knowing and loving You, no such limitation exists on Your side. You fully know me and fully love me. I am eternally thankful. Amen.

# The bottom line of faith

*"This is love: not that we loved God,*
*but that he loved us ..." (v.10)*

**For reading & meditation – 1 John 4:7–19**

T he fact that we are fully known and fully loved by God is one of
the most encouraging and reassuring truths in the whole of the
universe. We spoke yesterday of Dietrich Bonhoeffer's conclusions
while in prison. Permit me to focus on them once more today, but
this time in a little more detail. Listen to these lines taken from the
poem: "Who am I?"

*Who am I? They often tell me*
*I would step from my cell's confinement*
*Calmly, cheerfully, firmly,*
*Like a squire from his country house.*
*Who am I? They often tell me*
*I used to speak to my warders*
*Freely, friendly and clearly*
*As though it were mine to command ...*
*Who am I? They mock me, these lonely questions,*
*Whoever I am, thou knowest, O God, I am thine!*

**FURTHER STUDY**

Rev. 1:1–8;
Rom. 5:8;
1 Cor. 6:11

1. What was the
extent of God's love?
2. What did Jesus do
before He washed
us?

Nowhere in the poem (over thirty lines) does
he say: "My faith pulled me through." He didn't
even take solace in his knowledge of God. The
truth that kept him going in that dark and
depressing situation was the fact that God knew
*him*. It is frightening for some people when they
come face to face with the thought: *God knows me
through and through.* Ah, but there's more. He not
only knows us – He loves us. And the addition of
those three simple words makes all the difference.

## Prayer

O Father, help me hold on to this truth, so that no matter what happens, I shall
not lose touch with the fact that I am fully known and fully loved by You. In
Christ's peerless and precious Name I ask it. Amen.

# "This incredible *knowing*"

*"for he knows how we are formed, he remembers
that we are dust." (v.14)*

**For reading & meditation – Psalm 103:1–22**

Phillip Keller says: "God in Christ knows all the intricacies of my genetic make-up. He is fully aware of all the interrelated characteristics which were inherited from my grandparents and former forebears. He knows precisely why I am the unique, special person I am."

He goes on to make the additional point that not even our parents know this much about us. God alone knows us in this intimate way. He understands exactly what goes on inside us, and for that reason, He and He alone can treat us with utter integrity, complete understanding and full compassion. You see, it is this infinite, incredible *knowing* that enables God to deal with us in dignity, forgiveness and love. He knows everything that has gone into the shaping of our personality, all the stresses, strains and pressures, and thus He alone can properly appraise the impact made upon us by our parents, peers, friends, schoolteachers, and so on.

This does not mean that He excuses us – He always holds us responsible for the decisions we make – but He looks upon us with a knowledge, an understanding and a compassion such as no other person in the universe could give to us. In the light of this, we can begin to see what underlies the cry from the cross: "Father, forgive them, for they do not know what they are doing" (Luke 23:34). It is this dimension of being known to the utmost depths of my being that conquers my heart's antipathies, and overcomes all my rebellion, all my suspicion and all my distrust. I am fully known *and* fully loved.

**FURTHER STUDY**

Matt. 10:22–31;
Luke 10:20;
Phil. 4:3

*1. In what can we
rejoice?
2. How did Jesus
express our value?*

## Prayer

O Gracious Father, the knowledge that You fully know me and fully love me sends me to my knees in gratitude. I can hold on to this even when I can't hold on to myself. I am grateful more than any words of mine can tell. Thank You, dear Father. Amen.

# "Seeing God"

*"The unfolding of your words gives light; it gives understanding to the simple."* (v.130)

**For reading & meditation – Psalm 119:129–144**

Paul, in the second part of 1 Corinthians 13:12, states: "Now I know in part (imperfectly); but then I shall know and understand fully and clearly, even in the same manner as I have been fully and clearly known and understood [by God]" (Amp. Bible).

Does this mean that because we can never fully know God and His Son Jesus Christ until eternity, we sit back and give no further consideration to the matter of developing our knowledge and love for Him? No, for despite the inner struggle we have to "see Him" as He truly is, it is important to understand clearly the methods and means which God uses to reveal Himself to us now. Although we are surrounded by imperfection, we can still "see God", even though dimly or vaguely.

The primary means by which we come to "see God" is, of course, His Word, the Bible. It is not as good, of course, as seeing Him face to face, but while we wait for that experience yet to come, we look into His Word and we "see Him" in a way that nourishes our spirits and sets our hearts beating in eager anticipation for "the appearing of our Lord Jesus Christ". Those who try to know God without coming to the Bible end up with the strangest misconceptions and misunderstandings. In my youth, I had a friend who tried to do this and finished up spiritually beggared and bankrupt. He became subject to his own moods; self-centred instead of Scripture-centred – hence moody, irritable and off-centre.

**FURTHER STUDY**

2 Pet. 1:16–21;
Psa. 19:8; 119:105;
Prov. 6:23

1. What was the basis of Peter's conviction?
2. What do we have to guide us?

## Prayer

Father, I see that it is only the entrance of Your Word that gives light, and by implication, the neglecting of Your Word gives darkness. Help me to take a daily look into Your Word, for it is only in Your light that I can walk with a sure and steady tread. Amen.

# The Bible – self-correcting

*"All Scripture is God-breathed, and is useful …"*
*(v.16)*

**For reading & meditation – 2 Timothy 3:1–17**

We can see God to a high degree *only* through His inspired Word, the Bible. We can know *about* God through such things as Nature and Providence, but we can only *know* God through the revelation contained in the Scriptures.

I have met many people who have tried to come to God through the medium of their own thoughts and ideas. I remember a man I once knew who told me that he used to begin his day by focusing on God through meditation. It was not biblical meditation, I hasten to add. Did he get through to God? No, because the effort we make to "see God" through the medium of our own conceptions is doomed to failure. Human conceptions are man's ideas about God; the Bible is God's revelation of Himself. Unless our thoughts are constantly corrected by God's thoughts, our thoughts invariably go off at a tangent and revolve around ourselves.

When the man I am talking about came to see this and surrendered his life to Jesus Christ, he began his day by looking into the Bible, and then – what a difference! After a few months of reading the Bible he said to me: "I used to look into my own mind and all I saw is what I am – a sinner. I now look into the Bible and I see not only what I ought to be but what I can be – by the grace of God." To attempt to come to know or "see God" without the Bible is like the captain of a large passenger liner setting out to sea without a compass.

**FURTHER STUDY**

2 Tim. 2:7–15;
1 Pet. 1:25;
Psa. 119:103;
Jer. 15:16

1. What was Paul's word to Timothy?
2. How did the psalmist describe God's Word?

## Prayer

O Father, how can I ever sufficiently thank You for giving me this most marvellous book, the Bible? I know it is inspired because it inspires me. Help me to draw daily strength and encouragement from its pages. In Jesus' Name I ask it. Amen.

# "The silence of eternity – broken"

*"Thank God for his Son – his Gift too wonderful*
*for words." (v.15, TLB)*

**For reading & meditation – 2 Corinthians 9:1–15**

What makes the Bible such a powerful force in helping us know and "see God"? There can be many answers to that question. For example, it tells us what went wrong with humankind in the beginning and how we can be put back together again. The books it contains are like sixty-six steps that lead from the Garden of Eden in the book of Genesis to the New Jerusalem in the book of Revelation.

But the biggest single thing contributing to the unique power of the Scriptures is the revelation they bring to us concerning the character of God. The Bible is the only book in the universe that has been specially inspired, protected and preserved to give us the truth about God and tell us exactly what He is like. So what is He like? – He is like Jesus.

Lao-tzu, the great Chinese philosopher, said: "The word that can be uttered is not the divine word; that word is Silence." Many people have pondered that statement and wondered what he meant. I believe he was saying that the truth about God is too great to go into words. But the alternative is not silence. Lao-tzu did not know

**FURTHER STUDY**

John 1:1–14;
1 John 1:1;
Rev. 19:13

1. How does John describe the glory of "the word"?
2. List 6 things he says about "the word".

Jesus, so for him, the word had to be silence. But the silence of eternity has been broken by the appearance of Incarnate Love – Jesus. The Word became, not just words or printer's ink, but *flesh*. God appeared before us in human guise and the Bible has captured this revelation, bringing to us the thrilling reality that in Jesus, God is approachable, available, simplified, loveable. The Word has become *flesh*.

## Prayer

O Father, I am so thankful that when all other ways were inadequate, You opened a way to us that met our deepest need. When we couldn't come to You, You came to us. It is too wonderful for words. All honour and praise be to Your Name for ever. Amen.

# "Love came down"

*"The Word became flesh and made his dwelling among us … full of grace and truth." (v.14)*

**For reading & meditation – John 1:1–18**

The text before us today says that not only did Christ appear, but that He "made his dwelling among us". The revelation of God was not a momentary rift in the clouds that surround the Deity – a fleeting vision of what God is like. No, He "made his dwelling among us", from the manger at Bethlehem to the cross on Calvary.

It was not very long, but long enough to reveal God's character in operation amid the surroundings where our characters are wrought out. Another passage says: "He has come and has redeemed his people" (Luke 1:68). The only way to redeem His people was to visit them. He didn't sit on a cloud and pick us up with a celestial pair of tongs and take us to heaven, having not soiled His fingers with the messy business of human living. No, He showed us how to live by living among us, amid our poverty, temptations, problems and choices.

Suppose our text for today had read: "The Word … made his dwelling among us … full of truth and grace." What if truth had been put first and grace second? Then the emphasis would have been upon "truth" in God, not "grace" – a characteristic of love. The Bible does not say: "God is truth"; however, it does say: "God is love". Gandhi said: "God is truth", but he failed to see that He is more than that. The greatest thing about God is His love, and it was that, more than anything else, which He brought with Him when He came to us at the first Christmas.

**FURTHER STUDY**

Phil. 2:1–11;
Gal. 4:4;
John 3:16

1. What form was Jesus willing to take on?
2. Share what God's love means to you with someone today.

## Prayer

O Father, I am so glad that You put things in the right order – first "grace" and then "truth". It underlines the fact that the greatest thing about You is Your love. I bow at Your feet today and lay before You my special gift of thanks. Thank You, dear Lord. Thank You. Amen.

# Getting ready for eternity

*" … his work will be shown for what it is … the Day will bring it to light. It will be revealed with fire …" (v.13)*

**For reading & meditation – 1 Corinthians 3:1–17**

The last of Paul's statements concerning Agape love (God's love in us) in 1 Corinthians 13: "… these three remain: faith, hope and love. But the greatest of these is love" (v.13). Some interpret Paul as saying here: "At the coming of the Lord, faith and hope will disappear and love alone will remain." Thus they interpret the apostle's words as meaning that when that which is perfect is come, two of these three things will pass away – faith into sight and hope into fruition.

But Paul is not saying that. He is saying that faith, hope and love, in contrast to the transitory gifts, remain even at the coming of the Lord. The Greek verb is singular although the subject is plural, indicating the indissoluble unity of the three virtues. They will *all* remain, but *the greatest of them is love*. We know little about the life that is to come, but it would appear from this that there will be a place for both faith and hope in eternity. If that is so, then the conclusion is that these are the only qualities which we will take with us into eternity.

**FURTHER STUDY**

1 Pet. 1:15–25;
2 Cor. 4:18;
Heb. 12:27

1. How have we been born again?
2. What is our flesh like?

This passage shows us that on the threshold of eternity, there will be a review of our life's work and the only thing that will survive will be true character. And what forms character? Faith, hope and love. Only to the degree that these are present in us are we building for eternity. If a person invests their short life on earth in anything else, then their days are spent without profit.

## Prayer

My Father and my God, help me to bind tightly together in my life the qualities of faith, hope and love so that they will become a threefold cord that I will carry with me into eternity. In Jesus' Name I ask it. Amen.

# Three survivors

*"… your work produced by faith, your labour prompted by love, and your endurance inspired by hope …" (v.3)*

**For reading & meditation – 1 Thessalonians 1:1–10**

The story is told of a man who died and went to heaven. Arriving at the Pearly Gates, he was asked his name and, after identifying it in the Book of Life, an angel escorted him through the streets of heaven. As they walked together, the man said to the angel: "Where are we going?" The angel replied: "We are going to the dwelling place which has been prepared for you."

As they walked, the man looked at the magnificent dwelling places that were all around, and wondered which one had been prepared for him. Eventually they came to a small, tumbledown abode at which the angel stopped and said: "Here is where you are to spend eternity." The man was taken aback and said: "Surely – not this. Why couldn't my home be like the beautiful mansions we have just passed?" In solemn tones the angel said: "I'm sorry, but we did the best we could out of the materials that you sent up."

It is only a story, of course, and in some ways it has little scriptural support except perhaps the passage we looked at yesterday. That showed us that the only materials that survive the refining fires we shall all have to pass through before entering into eternity are the gold, silver and precious stones of pure motive and character. Faith, hope and love have one thing in common – they are survivors; they last. They are, as one writer put it: "a tightly intertwined three-strand cord, braided together to form the unbreakable line of Christ's character extended to us as our own lifeline of eternal duration."

FURTHER STUDY

Rom. 5:1–9; Psa. 66:10; James 1:12; 1 Pet. 1:7

1. How does Paul show the outworking of faith, hope and love?
2. What is promised to the person who endures?

## Prayer

O Father, help me to accept responsibility for what I am expected to do this side of eternity. I see, as I look back on my life, that if I had decided differently I would have been different. From now on, I want all my decisions to be character-building ones. In Jesus' Name I ask it. Amen.

# "A woman in love"

*"… even though you do not see him now, you believe in him and are filled with an inexpressible … joy" (v.8)*

**For reading & meditation – 1 Peter 1:1–9**

In his book *A Layman Looks at the Love of God*, Phillip Keller tells of a young woman falling in love with a handsome young man in whom she puts enormous faith and hope. Eventually they are married, but she soon discovers that her "Prince Charming" is a deceiver and a rogue. All her dreams crash into rubble and she is broken-hearted. Why? Because she lacked faith in him? No. Because she lacked hope? No. Because she lacked love? No, she had invested her faith, hope and love in a person who had no character.

In time, the man dies and she tells herself that she will never have faith in anyone again, but one day a man comes into her life who is unpretentious, simple and transparently sincere. A tiny spark of faith is ignited within her. In due course the man asks her to marry him, and with faith no more than a grain of mustard seed, she begins another marriage. Things turn out well, for the man has impeccable character and is extremely loving and kind. Her heart is healed. Her happiness is complete.

Why? Was it just the faith she had? No. Was it just the hope? No. It was largely the character of the man. And it is just the same, says Keller, with Christ. His character is impeccable, His integrity undeniable and His trustworthiness complete. It is for this reason that our faith, hope and love endure – they are rooted in Him. His character validates our faith, honours our hope and confirms our love. They remain sure because He remains sure.

**FURTHER STUDY**

Isa. 6:1–8;
Col. 1:15;
1 Tim. 1:17;
6:15–16

1. What aspect of God's character was revealed to Isaiah?
2. How did God prepare him?

# Prayer

O Father, grant that my faith, my hope and my love shall be for ever rooted in You. For I see that unless they are, they will come to nothing. Help me to keep my eyes firmly fixed on You, dear Father, so that Your character will become my character. Amen.

# Faith, hope and love in heaven

*"...a Lamb, looking as if it had been slain, standing in the centre of the throne ..." (v.6)*

**For reading & meditation – Revelation 5:1–14**

O nce we see the tremendous truth that faith, hope and love remain sure because Christ remains sure, then we will be delivered from self-preoccupation. We will lift up our gaze from our own feeble faith to the One who is totally reliable. Our hope will be centred in the One who never fails. Our love will pour itself out in a continual love offering at His feet.

Unless Christ is the object of our faith, hope and love, then they are rooted in the wrong things. Change the word "faith" to "confidence" and you might begin to get a better idea of what I mean. Now ask yourself: in eternity, will my confidence be in Christ? What's the answer? It must be "Yes". Change the word "hope" to "expectancy" and ask yourself: in eternity, will my expectancy be in Him? The answer again must be "Yes". There is no need to change the word "love" to anything else, mainly because there is no other word to which it can be changed.

Now tie all three things together. In heaven there will be a never-ending confidence in the eternal value of Christ's sacrifice for us on the cross. Our text today gives us a beautiful picture of a Lamb on the throne "as though it had been slain". Why, in this vision of the future, do we see "a Lamb as though it had been slain" – freshly slaughtered? It shows, so I believe, the tremendous immediacy of Christ's self-giving. He not only captures our faith, hope and love here on earth: He will continue to capture them in eternity.

> **FURTHER STUDY**
>
> John 1:29–36;
> 1 Pet. 1:19;
> Rev. 7:9–12
>
> 1. What did John declare?
> 2. How do those around the throne respond to the Lamb?

## Prayer

O Father, I am so grateful that heaven will be, not only a different place, but a dynamic place where my confidence, expectancy and love can find endless and everlasting expression. Thank You, Father. Amen.

# How to love

*"We love because he first loved us."*
*(v.19)*

**For reading & meditation – 1 John 4:19**

How do we go about the task of deepening our love for Christ on this side of eternity? By far the greatest way is to focus your gaze on how much He loves you. You see, the more we concentrate our attention on how much He loves us, then His love produces the same degree of love in us in return.

Our text today says: "We love because he first loved us." The more we focus on how much He loves us, the more we will love Him back. In the divine economy, love begets love. We cannot love until we are loved; we cannot serve until we are served. God, in His great love, has gone to the utmost lengths possible to let us know He loves us, and as we gaze at the greatest proof of that love – Calvary – the scales fall from our eyes and our love flames forth in response.

One writer says: "We can love God only with Eros love and not with Agape. We can love others with Agape, but not God, because Agape is love regardless of the worthiness of the character concerned. We could not love God if God were not of good character. We love Him because He is worthy. Hence our love for Him is Eros and not Agape." This writer fails to see one important thing – God's Agape produces Agape in me. This is what makes the Christian life so wonderful – the source of my love for Him is His love for me. I do not love Him with my love, I love Him with His love – true Agape.

**FURTHER STUDY**

Isa. Ch. 53;
John 15:13;
Gal. 3:13;
1 Pet. 2:24

1. What quality of love is revealed in Isaiah 53?
2. How does John describe it?

## Prayer

Father, I am so grateful that I do not have to love; I simply have to allow Your Agape love to love me into loving. Keep ever before me that I am not the spring of love, but just the channel of it. Flow through me in Agape love this day and every day. Amen.

# No love – no identity

*"But the fruit of the Spirit is love …"*
(v.22)

**For reading & meditation – Galatians 5:16–26**

On this, the last day of our meditations in 1 Corinthians 13, we consider our conclusions concerning Agape love (God's love in us). No matter how spectacular, gifted or dedicated a person I might be, without love it is all ashes at God's feet. I may be able to prophesy and predict the future, speak eloquently with the tongues of men (or in supernatural tongues) and have enough knowledge to unravel the deepest mysteries of the universe, but if I do not have love, I am nothing.

The subtraction of love is the great subtraction. No matter how much else I have or do, it will all come to nothing without love. It is very much like multiplying by zero in mathematics – no matter how large a number we take when we multiply by zero, the result is always the same. Paul points out three things that are true of the person who does not love: "I am nothing", "I gain nothing", and "I just make a noise."

What a picture of a lost identity. A person who does not have love is nothing, achieves nothing, is without purpose or meaning, and is just a loud nuisance. However, those in whom Agape love dwells remain for ever. A loving character is the universe's most precious value. It will survive all the ravages of time and go singing into eternity. Let the wonder of it grip you as you ponder it in the days ahead. And keep ever before you the thrilling fact that both in time and in eternity, *love holds the field*.

**FURTHER STUDY**

1 Cor. Ch. 13; John 13:35; Eph. 2:4–5

*1. Read 1 Corinthians 13, putting the name "Jesus" in place of the word "love".*

*2. Read verses 4–6 again, putting your own name in place of "love". Does it fit?*

## Prayer

O God, my Father and Fountain of Agape love, I am so glad that Your love never wears thin – it is always Agape. Let me grow in the wonder of it, surrender to the call of it and live to be the channel of it. In Jesus' Name I pray. Amen.

# The Wondrous Cross

# The cross – central

*"For I resolved to know nothing while I was with you
except Jesus Christ and him crucified." (v.2)*

**For reading & meditation – 1 Corinthians 2:1–16**

The theme engaging our attention in this section is the cross. All communication between God and humankind begins at Calvary. There are many reasons why this is so, some of which we will explore together.

Over the years I have written on the cross a number of times, but never before have I felt such an urgency to call the Church back to this, the central issue of our faith. There are signs that the Church (generally speaking) is playing down the message of the cross in favour of more contemporary topics, such as self-image, co-dependency, awareness of group dynamics, and so on. Not that we do not need to have a Christian view of these subjects and pronounce on them from time to time. However, nothing must be allowed to replace the centrality of the cross. As a young Christian I was taught that no one can come to Christ or get to know Christ except through the cross. P.T. Forsyth, a preacher of a past generation, said: "Christ is to us what His cross is. If you move faith from that centre you have driven *the* nail into the Church's coffin."

Time and time again when I hear on television or read somewhere the ridiculous statement that "all religions are the same" my mind runs involuntarily to Calvary. No other religion has a cross. It is absolutely unique. The time has come, I believe, to put the cross back where it belongs; not on the periphery but at the centre of our faith. No cross – no Christianity. It is as stark and as simple as that.

**FURTHER STUDY**

1 Cor. 1:18–31;
Gal. 6:14;
Eph. 2:16

1. What was Paul's view of the cross?
2. What did this mean for him?

## Prayer

My Father and my God, lead me once more to Calvary. Deepen my knowledge and experience of the cross I pray. May I, like the apostle Paul, determine to know nothing except Jesus Christ and Him crucified. In Christ's Name I pray. Amen.

# The glorious cross

*"For the message of the cross is foolishness to those who are perishing, but to us … the power of God." (v.18)*

**For reading & meditation – 1 Corinthians 1:10–25**

Throughout the long history of the Church, preachers and teachers have claimed that we cannot understand Christ until we understand His cross. Emil Brunner, the Swiss theologian, put it like this: "He who understands the cross aright … understands the Bible, he understands Jesus Christ." The better we understand the cross the better we will understand Jesus, and the better we understand Jesus the better we will understand the cross. Not that it is possible for us to grasp the full meaning of either.

Theologians have devised a number of theories in their attempt to explain the mystery of the cross, but no theory it seems to me is big enough to fit the facts. Just as Jesus broke the bars of death and stepped beyond the tomb, so the fact of Jesus dying seems to transcend all statements and theories. They are attempts to tell the untellable, to speak the unspeakable.

The highest mountain in my native Wales is Mount Snowdon. Many a traveller has been stopped in his tracks when he has first caught sight of the great mountain reaching up towards the sky. But Snowdon looks quite different when contemplated from Beaumaris than when surveyed from Capel Curig. The view from Rhyl is quite unlike that from Llandudno. Yet the mountain itself is the same. Just so with the cross of Christ. To see it in all its glory we must gaze at it from different vantage points. Looked at from one viewpoint it is wonderful, but looked at from a number of viewpoints it is more than wonderful. It is sublime.

**FURTHER STUDY**

Phil. 3:1–18;
Col. 1:19–22; 2:14

1. How do most people live?
2. What is the heart of the message of the cross?

## Prayer

O Father, as I stand and gaze at the cross from different vantage points may I come, like the apostle Paul, to the conviction that nothing is worth boasting in apart from Your cross. Only that survives. Amen.

# The cross – a kaleidoscope

*"… the Lamb that was slain from the creation of the world." (v.8)*

**For reading & meditation – Revelation 13:1–9**

One preacher I heard described the cross as kaleidoscopic, not because it changes but because there are so many different ways in which it can be viewed.

In looking at the first of these perspectives we survey the cross from the viewpoint of eternity. This is what I am choosing to call *the cosmic cross*. We can't begin to understand the cross until we see it in a cosmic and eternal setting. The crucifixion of Christ was not merely an earthly affair conducted clandestinely in an obscure corner of the Roman Empire. It spans all time and transcends all history. Ian Macpherson, a British writer, put it like this: "Before the cross was an *act* in time it was a *fact* in eternity." Take, for instance, the strange text that is before us today, which tells us that the Lamb was slain from the beginning of time. But you say: "I thought Jesus was killed 2,000 years ago on a hill just outside the walls of Jerusalem." I would not wish to derogate in the slightest degree from that unique act of self-sacrifice which took place in time, but it is clear from Scripture that Calvary was antedated in eternity past. Jesus was the Lamb slain from the creation of the world. As one theologian put it: "There was a cross in the heart of God before there was ever one planted on the green hill outside Jerusalem."

The cross of Christ, as it has been graphically put, casts its shadow on the cosmos. Let the thought thrill you – God had a Lamb before He had a man!

**FURTHER STUDY**

John 1:1–29;
1 Cor. 5:7;
1 Pet. 1:19

1. How did John present Jesus?
2. How did Paul describe Christ?

## Prayer

Father, I see that the cross did not come out of history but came into it. You anticipated my sin and planned my salvation from all eternity. Such love deserves not just part of me but all of me. I give my all to You today. Amen.

# Redemption anticipated

*"He is the image of the invisible God, the firstborn over all creation." (v.15)*

### For reading & meditation – Colossians 1:15–23

W hy was it necessary for the Lamb to be slain from the creation of the world? When God created the world and laid down the broad beams that formed the universe He foresaw that evil would enter His creation and prepared for it by building into it a cross.

Couldn't God have made a universe in which sin and evil were *impossible*? He could have done so but just think what kind of a world it would have been: one in which creatures would have been like robots and responded to His commands in the same way that the computer on which I am writing these lines responds to my touch. By creating the universe and endowing creatures with the dangerous gift of free will God brought into existence the conditions in which evil became a possibility. Evil was not His intention. Yet, for a reason known only to Himself, He decided that by creating a universe in which evil could break out, greater glory could be gained for Himself and a higher good achieved for humanity than if He allowed it to remain uncreated.

In designing the universe, however, God made sure that the possibility of sin was met by the possibility of redemption. Thus those broad beams on which the universe is built are in the shape of a cross. And as we shall see a little later, you don't have to look very closely at the universe to observe that. Like a watermark in paper, the cosmos has a cross imprinted in it. It is not something imposed on time but exposed from it.

**FURTHER STUDY**

Deut. 30:1–19;
Josh. 24:15;
1 Kings 18:21;
Psa. 119:30

1. What is fundamental to human functioning?
2. What was the psalmist able to say?

## Prayer

Father, how can I thank You enough that the cross is not an afterthought but a forethought? With masterly strategy You planned my salvation. I shall be eternally grateful. In Jesus' Name. Amen.

# Part of the structure

*"... without the shedding of blood there is no forgiveness." (v.22)*

**For reading & meditation – Hebrews 9:11–28**

We ended our prayer yesterday with a note of thanksgiving that the cross is not an afterthought but a forethought. Some do not accept this. One befuddled theologian has said: "God never intended Jesus to be crucified; He intended that He should be followed." Dr Albert Schweitzer may have been a humanitarian with a brilliant mind but he was in a spiritual fog when it came to the cross. "Jesus," he said, "expected the Kingdom to come at Jerusalem. And when it didn't He died on the cross of a broken heart, crying, 'My God, my God, why hast Thou forsaken me?' But in dying He left an ethic of love." Those who see the cross as an afterthought fail to understand its meaning. The cross is a forethought – a fact worked into the texture of creation. It is, as someone put it, the groundplan of the universe.

Some Christians in China were forbidden to worship, so they would sit in a room and let the sun shine on a mirror, which threw an outline of a cross upon the wall. The outline drew their thoughts to their Lord, they said, and helped focus their worship. If someone who was not a Christian came into the room, one of the group would simply adjust the mirror slightly so it would not catch the rays of the sun.

As we investigate and throw light on the facts do we find that the cross is in the groundplan of the universe? I believe we do. It comes out of the universe because it was built into the universe.

**FURTHER STUDY**

Psa. 111:1–9;
Luke 1:68–70;
Heb. 1:10–12;
1 John 1:1–5

1. How did the psalmist describe God's plan of redemption?
2. What happened in the beginning?

## Prayer

Father, I see so clearly that the cross is not only an integral part of the Scriptures but also of life. The universe is the work not only of Your hands; it is the work of Your heart as well. Your heart is written into it. I am so thankful. Amen.

# A cruciform cosmos

*"'He saved others,' they said, 'but he can't save himself!'" (v.42)*

**For reading & meditation – Matthew 27:32–44**

"The cosmos," as Brian A. Greet succinctly puts it, "is cruciform." John Wesley had two simple tests for any teaching he gave, and he required a positive response to both. His first test was this: Is it in the Bible? His second: Is it in experience?

Clearly, the cross – the ultimate expression of the spirit of self-sacrifice – is in the Bible, but is it in experience as well? I believe it is. When we look closely at life we see evidence of the spirit of self-sacrifice everywhere. Firemen will go into a burning building and risk their own lives in order to save others. A not-so-good swimmer will plunge into the sea to save a stranger in distress and endanger his own life because something deep within him prompts him to do so. What is this "something"? It is, in my view, the law of self-sacrifice which runs like a scarlet thread through history. When Jesus hung upon the cross some of the crowd called out: "He saved others, but he can't save himself!" They could not see that He was saving others and therefore He could not save Himself.

**FURTHER STUDY**

John 15:1–13;
Eph. 5:2;
Titus 2:14

1. What is the underlying key to self-sacrifice?
2. Why is Christ's the supreme sacrifice?

The law I am talking about – the law of self-sacrifice – seems to be found not only in the texts of Scripture but in the very texture of life. Those who save others cannot save themselves trouble, pain, suffering, even death. Where does this desire to save others at the cost of one's own life come from? Is it, perhaps, explainable by the fact that we are made in the image of God – a God who gave Himself up for others?

## Prayer

Father, your image in us has been clouded by sin but clearly not obliterated. There are traces of the divine in us still. You made us like Yourself and for Yourself – and even gave Yourself for our salvation. My gratitude knows no bounds. Amen.

# The cross – inherent

*"And being in anguish, he prayed more earnestly …"*
(v.44)

**For reading & meditation – Luke 22:39–46**

As we gazed around Winchester Cathedral together, a friend pointed to the rood-screen and said: "There's a cross up there." Then he pointed to the floor and said: "And there's a cross down here." Like so many ancient places of worship the whole cathedral is a cross – it is a cruciform building. Chancel and nave for the upright, the two transepts for the cross-beam. If you could have stood at the foot of the hill called Calvary where Jesus died you might have pointed to the top and said: "There is a cross up there." Then you could have pointed to the ground at your feet and said: "And there is a cross down here." The cross is inherent in life. It is life's foundation, not an incongruity. Our Saviour, when He died at Golgotha, focused in a moment of time a fact which is in reality timeless. On that first Good Friday the Lamb slain from the creation of the world was *seen* slain.

One commentator daringly suggests that the supreme crisis for our Lord did not take place during His passion in Gethsemane where, as the poet put it, "God fought with God, and all the lights of heaven were afraid." He claims it took place before time began when the Son of God was faced with the prospect of coming to earth as a man and dying on a grisly cross. What He faced and felt in Gethsemane He had faced and felt before. What a mystery! How can we ever penetrate the heart of this matter?

**FURTHER STUDY**

Isa. 53:1–12;
Gal. 3:13–14;
Heb. 2:9

1. How did Isaiah depict the cross?
2. How did Paul put it?

## Prayer

O Father, I have never thought before of how You may have felt the pain of Gethsemane back there in eternity as You contemplated coming to earth to die and procure my salvation. Yet You did it. How marvellous. How wonderful. Thank You my Saviour. Amen.

# "As the flash of a volcano"

*"He was chosen before the creation of the world, but was revealed in these last times ..." (v.20)*

**For reading & meditation – 1 Peter 1:13–25**

We spend one more day reflecting on *the cosmic cross*. We said earlier that we do not rightly read the cross until we see it in a cosmic and eternal perspective. The cross was in the heart of God aeons before it stood stark on the crest of the hill of Calvary, and the supreme crisis of the passion which short-sightedly we assume took place in Gethsemane may have been suffered by our Lord before time began. "as the flash of a volcano discloses for a few hours the elemental fires at the earth's centre," wrote the theologian Dinsmore in his *Atonement in Literature and Life*, "so the light on Calvary was the bursting forth through historical conditions of the very nature of the Everlasting."

Some words of Leslie Weatherhead elaborate this thought: "... one night in the Mediterranean we passed close to Stromboli, the famous island volcano, when suddenly there was a great burst of flame from the crater on the summit. Huge tongues of fire shot up hundreds of feet into the sky, lighting up the ocean for miles around. Through our binoculars we saw a steady stream of lava run down to the sea; that red-hot stream of lava like some awful open wound gashed the darkness. What did it mean? For a few hours we saw revealed those great fires which had been burning in the mountain's heart since the foundation of the world."

**FURTHER STUDY**

John 8:58; 17:5;
Heb. 7:1–3;
Micah 5:2

1. What did Jesus declare of Himself?
2. How did the writer of Hebrews put it?

Calvary was the bursting forth into history of the very nature of the Everlasting – the great love which like a fire is always burning in His heart.

## Prayer

O God, I realise that Your love is not something You feel now and again; it is a fire that is always burning in Your heart. You are the world's most aggressive Lover. I am grateful beyond words that I have come to know that love. Amen.

# "It could not be otherwise"

*"Concerning this salvation, the prophets … searched intently and with the greatest care …" (v.10)*

**For reading & meditation – 1 Peter 1:1–12**

We continue reflecting on the fact that the cross of Christ is multi-dimensional, and to comprehend it more fully we must study it from different vantage points. We have looked at the cross from the viewpoint of eternity; now we look at it from the viewpoint of prophecy. Our text for today tells us that the ancient prophets sought diligently to understand what the Holy Spirit was telling them about Christ's coming to earth and the suffering He would endure before returning to His Father.

From the very beginning of the Scriptures we catch sight of what we might call *the prophetic cross*. Dr A.C. Dixon in his book *The Glories of the Cross* likens the Bible to a sunrise: "It is interesting to stand on a hill top and watch the coming dawn; first, the grey streaks in the East, and then the brighter light until the full-orbed sun arises. *There is a sunrise with its dawn like that in the Old Testament Scriptures.*" One of the first gleams of light to fall on the prophetic cross comes from the promise of the curse that would afflict humanity. It grows brighter with Abel's sacrifice of blood. It becomes brighter still in the deliverance of the children of Israel from Egypt and the blood upon the door-frames. And it shines with even more brilliance from the ancient tabernacle sacrifices, the uplifted serpent of brass, and later the rituals of the Temple worship.

Just as the cross is written into the cosmos so is it written also into almost every page of the Old Testament. It could not be otherwise.

**FURTHER STUDY**

Gen. 4:4;
Ex. 12:1–13;
Lev. 16:23–34;
Num. 21:4–9

1. What was to be the sign for deliverance?
2. What other accounts in the Old Testament can you think of that foreshadow the cross?

## Prayer

Father, I recognise that the Old Testament references to the cross are like searchlights stabbing the darkness looking for the hill called Calvary. How glad I am that the cross was not merely typified and prophesied but also realised. Now I have hope. Amen.

# Foresight *and* feeling

*"... prophecy never had its origin in ... man ... men spoke
from God as they were carried along by the ... Spirit." (v.21)*

**For reading & meditation – 2 Peter 1:12–21**

Not only is the cross written into the universe but, as we saw
yesterday, it is written into the Old Testament also. The cross is
to be seen on almost every page of the Old Testament Scriptures.

I remember that when I first began to study the Bible I found it
incredible that hundreds of years before Christ died on the cross
people were predicting the event in fine detail. Someone has
computed that the likelihood of the Old Testament prophecies
concerning Christ's death coming true by chance is one in five
billion. Yet they did – to the very letter.

I also remember as a young man hearing my pastor say that
some of the most moving and poignant pictures of the cross come
not, as we might expect, from those who penned the Gospels but
from some of the Old Testament writers. This I found hard to
accept, so one day I read through the four Gospels to see what they
had to say about the crucifixion of our Lord and also the way in
which they wrote about it. I was struck by the fact that they
appeared to write so objectively about the cross. In some passages
their subjectivity comes through, but largely the
Gospel writers' reports of the crucifixion are more
objective than subjective. However, the Old
Testament writers who focus on the cross describe
our Lord's sufferings not from without but from
within. They seem to get *inside* the event, to touch
its beating heart, and thus portray it not only with
foresight but also with *feeling*.

FURTHER STUDY

Psa. 22:1–31;
69:20–21;
Isa. 50:6–7

1. How does David
depict the sufferings
of Christ?
2. How does Isaiah
portray them?

## Prayer

O Father, may I view the cross not only objectively but subjectively too. Help
me feel something of what it meant for my Lord to hang and suffer on the tree.
In Jesus' Name I ask it. Amen.

# "The Psalm of Sobs"

*"My God, my God, why have you forsaken me?" (v.1)*

**For reading & meditation – Psalm 22:1–18**

We commented yesterday on the fact that whereas the Gospel writers, generally speaking, viewed the cross objectively, the Old Testament writers viewed it subjectively. The psalm before us today illustrates this subjectivity and is considered by commentators to be one of the most clear prefigurings of the passion of Christ anywhere in the Old Testament. It would seem that the inspired writer had "inside information" as he appears to enter into the very feelings Christ endured while on the cross. This is why it is called "The Psalm of Sobs". The words come across like the gasps of a dying man whose breath and strength are failing and who can only utter a word or two at a time.

Sometimes it seems the Old Testament is like a voice and the New Testament like the echo. The Old Testament predicts and the New Testament records. Look with me at a few of these correspondences. The mockery spoken of in verse 7 of the psalm is echoed by the derision of the priests in Matthew 27:39. The dividing of the clothing in verse 18 is answered by the act of the soldiers referred to in John 19:23–4. And the powerful verses (vv.14–17) in which the psalmist describes such deep suffering are echoed by every one of the Gospel writers.

A genuine personal experience of the psalmist is used by the Holy Spirit to provide him with a foreshadowing of Christ's experience. As the NIV Study Bible comments: "It is not surprising that the Prayer Book appoints this psalm for use on Good Friday."

> **FURTHER STUDY**
>
> Psa. 41:9;
> Zech. 11:12–13;
> Isa. 53:4–5, 12
>
> 1. Find the corresponding New Testament fulfilment.

## Prayer

O Father, how grateful I am that the psalmists and prophets predicted beforehand the sufferings of Christ and the glories that would follow. This reinforces still more powerfully the fact that You are a God of forethought, not afterthought. Amen.

# A most moving passage

*"But he was pierced for our transgressions, he was crushed for our iniquities ..." (v.5)*

**For reading & meditation – Isaiah 53:1–12**

Perhaps the most perfect picture of our suffering Saviour in all the Old Testament Scriptures is that given by the prophet Isaiah. In chapter 49 we begin to catch a glimpse of the suffering Messiah – the One whom men despise, whom the nation rejects, yet who shall be worshipped by kings and given for a covenant to the people. In Isaiah 50 the sufferings increase. He who is given "an instructed tongue" (v.4) is not rebellious. He gives His back to the smiters, and He hides not His face from shame and from the taunts of His accusers. In chapter 52 we again see the servant of the Lord, His face "disfigured beyond that of any man" (v.14).

Then we come to Isaiah 53 – one of the most moving passages in the Old Testament. Several times in this chapter we are told He suffers to take away our sins. Take these for example. (1) He was pierced for our transgressions. (2) He was crushed for our iniquities. (3) The Lord laid on him the iniquity of us all. (4) By oppression and judgment He was taken away. (5) His life was made an offering for sin. (6) He will bear their iniquities. (7) He bore the sin of many.

**FURTHER STUDY**

Zech. 12:1–10;
Psa. 109:4; 69:4;
34:20; 16:10

1. Find the corresponding New Testament fulfilment.

How marvellously the words of Isaiah came to be fulfilled can be seen not only by an examination of the Gospels but of other New Testament writings also. Isaiah was not making an inspired guess or using informed conjecture. It was a divine prediction. None but God could have foreknown and foretold what was to transpire that dark day on Golgotha.

## Prayer

O Father, help me in a deeper way to enter into Your Son's sufferings. Not in a sentimental way but a spiritual one. Bring home to my spirit a full realisation of what it meant to You and Your Son for my sins to be forgiven. In Jesus' Name. Amen.

# Death by a broken heart

*"Scorn has broken my heart and has left me helpless …" (v.20)*

**For reading & meditation – Psalm 69:1–21**

We look at one more instance of an Old Testament writer anticipating the sufferings of Christ and feeling in his heart something of our Lord's pain long before the event. Here the psalmist speaks of several forms of suffering that can be compared to Christ's agony on the cross, but the one on which I want to focus is that of a broken heart. Did the psalmist sense as he talked about his heartbreak that there would come into the world One who, though perfect, would have His heart broken in the course of bearing mankind's sin? I think that somehow he did.

But what the psalmist talked about figuratively Christ experienced literally. A.M. Hodgin in his classic *Christ in all the Scriptures* claims that the one factor above all others that contributed to the early death of Christ on the cross was a broken heart: "Death from a broken heart is very rare. It is caused by intense mental emotion. The loud cry, the fact of death coming so soon, the effect of the spear-thrust, all point towards this being indeed the cause of our Lord's death." When one of the soldiers approached Jesus to accelerate His death by breaking His legs he found that Jesus was already dead. The soldier then pierced His side, which brought forth a sudden gush of blood and water. Why water? Because the pericardium, the sac surrounding the heart which contains water, had burst – evidence, say physicians, that our Lord's heart had broken. The bearing of our sins, and the hiding of the Father's face on account of it, literally broke His heart.

**FURTHER STUDY**

Isa. 61:1–3;
Luke 4:17–21;
Psa. 34:18; 147:3;
Heb. 4:15

1. Why were everyone's eyes fastened on Jesus?
2. What is He a specialist in?

## Prayer

O Father, I see this psalm not just as the cry of a man who was hurt but a prophecy of the way Your own dear Son would be hurt. You became possessed of a human heart in order that it might be broken. I stand in awe of such amazing love. Amen.

# The event of eternity

*"The Son of Man will go just as it is written about him." (v.24)*

**For reading & meditation – Matthew 26:17–30**

We have looked over the past few days at some of the prophetic forecasts of the sufferings and death of our Saviour. There are many more, yet the few we have examined reveal most clearly that the cross was not only built into the texture of the universe but also written of in the texts of the Old Testament Scriptures. With what precision and detail the Old Testament writers predicted the sufferings and the events associated with the cross. Charles G. Trumbull said: "There are no fewer than twenty-nine Old Testament prophecies bearing on the betrayal, trial, death and burial of our Lord Jesus Christ, uttered by many different voices, during five centuries from the year 1000 BC to 500 BC, which were all literally fulfilled within twenty-four hours at the time of the crucifixion."

How can anyone doubt the veracity of the Old Testament after such an impressive forecast of events I do not know. I heard one professor of Old Testament studies say that if the New Testament were somehow to be taken away from us and all record of it removed (a tragedy we cannot envisage), it would almost be possible to reconstruct the closing scenes in the drama of Christ's life from the relevant prophetic passages in the Old Testament.

So much of the Old Testament is prophetic, and a good deal of that prophecy focuses on the coming of Christ and His death on the cross. The shadow of the cross is not only on creation; it is cast over the Old Testament also. Is it any wonder? The cross is *the* event of eternity.

FURTHER STUDY

Mark 8:31–38;
Luke 9:22; 22:37;
John 3:14

1. How aware of prophecy was Jesus?
2. How did He graphically depict His death?

## Prayer

Father, thank You for reminding me that the Cross is the event of eternity. Nothing is greater than it and nothing more wonderful. And it was all accomplished for me. Thank You my Saviour. Amen.

# The divine secret

*"... he was filled with wisdom, and the grace of God was upon him." (v.40)*

**For reading & meditation – Luke 2:21–40**

We now look at the cross through the eyes of our Lord Himself. We shall attempt to understand how *He* saw the cross and what it meant for Him to walk in its shadow. In our meditations we shall describe this aspect as *the impending cross*.

I have often wondered just when and how our Lord first understood that He was the promised Messiah. Was it something that came to Him in a sudden flash of divine revelation? Or did it dawn on Him gradually over weeks, months, or even years? We will never really know. My own view is that in the period referred to in our text today (between His consecration as a baby and His Bar Mitzvah at the age of thirteen) as He read, prayed and pondered the Old Testament Scriptures, gradually the Holy Spirit revealed to Him that He was the One of whom the prophets spoke. Probably this occurred when He was about eleven. Certainly we know that at the age of twelve He was aware of His divine destiny for He said to His mother: "Did you not know that I must be about My Father's business?" (Luke 2:49, NKJ).

What a momentous time that must have been in His young life. Carefully and sensitively the Spirit brought home to His heart the fact that He was the Son of God incarnate and that He had come into the world to give His life as a ransom for many. Scripture treats the matter as if it is a divine secret. Thus we must be careful not to probe or speculate too much.

**FURTHER STUDY**

Matt. 11:1–14;
16:13–20;
26:63–64

1. How did Jesus respond to John?
2. How did Jesus respond to Peter?

## Prayer

O Father, though Your Word draws a veil over the matters I have been reflecting on and I do not wish to probe too deeply, enough is said to increase my sense of awe at the way in which You designed my salvation. I am truly grateful. Amen.

# The shadow of death

*"But his mother treasured all these things in her heart."*
(v.51)

**For reading & meditation – Luke 2:41–52**

We pause on the words of our text today, which tell us that Mary "treasured all these things in her heart". What things? These among others: His spiritual astuteness, His comprehension of Scripture and His clear awareness that He was in the world to fulfil His heavenly Father's will. Did Mary know that her Son would die upon on a cross? She had been told by Simeon that one day "a sword will pierce your own soul too" (Luke 2:35). But here again we can only conjecture.

Holman Hunt in his beautiful painting *The Shadow of Death* depicts the inside of the carpenter's shop in Nazareth and has Jesus stripped to His waist, standing by a wooden trestle table on which He has put His saw. He lifts His hands towards heaven as if stretching to relieve His aching arms, and as He does so the evening sunlight streaming in through the open door casts a shadow in the form of a cross on the wall behind Him. On the wall is a tool rack giving the impression of a horizontal bar, to which, in the painting, His hands appear to be nailed. Even the tools themselves are a grim reminder of the hammer and nails used in Christ's crucifixion. In the foreground Mary kneels among the wood chippings, and although her face cannot be seen fully she appears to be startled as she looks up and sees the cross-like shadow of her Son on the wall.

The idea may be fanciful but nevertheless it is true theologically. The shadow of the cross was over Jesus from His earliest years.

---

**FURTHER STUDY**

John 4:1–26;
8:21–30; 11:25

1. What did Jesus confirm to the woman?
2. How did Jesus refer to the cross?

---

## Prayer

O Father, I can only glimpse a small part of what it meant for Your Son to spend His life knowing He must one day die upon a cross. I cannot comprehend it yet I appreciate it. For it was all in order to accomplish my salvation. Amen.

# The Messianic secret

*"He then began to teach them that the Son of Man must
suffer many things … and that he must be killed …"* (v.31)

**For reading & meditation – Mark 8:27–33**

Howerver the truth came to Jesus that He was destined to die on a
cross, it is clear from the Gospels that by the age of thirty He
knew that in the not too distant future He would face an
ignominious death. The passage before us now makes this plain.
These verses are viewed as pointing to the watershed in our Lord's
public ministry and are described as the first prediction of the
passion.

Having withdrawn with His disciples to the northern district
around Caesarea Philippi, Jesus put to them this pointed question:
"Who do people say I am?" When Peter blurted out, "You are the
Christ [the Messiah]," Jesus warned them not to reveal that fact to
anyone else. He probably gave this warning for two reasons: first, He
did not want His Messianic role to be revealed until His character
had been more clearly established (the popular Messianic
expectation was of a political leader), and second, He wanted to
carefully unfold the revelation *Himself*. Jesus then began to fill in
some of the details concerning His death: He would be rejected by
the elders, chief priests and teachers of the law,
and would be killed but after three days rise
again.

When Peter heard this he was horrified and
sharply rebuked Jesus. But Jesus, in turn,
vehemently rebuked Peter and told him that his
attempt to deny the cross was prompted by Satan.
So deeply was He committed to His Messianic
mission that He would not allow anything to
deter Him. He had come into the world to die.

FURTHER STUDY
John 1:43–51;
Matt. 16:16;
John 4:29; 6:69;
11:27; 20:28

1. What responses
did Christ receive?
2. Who were the
6 people who
responded to Him?

## Prayer

Father, although I know that in a sense we all come into the world to die, Your
Son knew not only that He would die but how He would die. Yet with what
fortitude and determination He undertook the task. And again, all for me.
Thank You Lord. Amen.

# When afraid – avoid

*"But they did not understand what he meant and were afraid to ask him about it." (v.32)*

**For reading & meditation – Mark 9:14–32**

We looked yesterday at what commentators describe as the first prediction of the passion. Today we examine the second. This second prediction was made as our Lord was passing through Galilee. Please note the sentence "Jesus did not want anyone to know where they were, because he was teaching his disciples" (vv.30–32). Unfolding the plan that He was to die was so important to Him that He did not want anything to interrupt Him.

Here Jesus gives the disciples a little more information in that He makes plain that He would be betrayed into the hands of men – the first hint of the betrayal. The words He used are similar to those of the first prediction, but this time we are informed the disciples did not understand the meaning of what He said and were afraid to question Him.

Matthew adds these words: "and the disciples were filled with grief" (Matt. 17:23). Perhaps the first time Jesus predicted His death the disciples put it down to morbid pessimism but the second time He raised the matter they were more deeply taken aback. One

**FURTHER STUDY**

Luke 9:18–27, 44;
John 10:11;
12:23–24; 15:13

1. In what 2 different ways did Jesus refer to His death?
2. How did He describe the relationship between death and life?

commentator believes the reason for their fear was because of their infatuation with the popular notion that the Messiah would usher in the Kingdom. They were thinking more of a crown than a cross.

We are always afraid when things fail to go the way we think they should. Fear becomes a defence that helps us avoid the hard facts of reality. To avoid being disturbed the disciples were afraid to ask Jesus any further questions.

## Prayer

My Father and my God, I confess that sometimes I prefer not to know those things that might encroach on my comfort zone. Is it because I do not trust You enough? Help me, dear Father. I want to be real. In the Name of Christ my Lord. Amen.

# Determined to die

*"They were on their way up to Jerusalem ... the disciples were astonished ... those who followed were afraid." (v.32)*

**For reading & meditation – Mark 10:32–45**

Our Lord made His third prediction of the passion when He and His disciples were heading towards Jerusalem, and Mark's account of the incident shows how the fear and astonishment that gripped them following His second prediction was still with them: "Now they were on the road, going up to Jerusalem, and Jesus was going before them; and they were amazed. And as they followed they were afraid" (Mark 10:32, NKJ). But their fear and amazement does not deter Him from making the third prediction of His death, and He names the place of His death – the Holy City, Jerusalem.

Surely even the most casual reader of the Gospels cannot help but be impressed with our Lord's steadfast determination to move towards His final hours. And this was no death-wish either, as some critics suggest. He did not relish death (as is made plain by His struggle in the Garden of Gethsemane), but such was His commitment to doing His Father's will that He put aside His own feelings. John Stott says of our Lord's threefold repetition of the passion prediction found in Mark's Gospel that "It is Mark's way of preparing his readers, as Jesus deliberately prepared the Twelve, for the terrible events that would take place."

Although our Lord made at least ten predictions concerning His death, these three recorded by Mark give us a picture (as I said a moment ago) of our Lord's solemn determination to fulfil the Father's will. He was determined to die. Not because of a death-wish but out of a desire to serve the Father's purposes.

FURTHER STUDY

Matt. 26:36–45;
6:10;
Mark 14:36

1. What did Jesus teach us to pray?
2. What did He pray?

## Prayer

O Father, the more I see the determination of Your Son to commit Himself to Your purposes the more I long that I might have that same steadfast will and determination. Help me, my Father. I want to fulfil Your purposes also. Amen.

# Uppermost in His mind

*"… Jesus … looked towards heaven and prayed:*
*'Father, the time has come …'" (v.1)*

**For reading & meditation – John 17:1–19**

The three predictions our Lord made concerning His death, as recorded by Mark, form an interesting trio as each builds on the other. The Gospels, however, present us with eight more predictions made by Jesus about His death. Matthew tells us that when our Lord came down from the Mount of Transfiguration He warned that He would suffer at the hands of His enemies (Matt. 17:9–13). Mark informs us that in response to the selfish request made by James and John that they have the best seats in the Kingdom Jesus made clear that He had come not to be served but to serve and to "give his life as a ransom for many" (Mark 10:35–45). It is interesting that six of our Lord's allusions to His death were made in the last week of His life as the cross loomed large before Him.

Clearly, then, our Lord lived out His life on earth in the shadow of the cross. Though He saw His teaching as important, His example as crucial, and His miracles as an essential part of His ministry, none of these dominated His mind as did the thought of going to the cross. What seemed to be uppermost in His thoughts was not so much His life, but the giving of His life. This, as our text for today puts it, was the "time" (or "hour") for which He had come into the world. He was determined to fulfil what was predicted of Him no matter how painful or difficult it would be. For He had come, "to seek and to save what was lost" (Luke 19:10).

**FURTHER STUDY**

John 19:1–18; 7:30;
12:23; 13:1

1. What was Jesus continually aware of?
2. When did the shadow become reality?

## Prayer

Father, I am so thankful that Your Son's death on the cross, though a painful one, was not a purposeless one. Such self-giving moves my soul in a way that nothing else ever could. I am so grateful. Amen.

# A most incongruous thing

*"When they came to the place called the Skull, there they crucified him ..." (v.33)*

**For reading & meditation – Luke 23:26–43**

We now focus our attention on the fact of the cross as a means of execution. This is what I am choosing to call *the historic cross*. We should not shrink from looking at the horrible fact of crucifixion because it will bring home to our hearts more powerfully what it meant for our Lord to suffer and die for our sins.

The words of our text today – "there they crucified him" – describe in the minimum number of words what in reality was the most momentous event of all time. Ian Macpherson says concerning this: "Think what a modern imaginative writer would have made of it. Yet the verbal economy of Scripture is infinitely more moving and more telling than any attempt at literary sensationalism. The biblical account of the crucifixion as is stark as the cross itself." There are few detailed descriptions of crucifixion recorded in history. Most writers seem to have avoided the subject, and we can well understand why. Crucifixion was one of the most barbarous and horrifying forms of execution, in which a living, breathing man was fastened to some timbers and allowed to hang there for days. This form of torture was devised to produce the maximum amount of pain over the longest period of time.

How incongruous it seems that our Lord should die such a death. The Almighty God comes to earth, lives as a man ... and He is whipped, spat upon, skewered to a cross and hung up for sinners to jeer at. It was indeed the most incongruous thing that has ever happened on this planet.

FURTHER STUDY

Luke 23:23–33;
Matt. 20:17–19;
26:1–2; 27:54

1. What was crucifixion associated with?
2. What did the soldier observe?

## Prayer

Father, in all the incongruity of Your Son's death on a cross I see a blessed congruity as well. Had He not died then I would never have been saved. The bad happened to Him that the good might happen to me. My gratitude knows no bounds. Amen.

# The horrors of crucifixion

*"'What shall I do, then, with Jesus who is called Christ?'
Pilate asked. They all answered, 'Crucify him!'" (v.22)*

**For reading & meditation – Matthew 27:11–26**

The most awful word uttered by human lips in New Testament times was *staurotheto*. That is what the crowd shouted when Jesus was being tried by Pilate. It meant "Let Him be crucified." We said yesterday that the crucifixion was the most incongruous event that ever happened on this planet. But it happened nevertheless and we must face that fact no matter how distasteful it may be to us.

Crucifixion was the most dreadful method of administering the death penalty, having been devised, it seems, by some twisted mind in Persia or Phoenicia and then adopted by the Romans. So brutal and humiliating was it that only the worst class of criminals was executed in this way. Cicero, the Roman philosopher, described it as "a most cruel and disgusting punishment". Later he declared: "The very word 'cross' should be far removed not only from the person of a Roman citizen, but from his thoughts, his eyes and his ears." Joy Davidman wrote of crucifixion with graphic realism when she penned these words:

FURTHER STUDY
Mark 15:1–32;
16:6;

2 Cor. 13:4

1. What were some
of the indignities of
Christ's crucifixion?
2. What was Paul's
summary?

*A crucified slave beside the Roman road,
Screamed until his voice died,
And then hung – a filthy, festering clot of flies,
Sometimes for days.*

That our Lord should be subjected to death on a cross is so shocking that the human mind can scarcely comprehend it. One marvels that even in hell they could think of anything so fiendishly wicked as that.

## Prayer

O Father, this great mystery of Your Son dying upon a cross is something I find too staggering to take in. Yet I know it happened. How awful sin must be to demand such an awful solution. Help me grasp it, dear Father. In Jesus' Name. Amen.

# Three types of cross

*"Above his head they placed the written charge against him …"* (v.37)

**For reading & meditation – Matthew 27:32–44**

We continue reflecting on the horrors of crucifixion, not out of morbid curiosity but so that we might more fully enter into the sufferings our Lord endured for us on the cross.

Different types of crosses were used by the Romans. One was shaped like the capital letter T, another like the capital X, and the third one, with which we are most familiar, was an upright post with a horizontal crossbar. On which of these was our Lord nailed? Our text for today makes it clear: "Above his head they placed the written charge against him." Note the words "above his head". That superscription could not have been fixed there unless the gibbet was constructed in the way it is traditionally depicted – as a crossbeam and an upright post.

A few ancient manuscripts tell us how a crucifixion was conducted. First a victim was flogged, then forced to carry the horizontal piece of the cross to the place of execution. There the wood was laid on the ground and he was fixed to it with ropes or nails. Then he was lifted up and secured to the main post (which sometimes was a permanent structure left in position as a warning), whereupon his feet would be tied or nailed to the upright.

It was not unusual for a person to survive on a cross for days. Exposure, fever, hunger, shock and exhaustion were usually the immediate causes of death. No wonder people speak of Christ's death on the cross as a tragedy. Why should such a bad thing happen to such a good person?

**FURTHER STUDY**

Acts 2:14–23;
4:8–13

1. What charge did Peter lay?
2. What was the effect?

## Prayer

Father, I know the answer to that: Jesus took my place on that tree. He took my badness so that I might receive His goodness. I cannot understand it fully but I stand on it fully. All honour and glory be to Your wonderful Name. Amen.

# Nothing more wonderful

*"Christ redeemed us from the curse of the law by becoming a curse for us ..." (v.13)*

**For reading & meditation – Galatians 3:1–14**

The social stigma associated with crucifixion at the time of Christ can hardly be overstated. According to Deuteronomy 21:23 anyone who died upon a tree was under God's curse. This was understood by the Jews to mean that the very method of death – hanging from a tree – brought a divine curse upon the one concerned. The idea of a crucified Messiah was totally repugnant to the Jews. Often, in the days following the resurrection, they used the manner of Jesus' death as an argument to counter the claims of those who preached the gospel.

Yet here, in the passage before us today, Paul links the Deuteronomic curse with the thought that he had been crucified with Christ (Gal. 2:20). He showed there that the sentence of capital punishment which the law imposed on a sinner had been carried out in the body of Christ on the tree. The curse that is upon all sinners was taken by our Lord and dealt with on the cross. Thus the sinner who would be condemned to death by the law can now be alive to God. Free from the curse he is open to the blessing of God that comes through Christ.

This is a truth that many Christians pass over too quickly, saying it is too difficult to understand. But it isn't. It simply means that Christ, by His atoning sacrifice on the cross, has borne our shame and has put to death the demands of the law over us. We died in Him and because He lives we live in Him. Nothing in heaven or earth is more wonderful. Nothing!

**FURTHER STUDY**

1 Cor. 1:1–23;
2:2–8

1. What was Paul's central message?
2. Why was it so central?

## Prayer

Lord Jesus Christ, help me grasp the fact that when I identify with You I have transferred to me all the benefits You obtained through Your cross. I die with You and live with You. Open my eyes to see this more clearly than ever before. Amen.

# "He suffered ..."

*"He had Jesus flogged, and handed him over to be crucified." (v.15)*

**For reading & meditation – Mark 15:1–15**

We continue to reflect on the horror of what it meant for our Lord to die on a cross. Death by crucifixion was the most shameful, ignominious way of bringing someone's life to an end. Yet this was the manner of death assigned to the Son of God. As the Apostles' Creed puts it: "He suffered under Pontius Pilate." *Suffered!* The account of our Lord's death is not a sentimental tale spun on the loom of fantasy; it is a record of hard, terrible reality. Jesus, we should remember, did not die in a cathedral surrounded by choristers but was suspended above the earth and left limp and bleeding, a public spectacle on a hill outside a city wall.

Once, while in the Far East, I was offended when I entered a church by the sight of a cross on a wall bedecked with jewels. It was encased in bullet-proof glass and guarded day and night because of its obvious value. As I gazed at it I thought to myself: "This is not the kind of cross on which Jesus died. His cross was not adorned with precious stones. The only jewels on His cross were the knots of wood stained red by the blood of the most wonderful man in the world."

The glory of the cross lies in its starkness. This unadorned cross was at the centre of the colossal cosmic drama of redemption – might versus weakness, pomp versus powerlessness. A cross was a symbol of failure but Christ turned it into a symbol of achievement. Now the cross conveys to the world not its message but His.

FURTHER STUDY

Gal. 6:11–14;
Col. 2:13–15

1. How did Paul describe the triumph of the cross?
2. What was nailed to the cross?

## Prayer

O Father, the more I have dwelt on the shocking nature of crucifixion the more I have appreciated what You did for me. Help me never to take my salvation for granted. It cost me nothing, but You everything. Thank You my Saviour. Amen.

# The sublime paradox

*"Did not the Christ have to suffer these things and then enter his glory?" (v.26)*

**For reading & meditation – Luke 24:13–32**

The words of our text today provide us with another vantage point from which to contemplate the cross. Our Lord was at pains to point out to the two disconsolate disciples who were on their way to Emmaus *why the cross had to be*. "Did not the Christ have to suffer these things and then enter his glory?" *"Have to …"* There was an inevitability about the cross. *It had to be.*

The same thought is found in Hebrews 2: "In bringing many sons to glory, it was fitting that God … should make the author of their salvation perfect through suffering" (v.10). *"It was fitting."* "… he had to be made like his brothers in every way, in order that he might become a merciful and faithful high priest" (v.17). "He *had* to …"

The crucifixion is often spoken of as a stark and unrelieved tragedy, and is viewed as the most terrible and incongruous event that has ever occurred. God came to earth in the form of a man and was whipped, spat upon, pierced with nails and hung up naked for everyone to jeer at. Looked at in this way the crucifixion is, we've decided, almost too shocking for us to comprehend it. It is, as someone described it, "the great incongruity". But that is only half of the story. In the midst of "the great incongruity" there is a great congruity too. The cross is a sublime paradox. An enormous incongruity; a lovely congruity. The worst thing the world has ever done; the best thing heaven has ever done. A great crime; a great love.

**FURTHER STUDY**

Luke 12:35–50;
22:37;

John 3:14

1. What did Jesus teach?
2. What is a recurring word in these passages?

## Prayer

O Jesus my Saviour, draw near to me today as You did on the road to Emmaus with those two disconsolate disciples, and reveal to me even more clearly why the cross had to be. Teach me more of its inevitability. For Your own Name's sake. Amen.

# The unavoidable cross

*"For Christ died for sins once for all, the righteous for the unrighteous, to bring you to God." (v.18)*

**For reading & meditation – 1 Peter 3:8–22**

The cross, we are saying, was inevitable. It could not have been avoided. Not by the Saviour. This is how a hymnist put it:

*He did not come to judge the world,*
*He did not come to blame;*
*He did not only come to seek,*
*It was to save He came;*
*And when we call Him Saviour,*
*Then we call Him by His Name.*

Let us see if we can understand a little more clearly why the cross was necessary. One reason is this: *it took the cross to reveal the deep ugliness of sin.* One of the great tragedies of the human race is that we fail to realise the sinfulness of sin. We tend to call our sins "mistakes", "slips", "failures" or "indiscretions". And when we do use the word "sin" we use it lightly and with no sense of culpability.

What is sin? It is acting independently of God, treating Him as if He didn't exist, relegating the great Creator of the universe to irrelevance. Sin, when taken to its nth degree, would, if it could, push God out of the very universe He made. This is what was attempted at Calvary. Sin is a foul blot in God's universe and it takes the cross to make us realise what it is really like.

**FURTHER STUDY**

1 Pet. 2:13–25;
3:18;
1 John 3:5

1. What did Peter say about sin?
2. Write out your own definition of sin.

## Prayer

Father, day by day the meaning of the cross becomes clearer and clearer. You not only required a penalty for sin but You paid it too. Only a crucified Saviour could reveal the ugliness of sin. I fall at Your feet in adoration and worship. Amen.

# The ugliness of sin

*"... God ... made us alive with Christ even when we were dead in transgressions ..." (vv.4–5)*

**For reading & meditation – Ephesians 2:1–10**

We said yesterday that without the cross we would never have fully realised the sinfulness of sin. Every one of us must understand that sin is *deadly*. "The war between good and evil," said one preacher, "is to the death." We can enter into sin without realising what we have given ourselves to ... *until we see the cross*.

Whenever we lie and persuade ourselves that it was "only a little thing"; whenever we are greedy and catch ourselves saying "Well, one must look after oneself"; whenever we slander someone and excuse ourselves on the grounds that "They deserve everything they get"; whenever we are bigoted and convince ourselves that we are standing for the truth; whenever we are proud, selfish, self-indulgent, greedy, grasping and without any sense of shame – then we should look at the cross. That is where the real nature of sin is revealed.

We sometimes think that Christ was put to death by the serious sins of the religious leaders of His day, but it was by the accumulation of what we sometimes call "little sins" as well. Things like gossip, slander, greed, bigotry, fear were all present at Calvary. We might never have known the deadly nature of all sins – little or big – unless it had been placarded before our eyes. In the light of the cross it is impossible to discuss sin academically. For there it is seen for what it is. Think about this as you go about your duties this day: every one of us has been guilty of the sins that nailed Christ to His cross.

**FURTHER STUDY**

Gal. 1:1–6;
1 John 3:16;
Heb. 6:6

1. What was Paul astonished at?
2. How can we crucify Christ afresh?

## Prayer

O Father, how different the cross appears when I realise that all the different sins I have committed led to Your Son's crucifixion. I was there when they crucified my Lord. You have forgiven me; now keep me from sin. In Jesus' Name. Amen.

# No cross – no salvation

*"They spoke about his departure, which he was about to bring to fulfilment at Jerusalem." (v.31)*

**For reading & meditation – Luke 9:28–36**

Another reason why the cross had to be was this: only a *crucified* Saviour could save us from our sins.

For centuries people have pondered the question: Was it really necessary for Christ to be crucified in order that the Father could forgive us? The father in the story of the prodigal son, they point out, forgave the son without any talk of atonement. Couldn't God have done the same? But the parable of the prodigal son is not a complete picture of God's relationship with His wayward and erring children. It was never meant to be. The relationship of a human father and his son is a relationship of two sinners and is not, nor can it be, a complete and perfect parallel of the relationship that exists between a soiled sinner and a holy God.

Sin always has a price and somebody must pay. The punishment of sin is death, and it was necessary for someone to bear the piled-up debt of the human race – someone who was not only willing but worthy. The debt created by our sin was met by Jesus. What no other man could do this man did. By His death on the cross He paid for our sin in such a way that He bore it all away. He fought sin and defeated it. Let there be no serious talk about the cross being unnecessary. Perhaps the shortest answer to that suggestion is this: if the cross was unnecessary it would never have been.

**FURTHER STUDY**

Rom. 5:1–6:23

1. How did God demonstrate His love?
2. What was the cross an act of?

## Prayer

Father, I realise that where sin and love meet a cross is set up – inevitably. Because there was sin in me and love in You then there was just no answer other than a cross. You suffered so that I should not suffer. My heart is now Yours for ever. Amen.

# Why such violence?

*"With a loud cry, Jesus breathed his last."* (v.37)

**For reading & meditation – Mark 15:21–39**

While it is fairly easy to understand and accept the fact that Christ had to die a substitutionary death in order that we might be saved, it is not so easy to understand why His death had to be so *violent*.

I once read a novel in which the author depicted Christ as having been put to death by a robber who hit Him on the back of the neck while He was walking alone one night through the back streets of Jerusalem. The point was: Christ *had* to die, but God made a mistake when He allowed Him to be crucified, as all the benefits of His death could have still been ours if He had died from a quick blow. This is nonsense of course. I have always been indebted to Dr W.E. Sangster for his explanation as to why Christ's death had to be violent: "Could He [Christ] have exposed sin in all its foul horror if He had died in His bed ... or by accident? Only a *violent* death could have exposed sin in the way sin so sorely needed exposing."

What it amounts to is this: Christ had to die to save us and He had to die by way of the cross. He could have died as Stephen died, by stoning, but horrible though that manner of death was, it was not half as horrifying or as violent as crucifixion. I don't know about you, but I just can't put into words the gratitude I feel to my Saviour for submitting to such a death on my behalf.

**FURTHER STUDY**

Matt. 1:18–22;
Isa. 59:2;
Heb. 9:16–23

1. How was the cross written into the annunciation?
2. What is vital for the forgiveness of sin?

## Prayer

O Father, forgive me if I listen to the story of the cross and take it for granted rather than feeling intense gratitude. Help me to look at it not only from an objective view. Help me to feel something of what it cost You also. In Jesus' Name. Amen.

# "I have suffered too!"

*"...'Put your finger here; see my hands. Reach out your hand and put it into my side.'"* (v.27)

**For reading & meditation – John 20:24–31**

A third reason for the inevitability of the cross: only a suffering Saviour could meet us in the moments of our deepest agony. During my eighteen years in pastoral life almost every week I met people who were experiencing the most distressing situations. I will never forget one week in particular when I had to minister to a wife whose husband had killed another man in a fit of temper, a mother and father whose newborn baby had been born with a broken back, a woman who had just heard she had terminal cancer, a fourteen-year-old girl who lost both her parents in a car accident, and my own wife who had a miscarriage. I tell you, had I not had a suffering Saviour to talk about to those whose lives had suddenly been turned upside down and inside out, I would not have known what to say.

I love reflecting on the passage before us today in which we see Jesus standing before Thomas and saying to him in effect: "Behold the marks of My crucifixion." This is how our Lord deals with us when we are caught up in the most awful situations. He stands in front of us and says: "Look at these hands; they were nailed to a tree. I know how you feel. Let Me enter into your sorrows." As a preacher of the gospel I have been grateful on hundreds of occasions when confronted by someone writhing in deep mental anguish that I have a crucified Saviour I can talk about. More eloquently than any words, those pierced hands say: "I have suffered too!"

**FURTHER STUDY**

Heb. 4:14–16; 2:17;
6:20; 7:23–8:2

1. Why is Christ able to be our high priest?
2. What does this mean for us?

## Prayer

O Father, having spent these few days reflecting on why the cross had to be I think I see more clearly now why it was so fitting. Were it not for a crucified Saviour, life's deepest questions would have no answers. All I can say is "Thank You." Amen.

# At-one

*"God presented him as a sacrifice of atonement,
through faith in his blood ..."* (v.25)

**For reading & meditation – Romans 3:21–31**

The aspect of the cross that is perhaps one of the most profound of all is the atoning work of Christ. Hence our theme for the coming few days is *the atoning cross*.

The word "atonement" has a fascinating history and one which helps us understand its meaning. William Tyndale, when translating the New Testament into English, found the language of his day woefully inadequate to express the richness of the Greek. Particularly baffling was the word which Paul used to express the redeeming work of Christ on the cross – *"katallage"*. So joining together the simple words "at" and "one" he gave us the word "atonement", which has passed into theological currency. Its etymology, therefore, provides us with the clue to its meaning – the bringing together of God and man so that the two parties who were once separated by sin are now *at one*.

One preacher I know uses a wonderful word to describe Christ's role of reconciling mankind to God and making them one. The term he uses is *Middleman*. Sometimes you will see an advertisement in the newspapers or on television that goes something like this: "These goods are cheap because we have cut out the middleman." Believe me, any religion that cuts out the *Middleman* is cheap – and worthless!

**FURTHER STUDY**

Lev. 4:1–21;
Ex. 30:10;
Lev. 16:18–30;
Heb. 10:20;
Rom. 5:10–11

1. What was the "sin offering"?
2. Who and what was the "middleman" before Christ?

## Prayer

Father, how can I thank You sufficiently for providing a *Middleman* who has in Himself the nature of God and the nature of man? There could be no union between God and man without someone who was both. I am so grateful. Amen.

# Jesus is the Atonement!

*"... he had to be made like his brothers in every way ... that he might make atonement for the sins of the people." (v.17)*

**For reading & meditation – Hebrews 2:5–18**

We must remember that it is not the cross itself that provides atonement but the One who hung upon it. Dr Edwards, a famous Welsh theologian, was so gripped with the idea that the atonement centres on the Person of the Son of God that he ran into the street shouting excitedly: "Jesus is the Atonement!" Then going back into his study he wrote these words: "This is the Atonement – not the sufferings and not the death, but the *Person* of the Son of God in the sufferings and death. It is not that He made the atonement or paid the atonement. The Bible goes far beyond that. He is the Atonement – not He Himself without the act, but He Himself in the act." Thrilling words. But what does it mean when we say Jesus is the Atonement? How does our Lord bring God and humankind together?

First, *He brings God and mankind together in His Person.* Because Jesus is God and man He is both human and divine. This is the whole point of the incarnation – God took on human flesh and thus combined the two natures in one Person. Those who do not believe in the virgin birth of Christ will certainly not believe in the atoning death of Christ for the one depends on the other. If Jesus had not joined Himself to us in the incarnation then He would not have been able to join us to God in the atonement. "A Saviour who is not quite God," said Bishop Handley Moule, "is a like a bridge broken at the farther end." He is right.

FURTHER STUDY
1 Tim. 2:1–5;
Heb. 8:6; 9:15;
12:24

1. What does "Mediator" mean?
2. How does this relate to atonement?

## Prayer

O Father, help me see beyond all theories of the atonement to the fact that it is not a theory that saves but a Person. And that Person is none other than the Son of God, my Saviour. All honour and glory be to Your matchless Name. Amen.

# He who had no sin ...

*"God made him who had no sin to be sin for us ..."*
(v.21)

### For reading & meditation – 2 Corinthians 5:11–21

If Jesus had not united Himself to us in His Person then He could never have united us to God in His passion. Theologians use the word *passion* to describe the events connected with the crucifixion and death of our Lord, and it is on His passion that we focus now.

No verse in the whole of the New Testament puts the truth of the atonement more clearly than the one before us today: "God made him who had no sin to be sin for us ..." How can anybody be made sin for someone else? I don't know. And neither does anyone else. It is a mystery. But this I know: He who had no sin was made sin on our behalf. This goes beyond our understanding, but we can experience the benefits even though we do not understand it.

The most awful thing about sin is that it separates us from God. We know that much. When we sin, doesn't a cloud come between us and God? Our fellowship with Him is interrupted. We pray but the heavens seem as brass. And we have no peace until we bring the matter to God and ask for His forgiveness. Think of the intimate fellowship Jesus had with His Father, then think also of the cloud that rolled between Him and God when He hung upon the cross. He who had no sin entered into the experience of sin – the awful sense of separation from God. It was not that He became a sinner but that He was made to be sin. There is a difference.

FURTHER STUDY

1 John 3:4–10;
Matt. 5:17;
Gal. 1:4; 3:1

1. How does John define sin?
2. How did Christ fulfil the law?

## Prayer

O Father, the gospel is so clear that I wonder why more do not accept it. The punishment that should have fallen on me fell instead upon Your Son. He bore what I should have borne. Blessed Saviour. My heart is Yours for ever. Amen.

# "Fellow lepers!"

*"He himself bore our sins in his body on the tree ..."*
*(v.24)*

**For reading & meditation – 1 Peter 2:13–25**

Even though, as we said yesterday, we will never be able to fully understand the meaning of the atonement here on earth (and perhaps not even fully in heaven), an illustration may help.

Of all the illustrations I have heard, the one I love best is the story of Father Damien, a Belgian missionary who went to serve the Lord on the island of Honolulu. Whilst there he learned of a leper colony on the much smaller island of Molokai and obtained permission to go and minister to the 600 unshepherded souls who lived there. He was the only healthy man on an island of lepers and confessed at times to being terribly lonely. One morning as he was pouring boiling water into a pan some of it splashed on to his bare foot. And he felt nothing. Then the truth dawned on him. One of the signs of leprosy is immunity to pain. *He was a leper himself!* Most men would have been devastated but do you know what Father Damien did? He rang the church bell to summon everyone to the building. When all had gathered he leapt into the pulpit, stretched out his arms and said: "Fellow lepers." From that moment on his words gained greater credibility. The people who heard him speak all agreed: "He is one of us."

All analogies are inadequate. Jesus could never say "Fellow sinners" because He had no sin. Yet, as we saw earlier, He was *made* to be sin. He became what we are in order that we might become what He is.

| FURTHER STUDY |
|---|
| Eph. 2:11–16; |
| 2 Cor. 5:18; |
| Col. 1:20; |
| Titus 2:11–14; |
| Rom. 8:17 |
| |
| 1. What ministry has Christ given to us? |
| 2. What can we say we are jointly with Christ? |

## Prayer

O Divine Redeemer, I will never be able to understand what it meant for You, the sinless One, to be made sin, but I can be grateful for it. And I am eternally grateful. I shall sing Your praises for ever. Amen.

# A Good Friday perspective

*"... how much more, having been reconciled, shall we
be saved through his life!" (v.10)*

**For reading & meditation – Romans 5:1–11**

We have said that if Jesus had not united Himself to us in His Person in the incarnation He could never have united us to God in His passion. He first gave Himself to us, then gave Himself for us. "God made him who had no sin to be sin for us, so that in him we might become the righteousness of God" (2 Cor. 5:21).

And how does the One who had no sin, yet became sin, impart to us the righteousness of God? He does it by His continuing presence. It was not enough that God joined Himself to us in the incarnation or that Christ joined us to His Father in the atonement. For the benefits of the atonement to become a reality in our lives Christ had to come back from the dead and live in our hearts by faith. You see, you and I could never be righteous like Jesus. As well ask us to write a play like Shakespeare, paint pictures like Raphael or compose music like Beethoven. We just couldn't do it. The amazing fact, however, is this: ordinary folk like you and me can live like Jesus Christ – righteously – because He not only imputes His righteousness to us through the cross but imparts it by coming and living in us.

That is why Good Friday should never be considered in isolation. It is linked to Easter Sunday. Think on this: Christianity is the only religion in the world whose Founder rose from the dead and came back to live His life in and through His followers.

**FURTHER STUDY**

Rom. 10:1–4;
1 Cor. 1:30;
Phil. 3:9

*1. What is Christ the end of?*
*2. What was Paul's desire?*

## Prayer

Father God, thank You for reminding me that Good Friday is not an isolated event but a point in a line. And the line passes through an open tomb. Your Son died but lives again. And because He lives I can live also. Live! Amen.

# Unified personalities

*"... he who raised Christ from the dead will also give
life to your mortal bodies through his Spirit ..." (8:11)*

**For reading & meditation – Romans 7:14–25; 8:1–11**

We continue thinking through the issue we touched on yesterday, namely that Christ unites us to God not only by His Person and His passion but also by His *presence*. He brings God's righteousness to us and lives His pure and perfect life in our responsive and yielded hearts.

Have you ever considered what results from the presence of Christ in our hearts? Many things, of course, but consider just one: His presence unifies our personalities. As people we are terribly complicated. One psychologist said: "We are not the same person from one minute to the other." Our moods and thoughts are constantly changing. Edwin Sanford Martin put it like this:

*Within my temple there's a crowd:*
*There's one that's humble and there's one that's proud,*
*There's one that's broken-hearted for his sins,*
*And one who, unrepentant, sits and grins.*
*There's one who loves his neighbour as himself,*
*And one who cares for naught but fame and self.*

When Jesus Christ comes into the heart, however, all this is changed. The multiple personality is unified. Then we can say with the apostle Paul: "I no longer live, but Christ lives in me" (Gal. 2:20). And how!

**FURTHER STUDY**

Gal. 2:20;
Col. 1:27;
1 John 3:24;
Isa. 61:1–10

1. What is the hope of glory?
2. What are we able to sing with the prophet of old?

## Prayer

Gracious and loving Father, the presence of Your Son in my heart unifies my personality far more powerfully than any earthly therapy can. How grateful I am that He lived here on earth, but how much more grateful that He lives now in me. Amen.

# Two words – two worlds

*"Come and see the place where he lay."* (v.6)

**For reading & meditation – Matthew 28:1–15**

On Easter Day Christians celebrate the fact that though it was possible for our Lord to experience death, it was not possible for Him to be held by it. Christ's rising from the dead is God's great confirmation of the fact that His sacrifice for us on the cross was accepted by heaven.

Every year that passes sees the truth of the resurrection come under greater attack. One theologian is reported to have said recently: "We don't have to believe in the resurrection for Christianity to be perpetuated. It will survive without it." But would it? Perhaps it would survive as a system of moral philosophy or social reform but not as a dynamic faith. We see in the passage before us today that Mary was surprised when she found the tomb empty. But imagine the effect upon her and the ages if the Lord still lay there. As a poet put it:

> O, the anguish of Mary!
> O, the depth of despair!
> Had she gone to the tomb,
> And the dead Lord was there.

**FURTHER STUDY**

Rom. 10:5–9;
1 Cor. 15:3–18;
Eph. 1:20

1. What are the 2 key elements of salvation?
2. What level of importance did Paul put on the resurrection?

How wonderful it is that we do not have to say "Come and see the place where He *lies*," but "Come and see the place where he *lay*." Two different words – two different worlds. Hallelujah!

## Prayer

O Father, without doubt the first Easter morning was the most glorious dawn in history. There was a radiance in it that the world had never known before. And that radiance casts its glow over every other dawn. Hallelujah!

# "Horizons"

*"… his Son … was declared with power to be the Son of God, by his resurrection from the dead …"* (vv.3–4)

**For reading & meditation – Romans 1:1–7**

We are pausing in our meditations on the cross to reflect on the wonder of the resurrection. In the passage before us today we are told that Christ was "declared with power to be the Son of God". What does to be "declared with power" mean? The word "declared" in the Greek comes from the verb *horizo*, from which we get the word "horizon". The resurrection of our Lord has given a completely new horizon to the gospel. Perhaps an illustration (borrowed from another preacher) will help make the thought clear.

Imagine a television news studio before the high-powered lights are switched on and the cameras are set in motion. The news reader who sits there occupies just a few cubic feet of space. If someone were to look at him from a mile away he would not be visible, and no matter how loudly he spoke he would not be heard. But when the lights are switched on and the cameras begin to roll, what a difference. He can be seen and heard by millions all over the country, and if it is a CNN broadcast, all over the world.

This is analogous to what happened at the resurrection. Christ, whose bodily presence occupied only a few cubic feet in Palestine prior to the resurrection, became on Easter Day the One who was no longer limited, but unlimited. He rose from the dead to fill all space and all time. Our Lord, on that glorious resurrection morning, pushed back all horizons, and through His rising from the dead has opened up for us the unending vistas of eternity.

FURTHER STUDY

Matt. 28:16–20;
Mark 16:14–18;
Acts 1:8

1. What was the "horizon" set before the disciples?
2. What was Christ's "horizon" promise?

## Prayer

My Father and my God, I see Your Son's resurrection enabled Him to move beyond the restrictions of this earthly abode to fill all space and time. He has opened up for me new horizons – eternal ones. I am deeply grateful. Amen.

# Power from a tomb!

*"I want to know Christ and the power of his
resurrection ..." (v.10)*

**For reading & meditation – Philippians 3:1–11**

In the passage before us today Paul exults in the fact that the
resurrection was not only a powerful event in history but was an
explosive event in his life and experience also. Calvary, pronounces
the great apostle, constituted more than a date on a calendar: it was
a dynamic in his heart. Wistfully he cries: "I want to know Christ
and the power of his resurrection ..."

Think about that phrase with me for a moment – *the power of His
resurrection*. He could just as easily have said: "The power that
flowed from His tomb." Have you ever thought how strange it is
that power flows from a tomb? Power usually comes from a throne.
We don't normally associate power with a tomb. It is, as I heard one
preacher put it, somewhat verbosely you might think: "an
incongruous and incredible conjunction of concepts". Power from
the tomb means this: the energy that was focused in bringing Christ
back from the dead is available to you and me – to save us, sanctify
us and get us ready for heaven.

All the forces of earth conspired to keep Christ in the grave.
They put a large stone over the mouth of His
grave, sealed it with a Roman seal, and posted a
guard to stop anyone moving it. But the power
that was *in* the tomb was greater than any power
that was *without*. One writer worded it like this:
"On the day of the resurrection God took the seal
from off the tomb and put it on the gospel."
Hallelujah!

**FURTHER STUDY**

Eph. 2:1–6;
Rom. 8:11;
Col. 3:1

1. What heights
does the power of
God's resurrection
raise us to?
2. What does Paul
admonish the
Colossians?

## Prayer

Gracious Father, how thankful I am that like the apostle Paul I have experienced
something of the power that comes from the tomb. But like him, too, I want to
know more. Not only more of the power but more of the Person. In Jesus'
Name I pray. Amen.

# Crucified afresh

*"... to their loss they are crucifying the Son of God all over again ..." (v.6)*

### For reading & meditation – Hebrews 6:1–12

We return to our main theme: the wondrous cross. There is a sense in which though the crucifixion was a one-off event which took place nearly 2,000 years ago, *our Lord is being crucified still*. The text before us today tells us that it is possible to crucify the Son of God afresh. How is it possible for Christ to be crucified *afresh*? According to the writer to the Hebrews it happens when those who have "been enlightened, who have tasted the heavenly gift ... fall away" (vv.4–6) and deny the faith. Such a disavowal is tantamount to swinging the hammers that crucified Jesus once again and driving the nails into His flesh.

I think it is true to say that few believers would openly deny Christ and pledge to have nothing more to do with Him. But do we realise that to profess to be one of His followers and yet refuse to live as He commanded is in itself a form of denial? I speak metaphorically, of course, but the Saviour bleeds again when we choose not to obey His commands and act in a way that brings dishonour to His Name.

We stress the suffering of Christ for the world – and rightly so. That was once and for all. But what about this suffering He continues to undergo from those of us who say we love and bear His Name and yet in that very Name do some ugly things? Our Lord's pain did not end when He expired on the cross. The suffering of the cross continues every time we put our own interests before His.

**FURTHER STUDY**

Rom. 2:1–24;
Neh. 5:9; Ezek.
36:20; Gal. 4:9;
2 Pet. 2:17–22

1. What indictment did Paul lay against the Roman Jews?
2. What strong words did the apostle Peter utter?

## Prayer

Lord Jesus Christ, help me to so live that nothing I do brings You grief and pain. Forgive me if I represent You poorly to this world. I come to You for forgiveness, cleansing and a new touch of power. In Jesus' Name. Amen.

# Again He bleeds

*"They divided my garments among them and cast lots for my clothing." (v.24)*

**For reading & meditation – John 19:16–24**

Yesterday I suggested that although the crucifixion was a one-off event there is a sense in which the pain of the cross continues. I said that when we refuse to obey Christ's Word and deliberately choose our own way rather than His, again He bleeds. Is this taking things too far? Can we really be said to be crucifying Christ afresh when we act in a way that brings disgrace to His Name? In a certain sense – yes. We do not physically crucify Him when we do things that dishonour Him but we cause Him great agony nevertheless.

You may wonder why I have chosen this particular text for our focus today. It came to me when I was in the Far East and heard about a sad situation. A certain church building had been padlocked by the secular authorities because two factions in the church had quarrelled. Such was the violence that had erupted in the congregation that the local police had needed to intervene and subsequently denied both factions the use of the church building. The two factions then attempted to settle the matter of the building's ownership by going to court. You can just imagine what the local newspapers made of that.

FURTHER STUDY

1 Cor. 6:1–11;
Matt. 5:23–25;
2 Tim. 2:14;
Prov. 25:8

1. What did Jesus teach about disputes?
2. What did Paul teach about disputes?

As I heard that story my mind went immediately to the incident recorded in the passage we have read today. As Christ hung dying upon the cross some soldiers sat around and cast lots for His clothes. Casting lots for His clothes and gambling over court decisions for possession of property – is there any difference? In my opinion, little or none! *Again He bleeds.*

## Prayer

Loving and gracious Father, my heart feels sad at the thought that the ugly things we Your Church sometimes do perpetuate the pain of the Saviour's cross. Wake us up to see what we are really doing. And forgive us. In Jesus' Name. Amen.

# "Not on speaking terms"

*"First go and be reconciled to your brother ..."*
*(v.24)*

**For reading & meditation – Matthew 5:17–26**

Yesterday I mentioned a church where violence erupted because members of the congregation had differing views and then went to a secular court to solve their dispute. Were those Christians crucifying Christ? I have no hesitation in saying that they were. Our Lord still feels pain. The suffering of the cross continues.

Some years ago, there was an account in our British newspapers of a scandal involving an ordained clergyman and a woman who accused him of sexual misconduct. He was cleared by an ecclesiastical court but behind that story another, equally distressing, emerged. Several high-ranking clergymen were seen to be at loggerheads. One was even reported as saying: "We are not on speaking terms and as far as I can see, we never will be." I tell you, the blood drops of Christ are on that controversy, and all similar situations where a church or its members or officers misrepresent Him to the world.

Let us have done with thinking that we have to walk away from the faith and deny we ever had anything to do with Christ in order to crucify Him afresh. We do so also when we stubbornly refuse to follow the principles He has laid out for us in His Word – principles such as forgiveness and reconciliation. It is unrealistic to expect that Christians will never fall out with one another, but we need not and must not allow that situation to remain. We are to work at being reconciled to one another. When we fail to follow these directives then, believe me, the suffering of the cross continues. Our Saviour is in pain.

**FURTHER STUDY**

1 Cor. Ch. 3;
2 Tim. 2:1–24;
2 Cor. 12:20

1. What perspective did Paul put on the Corinthian dispute?
2. What was Paul's instruction to Timothy?

## Prayer

Blessed Lord Jesus, the pain You endured at the hands of Your enemies must have been agonising. But how much more agonising must it be to be hurt by those You count as Your disciples. Forgive us and help us, dear Saviour. Amen.

# Paul's pain – Christ's pain

*"… I fill up in my flesh what is still lacking in regard to Christ's afflictions …"* (v.24)

**For reading & meditation – Colossians 1:24–29**

The verse before us now is a strange one. Paul says that he rejoiced in his sufferings because it helped make up what was lacking in Christ's afflictions. What was lacking in regard to Christ's afflictions? Nothing, if we are talking about the price Christ paid for our redemption on the cross. There is no deficiency in the atoning work of Christ. No one can, or need, add to His finished and perfect work. Rather, Paul was referring to the afflictions he was called to bear "For the sake of … the church" when presenting the gospel. Dr E. Stanley Jones gave an intriguing interpretation of this verse. He said that when Paul was suffering "For the sake of the Church", Christ, too, was suffering in Paul's sufferings. In other words, Paul's pain was Christ's pain.

A very discouraged minister told me that his church had split over the issue of Holy Communion. Apparently it was the tradition in that church to drink communion wine from one cup but some, fearing the Aids epidemic, thought it would be more hygienic to purchase individual cups. Now there were several ways in which that problem could have been solved, but because the two sides became entrenched and would not even begin to consider each other's point of view the church divided and one group left to form another church.

**FURTHER STUDY**

1 Pet. 3:8–12;
1 Thess. 5:12–15;
Phil. 4:1–5

1. What is Peter's admonition?
2. What is to be evident to all?

The communion service brings moments of great blessedness, but in this case all it produced was bitterness. Does Christ bleed when divisions like this occur amongst His people? I think so. The blood drops of Christ are on this controversy also.

## Prayer

O Father, how is it possible that we Your people can turn a matter of blessedness into a cause of contention? We need a good shaking. Help us see the hurt we bring to our Saviour when we live contrary to the divine purposes. In Christ's Name. Amen.

# If only ...

*"... he will answer, 'The wounds I was given at the house of my friends.'" (v.6)*

**For reading & meditation – Zechariah 13:1–9**

Karl Barth, the well-known theologian, is reported to have said: "The church is a continuous crucifixion to Jesus." This is a generalisation, of course. I must confess that when I first read that statement of Barth's I wondered whether he had gone too far. But the more I have pondered it the more I have come to agree. The way some sections of the Church behave must bring deep pain to our Lord's heart.

During the days of the Inquisition when the Roman Catholic Church was attempting to deal with heresy, a judge put on his desk in court a wooden statue of Christ. The head of this statue was so designed that when the judge hit the desk with his gavel it nodded in approval. How do you think Christ felt about that? I think He must have been in pain. But coming to more modern times, in one country I visited I saw a sign outside a church that read: "This church is the only church authorised by God to represent the Lord Jesus Christ." Is such a church part of the true Body of Christ? If it is, then the attitude of its members must cause our Lord considerable grief. It is tantamount to crucifying Him afresh.

If only we who profess the Name of Christ could see what we do to our Lord when we choose to disobey His commands. If we did, then the Church would be very different. How tragic that our Lord was wounded at Calvary by His enemies but now He is being wounded in the house of His friends.

**FURTHER STUDY**

Psa. 41; 55:12–14

1. How were the psalmist's words prophetic?
2. What application do they have today?

## Prayer

Lord Jesus, I stand in awe at the fact that when You are hurt by the actions of Your Church You do not reject us but continue to move towards us in love. O Lord, help us be worthy of such love. For Your own dear Name's sake. Amen.

# "If it wasn't for You ..."

*"'Who are you, Lord?' Saul asked. 'I am Jesus, whom you are persecuting,' he replied." (v.5)*

**For reading & meditation – Acts 9:1–19**

Most Christians I have talked to about Christ's continuing crucifixion have no difficulty in accepting the fact that Christ suffers in the sufferings of His Church, but fail to see that He suffers also in being misrepresented by His Church. A friend drew my attention to the text before us today and commented: "It says quite plainly that Christ was suffering in Paul's persecution of the Church, but show me a text where it says or even suggests that He suffers also in the failures of His Church." I pointed him to the account of the seven churches in Revelation where clearly our Lord was hurting because of their gross misconduct and failures. He was not convinced.

What about you? Do you believe our Lord is pained when, for example, we make no effort to be reconciled to those we have offended, when we put denominational interests above Christian unity, or when we introduce our selfish ambitions into a kingdom that is based on self-giving? I believe He is in anguish when we do such things. "He was pierced *for* our transgressions," said the prophet Isaiah (53:5), but there is a sense in which He is wounded *by* our transgressions also.

**FURTHER STUDY**

Rev. 2:1–3:22

1. What are some of the things that grieved the Lord?
2. What are His responses?

A very sensitive and spiritually-minded Christian who witnessed people in her church buying lottery tickets (a clear form of gambling) became so upset she said to the Lord during one of her prayer times: "O Jesus, if it wasn't for You I wouldn't be Christian for five minutes." Thankfully He remains faithful to us even when we do not remain faithful to Him.

## Prayer

O Lord Jesus, bring Your Church worldwide face to face with the reality of the pain we give You when we profess to follow You yet depart from Your principles. Send Your Holy Spirit among us – to convict and to cleanse. In Your Name I pray. Amen.

# The true dynamic

*"But I, when I am lifted up from the earth, will draw
all men to myself." (v.32)*

**For reading & meditation – John 12:20–36**

We move on now to consider yet another vantage point from which we can contemplate the cross: the manner by which it *captivates* attention. In the text before us now our Lord predicted that when He was lifted up He would draw men and women to Himself. He was saying that though He attracted the attention of the multitudes by His teaching and miracles, His greatest drawing power would come when He was lifted up on Calvary. This we might refer to as *the magnetic cross*.

Throughout time it has been the custom to honour great men by putting statues of them in an elevated position. In England we have given prominence to Lord Nelson, whose statue stands on top of a column in London's Trafalgar Square, while Hull has done the same for William Wilberforce, who did much to end slavery in the British Empire. And in Scotland, Edinburgh has similarly honoured Sir Walter Scott. Now our Lord Jesus, by any assessment of personality, was a great man. His achievements earned Him the right to be lifted up above His fellows. And so He was. Not on a marble pillar, however, but on a grisly cross.

Some strange, powerful dynamic flows from the cross that draws more people than any other aspect of His ministry. As the centuries have proved, people can become interested in Christ for all manner of reasons – His pure personality, His moral teaching, His supreme example, and so on. But unless they are drawn to the Christ of the cross there can be no true salvation. It is the Christ of the cross who saves.

**FURTHER STUDY**

Matt. 27:33–44;
Mark 15:22–41;
John 19:19–27

1. Who were some of the people gathered round the cross?
2. What were some of their responses?

## Prayer

O Father, I know from personal experience that Your Cross is magnetic for it has drawn me. This divine lodestone has captivated my spirit – and I am glad. Thank You, my Father. In Jesus' Name. Amen.

# Why the cross draws

*"This is how God showed his love among us: He sent
his one and only Son into the world ..."* (v.9)

**For reading & meditation – 1 John 4:7–21**

The surprising thing, we discover, when we read the Gospels is
that though death on a cross was horrific, Jesus moved towards
it as eagerly as an Olympic racer holds out his hands towards the
finishing tape. There was almost a glint of anticipation in His eye as
He drew near to it. In the Garden of Gethsemane He appeared to
shrink momentarily from the prospect of being separated from His
Father, but on almost every other occasion recorded in the Gospels
we see Him approaching Calvary without flinching. Why?

Some of the reasons are matters we have already considered, but
a large part of the answer lies in the words of our Lord that we read
yesterday: "But I, when I am lifted up from the earth, will draw all
men to myself" (John 12:32). What is it about the cross that gives it
this strange drawing power? Wherein lies its mighty magnetism?
I think the cross draws people because it is *the exhibition of divine
love.* Pascal, the French philosopher, said: "If we could see God as
He really is then there would not be such a thing as a sinner left in
the world." Powerful words. What drives us away from God are our

**FURTHER STUDY**

Isa. 50:1–7;
John 2:1–4; 12:31;
17:1

1. What was Isaiah's
prophetic utterance?
2. How was this
fulfilled?

misconceptions of Him. When we see Him as He
really is – unbounding Love – then we are not
driven from Him but drawn towards Him.

Love, it has been said, is the greatest force in
the world. That being so, then Calvary is the
greatest exhibition of that force. Its magnetism
has touched my heart. I hope it has touched yours
too.

## Prayer

O Father, as I gaze on Your Son dying on a cross for me I see love and only
love. Love for everybody, everywhere. But best of all – love for me. I am so
deeply, deeply thankful. Amen.

# Heaven's strategy

*"Just as Moses lifted up the snake in the desert, so the
Son of Man must be lifted up …" (v.14)*

**For reading & meditation – John 3:1–21**

Sin has blinded our eyes to the reality of God. We are not sure that
He loves us enough to provide a way out of our sin and back to
Himself. The cross, however, lays that idea to rest. The uplifted
Christ shows us that God loves us enough to give His own Son to
die for us, and when we see God as He is – true unbounding Love –
we are strangely drawn to Him.

We all carry in our hearts, prior to our conversion, a
misconception of God. The cross says: "What you have believed
about Him is wrong. This is what He is really like – pure infinite
Love." It is only when we see how much we are loved that we can
love. The Bible puts that truth in this form: "We love *because* he first
loved us" (1 John 4:19). Our love for God begins in His love for us.
If we were unable to see how much we are loved then we would not
be able to love. Heaven's strategy for begetting love in human hearts
is this: we are invited to look at the cross and then, as we look, the
scales will fall from our eyes, our sin-dulled gaze will be
transformed, and seeing how much we are loved our own love will
flame in response.

Our Lord talked much to the multitudes
about the love of God but they never
comprehended His love fully until they saw it at
Calvary. There He revealed the beauty and
perfection of His love. Nothing unveils the heart
of God like the cross.

FURTHER STUDY
Rom. 5:1–8;
Jer. 31:1–3; Hosea
11:4; Eph. 2:4–5;
1 John 3:1

1. How does John
describe the demon-
stration of God's love?
2. How is the cross a
demonstration of
mercy?

## Prayer

O Father, now I see why the cross has such a magnetic effect on my heart. It
shows me as nothing else what lies at the core of the divine nature – everlasting
love. My heart responds to that heart. Thank You my Father. Amen.

# A word with a stoop in it

*"… so that, having been justified by his grace, we might become heirs …" (v.7)*

**For reading & meditation – Titus 3:1–11**

One reason why the cross draws men and women is because it is the expression of divine love. Love is a response – we love *because*. When we take a serious look at the cross and see how much we are loved something moves in our hearts and we are drawn not against our will but *almost* against our will to the source of that mighty love. This is divine magnetism at work. But look with me now at another reason for the drawing power of the cross: *it is the exhibition of divine grace.*

Frequently I am asked: "What is the difference between love and grace? When I reply I think of the words of an elderly Welsh preacher: "Love reaches out on the same level, but grace always has to stoop to pick one up." The great preacher D.L. Moody used to say: "Grace is a word with a *stoop* in it." Some people attempting to define grace like to use this acrostic: God's Riches At Christ's Expense. When, many years ago, I looked at the cross and saw what Christ did for me, a lost and hell-deserving sinner, the sight of it drew my heart out through my eyes in hot adoring tears of love.

**FURTHER STUDY**

Titus 2:1–11;
Acts 15:11;
Rom. 5:15

1. What has appeared to all men?
2. Can you make another acrostic from the word "grace"?

Alexander Whyte, the great Scottish preacher, stood in his pulpit one Sunday and announced: "This past week I have discovered who is the most wicked man in Edinburgh. And I am now going to name him." As the congregation waited with bated breath to see whom he would name he said very quietly and with tears running down his face: "Alexander Whyte."

## Prayer

O God, Your love is wonderful, but how much more wonderful is divine grace. It stooped to where I was and has lifted me up to where You are. I will sing of its power in time and in eternity. Blessed be Your Name for ever. Amen.

# "Beer into furniture"

*"... the gospel ... is the power of God for the salvation
of everyone who believes ..." (v.16)*

**For reading & meditation – Romans 1:8–17**

The cross draws people firstly because it is the exposition of
divine love. When we see how much God loves us – nowhere is
that shown more clearly than at the cross – our hearts run to their
rightful Lord. Secondly, the cross draws people because it is the
exhibition of divine grace. When we really *see* what grace is – God's
Riches At Christ's Expense – our spirits are taken captive. The third
reason, I suggest, why the cross draws is this: *it is the expression of
divine power*. Our text for today tells us that the gospel (the message
of the cross) is the *power* of God for salvation.

When I think of magnetic power my mind goes back to the days
when I was an apprentice in an engineering works. The company
decided to invest in a powerful electromagnet and had it installed in
the foundry. As soon as it was switched on, pieces of iron ore that
were buried in the sand of the foundry floor began to fly upwards,
drawn by the awesome magnetic force. The cross is like that. It lifts
us out of sin and lifts sin out of us.

A newly converted man, previously known for his irresponsible
behaviour, was speaking in an open-air service
about Christ's power to change. Suddenly his
message was interrupted by a heckler who
shouted out: "You don't really believe Christ
turned water into wine, do you?" Quick as a flash
he replied: "He has done something better than
that. He has turned beer into furniture in my
house." It takes power to accomplish that – the
power of the cross.

FURTHER STUDY

2 Cor. 5:11–15;
Rom. 15:17–20;
1 Cor. 9:16

1. What was it that
   gripped Paul?
2. What did it cause
   him to say?

## Prayer

Gracious and loving heavenly Father, thank You for these days when I have been
reflecting on the magnetic power of the cross. Love, grace and power have an
irresistible pull on my heart. I am still being drawn. Thank You, my Lord.
Amen.

# "Come and die"

*"If anyone would come after me, he must ... take up his cross ..." (v.34)*

**For reading & meditation – Mark 8:31–38**

We now look at a somewhat different aspect of the cross. It can best be understood, I feel, by the term *the symbolic cross*. In our passage today we read that before Christ challenged His followers to deny themselves and take up their own cross *"he called the crowd to him"* (v.34). The need to take up one's cross was not an esoteric secret to be divulged to a close group of the spiritually elite but a condition of discipleship that was openly announced to all. Summoning the crowds, our Lord told them bluntly that if they decided to be His followers then they must be willing to carry a cross.

Obviously our Lord was not intending His followers to understand they would be literally crucified, but was using the word "cross" in a symbolic sense. He meant that His followers should be prepared to have a deathblow delivered to their natural self-interest and to live for God's interests. And this was not intended to be one dramatic gesture of self-abnegation but a continuous one. It was to be done *daily*. Paul was so prepared to disregard his own interests and safety for the sake of the gospel that he declared "I die every day" (1 Cor. 15:31), referring to the physical danger he constantly faced.

Dietrich Bonhoeffer, who was executed by the Nazis just a few weeks before the end of World War II, put it well when he said: "When Christ calls a man He bids him come and die." Though this aspect may be described as the *symbolic* cross, believe me, it represents something very real.

**FURTHER STUDY**

Matt. 10:32–38;
16:24–28;
Luke 9:57–62

1. What hard words did Jesus say to some who wanted to follow Him?
2. What is their significance?

## Prayer

Lord Jesus, I see that just as You took up a cross so I too am to carry one. Help me dedicate myself to this task in the way that You did so that like You I will be able to say: "I have finished all that the Father asked me to do." For Your own Name's sake. Amen.

# "Outside the camp"

*"Let us, then, go to him outside the camp, bearing the disgrace he bore." (v.13)*

**For reading & meditation – Hebrews 13:7–21**

Though we are thinking of the cross in a symbolic sense, the issues involved are very *real*. Taking up the cross means far more than putting up with frustrations – things that usually we *cannot* avoid. The cross we are told to take up on Christ's behalf is a chosen cross. It is something, if we so desire, we can avoid. It has to do, I believe, with living so closely to Christ that the disgrace He suffered falls on us. Get this fact firmly fixed in your mind – there is a shame at the heart of the cross and it must be borne.

In the passage before us today the writer is addressing people who had endured the shame of the gospel (see Hebrews 10:32–34) and who had still more persecution to endure. "Let us, then, go to him outside the camp," he says, "bearing the disgrace he bore." Students of Scripture see in Jesus' death the fulfilment of the sin offering that was tendered in ancient Israel when an animal was killed, offered as a sacrifice for the sins of the people and then carried outside the camp so that it would not pollute the place where the people lived. Our Lord too was taken "outside the camp".

The old hymn puts it like this: "There is a green hill far away, *without a city wall.*" "Without the camp." Jesus was cast out, despised and rejected by men.

The issue then is this: those who follow Christ and commit themselves to Him wholeheartedly can expect to suffer the same obloquy and shame.

**FURTHER STUDY**

Matt. 5:11–16;
10:22;
2 Tim. 3:10–12

1. How are we to respond to reproach for Christ's sake?
2. What did Paul underline to Timothy?

## Prayer

Father, help me not to draw back from bearing the shame of the cross. If I am sent "outside the camp" because of my commitment to You let me not be ashamed of it. Let me *exult* in it. In the Name of my Lord Jesus Christ I pray. Amen.

# Not our shame – *His*

*"In fact, everyone who wants to live a godly life in Christ Jesus will be persecuted ..." (v.12)*

**For reading & meditation – 2 Timothy 3:10–17**

There is disgrace associated with the gospel. Just as our Lord willingly bore a cross of shame so it falls to those of us who are His disciples to do the same. It is not possible to have the hearty friendship of the world and the saving friendship of Christ. There is a choice to be made, and if you are willing to be definite in discipleship – committed to taking up your cross – then you must be prepared for a degree of suffering.

Some of Christ's disciples suffer social ostracism because of their commitment to Him. They are excluded from the camp, barred from general social acceptance. Because they refuse to join in with activities that dishonour Christ, people think they are killjoys. Sometimes Christians suffer in their professional advancement because of their commitment to Christ. I know many who could have reached the top of their profession had they been willing to compromise on certain issues – but they would not. So they found themselves "outside the camp, bearing the disgrace he bore".

Many reading these lines will know what it means to be the butt of a joke or the object of ridicule because they "stand up for Jesus" in their social circle, school or place of work. You are made to feel you are not part of the set – "outside the camp". Don't fret about this – bear it willingly. Say to yourself: "I am going to thrust my shoulder underneath His cross and bear whatever I can of His disgrace. It is an honour of which I am unworthy." Remember, it is not your disgrace. It is *His*!

**FURTHER STUDY**

Acts 5:33–42;
1 Cor. 4:10;
2 Cor. 4:11;
11:23–29

1. Why were the apostles rejoicing?
2. What did Paul constantly face?

## Prayer

Father, help me remember the shame of Jesus – crucified stark naked on a cross – is not my shame, but His. I count it a privilege and an honour that I am allowed to bear something of His shame. Thank You my Father. Amen.

# "The seventh scar"

*"And anyone who does not carry his cross and follow me cannot be my disciple." (v.27)*

**For reading & meditation – Luke 14:25–35**

There is a church in the Far East known as "The Fellowship of the Seventh Scar". This is why: Our Lord was wounded in six places: His two hands, His two feet, His side and His head. But there would have been another wound also – the bruise on His shoulder due to carrying a heavy cross. Maybe a bruise cannot properly be called a wound – it probably would not have left a scar – but one can sympathise with the idea nevertheless. The members of this particular church emphasise the fact that Christians must be willing to thrust their shoulders under a cross in the same way that Jesus did. They say if there is no metaphorical bruise on a Christian's shoulder, they have not entered into true discipleship.

Ian Macpherson tells of a couple who went to see the famous Passion Play in Oberammergau, in which the story of Christ and His crucifixion is acted out. The husband, seeing the actor who played the part of Christ laying down the cross during an interval, thought it would be a good idea to have his wife photograph him bearing it. But as he tried to lift it he found it was too heavy for him. "It's heavier than I thought," he remarked and, turning to the actor who was standing nearby, said: "Why is it so heavy?" Drawing himself up to his full height the actor replied: "Sir, if I did not feel the full weight of His cross I could not play His part." We must all feel the weight of the cross if we are to play His part.

**FURTHER STUDY**

Mark 8:34–38;
Phil. 3:8;
1 Cor. 9:27

1. What are we to do before taking up our cross?
2. What is Christ's condition of discipleship?

## Prayer

Lord Jesus Christ, I see that if I am to play the part You have for me in this world then I must feel the weight of Your Cross. I would not go through this life unscarred. Help me put my shoulder under the cross and bear it as courageously as You bore Yours. Amen.

# Another shoulder

*"For my yoke is easy and my burden is light."*
*(v.30)*

**For reading & meditation – Matthew 11:25–30**

Though actual bodily impalement is not what we are called to endure, the symbolic cross represents something very real. Taking up our cross involves (as we have seen) a daily commitment to serving Christ which carries with it a sense of disgrace and shame. We referred the other day, you will remember, to the words of Dietrich Bonhoeffer: "When Christ calls a man He bids him come and die." True disciples deem it an honour to suffer for Christ and to bear His shame. They sing with the hymnist Isaac Watts:

> I'm not ashamed to own my Lord,
> Or to defend His cause,
> Maintain the honour of His Word
> The glory of His Cross.

Christians who bear Christ's cross, however, find to their delight that there is another shoulder beneath it in addition to their own. One preacher, B.D. Johns, put it like this: "He who has been *on* the cross *for* us has promised to be *under* the cross *with* us." So the next time you undertake some uncongenial task for the sake of Christ, need to subordinate your own interests, suffer some mild or not so mild ostracism, experience setbacks in your vocation or profession, or become the subject of covert sneers, then take heart – under the cross is not only your shoulder but the shoulder of the Crucified One. And Christ helps lift us as well as the cross by His sustaining power.

**FURTHER STUDY**

1 Pet. 5:1–7;
Matt. 8:17;
Isa. 53:4;
1 Pet. 2:24

1. What can you take comfort in today?
2. Is there someone you can help with their cross today?

## Prayer

O Father, how glad I am that You thrust Your shoulder beneath the cross I am called to carry. Because of this what I thought was a burden becomes a blessing. On the cross for me; under the cross with me. What more can I ask? Amen.

# "Me"

*"... the Son of God, who loved me and gave himself
for me." (v.20)*

### For reading & meditation – Galatians 2:11–21

There is one final aspect of the cross we must look at if we are to
truly understand its meaning, preciousness and power. This I
shall refer to as *the personal cross.*

The priests, the people of Jerusalem, and the Romans were not
the only ones responsible for putting Christ on the cross; *we were
implicated in it too.* Unless we can see that we were involved in the
cross, unless we can say with the apostle Paul, "The Son of God,
who loved *me* and gave himself for *me*," then it will have no more
effect on us than any other great event in history. The cross is only
meaningful as we realise our personal involvement in it.

You are familiar, I am sure, with the story of Martin Luther's
conversion. For years he was a monk, laboriously "working his
passage to heaven". But despite his many religious exercises, he
never had the assurance that his sins were forgiven. But after a long
time the pronouns in the text before us came alive to him and he
cried: "The Son of God, who loved *me* and gave himself for *me*." In
his commentary on Galatians, which he wrote many years later, he
said: "Read therefore with great vehemency these
words '*me*' and 'for *me*' and so inwardly practise
with thyself, that thou, with a sure faith, mayst
conceive and print this '*me*' in thy heart and apply
it to thyself, not doubting but thou art of the
number of those to whom this '*me*' belongeth."
The cross will come alive only when we
understand it was for *me*.

FURTHER STUDY

Rom. 6:1–6;
2 Tim. 2:11;
Gal. 5:24

1. What was Paul
able to say?
2. What is a
trustworthy saying?

## Prayer

Heavenly Father, help me now as I near the end of these meditations to make
sure that I have understood the "me" in the cross. Show me even more clearly
my personal involvement in that ghastly event. In Jesus' Name I pray. Amen.

# It matters – eternally

*"I tell you the truth, whoever hears my word and believes him who sent me has eternal life ..."* (v.24)

**For reading & meditation – John 5:16–30**

The essential difference between a Christian and a non-Christian is that the Christian has understood the "me" in the cross. One theologian gave his testimony before a large crowd: "I had a degree in theology (a PhD) and I could read the Bible in its original languages, but I never saw that Christianity was not so much a matter of religion but a matter of relationship. One day a young evangelist came to our church and though he broke almost every rule of hermeneutics [the art of interpreting the Bible] he brought home to me that I was not a Christian because I did not have a personal awareness of what Christ had done for me. It was this realisation, then later my commitment, that has made Jesus not the centre of religion but the centre of my life."

John Wesley, you may remember, said something similar. On the night of his conversion in Aldersgate Street, London – 24 May 1738 – the pronouns came alive and as he himself worded it: "... an assurance was given me that he had taken away my sins, even mine, and saved me from the law of sin and death." His brother Charles Wesley, the great hymn writer, put it like this:

**FURTHER STUDY**

Col. 3:1–4;
John 14:20:
1 John 3:24

1. What did Paul assure the Colossians?
2. How can we be sure that we live in Him?

*I felt my Lord's atoning blood*
*Close to my soul – applied;*
*Me, me He loved – the Son of God ...*

Every Christian will tell you the most memorable day or period of their lives was when the "me" came into the cross. Understanding the "me" in the cross makes the difference between spending eternity in hell or heaven. It matters eternally.

## Prayer

Loving heavenly Father, I must question myself to see whether I am in the faith or not. I cannot rest on my good works or even my attendance at church. I must rest my faith on You. Help me settle this issue beyond all doubt. In Jesus' Name. Amen.

# "I did that!"

*"Look, the Lamb of God, who takes away the sin of the world!" (v.29)*

### For reading & meditation – John 1:29–34

Some may think that it was easy for Paul to say, "The Son of God, who loved me and gave himself for me." Because Paul was one of Christ's contemporaries, he could talk with those who had known Him well. But how can we, who are separated by 2,000 years of history, utter those words with any intelligent meaning? We weren't thought of then – humanly speaking anyhow. More than sixty generations separate us from those who stood on that first Good Friday outside the city wall. How can we say with any conviction that He loved *me* and gave Himself for *me*?

A man once asked me: "How could Jesus have died for my sin when I wasn't around at the time He died to commit any sin?" What answer would you give to that question? Well, the answer didn't come easily but thank God it came. My reply went something like this: "Jesus Christ died not only *for* your sins but *by* your sins. The sins that put Him on the cross were the same that you and I commit. There was the bigotry of the Pharisees, the self-seeking of the Sadducees, the cowardice and disinterest of Pilate, the taunts of the crowd. I cannot say that I have never been bigoted, self-seeking, cowardly, or disinterested in what God wants. Can you?" He got the point.

The next time we catch sight of a cross or a crucifix the event it symbolises might come home to us more forcibly if we say to ourselves: *I did that!*

FURTHER STUDY

Col. 1:9–14;
John 15:13; 1 John
3:16; Rev. 1:5

1. What does Christ's
sacrifice rescue
us from?
2. Do you need to
ask God to cleanse
your sin today?

## Prayer

Father, I see more clearly now how I was implicated in the cross. My sins did that to You. My sins. Even though I was not there, I was implicated. O God, I must be forgiven for this. Help me. In Jesus' Name. Amen.

# "Go to the cross"

*"Who may stand in his holy place? He who has clean hands and a pure heart …"* (vv.3–4)

**For reading & meditation – Psalm 24:1–10**

Why do we need a Saviour at all? The simple answer is that we are all sinners and as such we need a Saviour. We have only to look into our hearts to see (as I have said) that the sins which nailed Jesus Christ to the tree are in all of us – bigotry, self-interest, disregard of God's purposes, and so on. Our hearts are shot through with sin. We are deep-dyed sinners – "dyed in the wool" as the saying goes.

What can we do about it? The Bible makes clear (note again our text for today) that we cannot expect to come into God's presence with sin in our hearts. Reverently we have to stand before Him and say: "God, help us." We cannot undo our past and we cannot go into the future thinking that by resolving to be different the matter can be solved. Do we really believe that we can make up our mind never to sin again and keep that resolution on our own? It cannot be done. That is why I advise people: go to the cross. Stand before God in Christ and plead for mercy. Don't try to defend yourself for there is no defence. Your case will be lost if you try to do that. No one has come from the cross feeling justified because they based their plea on justice. The plea must be based on mercy. We must ask God for Christ's sake to forgive us our sins.

If you have never done this then I urge you – do so now. Pray this prayer with me.

---

**FURTHER STUDY**

Acts 3:11–26;
Matt. 5:20; 18:3;
John 8:24

1. What did Peter call on people to do?
2. Why not turn to God today?

---

## Prayer

O Jesus, Lord and Saviour, I ask You to forgive my sins, cleanse me of all unrighteousness and make me a member of Your eternal family. I believe You have heard my prayer. Now give me the assurance that I am saved. In Your most merciful Name I ask it. Amen.

# Glorying in the crucified

*"May I never boast except in the cross of our Lord Jesus Christ ..." (v.14)*

**For reading & meditation – Galatians 6:7–18**

Today we bring to an end the meditations in which we have contemplated the cross from different vantage points. We have looked at the cosmic cross, the historic cross, the inevitable cross, the atoning cross, the continuing cross, the magnetic cross, the symbolic cross and the personal cross. Viewing it from various angles we get different perspectives, yet there is an organic relationship between them all.

People of the world look at the cross in a different way from a Christian. They see it as nothing more than a couple of wooden beams, an instrument of capital punishment. Paul's outlook on the cross was different. He saw it as something to be gloried in. Sir John Bowring shared Paul's view when he wrote:

*In the cross of Christ I glory,*
*Towering o'er the wrecks of time,*
*All the light of sacred story*
*Gathers round its head sublime.*

Dr A.C. Dixon pointed out that although Paul's first vision was of the glorified Christ on the road to Damascus, he did not glory in the glorified. He gloried rather in the crucified. That is where our glorying must be too.

**FURTHER STUDY**

2 Cor. 5:1–17;
Titus 3:5;
1 Pet. 1:23;
John 12:25

1. Why is the cross
so fundamental to
our faith?
2. Talk to someone
about the cross today.

## Prayer

Father, may I like the apostle Paul glory for ever in Your cross. Let what I have learned about it so grip me that Christ and the cross will be at the centre of my life and the inspiration for every step I take into the future. In His Name I ask it. Amen.

# The Treasures
## of Darkness

# Hidden treasures

*"I will give you the treasures of darkness, riches stored in
secret ... that you may know that I am the Lord ... (v.3)*

**For reading & meditation – Isaiah 45:1–17**

We begin a new theme: *the treasures of darkness.* In writing Bible
notes it is my custom to approach every theme from a
different angle. Sometimes I focus on a book or passage, and thus
the approach is analytical and expositional. Sometimes the purpose
is functional and practical, giving insights on how to be a more
effective disciple of the Lord Jesus Christ. And on occasions (such
as this) the approach is devotional and inspirational – portraying
biblical truths that are designed to warm the heart and set fire to the
soul. In this way a varied spiritual menu is presented – a method
necessary not only to assist spiritual growth but to satisfy wide
tastes among the readers.

This devotional theme brims over with hope and confidence,
which are much needed, for many times we are called to walk in
darkness. Perhaps you are there at this moment. The secret of why
God chooses to lead us into the darkness is revealed to us in our text
for today: "I will give you the *treasures* of darkness."

Are there treasures which can only be found in the dark? It
would seem so. John Bunyan found them in the
darkness of prison and wrote the immortal story,
*Pilgrim's Progress.* Helen Keller, blind and deaf and
dumb, found treasures in her darkness and shared
them with the world through her glowing spirit.
In a deep dark well you can look up and see the
stars, even when people in the light above can't
see them. We can discover treasures in the
darkness that we would never be able to find in
the light.

| FURTHER STUDY |
| :---: |
| Psa. 18:1–28; |
| 2 Sam. 22:29; |
| Psa. 112:4; |
| Col. 2:2–3 |
| 1. What was David's testimony? |
| 2. Where is treasure hidden? |

## Prayer

O Father, help me learn the secret of turning all my periods of darkness into
occasions of delight – delight at the discovery of Your hidden treasures. In Jesus'
Name I ask it. Amen.

# "Next summer's apples ..."

*"Although he was a son, he learned obedience from
what he suffered" (v.8)*

**For reading & meditation – Hebrews 5:1–14**

Yesterday we said that many people have made discoveries in the
darkness that they might not have made in the light. A Christian
woman woke up one morning in the dead of winter with the words
ringing in her mind: "Next summer's apples are already on the tree."
How strange, she thought, for as she looked out through her
window she saw nothing but snow and ice. Then the Spirit said:
"You may not see the apples yet, but they are there, nevertheless.
And in the same way, the treasures of summer are already in the tree
of life, caught at this moment in the darkness of the winter's cold. Be
patient, for love will soon bring them out."

I have chosen the verse for today: "... he learned by all he
suffered how to obey" (Moffatt), because it emphasises the point I
want to make throughout this theme, namely, that the place of
darkness can be the place of delight. Jesus, we are told, learned by
all He suffered. How strange that the Son of God should learn
anything. Did He not have all knowledge and wisdom? Yes He did,
but when He took upon Himself our flesh He deliberately and
voluntarily limited Himself to finding out about
life in the way we find out – by grappling with
issues day after day. He learned that "treasure" is
found in "darkness" – the darkness of suffering.

Milton found great treasures in the darkness
of his blindness and revealed them to the world in
immortal verse. Sometimes a dark tunnel is the
shortest way around a hill.

FURTHER STUDY

Heb. 10:19–39;
2 Tim. 2:3–12; 4:5

1. What is the theme
of the writer to the
Hebrews?
2. What was Paul's
exhortation to
Timothy?

## Prayer

Father, help me to remember that no matter how dark and cold the winter, the
treasures of summer are already in the tree. Etch this truth so deeply into my
spirit that it will never be effaced. In Christ's Name I pray. Amen.

# "Dig – dig for meaning"

*"You, O Lord, keep my lamp burning; my God turns my darkness into light." (v.28)*

**For reading & meditation – Psalm 18:16–30**

W hen we find ourselves surrounded by darkness, we must look for the *meaning* that lies within it. Whenever you find yourself engulfed in darkness, begin to dig by the light of your flickering torch of faith for the treasures of meaning that are hidden there. For the treasures of darkness are found only by those who dig – dig for meaning. Many Christians have allowed darkness to drag their spirits down so much that they have lost their faith. They did not know how to search out the treasures that lay all around them.

Paul must have inwardly chafed when he found himself in the darkness of a prison cell – confined for the crime of announcing the good news. The curtailment of his personal liberty was hard, but it was harder still to be shut off from the opportunity of telling people about his beloved Saviour. What could compensate for that? But in the darkness he found a treasure. Paul's letters, mostly written from prison, have enriched Christians down the centuries and will continue to do so, if the Lord tarries, for centuries to come. They could not have been written except in the darkness of a prison experience. Paul dipped his pen in the blood of his sufferings and wrote words that are deathless. In long days and nights of pondering upon Jesus, his thoughts crystallised into immortal phrases through which men and women have looked into the heart of a redeeming God.

One thing is sure – God will never allow us to be surrounded by darkness without handing us a pick so that we can dig for treasure.

**FURTHER STUDY**

Acts 16:16–40;
2 Cor. 11:23; Eph. 3:1

1. How did Paul respond to his prison experience in Philippi?
2. When writing to the Ephesians, how did Paul describe his imprisonment?

## Prayer

Father, I see that the treasures of darkness come only to those who dig for meaning. Help me not to rebel against the darkness but rejoice in it – rejoice because with Your help I can turn the place of darkness into the place of discovery. Amen.

# Having the right attitude

*"If God is for us, who can be against us?"*
*(v.31)*

**For reading & meditation – Romans 8:28–39**

The first thing we need to understand when we are surrounded by deep darkness is that we are not going to be exempt from the difficult periods of life just because we are Christians. If we react to dark experiences by saying: "I'm a Christian, why should this happen to me?" then this will hinder us from finding the treasures that lie all around. Richard Baxter wrote concerning the Great Plague: "At first so few of the religious people were taken away that they began to get puffed up and boast of the great differences which God did make. But quickly after that, they all fell alike."

There is little we can do to stop the darkness descending, but there is a lot we can do to make it give up its hidden treasures. So whenever you find yourself in a period of darkness, hold fast to the idea that what matters is not so much what is happening to you as the meaning that you can get out of it. Sorrows, griefs, losses, disappointments, frustrations, sickness, failures – these can be dark and difficult experiences. They can, however, be times of great spiritual advance, providing we stand up to them with the right attitude – God will allow nothing to come into my life unless it can be used.

If you say to yourself: "This should not have happened to me because I am a child of God", then your attitude will prevent you from discovering the treasures that are all around. When you realise that you can use everything, then you need not be afraid of anything.

**FURTHER STUDY**

1 Tim. 1:8–14;
2 Cor. 12:9;
Phil. 4:19;
Eph. 2:6–7

1. What was Paul's strength?
2. How did he respond?

## Prayer

O Father, help me to have the right attitude to all my circumstances for I realise that I am more influenced by my attitudes than by my arteries. When I serve You, then all things serve me. I am so grateful. Amen.

# "Grace enough, and to spare"

*"I, Paul, write this greeting in my own hand.
Remember my chains. Grace be with you." (v.18)*

**For reading & meditation – Colossians 4:7–18**

Some years ago a friend asked: "Can you help me out of the darkness I'm passing through?" After questioning him for a few moments, I said to him: "I can't help you to get out of the darkness, but I can help to get the darkness out of you." His eyes lit up and he said: "Quickly, tell me how." I was not able to give him any "quick" answers, but I was able to give him clear answers – answers that enabled him to find treasures in his darkness. Many of those answers I will share with you.

In the text before us today Paul shows how he had developed the attitude that enabled him to stand fast in the midst of the most depressing circumstances. Moffatt has: "This salutation is in my own hand, from Paul. 'Remember I am in prison. Grace be with you.'" We might have expected Paul to have written: "I am in prison; God give me grace." But no, he puts it the other way round: "I am in prison; grace be with *you*." It is as if he is saying: "I have found grace in the darkness of a prison experience – enough and to spare. I pass it on to you."

The experience of being engulfed in darkness can either make or break us. Some it shatters; others it strengthens. When our souls are open to the grace that constantly flows towards us from heaven, then every limitation, every difficult situation, every perplexing circumstance can be the setting for a new discovery of God and a new revelation of His love.

FURTHER STUDY

Eph. 4:1–7;
Phil. 1:7, 14;
2 Tim. 1:8–10

1. What has been
given to each
one of us?
2. What was one
result of Paul's
chains?

## Prayer

O Father, help me whenever I am engulfed in darkness to find grace – and not only grace enough for my need but "enough to spare". May its flow contribute to my overflowing. This I ask in and through the peerless and precious Name of Jesus. Amen.

# Is darkness God's punishment?

*"… every branch that does bear fruit he prunes so that it will be even more fruitful." (v.2)*

**For reading & meditation – John 15:1–17**

The darkness I am discussing is not the cloud of guilt that descends upon us because of some sin we have committed, but the darkness allowed by God to deepen our understanding of Him and His love. We live in a world of moral consequences and sin does produce darkness in the soul, but if, when we are in darkness, there is no conscious sin in our lives, we ought not to beat ourselves over the head with a spiritual club, saying: "This is happening to me because I am such an awful person." See the darkness from the same perspective as the poet:

> *Why do I creep along the heavenly way*
> *By inches in the garish day?*
> *Last night when darkening clouds did round me lower*
> *I strode whole leagues in one short hour.*

The darkening clouds may only serve to quicken our pace towards Home. An Indian proverb says: "The bursting of the petals says the flowers are coming." So when your heart bursts with pain, it is only the bursting of the cramping sheaf to let the flowers out.

**FURTHER STUDY**

Matt. 26:36–46;
Mark 14:36;
Luke 22:42

1. What was Christ's response to His moments of darkness?
2. What was His decision?

The heartbreak of Gethsemane was the bursting of the sheath to let the Passion flower out. And because of that, the world today is filled with its perfume. As someone said: "It's wonderful what God can do with a broken heart if He is given all the pieces."

If at this moment you find yourself in darkness and your heart is broken, then give God all the pieces. He is more than able to put your life together again, perhaps in a new and more glorious pattern.

## Prayer

Father, help me to learn the important spiritual lesson that every branch in You that bears fruit is pruned that it might bear more fruit. Prune me that I might be more fruitful. In Jesus' Name I ask it. Amen.

# Never alone

*"... And God is faithful; he will not let you be tempted beyond what you can bear ..." (v.13)*

**For reading & meditation – 1 Corinthians 10:1–13**

What are some of the dark experiences through which we are called to pass, and how do we find meaning in them? The first that we focus on is the darkness of fierce temptation. Perhaps at this very moment you are engulfed by a cloud of temptation that threatens to upset your spiritual equilibrium. Take heart, today's text tells us that God is committed to standing with you in the hour of temptation and providing a way of escape. You will find treasure in the darkness.

Note again what the text says: "God is faithful; he will not let you be tempted beyond what you can bear." God owes it to Himself, His Word, His love and His character to succour you in any temptation that comes your way. He knows that you can do nothing without Him and that you will certainly fail if He abandons you, so the Almighty will not let you down. If God were to remove Himself from you in the moments when you are overtaken by powerful temptation, He would be untrue to Himself. So right now drop your anchor into the depths of this encouraging revelation – He has promised to stand by you and there is no way He will ever abandon you because He cannot be untrue to Himself.

But what does this faithfulness mean? It does not mean that He will prevent the darkness of temptation from descending; what it does mean is that He will never allow the temptation to go beyond your power to resist. That's the escape route He promises. Rest in that promise – it will never fail.

**FURTHER STUDY**

Heb. 4:12–16;
2:18;
James 1:12

1. What is available in our time of need?
2. What are we to do?

## Prayer

O Father, I am so thankful that when I enter into the darkness of temptation I am never alone. Let me be gripped by this glorious truth that no matter how powerful the temptation, You will never allow it to get beyond my ability to resist. I am deeply grateful. Amen.

# Unbeatable and unbreakable

*"… no weapon forged against you will prevail …"*
(v.17)

**For reading & meditation – Isaiah 54:11–17**

One treasure in the darkness of temptation is that God always keeps His promises. How could we ever understand the faithfulness of God unless we saw it at work in difficult situations?

Temptation, though you may not think so when you are going through it, has a beneficial purpose. Goethe said: "Difficulties prove men. As we grapple, we grow." The greatest treasure we can discover in the darkness of temptation is the understanding that we can do more with temptation than just bear it – we can use it. How to turn temptation to our advantage is one of life's greatest secrets. Once we have learned it we are unbeatable and unbreakable. And it is one of those priceless treasures that can only be found in the dark.

A Sunday-school teacher told me that when she was talking to her class about the cross a little boy raised his hand and said: "Jesus didn't just carry His cross – He used it." What a powerful truth lies in the words of that little boy. God does not want us just to bear a cross of temptation; He wants us to use it. A Stoic bears a cross; a Christian uses it and makes it bear him.

**FURTHER STUDY**

Isa. 61:1–7;
Psa. 126:5;
Neh. 8:10

1. What does God bestow in place of ashes?
2. What will God do with our mourning?

I once heard the singer Sammy Davis take words that were shouted to him from the audience and put them to music. Someone handed him a shopping list which he promptly set to a tune. Everything can be used – even temptation. So before going any further, settle for this as a life conviction – it's not what comes, it's what we do with it, that's important.

## Prayer

Father, I see so clearly that when I am in You and You are in me, them everything can be used – even temptation. Help me to discover even more of the treasures that lie in its oppressive darkness. In Jesus' Name I pray. Amen.

# "It hurts good"

*"Consider it pure joy … whenever you face trials … the testing of your faith develops perseverance."* (vv.2–3)

**For reading & meditation – James 1:1–8**

When we find ourselves engulfed by the darkness of oppressive temptation, we ought not to allow ourselves to sink back in despondency and say: "Why should this happen to me?" but remind ourselves that the darkness contains hidden treasures.

Philosophers have told us repeatedly that life is determined more by our reactions than by our actions. Temptation sweeps in upon us and forces its way into our lives without asking (and sometimes without our acting) and it is then that our reaction plays an important part. We can react in self-pity and frustration, or we can act with confidence and courage and let the temptation cause us to sink down even more deeply into the everlasting arms. If you have been seeing temptation as a groaning point, change your perspective and begin to view it as a growing point.

I am told that whenever they are sick, some South American Indians push aside modern medicines that are available, preferring instead the medicines that their ancestors have used down the centuries. One reporter was told: "The trouble with modern medicine is that it is not bitter and we are suspicious of anything that does not cause us distaste." They have a saying which they use when taking their bitter medicines: "It hurts good." You can make temptation "hurt good" when you see it as an opportunity to increase your dependence upon God, develop your trust, improve your character and make you more and more like Jesus Christ. The darkness yields a treasure – a deeper awareness and understanding of the importance of absolute dependence on an all-sufficient God.

**FURTHER STUDY**

2 Pet. 2:1–9;
James 1:12;
Rev. 3:10

1. What has God promised to those who trust Him in the hour of trial?
2. When are we blessed?

## Prayer

Lord Jesus, You who faced the bitterness of a wilderness temptation and used it in the purposes of redemption, teach me to do the same. May I face the bitter in the assurance that when You are with me all it can do is make me better. In Jesus' Name. Amen.

# Why God allows temptation

*"Blessed is the man who perseveres under trial ..."*
*(v.12)*

**For reading & meditation – James 1:9–20**

Why does God allow temptation? To understand that, we must look at the Greek word for temptation – *peirasmos* – which means to test, try or prove. The biblical use of the word (unlike its modern use) does not contain the idea of seduction or entrapment but rather, putting a person to a test for the purpose of deepening qualities of character.

The purpose, then, behind every temptation which God allows is the development of character. One writer says: "The conversion of a soul is the work of a moment but the making of a saint is the work of a lifetime." Oswald Chambers, expressing the same truth differently, said, "God can, in one single moment, make a heart pure, but not even God can in a single moment give a person character." Character would not be the precious thing it is if it could be acquired without struggle, combat and contradictions. Virtue that has not been tried and tested in the fire is not worthy of the name of virtue. In a world such as this, it is essential that temptation should come to try us, for without it there can be no advance in virtue, no growth in holiness and no development in character.

**FURTHER STUDY**

Rom. 12:9–21;
Heb. 12:1; 1 Pet.
1:13; James 5:11;
Job 13:15

1. What example does James point us to?
2. What lessons can we learn from this example?

But what is character? The definition I like is this: "Character is what we are in the dark." Reputation is what others think of us – character is what we are on the inside. It is the strength of soul we develop as we stand against the tide of temptation. When we grapple, we grow. And out of the growing comes character.

## Prayer

O Father, if character is something slowly achieved rather than suddenly acquired, then help me in achieving. And if temptation is a way of deepening my personal qualities, then I welcome it. Help me to turn it all to good. In Jesus' Name. Amen.

# A purpose in all things

*"These have come so that your faith ... may be proved genuine ..."* (v.7)

**For reading & meditation – 1 Peter 1:1–9**

To many people, Christians included, the idea that God allows His children to be tempted by the devil is inconsistent with His omnipotence. "If God is Almighty," they reason, "then He should intervene in Satan's attempts to seduce us and should prevent Satan damaging our personalities." But it is because God is omnipotent that He permits us to be tempted.

P. Harton says: "A conquering nation that is not sure of its own strength, refuses the people any kind of independence at all, and keeps control with a strong hand, is governed not by a love for the people but by a fear of the people." God does not control the lives of His people by fear but by love, justice and the desire always to do what is right. He will not deliver us from temptation, but He will deliver us in it. Whenever we are under attack, it is one of Satan's strategies to persuade us that because God does not deliver us from temptation, He is not able to help us. God is well able to help us and the help He gives is to supply us with the grace to overcome it.

God clearly allows temptation as part of His purposes for our spiritual development, so why fear it? Humility will not permit us to desire temptation – that would be to presume on our own strength – but zeal for our Christian advancement should result in our not dreading it and not being unhappy when it comes. Holiness would not be as awesome to our carnal natures if it could be acquired without a struggle.

> **FURTHER STUDY**
> Matt. 6:5–18;
> James 1:13–15;
> 2 Cor. 11:3
>
> 1. What did Jesus pray about temptation and the evil one?
> 2. What follows evil desire?

## Prayer

My Father and my God, thank You for unveiling to me the treasures that are hidden in the darkness of temptation. Help me in future to face all temptation in the sure knowledge that You are in control. In Jesus' Name. Amen.

# Shattered hopes and plans

*"Then all the people ... asked Jesus to leave them, because they were overcome with fear ..." (v.37)*

**For reading & meditation – Luke 8:26–39**

What is another form of darkness in which God invites us to take the pickaxe of faith and dig for meaning? It is the darkness of shattered hopes and plans. The time when all our plans seem to go wrong is one of the most difficult periods of life. It throws confusion into everything for so much can be geared to those plans. But listen carefully to me – there are treasures to be found even in this deep darkness.

Look with me at how Jesus reacted to the blocking of His plans in the incident that is before us today. After He had healed the man possessed with devils, the people came to see what had happened and found the man "sitting at Jesus' feet, dressed and in his right mind" (v.35). The passage goes on to say, "and they were afraid". Afraid of what? They were afraid of something they could not understand. They could handle insanity better than they could handle sanity. Insanity was familiar to them, but the deliverance of the demonic was something very unfamiliar. So they begged Jesus to leave.

**FURTHER STUDY**

Luke 3:1–6;
Isa. 40:4; 45:2;
Matt. 16:18

1. What was prophesied of Jesus?
2. What did Jesus declare?

How did Jesus react to this apparent blocking of His ministry in that region? He turned in another direction and when you read the next two chapters you find one astonishing miracle after another. He turned the blocking into a blessing. If He couldn't do this, He could do that. The frustration turned to fruitfulness. So when your plans are upset do what Jesus did – utilise the grace that flows from God and prepare to turn in another direction.

## Prayer

Father, help me not to be deterred by the blocking of my plans. Give me a resilient spirit to forget the broken plans and by Your grace make new and better ones. In Jesus' Name I ask it. Amen.

# Isolation becomes revelation

*"I, John ... was on the island of Patmos because of the
word of God and the testimony of Jesus." (v.9)*

**For reading & meditation – Revelation 1:4–20**

There are treasures to be found in every difficulty, a dawn in every midnight, opportunities in every opposition. I know I am talking to someone now whose plans have been completely overturned. Maybe you are sitting reading these lines feeling as if the world has caved in on you. Lift up your heart – the eternal God has a word for you. His grace and power are flowing towards you at this very moment, and if you avail yourself of them, then the block can become a blessing, the frustration can be turned into fruitfulness, and the setback become a stepping stone.

When John found himself on the Isle of Patmos, incarcerated for the sake of the gospel, it must have seemed that his ministry and all his plans had been rudely shattered. He says, "I John ... found myself in the island called Patmos, for adhering to God's word and the testimony of Jesus" (v.9, Moffatt). However, he continues: "On the Lord's day I found myself rapt in the Spirit, and I heard a loud voice ... calling, 'Write your vision ...'" (vv.10–11). Isolated, and prevented from preaching the gospel, he wrote a book that has blessed men and women down the centuries. The place of isolation became a place of revelation.

This is what can happen to you today if you do not allow yourself to sink into self-pity and instead receive the grace that God is offering you now. Sit down amongst your broken and shattered plans and "write out" the vision of the new and better ones that God will give you.

**FURTHER STUDY**

Hab. Ch. 1;
2:1–3

1. What was
Habakkuk's
complaint?
2. What was God's
response?

## Prayer

Lord Jesus, strengthen me and guide me to "write out" my personal vision of Your coming victory. Help me to see that the break up of present plans can lead to bigger and better ones. For Your own dear Name's sake I pray. Amen.

# Working with a wound

*"When Jesus heard what had happened, he withdrew by boat … to a solitary place … the crowds followed him …"* (v.13)

**For reading & meditation – Matthew 14:1–14**

L ook at the picture before us today. Jesus had just heard that John the Baptist, his cousin and forerunner, had been beheaded. The account says: "When Jesus heard it, he withdrew by boat to a desert place in private" (v.3, Moffatt). No doubt the Saviour longed to be alone with His grief, but verse 13 continues, "but the crowds heard of it and followed him on foot from the towns." They broke up His plans. Now what did Jesus do? Did he turn on the people and reprimand them for invading His privacy? Listen again to what the account says: "So when he disembarked, he saw a large crowd, and out of pity for them he healed their sick folk" (v.14, Moffatt). He turned His hurt into healing and responded to the situation with infinite tenderness and compassion. Our Lord had a wound in His heart but that wound became healing for others.

Now you may think that it is insensitive of me to talk about ministry to others when you are hurting, but this is precisely what you need to hear. I am not unmindful of the hurt you go through when important plans are thwarted, but if self-pity is to be challenged and your life turned in a new direction, you must let me tell you in the most loving way I can that your wound can become healing for others. The same Lord who ministered with a wound in His heart can both minister to you and through you. Oh, I pray that you may feel His touch at this very moment – this very hour.

**FURTHER STUDY**

Acts 20:25–35;
Eccl. 11:1;
Matt. 10:8;
Luke 6:38

1. What is it more blessed to do?
2. What is God's way of working?

## Prayer

Blessed Lord Jesus, I am comforted to know that You too must have winced when wounded, but You used your wounds to reach out to others. Now let your wounds heal my wounds and my wounds heal someone else's. For your own dear Name's sake. Amen.

# "The show will go on"

*"He alone is my rock and my salvation; he is my fortress, I shall never be shaken." (v.2)*

### For reading & meditation – Psalm 62:1–12

Someone has spoken of "getting meaning out of life's remainders". Sometimes everything we longed for has gone and we are left with just "remainders" which are nothing more than reminders of what might have been. But we can get meaning out of those "remainders". "A Christian," says Billy Graham, "is someone who, when he or she comes to the end of a rope, ties a knot and holds on." Are you at the end of a rope at this moment? Then take his advice – tie a knot and hang on.

A passage in the book of Revelation says: "… there was silence in heaven for about half an hour" (Rev. 8:1). I heard a preacher say: "That was because God was moving the scenery for the next act." Can you dare believe that in the period when important plans have broken up God is at work moving the scenery for the next act? Hold steady – the show will go on. In the meantime, prepare to let God give you the assurance that there is a purpose to what has happened to you. Let the "remainders" be your reminders that with God all things are possible.

A man once told me that a year earlier his plans to emigrate and start a new life with his family had been overturned just days before he was due to leave the country. "I thought life had come to an end," he told me, "but within weeks God moved me into an exciting new career that hitherto I could not have dreamed was possible." The upset served only to set him up.

**FURTHER STUDY**

Mark 10:17–27;
Matt. 17:20; 19:26;
Luke 1:37; 18:27

1. What did Jesus declare to the disciples?
2. What is He saying to you today?

## Prayer

O Father, drive the truth deeply into my spirit that there are treasures to be found in every darkness. Show me how to take the pickaxe of faith and dig for meaning in every puzzling and perplexing situation. This I ask in Christ's all-prevailing Name. Amen.

# The hidden "better"

*"In a little while you will see me no more, and then
after a little while you will see me." (v.16)*

**For reading & meditation – John 16:5–16**

How it must have upset the plans of the disciples when they were told by Jesus that He was about to leave them! After just three years it seemed His ministry was beginning to make its mark and their hearts must have sunk within them as they heard him say: "I am about to leave you." Those disciples, remember, had given up their jobs to travel with Him. Our Lord's announcement that He was soon to go away must have sounded like a thunder clap in their souls. It was the collapse of all their expectations.

However, His going brought them an even greater blessing. Our text puts it most beautifully when it says: "It is for your good that I am going away" (v.7). In effect, Jesus was saying something like this: "I will take away My physical presence but instead you will experience My omnipresence. I will be closer to you than I have ever been before. The Holy Spirit will bring Me back, not just to be alongside, but within you. You will just have to drop into the recesses of your own heart and I will be there – burningly, blessedly there."

FURTHER STUDY

John 15:18–27;
Acts 1:4–8; 2:1–4

*1. What did Jesus promise to the disciples?*
*2. What would have happened if they had gone home after the Ascension?*

The disciples were to learn, as you and I must learn, that God never takes away the good unless He plans to replace it with the better. After Pentecost, the disciples must have said to each other: "It is true He has gone, but somehow He is closer to us than ever." Oh, if only we could learn that the shattering of our plans is but the prelude to the advancement of His!

## Prayer

O Father, when some "good" is taken away and I am left feeling bereft, help me believe for the hidden "better" that may be just round the corner. This I ask in Christ's peerless and precious Name. Amen.

# "Mankind's biggest problem"

*"I will say of the Lord, 'He is my refuge and my fortress, my God, in whom I trust.'"* (v.2)

**For reading & meditation – Psalm 91:1–16**

Yet another form of darkness in which people sometimes find themselves is the darkness of loneliness. Can divine treasures be discovered there? With all my heart I say – they can.

By "loneliness" I don't mean "aloneness". It must be understood at once that there is a great difference between loneliness and aloneness: it is possible to be alone and yet not lonely. The well-known psychiatrist and author, Dr Leonard Zunin, said: "Loneliness is mankind's biggest problem and is the major reason behind the many and varied symptoms which I see in the people who present themselves before me day after day." So what is loneliness? It is the feeling we get when we are bereft of meaningful human companionship; it is a sense of isolation, of inner emptiness, deprivation and worthlessness.

The poet Rupert Brooke records how, when he first set sail from Liverpool for New York, on May 22nd, 1913, he felt terribly lonely because no one had come to see him off. Everyone else had friends waving them goodbye – but not he. Looking down from the deck, he saw a scruffy little boy and swift as thought he ran down the gangway and said to him: "Will you wave to me if I give you sixpence?" "Why, yes," said the little boy. The sixpence changed hands and that day Rupert Brooke wrote in his diary, "I got my sixpenceworth in an enthusiastic farewell – dear, dear boy."

It is a desolating experience to be lonely, yet the divine presence can so reveal itself that even this deep darkness is made bearable.

FURTHER STUDY

Matt. 26:36–75;
Psa. 102:7;
John 16:32

1. How was Christ's loneliness increased?
2. Which lonely person will you befriend today?

## Prayer

O Father, help me understand that whenever I feel alone, forsaken or forgotten – in truth I am not alone, for You are constantly with me. But make this more than just a theory; turn it into fact in my life and experience day by day. In Jesus' Name I ask it. Amen.

# No one as lonely as He

*"Then all the disciples deserted him and fled."*
(v.56)

**For reading & meditation – Matthew 26:36–56**

It is possible to be alone and yet not feel lonely. To feel lonely is quite terrifying. The feeling of loneliness is not diminished in a crowd, or, for that matter, in a Christian church. Someone has described some churches – thankfully not all – as "lonely places where lonely people go so that everyone can be lonely together". One can be *in* a crowd and not *of* it.

Did Jesus ever feel lonely? I cannot think that He would be able to sympathise with this problem had He not at some time in His life felt lonely. Since He was sinless, He would not have experienced the associated feeling of worthlessness, but there were times when He was bereft of human companionship and in that dark hour on the cross He was bereft of divine companionship, too. The disciples were incapable of entering into our Lord's feelings as He agonised in the Garden of Gethsemane. On the eve of His death they argued about precedence; they slept while He wrestled in prayer; when He was arrested, they ran away. Most who have been willing to die for a cause have been able to comfort themselves that there were those who sympathised with them – but even this was denied Jesus. His self-sacrifice mystified the people who were His closest companions. Not one single soul understood why He allowed men to take Him and string Him up on a cross.

However difficult it may be to face the darkness of loneliness, at least Jesus knows how it feels. Others may not be able to understand it, but our Lord most certainly does.

**FURTHER STUDY**

Isa. Ch. 53; 50:6;
Psa. 22:1;
Matt. 27:46;
Psa. 37:25

1. What words of the psalmist did Christ echo?
2. What had the psalmist never seen?

## Prayer

Lord Jesus, clearly no one has ever touched some depths of loneliness in the way You have. Draw close to me in my own moments of loneliness so that I might learn how to find the treasures that are hidden in its darkness. For Your own dear Name's sake. Amen.

# Solitariness – a trifle?

*"And surely I am with you always, to the very end of the age." (v.20)*

**For reading & meditation – Matthew 28:16–20**

The treasure that can be discovered in the depths of loneliness is – a deeper sense of the presence of God. An acquaintance of mine, a preacher who never married and who spends a great deal of time on his own, said this: "Loneliness, that precious opportunity for discovering more of God." He went on to say that he noticed that the times of his deepest loneliness were the times when Christ was most real to him.

F.W. Robertson, the prophetic preacher of Brighton, proved this. He was bitterly attacked by fellow Christians for his views, and as his brief life sped away his friends got fewer and fewer. It was in one of these dark periods, when it seemed that all his friends had gone, that he wrote: "I am alone, lonelier than ever, sympathised with by none, because I sympathise too much with all, but the All sympathises with me … I turn from everything to Christ. I get glimpses into His mind, and I am sure that I love Him more and more. A sublime feeling of His presence comes about me at times which makes inward solitariness a trifle to talk about."

Look at that last sentence again: "A sublime feeling of His presence comes about me … which makes inward solitariness a trifle to talk about." What a testimony! He found treasure in the darkness. With the assurance of Christ's presence vouchsafed to every Christian, there need not be utter loneliness in the hearts of God's children. Christ walked that way so that no one need ever walk it again.

**FURTHER STUDY**

Rev. Ch. 1;
Acts 23:11;
Phil. 4:13

1. What was John's experience on Patmos?
2. How was Paul strengthened during his confinement in Jerusalem?

## Prayer

Father, I see that though I might feel lonely, I need not feel desolate, for You are ever with me. Show me how to drop all my barriers so that You can enter into the deepest depths of my being. In Jesus' Name I ask it. Amen.

# Pause – and consider

*"Share with God's people who are in need. Practise hospitality." (v.13)*

**For reading & meditation – Romans 12:1–21**

It would be impossible to discuss the subject of loneliness properly without making the point that some people bring loneliness upon themselves – they are lonely through their own fault. "Loneliness," says one writer, "is more of an attitude than a circumstance; more self-inflicted than outwardly caused. It is not just a matter of isolation, it is more a matter of insulation. Lonely people build walls around themselves and then complain of their loneliness." If we are in love with no one but ourselves, we can end up disliking everyone but ourselves.

Those who, like myself, find themselves in circumstances that compel them to live alone must watch that they do not become morose, critical, self-pitying and inward-looking. These attitudes will reinforce even the slightest feelings of loneliness and quickly drive people away. "In a needy world like ours," said W.E. Sangster, "anybody can have friendship who will give it." And Emerson said many years ago: "The only way to have a friend is to be a friend." When anyone says, "I am friendless", they come dangerously near to self-condemnation. The statement begs the rejoinder: "Have you *been* a friend?"

**FURTHER STUDY**

John 11:1–17;
Prov. 18:24;
27:10, 17

*1. How did Jesus describe Lazarus?*
*2. Do something to foster a friendship today.*

The Greek word *charis*, usually translated in the New Testament as "grace", also means "charm". God's grace can add charm even to the most morose personality. Have you noticed how two people in love sometimes become radiant? They not only demonstrate love to each other but it spills over to everyone else as well. Christ's presence in your heart will help you to be a friend, and that means you will never have to concern yourself about having a friend.

## Prayer

Father, help me to be open to the fact that sometimes my feelings of loneliness might be self-induced. If this is so, give me the courage to change. Illumine my life with Your friendship and then help me to pass it on to others. Amen.

# Where do you live?

*"For in him we live and move and have our being."*
(v.28)

**For reading & meditation – Acts 17:22–34**

We must be careful that in looking for the treasures that lie in the darkness of loneliness, we don't make the mistake of pretending that loneliness is not a painful experience. There are some Christians who, whenever they sense that there is pain in an experience, pull away from it and pretend that it is not painful at all. That is an escape into unreality. Loneliness can be pretty painful and if it is, don't pretend that it is not. Christianity is not a religion of pretence; it is a religion of reality. We face the pain knowing that Christ can help us through it and turn the pain into something of benefit to Him, to others and to ourselves. The important thing is to recognise that in all pain there are advantages. And the art is to admit the pain but focus on the advantages.

And what are the advantages of loneliness? What are the hidden treasures that lie within its darkness? The hurt or the pain brings deeper sensitivity to the problems of others, greater awareness of God's tenderness and nearness, increased self-understanding and the realisation that out of every pain God can produce a pearl. A visitor to an old people's home saw a man he knew, a Christian, and said to him: "I'm sorry to see you living in this old people's home." The old man drew himself up to his full height and said: "My friend, I do not live in an old people's home – I live in God."

What about you, my lonely friend? Where do you live? All alone – or in God?

**FURTHER STUDY**

Psa. 42:1–11; 71:5;
Jer. 17:7

1. What was the
psalmist's
predicament?
2. What was the
psalmist's
conclusion?

## Prayer

O Father, sweep into my soul with such a consciousness of Your presence that although I may be bereft of human companionship, loneliness will be a minor problem and not a major one. This I ask in and through my Saviour's precious Name. Amen.

# "Music in the making"

*"For the revelation awaits an appointed time ...
Though it linger, wait for it ..." (v.3)*

**For reading & meditation – Habakkuk 2:1–4**

Another form of darkness in which some Christians on occasions find themselves is that of spiritual silence. I mean by this those times when it seems the heavens are silent and God no longer directs us. We are not conscious of any sin, we pray and read the Scriptures daily, but nothing we do seems to bring guidance for the next step forward. Is this where you are at the moment? Take heart – there are treasures to be found in even this darkness.

For some people, a period of spiritual silence is harder to bear than persecution or suffering. People who have experienced this have said to me: "I can handle anything as long as I hear God's voice speaking to me, but when there is silence I find it hard, if not impossible, to cope." But we must understand that a silent heaven does not mean an unconcerned heaven. There are always reasons for everything God does and learning to trust these reasons when we cannot understand them is a mark of spiritual maturity.

Someone has said that pauses in music are "music in the making". A momentary pause in a musical composition produces a suspense that makes the music more beautiful than before. The pause prepares those who listen for finer music. I have sat with many who have thought that the period of spiritual silence in which they have found themselves was a sign of God's displeasure, but they came to see that the silence was really "music in the making". The music when it came was all the richer for the silence that preceded it.

FURTHER STUDY

Ex. Chs. 1–2;
Ezek. 12:25;
Matt. 5:18;
Phil. 1:6

1. Why was there a pause in Moses' life?
2. What was God teaching him?

## Prayer

O Father, whenever I enter into the darkness of spiritual silence, teach me never to let go of what I learned in the light. Help me now to grasp the lesson that the silences are but "music in the making". In Jesus' Name I pray. Amen.

# "The silent years"

*"… when God … was pleased to reveal his Son in me so that
I might preach him … I went … into Arabia …" (vv.15–17)*

### For reading & meditation – Galatians 1:13–24

We often talk about the public life and ministry of Jesus, but
little is said concerning what theologians call "the silent
years". Just picture it – the Son of God making yokes for the farmers
of Palestine when He yearned to lift the yoke of sin from the neck of
humanity, making ploughs to till the soil when He longed to plough
deep furrows in the hearts of men and women. But this does not
mean that He became impatient: clearly He knew that the silent
years were a preparation for the great ministry that lay ahead of him.
Thirty years of silence; three years of song. But the song was all the
richer for the silence that preceded it.

When I was in Nairobi once, I met a man who described himself
as a "missionary casualty". This is someone who has to return from
the mission field because of an inability to adjust. He told me: "I
decided to take a short cut to learning the language by closing my
textbooks and just going out among the people. I learned the
language in a way but when I got into the midst of the people it was
clear that I didn't make sense. They knew that I could not
communicate in the way the other missionaries
did and I did not have their ear. Gradually things
got to me and I had a breakdown."

He had longed to get among the people, but
was not willing to bear the silence – hence he
became unproductive. He was not prepared for
the pause, and lived to regret it.

**FURTHER STUDY**
Lam. Ch. 3;
Psa. 77:9; 88:8–9

*1. List some of the
feelings of the writer
of Lamentations.
2. List his
affirmations
concerning the Lord.*

## Prayer

Father, I see that without a pause there is no "music in the making". Help me to
understand that Your delays are not Your denials. The silences are working for
me; treasures are to be found in the darkness. I believe it. Thank You, Father.
Amen.

# "The prelude to the light"

*"… 'Never will I leave you; never will I forsake you.'"*
*(v.5)*

### For reading & meditation – Hebrews 13:5–21

The thought that has been engaging our attention is that silence is "music in the making." Pauses create a suspense which makes the music even more lovely.

A minister, who was on the point of giving up the ministry because he was going through a period of spiritual silence, picked up a copy of *Every Day with Jesus* and read some words that I have used several times over the years (and referred to again at the beginning of this theme): "A dark tunnel is often the best way of getting round a hill." He wrote: "God used those words to show me that the darkness in which I was enveloped was really the prelude to the light. I had wanted to move on into something that I felt sure was the divine will but every time I talked to God about it there was from His side nothing but silence. The words you wrote were like a new injection of life to my spirit and I held on, believing that when the light came I would find that God had been working for me in the darkness. One day the light shone and with such radiance that I could never have believed it possible. In that moment there was enough light to compensate for every hour of the darkness."

**FURTHER STUDY**

Matt. 26:57; 28:20;
John 2:18–22

*1. How did the disciples respond to God's silence between the Crucifixion and the Resurrection?*
*2. What happened when the silence was broken?*

And just as darkness is the prelude to the light, so is silence "music in the making". Never forget that God has music to play in your life which may not reach its full beauty if it is not preceded by a few silent pauses.

## Prayer

Father, what can I say? Let this truth take hold of my inner being so that when I am next engulfed in darkness I may walk on in faith, knowing that the fact that I cannot hear You does not mean that I am forgotten by You. In Jesus' Name I ask it. Amen.

# The divine perspective

*"But he knows the way that I take; when he has tested
me, I shall come forth as gold." (v.10)*

**For reading & meditation – Job 23:1–17**

Job was engulfed in silence and said: "But if I go to the east, he is
not there; if I go to the west, I do not find him. When he is at
work in the north, I do not see him; when he turns to the south,
I catch no glimpse of him" (vv.8–9). Here is a man suffering great
physical affliction, bereft of his children, and shut up with a nagging
wife. He is heavy of heart and goes out at night looking for God. He
glances up into the heavens and says: "I look and he is not there."
I think it is safe to say that perhaps no other human being (with the
exception of our Lord Jesus Christ) experienced such deep darkness
and desolating silence. When you have been through a time of
silence such as Job went through, then you know exactly what he is
saying. But despite the silence, Job has the right perspective.

Listen again to what Job says in the midst of his darkness: "But
*he* knows the way that I take; when he has tested me, I shall come
forth as gold." *He!* I may not know, but He does – and that makes all
the difference. If you are surrounded by darkness at this moment,
then let the word that Job spoke those many centuries ago bring
comfort and joy to your spirit. You may not know
why you are going through this but He does.
If you can learn to look at life from God's point
of view, then you have discovered the secret of
everything.

**FURTHER STUDY**

Job Ch. 42;
Psa. 10:1; 13:1;
89:46

1. Despite the silence
what was Job's
conviction?
2. When did the Lord
change his
circumstances?

## Prayer

O Father, if your servant Job could do it, I can do it, too. From now on I will
look at what is happening to my life, not from my point of view, but from
Yours. Help me to remember it, not just today but every day. In Jesus' Name.
Amen.

# The language of silence

*"… a time to be silent and a time to speak"* (v.7)

**For reading & meditation – Ecclesiastes 3:1–14**

We spend one more day meditating on the thought that a time of spiritual silence does not necessarily mean that God is not interested in us. Susan Lenzkes, the poet, talks in one of her books about "the language of silence". Her point? Not all communication needs words. God has gifted us with words to convey our thoughts, but we communicate our feelings in many different ways – touch, tears, laughter, expression of the eyes. "Sometimes words can be an intrusion," she says, "an obstacle."

I am sure you have heard the beautiful story of a man whose life was marked by one hardship after another. He felt at times that God had left him and that he was engulfed in spiritual silence. One night he had a dream. He was with the Lord looking back upon his life, portrayed as footprints along a sandy beach. Usually there were two sets of footprints – his and the Saviour's. But as he looked more closely, along the very rugged places he saw only one set of footprints. He frowned and said to the Lord: "Did you leave me at those moments when I most needed you?" "No", said the Lord, "the single set of footprints you see in the perilous places are Mine. Those were the times when I picked you up and carried you."

**FURTHER STUDY**

Psa. 139:1–12;
Gen. 28:15;
Ex. 3:14

1. What did the psalmist say about darkness?
2. What was God's promise to the Israelites?

Such is the language of love, wordless but sustaining, nevertheless. In the silence you may feel forgotten, but realise that His arms are about you all the time. In periods of spiritual silence God does not speak in words; He picks us up and holds us close.

## Prayer

Thank you, Father, I needed to be reminded of this. Help me never to forget it and let me take comfort from the thought that You do not always communicate with words. You can reach me even in the silence. I am so deeply, deeply grateful. Amen.

# A believer – and an achiever!

*"Thomas said to him, 'My Lord and my God!'"*
(v.28)

**For reading & meditation – John 20:19–31**

Almost every Christian struggles at times with another form of darkness – deep and desolating doubts. Some go through such agony of soul that they end up spiritually exhausted. Someone once told me: "Things are happening at such a speed in the world, I'm afraid I'll wake up one day and find that science has completely disproved the Scriptures." I assured her that her doubts were groundless, for *true* science will never disprove Scripture – just confirm it. The God who built the universe is the God who wrote the Bible.

I suppose the classic example of doubt is the disciple Thomas. We call him "doubting Thomas" – an unfair label if there ever was one. It's sad how we pick up what we consider a negative in a person and make them carry that label for a lifetime, or, in Thomas's case – two millennia. Thomas entered for a little while into the darkness of spiritual doubt, but he came out of that experience with a firmer faith than ever before. The darkness served only to deepen his love for the Master. When in Madras, India, I heard of some of the treasures that came out of Thomas's darkness as I was told how Thomas visited that continent and gave his life for the founding of a church which is there to this day. The "St Thomas Christians", as they are called, are some of the finest believers I have ever met.

Thomas had his doubts allayed in one glorious moment of illumination. He became a believer and an achiever – and then he went places. So, my friend, can you!

---

**FURTHER STUDY**

Acts 12:1–17;
Isa. 53:1;
1 Tim. 2:8

1. What did Peter say about his miraculous escape?
2. How did the praying congregation respond?

---

## Prayer

Gracious and loving Father, help me to understand that with You I can find treasures even in this darkness – the darkness of doubt. Show me how to turn this stumbling block into a stepping stone. In Jesus' Name I ask it. Amen.

# Truth – in the inner parts

*"Surely you desire truth in the inner parts ..."* (v.6)

**For reading & meditation – Psalm 51:1–19**

There is a difference between defensive and honest doubts. Some of the doubts that arise within us concerning our faith are unconscious attempts to hide some moral weakness or failure.

Not all doubts fall into this category, but many do. I have often talked to people, particularly young people, who are committed to Jesus Christ but are plagued with all kinds of doubts about the faith. On questioning them, I have found so many times that the doubts are really defensive attempts of the personality designed to relieve the young people of the responsibilities of their commitment.

I remember when I was a young Christian hearing a challenging sermon that showed me there was something about my Christian life that needed immediate correction. Then I came up against Brunner's Law: "The more a decision will affect your way of life, the more your sinful nature will enter into the debate." So what happened? My defensive carnal nature supplied me with doubts about the validity of the exposition I had heard and I used these doubts to "get me off the hook". Rather than face the issue with which I was being challenged, I preferred the safety of doubt. It was only when my pastor said to me: "If you believed the truth of what you heard, would there be anything in your life that would have to be changed?" that I saw what I was doing. I was using doubt as a defence. I preferred to believe that what I heard was not true because to believe it meant I had to change.

**FURTHER STUDY**

Jer. 17:5–11;
Mark 7:18–23;
Heb. 3:12;
Psa. 139:23–24

1. How is the heart described?
2. What was the psalmist's prayer?

## Prayer

O Father, whenever I am assailed by doubts, give me the ability to identify whether the doubt is a ploy of my personality or an honest and genuine concern. You desire "truth in the inner parts". So help me be honest. In Jesus' Name I pray. Amen.

# Our legacy from Adam

*"But the Lord God called to the man, 'Where are you?'"*
*(v.9)*

**For reading & meditation – Genesis 3:1–15**

Young people are often assailed by defensive doubts. Fallen human nature shrinks from facing up to God's challenges and it quickly fights back when we are caught in the challenge of moving on with God or staying where we are.

Deeply embedded in our nature is a defensive system that is a legacy from our first parents – Adam and Eve. Look at what happened immediately Adam and Eve sinned. God came down and confronted them with their sin. And what did they do? Instead of facing up to the issue as responsible human beings, they employed defensive manoeuvres in order to escape from the Creator's challenge. Adam said: "The woman you put her with me – she gave me some fruit from the tree, and I ate it" (v.12). Notice something that is often overlooked by Bible expositors here? Adam not only blamed his wife but also implied that the predicament he found himself in was partly God's fault: "it was the woman you gave me" (Living Bible). Notice also how Eve handled the situation: "The serpent deceived me" (v.13).

When caught violating God's principles we are perfectly capable of using anything to protect ourselves – including doubt. How we need constantly to come before God in the words of Charles Wesley:

*Jesus the hindrance show*
*Which I have feared to see,*
*Yet let me now consent to know*
*What keeps me out of Thee.*

**FURTHER STUDY**

Matt. 19:1–12;
15:1–10; 16:1–12

1. How did the Pharisees use doubt as a defence against what Jesus was saying?
2. How does the defence of doubt often reveal itself when we receive a challenge?

## Prayer

Father, I see that my fallen human nature can be ruthlessly self-protective. Help me, therefore, to be ruthlessly honest. I ask it in and through our Lord's peerless and precious Name. Amen.

# Doubt – faith in two minds

*"... they received ... message with ... eagerness ... examined the Scriptures ... to see if what Paul said was true." (v.11)*

**For reading & meditation – Acts 17:1–15**

Today we examine the nature of honest doubts – those doubts that arise from the perplexing situations in which we find ourselves and which appear to give the lie to the promises of God. For example, it is difficult sometimes to equate the truth of God's love with such things as natural disasters, physical suffering or child molestation.

Some Christians attempt to resolve the problem of doubt by saying: "A true believer ought not to doubt – that's the end of the matter." What kind of answer is that? The truth is that sometimes we do doubt and we must face that fact, unpleasant though it may be. A painful crisis arises which doesn't seem to have any quick resolution and we wonder about all those promises of a prayer-answering God. Some particular part of Scripture (as we perceive it) does not stand up to our experience. The fellowship of the Church lets us down and a doubt comes into our minds: "Perhaps God will let me down, too." These I regard as honest doubts; they arise in the hearts of even the best and most mature Christians.

**FURTHER STUDY**

James 1:1–8; 4:8;
Matt. 6:22

1. What will continual double-mindedness bring?
2. What brings light?

Whenever you are assailed by honest doubts, remind yourself that doubt is not the same as unbelief. Os Guinness puts it like this: "Doubt is a state of mind in suspension *between* faith and unbelief so that it is neither of them wholly and it is only each partly." When we have an honest doubt, we are not betraying our faith or surrendering to unbelief. We are simply saying we are in two minds – and asking which way to go.

## Prayer

Gracious and loving Father, what a relief it is to know that doubt is not the same as unbelief but that it is faith in two minds. Help me in every period of doubt to make up my mind in conjunction with Your mind. In Jesus' Name I ask it. Amen.

# Bring your doubts to Jesus

*"Are you the one who was to come, or should we expect
someone else?" (v.3)*

**For reading & meditation – Matthew 11:1–11**

A lthough we can't stop doubt arising in our minds, we can use it
to ask questions that will enable us to take a firmer grip on God.
This is the treasure we can rescue from the darkness. Doubts can be
valuable if they motivate us to search God's Word more deeply for
the answers which are surely there.

Unfortunately, in most of today's evangelical churches there is
very little sympathy with those who doubt. This is why Francis and
Edith Schaeffer established a centre for those with doubts about
their faith and called it L'Abri, which is French for "The Shelter".
Hundreds made their way there and came back with a faith deeper
than ever before. Jesus did not reject Thomas because of his
doubting attitude but said: "Put your finger here; see my hands.
Reach out your hand and put it into my side. Stop doubting and
believe" (John 20:27). John the Baptist, who witnessed the descent
of the Holy Spirit upon Christ and said: "Look, the Lamb of God,
who takes away the sin of the world" (John 1:29), later entertained
some doubts about Jesus. How did Jesus respond to those doubts?
With love and sensitivity: "Go back and report to
John what you hear and see: The blind receive
sight, the lame walk …" (Matt. 11:4–5).

Those who doubt and use their doubts to ask
deep questions of God and Scripture will find
themselves coming out with a faith stronger than
ever before. Those who have doubted most have
become some of Christ's strongest disciples.
Treasures have been found in the darkness.

**FURTHER STUDY**

Luke 7:18–28;
Matt. 28:17

1. How did Jesus
describe John the
Baptist?
2. How did some of
the disciples respond
to the risen Christ?

## Prayer

O Father, what a prospect – I can use all things to serve me, even doubt. Hold
me fast whenever I am assailed by doubt so that I am able to doubt my doubts
and believe my beliefs. In Christ's peerless and precious Name. Amen.

# After the avalanche

*"In all this, Job did not sin by charging God with wrongdoing."* (v.22)

### For reading & meditation – Job 1:1–22

Another form of darkness in which we sometimes find ourselves engulfed is that of suffering and pain. A woman writes: "My sister was a very godly woman but she suffered so dreadfully in childbirth. Why didn't God spare her this suffering since she was such a godly woman?" A professor in a great Christian university in the United States of America was hit by a truck, knocked down and suffered a broken leg. After he recovered, he told the students in the morning chapel: "I no longer believe in a personal God. If there were a personal God, would He not have whispered to me to beware of the danger of the coming truck and have saved me from this calamity?" The professor was struck and in his fall his faith crashed too.

Can God hold us fast in such times? Can we find treasures in this darkness, too? With all my heart I say – we can. The ancient patriarch Job could describe intense suffering in the first person because of his own sea of pain. Blameless, upright, clean-living and respected by everyone – God included – he experienced a wave of calamity that almost blotted him out. He lost his livestock, crops, land, servants, and every one of his ten children. Soon after that he lost his health, his last human hope of earning a living. How did he react to all this? Well, you read his response in the words of our text for today.

Right now I'm shaking my head with amazement as I consider his words. Would I have responded in such a way? Would you? I wonder.

**FURTHER STUDY**

Psa. 84; Isa. 40:31; 41:10; Eph. 3:16

1. What is the reward of the upright?
2. Consider how the RV brings out the meaning of Psalm 84:6: "Passing through the valley of Weeping they make it a place of springs."

## Prayer

O Father, is it really possible that You can give us such grace at such a moment? It is written in Your Word – thus I must believe it. Give me Job's secret so that I, too, might respond to all suffering with grace and not a grudge. In Jesus' Name. Amen.

# A recipe for handling problems

*"I know that you can do all things ... Surely I spoke
of things I did not understand ..." (vv.2–3)*

**For reading & meditation – Job 42:1–17**

How could Job go through all his sufferings and not rail against the Almighty? Bankruptcy, pain, ten fresh graves – yet we read that he worshipped God. He did not sin, nor did he blame his Maker. The question raises itself to almost cosmic proportions: why could he ward off bitterness and still maintain his faith?

I think one reason was because Job accepted the fact of God's sovereignty. He sincerely believed that the Lord who gave had every right to take away. He had no arguments over God's rule in his life and believed that God's sovereignty was laced with love. Another reason was: "I know that my Redeemer lives, and that in the end ... I will see God" (Job 19:25–26). He not only looked *up* – he looked *ahead*. He counted on God's promise to make all things clear at the Resurrection. He knew that at that time all pain, death and sorrow would be removed. Job endured the day-to-day happenings in the light of the next day's envisioning. A further reason was because he looked *within* and confessed his own lack of understanding. Our text for today puts this point most effectively. Job confessed his inability to put it all together and did not feel compelled to know just why God allowed things to happen to him in the way they did. God was the judge: that was fine with Job.

That was how Job picked up the pieces after the avalanche had struck. It takes a firm faith to respond like that, but the fact that Job did it shows it can be done.

**FURTHER STUDY**

Rev. Ch. 21;
Psa. 30:5; 34:19;
Isa. 43:2

1. What is the hope of the believer?
2. What is the promise for the present?

## Prayer

O God, how I long with all my heart to be able to respond to the problems in my world in the way Job responded to his. Help me to begin to practise these principles today and then go on to master them in the weeks that lie ahead. For Your own dear Name's sake. Amen.

# The inevitability of suffering

*"Yet man is born to trouble as surely as sparks fly upward." (v.7)*

### For reading & meditation – Job 5:1–18

It's surprising how many believe that God should spare good-living people from calamities and troubles. Suppose it could be guaranteed that calamities would always strike the wicked alone and that the righteous would always be saved – what kind of world would it be? Its laws would always be in a process of suspension to accommodate the righteous. Gravity wouldn't pull you over a parapet even though you leaned out too far – provided, of course, you were a Christian. The universe would no longer be dependable, for in any situation involving another person you would never be sure which laws would act for you. Much would depend on the character of that other person – and that would only be clear after the event had taken place – one way or the other! Such a situation would be ridiculous.

I do not question that God can and sometimes does intervene and save His children in particular situations, for one thing is sure – you cannot put God into a straitjacket in His own universe. The laws He has designed for the running of the universe are His habitual way of maintaining it, but He is perfectly capable of suspending those laws when He sees fit. Such an event we call a miracle. But miracles, by definition, cannot be the norm.

When Jesus hung upon the cross, the crowd cried: "He trusted in God; let Him deliver Him" (Matt. 27:43, NKJV). God did not deliver Him; *He did something better.* And it is along the line of "something better" that we must search for the Christian solution to the problem of suffering.

**FURTHER STUDY**

Job Ch. 19;
Psa. 27:1–14;
Mal. 4:2

1. What was Job's affirmation, despite his pain?
2. What was the psalmist's declaration?

## Prayer

Father, I realise that I am looking into the heart of one of the deepest mysteries of the universe – suffering and pain. Help me to believe that when You don't deliver me it is because You have something better. Amen.

# God has suffered too

*"Surely he took up our infirmities and carried our sorrows ..." (v.4)*

**For reading & meditation – Isaiah 53:1–12**

When all human attempts to relieve suffering do not work and even prayer seems not to prevail – what then? We must believe that God is still at work and is with us in the pain. God did not rescue Christ from the sufferings of the cross because it was only through those sufferings that His perfect purposes could be achieved. This is the key – *God allows only what He can use.*

Christianity is the only religion that dares to ask its followers to believe that God can work through suffering, because it is the only religion that can say its God has suffered too. How much has God suffered? Some think he suffered only during the hours that Christ hung upon the cross, but there is much more to it than that. Christ was the "Lamb that was slain from the creation of the world" (Rev. 13:8). Ages before the cross was set up on Calvary, there was a cross in the heart of God. The piercing pain of Calvary went through the heart of the Almighty the moment He laid the foundations of the world. Throughout the long millennia of history God carried with Him the pain of being parted from His only begotten Son. Then came the awful moment when it happened on Calvary. And was that the end of God's sufferings? No, now His sufferings continue in the world's rejection of His Son and at times in the indifference of some of His children – you and me.

Though living in this world costs us pain, it costs God more. I find this thought deeply comforting.

FURTHER STUDY

Mark Chs.14–15;
Heb. 4:15–16

1. List 10 aspects of pain suffered by Christ.
2. How was He able to face it?

## Prayer

O Father, my suffering seems so small when placed against the suffering You must have experienced in the giving of Your only Son. You turned Your pains to good account; help me to do the same. In Jesus' Name I ask it. Amen.

# A priceless treasure

*"Praise be to ... the God of all comfort, who comforts us ...
so that we can comfort those in any trouble ..." (vv.3–4)*

**For reading & meditation – 2 Corinthians 1:1–11**

Of all the letters Paul wrote, 2 Corinthians is regarded as the most autobiographical. In it the great apostle lifts the curtain that hung over his private life and allows us to catch a glimpse of his human frailties. You really need to read the whole letter in one sitting to catch the emotion that surges through Paul's soul. Here he records the specifics of his anguish, tears, afflictions, satanic opposition, beatings, loneliness, imprisonment, hunger, shipwrecks and sleepless nights. What were the treasures that were discovered in the darkness?

One treasure is found in the word "comfort". The word appears again and again in the passage before us today. Because he had suffered, the apostle was able to enter into other people's problems with a capacity that he would never have had if he had not gone through those experiences. Have you noticed that when you have gone through a time of personal suffering and pain you are able to enter into other people's problems with more that a shallow pat on the back and a tired "May the Lord bless you"? Now you have genuine, in-depth understanding and sympathy. And you know exactly how to comfort others because you yourself have received the comfort of God.

**FURTHER STUDY**

2 Cor. Ch. 3;
11:16–33; 4:7–10

*1. List 15 ways in which Paul was afflicted.*
*2. Where was Paul's sufficiency?*

Are you suffering right now? Our loving heavenly Father is never preoccupied or removed when we are enduring sadness and affliction. He is there at your side this very moment. Let Him surround you with His special comfort and then, perhaps weeks or months later, you will be able to pass on that same powerful comfort to others.

## Prayer

O God of all comfort, help me to be not only a receiver of comfort but also a giver of it. And Father, if I can unearth just this one treasure from the darkness of suffering and pain, then I will be rich indeed. In Jesus' Name. Amen.

# Our most vulnerable moment

*"Come to me, all you who are weary and burdened,
and I will give you rest." (v.28)*

**For reading & meditation – Matthew 11:20–30**

A nother form of darkness that almost everyone has to face is the darkness of bereavement. In the very nature of things, hundreds of you reading these lines will be there right now. Others may have to face bereavement in the very near future, so we must learn how to enter this darkness with the confidence that there are treasures to be found even here.

It has always struck me whenever I have been with people who are in bereavement that no matter how strong they may be at other times, whenever they are bereaved they become extremely vulnerable and thus open either to pain or consolation. J. Pierpoint Morgan, the American financier, was regarded as a tough and callous man; his biographer said that the strongest quailed before him. Yet when his wife died, he was so distraught that he cried out, "Won't someone please give me some comfort?" How human that is!

Let's examine some of the "comforts" that the world offers to those who are bereaved. One is to drown one's sorrows in drink. Many faced with the loss of a loved one try to find refuge by soaking themselves in alcohol. Wanting to soften the pain inside them, they take what seems to be the easiest way to that end. But it is a failure. In the first place, it is horribly vulgar, and in the second, it is thoroughly ineffective. There is always the morning after, and the poignant memories return to haunt the mind – again and again and again. There is no true comfort in the "cup that cheers" – lasting comfort comes only through Christ.

**FURTHER STUDY**

Rom. Ch. 12; 15:1;
Acts 20:35;
James 1:27;
Gal. 6:2

1. How are we to respond to those who weep?
2. How can we be supportive?

## Prayer

Father, help me to learn that there can be no escaping from reality, but with You I can face anything that comes, knowing that though You will not save me from it, You will save me in it. And for that I am deeply grateful. Thank You, dear Father. Amen.

# Supplements are not solutions

*"You will keep in perfect peace him whose mind is
steadfast, because he trusts in you." (v.3)*

**For reading & meditation – Isaiah 26:1–11**

O ne day someone showed me a statement made by a well-known
"Agony Aunt" who has a regular column in a women's
magazine. She was giving advice to someone who had been
bereaved: "find comfort in literature. The anodyne you need is good
reading. Go along to your local library and get a good book. Lose
yourself in it and you will find that it will do for you what it does for
countless others – brings relief to your aching heart."

I have no doubt that this advice is well-meaning but the worth
of it can only be judged by those who love books. Not everyone
does. People who have little interest in literature would find little
help in this advice. A book can be a wonderful extra to those who
need comfort, but it is absurd to expect a piece of literature to heal a
wounded spirit.

Another way of the world is to recommend that one turn to
nature. Lord Avebury, in his preface to his two volumes, *The Marvels
of the Universe*, says: "Nature does much to soothe and comfort and
console." I do not deny that there is a healing touch in nature.

**FURTHER STUDY**

John Ch. 14;
Rom. 8:11, 16;
Gal. 4:6

1. What name does
Christ give to the
Holy Spirit?
2. How does He
carry out this
ministry?

Multitudes who have been bereaved have gone
out into the hills and felt ministered to by the
power of nature but, once again, though it is a
good supplement, nature is not a good substitute
for the precious and powerful comfort that flows
from Christ.

Art, nature, literature – all these may have a
part to play in the life of those who are bereaved.
They can help, but listen – listen – Jesus alone can
heal.

## Prayer

Lord Jesus Christ, I am grateful for the supplements that can help me in the
hour of need, but help me see that they are only supplements and they can
never be a substitute for You. I glance at them, but my gaze must be ever on
You. Amen.

# "Vita! Vita! Vita!"

*"… everyone who looks to the Son and believes in him
shall have eternal life, and I will raise him up …"* (v.40)

**For reading & meditation – John 6:35–51**

I wish I could write on the sky in letters of fire, so that the whole
world might see, the fact that *the Christian faith is the only faith that
lights up that dark area of life which we call death.* It lights it up with the
word made flesh. Jesus went through death and thus the word of
resurrection became flesh in Him. What was said of Emerson: "He
did not argue; he just let in the light," can be said of Jesus: He did
not argue immortality; He simply showed Himself alive.

A missionary in Thailand was teaching a group of children
about the cross and death of Jesus, and as time was short she was
forced to end the story at the point where Jesus was laid in the
grave. A boy jumped up, saying: "It's not fair – he was a good man!"
One little girl, who knew the full story, pulled him back to his seat
and said: "Ssh! Don't make a fuss – He didn't stay dead." Well, if he
didn't stay dead, neither will we stay dead.

A biographer says of Tennyson, "He laid his mind on the mind
of others and they believed his beliefs." This is what our Lord does,
only in an infinitely greater way. And our Lord believed in and
demonstrated immortality. No wonder the early
Christians, shut up within the dark underground
prisons, wrote on the walls: "Vita! Vita! Vita!" –
"Life! Life! Life!" Prison walls could not quench
or stifle this life, nor can death extinguish it. Can
death stop a Christian? Stop him? It only frees
him – for ever.

> **FURTHER STUDY**
>
> 2 Tim. 4:6–18;
> Rom. 14:8;
> Phil. 1:21;
> Psa. 23:4
>
> 1. How did Paul
> describe death?
> 2. How does the
> psalmist describe the
> presence of death?

## Prayer

O Jesus, Saviour and Lord, You have laid Your mind upon my mind so that
now I believe Your beliefs. You believed in eternal life and demonstrated it – so
now, do I. I shall write on all my confining walls – "Vita! Vita! Vita!" Amen.

# When diamonds look their best

*"The eternal God is your refuge, and underneath are the everlasting arms ..." (v.27)*

**For reading & meditation – Deuteronomy 33:24–29**

What are some of the treasures we can expect to find in the darkness of bereavement? It is now some years since I laid my wife to rest, and I have been asking myself what treasures I discovered in the darkness of my own bereavement. One that immediately comes to mind is a new discovery of God and the truths contained in His Word. I had walked with the Lord for forty years before my wife was taken from me by cancer, and I had thought my intimacy with the Lord was about as good as it could ever be. I found, however, that the death of my wife produced in me a degree of grief and sorrow that I had never thought possible. I had known for several months that my wife's condition meant that her death was imminent but I was not prepared for the shock wave that went over me when it actually took place.

The text I have chosen for today is one that had always been a great favourite of mine, but now, since I have passed through the darkness of bereavement, it has taken on a dimension that is almost impossible for me to describe. Just as a precious diamond is best seen against a dark velvet background, so does the truth of God shine more beautifully when set against those black moments of life such as death and bereavement. The truth of God shines most beautifully at any time, but believe me, never more illustriously than when set against the darkness of a bitter and heart-rending experience.

**FURTHER STUDY**

Psa. 27:1–6;
31:19–21; 32:7,
119:14

1. What had the
psalmist discovered?
2. What are you
discovering?

## Prayer

Father, I see that grief and sadness can be the backdrop and setting against which Your truth and comfort shine more beautifully that ever. Help me, whenever I am engulfed by such feelings, to expect and await a new discovery of You. Amen.

# Grace that abounds

*"And God is able to make all grace abound to you ...
so that ... you will abound in every good work." (v.8)*

**For reading & meditation – 2 Corinthians 9:6–15**

We will never really understand a truth of Scripture until that truth is the only thing we have left to hold on to. Deuteronomy 33:27 (the text we looked at yesterday) is now more than a favourite text of mine – it is a spiritual lifeline. I know its power in a way I never knew it before because it held me in one of the darkest moments of my experience – bereavement.

Another treasure that we can find in this type of darkness is a more effective spiritual contribution to the life of the Church. Out of our personal sorrow comes a concern for others that impacts their lives in a greater way than ever before. A couple of years after my wife died, a woman said to me: "I used to listen to you twenty years ago when you were a pastor in London, and although I was blessed by what you said, I always felt you were a little hard. Now you are so different. The hardness has gone and a wonderful softness flows out of you." I tell you, a tear came to my eye as she talked because I recognised the truth of what she was saying. People have told me that there has been a new note in my writings, in my preaching, and in my teaching. This is the treasure I found in my darkness.

If you are bereaved at this moment, or facing a possible bereavement, take heart – you will find treasures in the darkness that will remain with you for the rest of your life. He gives most when most is taken away.

**FURTHER STUDY**

2 Cor. Ch. 1;
Matt. 5:4;
Psa. 86:17

1. What was the psalmist's testimony?
2. Why are we comforted?

## Prayer

Father, the need for consolation lies deep within me and is therefore inescapable. But help me understand also that while You meet me in grief, You want to take me beyond it – to a greater understanding of You and a greater usefulness for You. Amen.

# When money takes wings

*"Do not wear yourself out to get rich ... glance at riches, and they are gone, for they ... sprout wings ..." (vv.4–5)*

**For reading & meditation – Proverbs 23:1–8**

Another form of darkness is that of financial failure or material loss. Dare we believe that God can help us find treasure when there has been a financial catastrophe? He can!

Many years ago I had a friend who lost literally everything. He came out of it, however, with a philosophy of life that enabled him to say: "Never again will I be broken by material loss." Why? Because out of his downfall he built a biblical framework which enabled him to see finance from God's perspective. He has come back now from bankruptcy and is once again a wealthy man, but this time around he holds his possessions more loosely and sees himself, not as a proprietor, but as a steward. Sometimes it takes an upset to set us up, in the sense that we do not gain the right perspective on things until we are brought down into a crisis.

Do you find yourself this moment in a financial reverse? Have you been stripped of many, if not all, of your assets? Then follow me carefully over the next few days, for I want to share with you some principles that will help to rebuild your life and bring you into a deeper understanding than ever before of the biblical purpose of possessions. This also applies to those who may not at this moment be in reduced financial circumstances because in a world such as this a financial reverse can come at any time. It behoves us all to learn how to live independently of our possessions because one day we may be called upon to do just that.

**FURTHER STUDY**

Deut. 8:1–18;
1 Chron. 29:12;
Eccl. 5:19

*1. What was the admonition to the Israelites?*
*2. What were they to remember?*

## Prayer

Father, help me, once and for all, to settle my attitude to my possessions. I know I can never be a true disciple of Yours until I see my discipleship in terms, not of what I own, but of what I owe. Help me, dear Father. Amen.

# Transferring ownership

*"... because you have done this and have not withheld your son, your only son, I will surely bless you ..." (vv.16–17)*

**For reading & meditation – Genesis 22:1–19**

Some Christians speak scornfully of those who have a good deal of money. The Bible never does that; bringing to task those who make money their god, it never rails against money as such. Money in itself is not evil; it feeds the hungry, clothes the naked and through it many errands of mercy are performed. It is true that money cannot bring happiness, but as someone said, "It can certainly put our creditors in a better frame of mind."

Whether you have a little or a lot of this world's goods, I suggest that if you have never taken the following step, then you do it now – *in a definite act of commitment, transfer the ownership of all your possessions into the hands of God.* Those of you who have been stripped of everything will need to do this as an act of faith, indicating that should God allow you to have possessions again, you will see yourself as a steward and not a proprietor. The friend to whom I referred yesterday – the one who lost everything – told me that after reading the passage which is before us today, he got on his knees and by faith said to God: "Whatever comes into my hands again, I will hold in trust for You." That act of dedication becomes the point of transformation. God took him at his word and helped him rebuild his life.

If in reality we do not own anything, but are given things from God, then the common-sense thing is to say: "Lord, I'm not the owner, but the ower." We must never forget that.

**FURTHER STUDY**

Matt. 25:14–30;
1 Cor. 4:2;
Rom. 14:12

1. What is required of a steward?
2. What were "talents"?

## Prayer

Father, I am one of Your followers, but so often I am afraid to follow You all the way. Give me the faith of Abraham to believe that all things are in Your hands. Right now I lay everything I own on Your altar. It's no longer mine; it's Yours. Amen.

# Hitched to a plough

*"Set your minds on things above, not on earthly things."* (v.2)

**For reading & meditation – Colossians 3:1–17**

Once we have transferred ownership of all our possessions to God, next we should *streamline our lives for the purposes of God's Kingdom.* David Livingstone said: "I will place no value on anything that I have or possess except in relation to the Kingdom of Christ. If anything I have will advance that Kingdom, it shall be given or kept, whichever will best promote the glory of Him to whom I owe all my hopes, both for time and eternity."

Commenting on Livingstone's words, one writer said: "That first sentence of Livingstone's should become the life motto of every Christian. Each of us should repeat it slowly to ourselves every day: 'I will place no value on anything I have or possess except in relation to the Kingdom of Christ.'"

In the days when missionaries were able to work in China, John Wanamaker, a Christian businessman, visited to see that the donations of people were being used wisely. One day he came to a village where there was a beautiful little church. In a nearby field he caught sight of a young man yoked to an ox, ploughing a field.

**FURTHER STUDY**

1 Kings 17:7–24;
Matt. 26:7;
2 Cor. 8:1–5

*1. What was the experience of the widow of Zarephath?*
*2. What did Paul testify of the saints in Macedonia?*

He went over and asked the reason for this strange sight. An old man who was guiding the plough from behind said: "When we were trying to build our church, my son and I had no money to give. My son said: 'Let us sell one of our two oxen and I will take its yoke.' We did so and were able to give the money we made towards the building of the church." Wanamaker wept!

## Prayer

Father, perhaps I should be weeping, too, but for a different reason – weeping when I ask myself how much of my life is streamlined for Kingdom purposes. Would I be willing to be yoked to a plough for the Kingdom? Help me, dear Father. In Jesus' Name. Amen.

# "Above all distinctions"

*"... I have learned the secret of being content in ... every
situation ... whether living in plenty or in want." (v.12)*

**For reading & meditation – Philippians 4:4–13**

A third principle of rebuilding after a financial catastrophe is this
– *learn what it means to be free to use either poverty or plenty.* As a
rule people try to defend themselves against financial disaster in one
of two ways. One is by saving as much as possible, and the other is
by renouncing all interest in money or material things. If, in
building up financial reserves, people allow their trust and
confidence to be focused on amassing riches and material
possessions rather than on God, they become as metallic as the
coins they seek. They are in bondage to material gain. But the other
type can be in bondage too, for washing one's hands of material
things shows a bondage, not to riches, but to poverty.

The person who is only free to use plenty is bound by that, and
the person who is only free to use poverty is bound by that. Both are
in bondage. But the person who, like Paul in the text before us
today, has learned the secret of being content whether living in
plenty or in want, experiences a true freedom.

I remember reading the story of a missionary in India who got
into conversation with a high caste Indian at a
remote railway station. "Are you travelling on the
next train?" asked the missionary. "No," replied
the Indian, "the train has only third class
carriages. It's all right for you, because you are a
Christian and you are above such distinctions."

"Above such distinctions" – that is true
Christian living. Third class doesn't degrade us
and first class doesn't exalt us. Hallelujah!

FURTHER STUDY

Luke 3:1–14;
Prov. 15:16;
1 Tim. 6:6–8;
Heb. 13:5

1. What did John the
Baptist say to the
soldiers?
2. What was Paul's
word to Timothy?

## Prayer

Loving heavenly Father, help me to know what it is to be free – really free. Save
me from being entangled by plenty or broken by poverty. Do for me what You
did for the great apostle Paul. In Jesus' Name I ask it. Amen.

# Staying on course

*"… we have conducted ourselves in the world … not according to worldly wisdom but according to God's grace." (v.12)*

**For reading & meditation – 2 Corinthians 1:12–23**

One more principle to help us rebuild our lives when overtaken by a financial disaster is to *learn to differentiate between a need and a want*. Someone has defined a need: "We need as much as will make us physically, mentally and spiritually fit for the purposes of God, and anything beyond that belongs to the needs of others." Deciding what belongs to our needs and what belongs to the needs of others is a matter that each of us must work out between ourselves and God. Go over your life in God's presence and see what belongs to your needs and what really comes under the category of wants.

"But," someone may say, "what about luxuries?" Again, these things must be worked out in prayer between yourself and God. Only the Holy Spirit can sensitise our consciences and tune us to His purposes for our lives, and each of us may come out with different conclusions.

A fisherman said: "Some time ago I was on a lake. I pulled in my oars and let the boat drift. As I looked at the surrounding water I could see no drift at all, and only as I looked at a fixed point on the shore could I see how far I was drifting." The story is a parable. If you look around to see what others are doing and merely follow them, you will have no sense of drift. Only as you keep your eyes on Christ and remain fixed on Him will you know whether you are staying on God's course – or drifting from it.

**FURTHER STUDY**

Phil. 4:10–20;
Isa. 58:11;
Psa. 1

1. What has God promised to supply?
2. What is a condition of prosperity?

## Prayer

Gracious Father, sensitise my inner being so that I hear your voice in everything I do. Teach me what belongs to my needs and what belongs to the needs of others. In Jesus' Name I pray. Amen.

# "More to follow"

*"And God is able to make all grace abound to you ..."*
*(v.8)*

**For reading & meditation – 2 Corinthians 9:1–15**

We move on now to consider a form of darkness that can be filled with deep trauma – the darkness of broken relationships. I doubt whether there is any person reading these lines who has not experienced the hurt that comes from a broken relationship. At this very moment some of you will be going through traumatic experiences, perhaps the discovery of infidelity by a marriage partner, or a separation, a divorce, a rift between parents and children, or a broken engagement or friendship. Out of loyalty to their families, many face the world with a smile, but inwardly they are torn and bleeding.

Whatever the specifics of the situation, any rift in a relationship can be a deeply wounding experience. Are there treasures to be found in the darkness of a broken relationship? If you are in this kind of situation at present, it may be difficult for you to believe that you can come through spiritually enriched, but I want to assure you that you can. A little patient "digging" in the darkness that surrounds you can yield the most priceless treasures.

*How?* First, remind yourself that God provides sufficient grace and strength for us to deal with every situation. Others have been in the same situation, and have proved that God gives grace upon grace. An anonymous donor sent a poor man a £5 note every week with the message: "This is yours; use it wisely, there is more to follow." God does something similar with His grace. Every time you receive it there is always a note attached that says: "more to follow".

> **FURTHER STUDY**
>
> Psa. 55;
> Heb. 12:25–29;
> 2 Cor. 4:18
>
> 1. What caused David deep distress?
> 2. Where must we fix our eyes?

## Prayer

Father, help me see that You do not just supply me with grace; you overwhelm me with it. Help me to be a living illustration of the truth that You give grace upon grace. In Jesus' Name I ask it. Amen.

# A searching question

*"See if there is any offensive way in me, and lead me in the way everlasting." (v.24)*

**For reading & meditation – Psalm 139:13–24**

Keep in mind that the treasures in the darkness of broken relationships are found only as you dig for them. They don't just appear out of nowhere; they have to be searched for – with diligence, patience and trust.

Remind yourself that God provides "grace upon grace", then face this question: "How much may I have contributed to the problem?" In the midst of your pain, this might be a difficult thing for you even to consider, and if you can't, don't worry – when the pain subsides you can come back to it. But whether you do it now or later, face it you must. Our tendency whenever we are hurt is to see ourselves as a victim and forget that we may have contributed in some way to the problem. It may well be that you are an innocent victim but be ready and willing, nevertheless, to see if there is any way in which you may have contributed to the difficulties.

If, in looking at yourself, you find there are things that you are responsible for, then confess them to God and ask His forgiveness. This will help you make a clearer assessment of the situation. If you discover that you have hurt others, don't go running to them right away to ask for their forgiveness. You will need to know God's timing in this. It is always right to ask forgiveness of those we have hurt, but if it is not done at the right time it can create a wrong impression – they may, for example, feel that you are doing it to gain an advantage over them.

**FURTHER STUDY**

1 Cor. 11:23–32;
Lam. 3:40;
2 Cor. 13:5;
Gal. 6:4

1. What was Paul's exhortation to the Corinthians?
2. What are we to test?

## Prayer

Father, I see that right motives and right actions are not always enough; right actions must be done at the right time. Help me to grasp this lesson, for I see that a mistimed word can hinder rather than help. In Jesus' Name I pray. Amen.

# In whom do we trust?

*"When I am afraid, I will trust in you."*
*(v.3)*

**For reading & meditation – Psalm 56:1–13**

A woman whose husband left her took the first two steps I have suggested: first, she reminded herself that God was with her and, second, she faced with great courage the possibility that in some way she may have contributed to the problem. She asked God for His forgiveness and then immediately went searching for her husband to ask for his forgiveness. He interpreted this as manipulation and was not ready to receive it. Instead of drawing him to her, it drove him further away. We must be strong enough and trustful enough to await God's timing in all situations.

This brings me to my next suggestion – *learn how to become a truly secure person*. The secret of living successfully in this world is to remember that we are designed by God to draw our security as persons primarily from Him and not from our earthly relationships. Most of us get this wrong and draw our life from our horizontal relationships – the people around us, family, friends and so on – rather than from our vertical relationship with God. And we never know how flimsy that vertical relationship is until the horizontal relationships in which we are involved fall apart.

Many have told me that they never realised how dependent they were on others until the others were no longer there; then they were devastated. We are to enter into earthly relationships and enjoy them, but we are never to be dependent on them for our life. We are to be dependent only on God.

FURTHER STUDY

Psa. 118:1–8; 37:5;
Isa. 26:4; 2:22

1. What must we
stop doing?
2. What is it better
to do?

## Prayer

O Father, I see that when I draw my life from earthly relationships, then when they fail my life seems over. But when I draw my life from You, then life can never fail – for You are unchanging and unfailing. Thank You, my Father. Amen.

# In God we trust

*"He who dwells in the shelter of the Most High ... will say of the Lord, 'He is my refuge and ... fortress ...'"* (vv.1–2)

**For reading & meditation – Psalm 91:1–16**

Relationships can hurt. A friend of mine says: "God calls us to relate to people who are guaranteed to fail us." This is why we must find a source of security that is not in people, but in God, the unfailing One. This does not mean we must withdraw from people, but that we do not use them as the source of our life. Once we see that God alone is our true security, then when earthly relationships fail we are shaken but not shattered. There is a five foot drop and not a thousand foot drop.

When secure people are engulfed in the darkness of broken relationships – having reminded themselves that God's grace is ever-sufficient, and having looked at any way in which they may have contributed to the difficulty and thrown themselves in utter dependency upon God – they will be strong enough to sit back and wait for God to show them exactly what to do. They will not act precipitately because they are no longer dependent on their earthly relationships to hold them together but are dependent on God. They will move with poise and prayerful determination into the

**FURTHER STUDY**

Psa. 13; 33; 21:7; 32:10; 36:7

1. What was the psalmist convinced of?
2. Where was his trust?

situation. They know that there is no guarantee that poise and prayerful determination will bring about a resolution of the problem, but having done what God wants them to do, they are able to relax and leave the outcome to Him.

Once you have moved your point of dependency from the horizontal to the vertical, and are following God's direction and guidance in all things, then, though you may still hurt, you will not be destroyed.

## Prayer

O Father, I am so thankful that there is a way to live which guarantees, not that I will never be hurt, but that I will never be destroyed. Help me settle for that. In Jesus' Name I pray. Amen.

# The priceless pearl

*"Even in darkness light dawns for the upright ..."*
*(v.4)*

### For reading & meditation – Psalm 112:1–10

Once we know that if we draw our security directly from Christ and not from our earthly relationships, we may still get hurt but not destroyed – then we have discovered one of the most priceless treasures in the universe. Unfortunately, many do not find this treasure except in the darkness of broken relationships. Like Isaiah, they do not see the glory and sufficiency of the One on the throne until they go through an experience that seems like death. "In the year that King Uzziah died, I saw the Lord ..." (Isaiah 6:1).

Some broken relationships can be healed, but some cannot. Our part is to ensure that we do everything we can to restore them and then leave the matter in God's hands. If restoration comes, then fine, but if not, providing we are open all the time to doing what God wants us to do, then God will continue to bless us, even though the relationship is not restored.

Day by day, many Christians in broken relationships are doing what the oyster does when it gets an irritating grain of sand in its shell – they form a pearl around the problem. Just as the oyster down there in the darkness of the ocean builds a pearl around an irritant, so will God enable you to throw around all your difficult situations, especially broken relationships, a priceless pearl of character. The darkness then becomes a trusting place where daily you and the Lord work things out in ways that glorify His name. And had the darkness not come, you might never have discovered the treasure.

| FURTHER STUDY |
| --- |
| Heb. 12:1–15; |
| Rom. 13:8; |
| Lev. 19:18 |
| *1. What must we be careful not to miss?* |
| *2. What must we not seek?* |

## Prayer

O Father, I see so clearly that I am not motivated to dig for treasure until I am engulfed by darkness. But the treasures I can find there are worth much more than they cost. Help me to believe that, not just with my head, but with my heart. Amen.

# "Christmas depression"

*"And a sword will pierce your own soul too."*
(v.35)

**For reading & meditation – Luke 2:21–35**

We focus now on a type of darkness which engulfs many at festival seasons – the darkness of depression. Statistics show that more people get depressed at Christmas than at any other time of the year. It is also the time when the suicide rate rises to its highest level. These facts have given rise to the term "Christmas depression". Can we find treasure in this type of darkness? Once again, I hope to show you that we can!

In the passage before us today you will no doubt have noticed the strange and startling words with which Simeon ended his remarks to Mary: "And a sword will pierce your own soul too". I wonder what Mary thought of that deeply disturbing statement! One moment she was enjoying the thrill of holding the incarnate Son of God in her arms and the next moment she was told that as a result of His presence in the world a sword would pierce her soul. Simeon's prediction, I believe, had reference to such things as the flight into Egypt, the slaughter that would take place at Bethlehem, the later rejection of our Lord by His family and, above all, His crucifixion on the cross.

**FURTHER STUDY**

Psa. 42; 1 Pet. 5:7; Psa. 55:22; 43:5

1. How does the psalmist deal with his own downcast soul?
2. What is promised as we cast our cares on the Lord?

But isn't it strange that the prediction made by Simeon to Mary seems to apply to millions of people the world over? The period surrounding the celebration of Christ's birth seems to contain a sword that pierces their soul. Festivals may bring joy to some, but to others they bring gloom and sadness. I wonder why?

## Prayer

Father, help me come to grips with this issue for I sense that in understanding what lies behind it I shall have a better idea of how to relate to others at festival times, and be more sensitive to their deep inner needs. In Jesus' Name I ask it. Amen.

# "Celebrate – be happy"

*"Each of you should look not only to your own interests, but also to the interests of others." (v.4)*

**For reading & meditation – Philippians 2:1–11**

What is it about Christian festivals that brings both joy and sorrow to the world? Why is it that at such times so many fall into depression and find a sword piercing their soul? One reason is because at festival seasons people feel under pressure to "be happy". The expectation from almost everyone around is: "This is Christmas (or Easter) – so drop all expressions of sadness and put on a happy face." It reminds me of those experiences some children go through when they are taken to the seaside and told by their parents: "Now we've brought you here to enjoy yourself, and enjoy yourself you will!" Those who are feeling sad but are under pressure from society not to show that sadness may become resentful about this state of affairs and then push the resentment deep down inside them. And repressed resentment can soon turn into depression.

A psychologist, Dr Thomas Holmes, produced an interesting scale of factors which produced stress. He measures stress in terms of "life-changing units". On this scale, the death of a spouse rates 100 life change units; divorce, 73 units; pregnancy, 40 units; remodelling a home, 25 units. And *Christmas rates 12 units*. His conclusion is that from a strictly human point of view no one in their own strength can handle more than 300 units in a twelve-month period without suffering physically or emotionally within the following two years.

What does all this say to us? It says that we who are Christians need always to be sensitive to one another's circumstances and problems *but never so much as at festival times*.

### FURTHER STUDY

Acts 20:30–35;
Isa. 58:6–7;
Rom. 15:1;
Gal. 6:2

1. What words of Christ did Paul remember?
2. How do we fulfil the law of Christ?

## Prayer

O God, help me be aware! Stab my soul fiercely with an awareness of others' pain. Let my hands find other hands and give me a heart that divines, senses and enters into the sorrows of others. May I not just *bring* the Christian message but be it. In Jesus' Name. Amen.

# How much are you worth?

*"Praise ... to ... God ... Father of our Lord Jesus Christ,
who has blessed us in the heavenly realms ... in Christ" (v.3)*

**For reading & meditation – Ephesians 1:1–14**

The expectation our society places upon people to "be happy" sometimes produces deep resentment which, when repressed, turns into depression. Another cause of depression has to do with memory. Our memories are capable of remembering both good and bad things – and either can trigger depression.

A depressed teenager told me: "My main memory of Christmas is of my father coming home with a tree, but now he is gone and will never do that for me again." A depressed woman, also suffering from "Christmas depression" said, "My childhood Christmases had so many disappointments and bad memories that no matter how I try I can't enter into the spirit of the season." Two different memories, one good and one bad, but each in its own way triggering the same reaction.

Yet another cause of "Christmas depression" arises from the traditional receiving and giving of gifts. How can receiving a gift throw a person into depression? Well, when some people are given a valuable gift at Christmas they interpret it as being more than they deserve or, if the gift is not valuable, they interpret is as being less than they deserve. It is not the gift, of course, that causes the depression, but the person's perception of how the gift relates to his or her worth. This is why the biggest barrier against depression is to have a sense of worth that can stand anything that happens to you – gain or loss, increase or decrease, success or failure. And that comes only from an understanding of how much you are worth to God.

**FURTHER STUDY**

Matt. 10:26–31;
Luke 12:22–31

*1. How does Jesus illustrate our value?*
*2. Make someone feel worthwhile today.*

## Prayer

O Father, I see I need a sense of value that does not go up and down with the kinds of gifts I receive at Christmas time. Give me, therefore, a clear vision of how much I am worth to You. In Jesus' Name I ask it. Amen.

# An important "but"

*"For the law was given through Moses; grace and truth came through Jesus Christ." (v.17)*

**For reading & meditation – John 1:1–18**

We pause to drink in the wonder of the Incarnation. Today's text puts in one clear sentence the essential difference between the Hebrew religion and Christianity. When we speak of the Judaeo-Christian heritage and hyphenate those two words, we must be clear what they mean. In one sense, the Hebrew religion is the foundation on which Christianity was built – the two faiths are continuous. In another sense, however, they are discontinuous. There is a break – a radical break. The New King James Version of the verse before us today identifies that break by the word "but": "For the law was given through Moses, but grace and truth came through Jesus Christ."

The Christian faith stands in contrast to the basic precept of Judaism. Judaism says, "The law was given to Moses," that is, the word became word. The word (the expression of God's thought) was translated into another word – the Ten Commandments. But Christianity says, "Grace and truth came through Jesus Christ." Ah, that is so different – now the Word becomes flesh.

The Jewish religion is built around a law; the Christian religion is built around a Person. This is not a difference in degree, it is a difference in kind. The end product is different: one produced the Pharisee, correct, legal, proud, separate; the other produced the Christian, humble, receptive, loving, self-giving. The Jews say, "We have a law"; Christians say, "We have a Person" – and what a Person! The babe wrapped in swaddling clothes and lying in a manger is God. We gasp at such a revelation, but it's true. The Word has become flesh.

**FURTHER STUDY**

Phil. 2:1–11;
Isa. 9:6;
Gal. 4:4

1. What does being a
Christian mean to
you?
2. Share it with
someone today.

## Prayer

Father, help me see that the Christian spirit is to extend through the whole year. Let the Word show Himself through me. May I be the Christian message. For Your own dear Name's sake. Amen.

# "Wounded healers"

*"He heals the broken-hearted and binds up their wounds." (v.3)*

**For reading & meditation – Psalm 147:1–20**

As a counsellor, it has been my task over the years to talk with hundreds of depressed people, and if there is one thing I have learned, it is this – in almost all cases, unless there is a chemical or biological cause, there comes a point when the depression lifts and goes away. Some experience the deep darkness of depression for days, others for weeks or even months, but eventually the sun breaks through again. Now here's my point: when it does, the personality seems to have a sensitivity to the needs and problems of others that is quite astonishing. Some of the greatest counsellors I have ever met are those who have struggled with and come through deep depression.

For years now I have noticed something very interesting when I address groups of people on the subject of depression. If I am in a church and ask a general audience of people how many have suffered with depression, about twenty-five per cent of the congregation will raise their hands. In a training session for counsellors, the same question will bring a ninety per cent response. What does this say? It says that those who have struggled somehow become highly motivated to help others. It's one of the treasures that come out of the darkness – a deeper sensitivity and a more powerful motivation to reach out and heal the hurts of others. It is a fact that cannot be gainsaid – the best "healers" are "wounded healers".

**FURTHER STUDY**

1 Thess. 5:1–14;
2 Cor. 1:3–4; 7:6–7

1. What are we to do with the comfort God gives us?
2. What did Paul say about Titus?

## Prayer

My Father and my God, help me see that everything can be redeemed – even depression. I pray that I may do more than just experience sorrow – I may learn how to use it. In Jesus' Name I pray. Amen.

# The dynamics of confusion

*"He reveals the deep things of darkness and brings deep
shadows into the light." (v.22)*

**For reading & meditation – Job 12:13–25**

We end our meditations on the theme *the treasures of darkness* by looking at a form of darkness into which almost every Christian is plunged at some time or other – the darkness of spiritual confusion.

Perhaps you are there at this moment. You thought you had things all figured out and you anticipated God moving in a certain direction, but suddenly He seems to have moved in an entirely different way than you expected – and now you are confused. None of us likes confusion because it makes us feel so utterly helpless and out of control. Let me assure you that the treasures that are to be found in the darkness of spiritual confusion are amongst the finest and most valuable we can ever discover.

But before we look at some of those treasures, let's examine what I am going to call the dynamics of spiritual confusion. The unnerving thing about spiritual confusion is that it erodes our sense of competence. We all feel better when we know the outcome of any situation or when we can predict with some degree of certainty the way things will turn out. The trouble is, however, that although God tells us enough to establish, direct and nourish our faith, He doesn't always tell us enough to end confusion. I look back over my own Christian career and can remember times, many times, when what God did and what He allowed seemed baffling, even maddening. Yet I know also that from those times I have unearthed treasures that are now worth more to me than the greatest riches on earth.

**FURTHER STUDY**

Psa. 31; 73

*1. Why was the psalmist confused?
2. How did he handle it?*

## Prayer

O Father, whenever I am plunged into the darkness of spiritual confusion, help me dig for those treasures that are worth much more than they cost. Lord, I believe; help my unbelief. In Jesus' Name. Amen.

# In whom do we trust?

*"Those who trust in the Lord are like Mount Zion, which cannot be shaken but endures for ever." (v.1)*

**For reading & meditation – Psalm 125**

What is it about spiritual confusion that makes us feel so utterly bewildered? One reason is that it presents a serious challenge to our desire to be in control.

Once when I was in the USA, the car I had rented broke down on a deserted stretch of highway. Although I tied a white handkerchief to the wing mirror (the usual procedure there to show that help is needed) no one responded. As it grew dark, my anxiety level increased and I felt more fearful than I had done for years. I thought of all the American films I had seen where people had been attacked when stranded, and my prayers took on an unusual intensity. There was some physical danger and inconvenience, but I remember thinking that my high anxiety level suggested that something more was going on inside me than just that. Then it came to me – I was not in control of the situation. I just didn't know what to do or where to turn and I felt stupid, inadequate and incompetent. My destiny was out of my hands, even if only for a few hours, and I didn't like the feeling.

**FURTHER STUDY**

Luke 24:13–33;
2 Sam. 22:29

*1. Why were these 2 disciples confused?*
*2. How was their confusion resolved?*

Confusion is an enemy to those who want to be in control and if we are honest we will confess that most of us experience some panic whenever we find ourselves in a difficult situation where we are unable to take charge. What does all this tell us? Doesn't it bring home to us the solemn truth that, when it comes down to it, real trust is more difficult than we thought?

## Prayer

O God, I am so good at talking about trust but so poor at actually trusting. Forgive me for my desire to be always in control. Help me to be a more trusting person. In Jesus' Name I ask it. Amen.

# Three popular strategies

*"Woe to those who go down to Egypt for help, who rely on horses ... but do not ... seek help from the Lord." (v.1)*

**For reading & meditation – Isaiah 31:1–9**

Let me spell out three strategies that we use to cope with the panicky feelings that come whenever we are spiritually confused. One is to sidestep the feelings altogether and deny that we are confused. Integrity requires, however, that whatever is true must be looked at. Pretence gets us nowhere but I am afraid it is a popular strategy of many Christians. Don't run into denial, for when you do, you are not being real.

Another strategy is to admit the confusion but immediately go to work to replace it with some form of understanding. I have often said to people in counselling: "Why do you think God has let this happen?" only to hear an explanation that was so unrelated to reality it was ridiculous. One day it hit me why people did this – they were so disturbed by confusion that they felt compelled to impose some "order" on their world by coming up with an explanation which, although it really made no sense, was easier to live with than the uncertainty of confusion. They were not concerned about being right; they were concerned about being powerful, in control. Clarity took precedence over accuracy.

A third strategy that is used to reduce spiritual confusion is to move into confusing situations with firm, positive action and thus "take charge". Some situations have to be responded to in this way, but we must always be sure that our firm response to any situation and our eagerness to "take charge" spring, not out of a desire to relieve discomfort, but out of a desire to please God and do His perfect will.

**FURTHER STUDY**

John 11:1–44;
Psa. 46:2–5

1. In what way was the situation out of the control of Martha and Mary?
2. How did Martha use her reason to cope with Lazarus' death?

## Prayer

O God, I see yet again how prone I am to deal with my discomfort in ways that point to the fact that I am not trusting You. Forgive me and help me become a more dependent and trusting person. For Your own dear Name's sake. Amen.

# "As bad as that?"

*"Blessed is the man who makes the Lord his trust ..."*
(v.4)

### For reading & meditation – Psalm 40:1–17

One of the treasures we can expect to find in the darkness of spiritual confusion is an increased sense of dependence on God. All of us struggle with dependence, and those who say they don't are probably locked into denial. We find it difficult to rely totally on God. Although we lay great emphasis on trust in our songs and prayers, it's another matter when it comes to doing it. A Christian couple who were being counselled by their minister heard him use these words: "I rather think you have come to the position where you must trust God." "Oh dear," they replied, without realising the import of the words they were using, "has it got as bad as that?" It cuts across the grain of our carnal nature to be dependent on God to make our lives work; we feel utterly helpless. We are afraid of *real* trust.

Confusion is not as bad an experience as it might seem, for in the midst of it we become aware of our desire to be in control. We can then submit that to God and experience a deeper sense of dependence than we have ever known before. God does enlighten us on certain points but there are some levels of confusion that take a long time to disappear, and some may go on for a lifetime. At such times we can learn to relax and say to ourselves: "With God in control, I don't need answers. If He chooses to give them to me – fine; if not, that's fine too." In such a climate, dependence not only survives – it thrives.

**FURTHER STUDY**

2 Chron. 20:1–12;
Jer. 10:23;
John 15:5

*1. What was the essence of Jehoshaphat's prayer?*
*2. How did Jesus illustrate the need for dependency?*

## Prayer

O Father, bring me to a place in my Christian life where I can still go on even though I lack clear answers. I'm not there yet, but I'm growing. Take me further down this road, my Father. In Jesus' Name I ask it. Amen.

# Confidence in confusion

*"How long, O Lord, must I call for help, but you do not listen ...?" (v.2)*

**For reading & meditation – Habakkuk 1:1–17**

We spend one final day looking at a typical treasure that can be dug up in the darkness of spiritual confusion – a deeper dependence on God. It has been said that when moments of confusion shred our soul, there are three paths we can take: to abandon any claim to Christian belief and search for immediate relief; to run from confusion as a woodsman would flee from a hungry bear; or to cling to God with disciplined tenacity, reminding ourselves of who He is, even though our struggle with confusion continues unabated.

In the passage before us today, Habakkuk took the third course. His story begins in great bewilderment and the more he questions God, the more confused he becomes. Notice he does not run away and pretend his confusion isn't there – he faces it, feels it and presents some pretty tough questions to the Almighty. Notice also that Habakkuk does not become silent until after he has fully entered into and expressed his confusion (2:1). God then reveals Himself to His servant in a way that leads Habakkuk to proclaim a confidence in God that no amount of confusion can shake (3:17–19).

Wouldn't it be wonderful if we could all come through the darkness of confusion with such a treasure? Well, we can. Be open to looking at everything that is happening to you. Don't run too quickly from disturbing events into explanations that are more contrived than real. Contrary to popular Christian opinion, confusion is not bad. Right in the midst of it you can come to know God in a way you never knew Him before.

FURTHER STUDY

Psa. 37:1–8;
115:11; Prov. 3:5–6;
Isa. 50:10

1. What are we to do
when we walk in a
dark place?
2. Will you put your
trust in Him today?

## Prayer

Father, help me go on with a confidence that stands fast even in the midst of confusion. Let this be a turning point in my spiritual experience. In Jesus' Name I pray. Amen.

# The Pursuit of
# Excellence

# What's in a name?

*"The words of Jeremiah son of Hilkiah ..."*
(v.1)

### For reading & meditation – Jeremiah 1:1–3

The prophecy of Jeremiah is among the most powerful and spiritually productive books of the Old Testament. It is also the longest, so we will look only at some of its key passages.

Jeremiah lived approximately 600 years before Christ and was called to minister to Judah during the reign of its last five kings: Josiah, Jehoahaz, Jehoiakim, Jehoiachin and Zedekiah. He lived for about sixty years, most of which he spent in proclaiming God's Word. His ministry is reflected in his name; it means *the Lord hurls*. We read that the "word of the Lord came to him in the thirteenth year of the reign of Josiah" (v.2). But it not only came to him; it came *out* of him. He never failed to pass on what God had given him – sometimes hurling it into the midst of a rebellious nation with all the force of a thunderbolt.

Nowhere does Scripture reveal more clearly the meaning of spiritual faithfulness than in the life of Jeremiah. He kept true to the Word of God despite all the struggles he was called to endure. At times the fiery darts of doubt pierced his heart but they were always quenched when, through open and honest prayer, he allowed God's presence to flow into his soul. If you feel stressed as you try to live for God in difficult circumstances or if you are plagued with doubts concerning the path to which God has called you, then Jeremiah is the book for you. The greatest thing anyone can do in this life is to fulfil their spiritual destiny. Jeremiah shows us how.

**FURTHER STUDY**

Eph. 1:17–23;
Gen. 12:1; Judg. 6:14;
1 Kings 19:19; Isa. 6:8

1. What did Paul pray that the Ephesians would know?
2. What is apparent about the Old Testament characters in the above references?

## Prayer

Loving Father, I live in difficult times. Help me to hold tight to the fact that You never call me or lead me where You cannot help me. Teach me to trust myself less and You more. In Jesus' Name. Amen.

# The larger story

*"Before I formed you in the womb I knew you …"* (v.5)

**For reading & meditation – Jeremiah 1:4–5**

Jeremiah must have been encouraged to learn that before he became interested in God, God was interested in him. "Before I formed you in the womb," says the Almighty, *"I knew you."* This statement is intended to help Jeremiah understand that he is part of a larger story. It is God's reassurance that Jeremiah had *always* been known. It is a statement designed to warm his heart, not to satisfy his intellect. God is saying in effect: "Jeremiah, you have *always* been known and *always* will be known. You are not an accident of birth. You are part of a larger story. I appointed you as a prophet before you were ever formed in your mother's womb."

We do not discover our identity as persons when we know ourselves but when we realise that someone else knows us. We don't know who we are until we know whose we are. God knew us before our parents even knew we were on the way. Keep hold of this thought and you will never have an identity crisis.

Derek Kidner suggests in his commentary that this first word of God to Jeremiah gives the prophet a centre of gravity not in himself or his circumstances but in his Creator. Jeremiah was a prescription baby – made for the task which God had foreseen he could best accomplish. And so are you. You too have been chosen for something important that God is doing in this generation. It is something that nobody other than you can do.

**FURTHER STUDY**

Psa. 139:1–18;
Ex. 3:10–15;
Psa. 119:73

1. What was the psalmist's conviction?
2. What was God's assurance to Moses?

## Prayer

O Father, help me to understand that my destiny is not to be a spectator but a participant in your eternal purposes. Make even more clear to me the work You want me to do. Then enable me to do it, as You did for Jeremiah. In Christ's Name. Amen.

# Not my ability but His

*"Then the Lord … said to me, 'Now, I have put my words in your mouth.'" (v.9)*

**For reading & meditation – Jeremiah 1:6–10**

The Bible is full of examples of people who, whenever they were asked by God to do something special for Him, started pleading their inadequacy. Moses, Isaiah and Gideon did it. And as we see in this passage, Jeremiah did it. We are all good at inventing reasons why God should let us off the hook. God must get wearied with excuses!

The truth is that each person is utterly inadequate for the tasks God asks us to do for Him. We are not bright enough, smart enough, or efficient enough. God has to have a part in our lives if His work is to be accomplished through us. And it must be the *greater* part. God assures Jeremiah that He will be with him, then He touches his mouth and puts into his mind the very words He wanted him to speak. The God who made his mouth could provide him with the words to say.

It is not wrong to feel inadequate. But we must be careful not to let those feelings lead us to despair. Rather they should lead us to a deeper dependency on the Lord. I know that everything I have ever accomplished for God was done not out of a sense of adequacy but of inadequacy. It's not our ability but our response to His ability that is the key to service. "God does not send us into the dangerous and exacting life of faith because we are qualified," said Eugene Peterson. "He chooses us in order to qualify us for what He wants us to be and do."

**FURTHER STUDY**

Luke 14:15–24;
John 15:22;
Rom. 1:20; 2:1

1. What was the master's reaction to the excuses?
2. Why does Paul say we are inexcusable?

## Prayer

Father, I know that I cannot escape the tasks You have set for me by pleading my own inadequacy. The issue is not what I decide but what You decide. Help me to understand that where Your finger points Your hand always provides. In Jesus' Name I pray. Amen.

# Shaped by a vision

*"Today I have made you a fortified city, an iron pillar and a bronze wall …" (v.18)*

**For reading & meditation – Jeremiah 1:11–19**

God pictures Jeremiah as a strong fortified city, as immovable as an iron pillar, and as impregnable as heavy brass gates (v.18). How did he change from lacking confidence to being secure in God? It came about through two remarkable visions.

In the first, he saw a rod of almond. When Israel is still chilled by winter the blossoming almond tree shows that spring is on the way. It showed Jeremiah that just as surely as spring follows winter God is watching over His Word to fulfil it; the words for "almond" and "watch" are similar in Hebrew. Next he saw a pot of boiling water that was tipped; its scalding waters were spilling towards the south. Both the village of Anathoth where Jeremiah had been brought up and the city of Jerusalem (an hour's walk away) were directly in its path. The boiling water cascading down to the holy city represented enemy armies that were poised to invade. Judgment was coming because of the sinfulness and rebellion of the people.

These two visions, the blossoming almond branch and the pot of boiling water, have been described by one writer as "Jeremiah's Oxford and Cambridge" – his core curriculum. He was being taught that he must never under-estimate God and never over-estimate evil. We too, if we are to stand strong as iron pillars in difficult situations, must learn the same lesson. God never goes back on His Word and evil cannot triumph in the end. Only when we are shaped by that vision will we have the strength and courage to pursue the path that God has planned for us.

**FURTHER STUDY**

James 5:1–18;
Eph. 6:13–14;
Gal. 5:1;
2 Thess. 2:15

1. What qualities does James encourage?
2. What was Paul's admonition to the Early Church?

## Prayer

O God, as Jeremiah was shaped by this vision, shape me by it too. Help me never to under-estimate You and never to over-estimate evil. Grant that I might always be gripped and guided by this vision. In Jesus' Name I ask it. Amen.

# How problems develop

*"My people have ... forsaken me ... and have dug their
own cisterns ..." (v.13)*

**For reading & meditation – Jeremiah 2:1–18**

This was probably Jeremiah's first ever sermon. But perhaps the
word "sermon" is hardly the word to describe it. It is more of a
"case for the prosecution". Jeremiah, speaking on behalf of the
Almighty, issues a powerful indictment against the people of Israel
accusing them of spiritual promiscuity. Like an expert prosecutor he
challenges them to answer some sharp and incisive questions. What
fault have you found in me? Has any other nation ever changed its
gods? Where are the gods you made for yourselves? The challenges
ring out one after another.

Then in one of the most powerful statements in the whole of
Scripture Jeremiah sums up their spiritual condition. It consists of
two great sins: first, forsaking the spring of living water and second,
digging their own water-storage cisterns. This illustrates the root
cause of many of our problems. When I train counsellors I use this
verse to show them from a biblical perspective how problems
develop in the human personality. When we dig beneath the layers
of psychological symptoms ultimately we come to a *person*. This
person refuses to slake their thirst in God, preferring instead to find
stagnant water in a "cistern" of their own making

– money, power, status, and so on.

But why would anyone choose a stagnant
cistern over a fresh spring? There is only one
explanation. We like to feel we hold the resources
for our well-being in our own hands. We don't
like feeling dependent; we prefer to feel
independent. This attitude of independence is the
energy that makes many of our emotional and
psychological problems grow.

> **FURTHER STUDY**
>
> Isa. 55:1–5;
> John 4:14;
> 7:37–38;
> Psa. 36:8; 63:5
>
> 1. What is promised
> to those who thirst
> for God?
> 2. What was the
> psalmist's testimony?

## Prayer

O Father, I sense that even though I belong to You this stubborn commitment
to my independence is still in my heart. Teach me how to depend more on You,
not merely at some times, but at all times. And in all things. For Jesus' sake.
Amen.

# Shocking language

*"You are a swift she-camel running here and there ..."*
(v.23)

**For reading & meditation – Jeremiah 2:19–32**

One wonders how anyone listening to this damning and impassioned indictment of Judah's spiritual condition could have remained unrepentant. But clearly the people had become complacent – one of the most terrifying maladies that can afflict anyone. One of the seven churches in the book of Revelation was in this condition. When addressing the Christians in Laodicea, our Lord threatened to "spit you out of my mouth" (Rev. 3:16). Why does he use such uncharacteristic, even shocking language? Because complacent people *need* to be shocked. Perhaps this is why the Almighty chooses these vivid and unflattering word pictures to describe the condition into which Judah had fallen.

One graphic metaphor after another illustrates their spiritual depravity: a degenerate vine (v.21), ineffective ablutions (v.22), a wild ass on heat (v.24), a disgraced thief (v.26) and a forgetful bride (v.32). And in the verse I have highlighted for today God described them as: "a swift she-camel running here and there".

God was saying in effect: "You are like a female camel in heat, racing up and down the desert looking for sexual satisfaction from a mate. Your behaviour is a disgrace to your calling. You are no better than animals." The metaphor implies that Judah is actively engaged in seeking out idolatrous experiences like a camel sniffing at the wind to detect the male scent. When God's people desire the things that lie outside of God's will so much so that they will do anything to get it, then it is a sure sign of a dire spiritual condition that needs to be sternly confronted.

FURTHER STUDY

Amos 6:1;
Matt. 22:1–7;
24:1–12

1. What enraged the king?
2. What did Jesus say will be one of the signs of the end times?

## Prayer

O God, help me to examine myself today to see if the cancer of complacency has eaten its way into my soul. If it has, perform whatever surgery or treatment is necessary to rid me of it. In Christ's precious Name I pray. Amen.

# Sin breaks God's heart

*"'Return, faithless Israel,' declares the Lord, 'I will frown on you no longer ...'"* (v.12)

**For reading & meditation – Jeremiah 3:1–25**

Complacent people need to be shocked, so Jeremiah adds another shocking statement. Continuing the analogy of a broken marriage (2:2) he reminds them of the law given to Moses that forbade a divorced couple to be reunited to each other (v.1; Deut. 24:1–4). The purpose of this law was to maintain a high view of marriage and to protect relationships from being degraded to the casual level in which a man could divorce his wife and have her back whenever he felt like it. The point God is making is that Judah's spiritual adultery has put her in danger of being utterly separated from God. And if that happens, then she might not be able to return. They are startling words. God then compares the southern kingdom of Judah to her northern sister Israel (vv.6–11). He points out that whereas Israel had defected from God and had suffered the consequences of being destroyed, Judah had also sinned but pretended to repent (v.10).

In the course of this rebuke God's tone suddenly changes. He turns from upbraiding and shocking them to wooing them. Passionately and plaintively the Almighty cries out: "Return ... and I will cure you of backsliding" (v.22). If you listen to this cry from the heart of God you will see sin in a new way. Sin hurts God in a way that perhaps we as human beings can never conceive or understand. But it might help us to understand if we keep in mind that the most awful thing about sin is not simply that it breaks God's laws, but that it breaks His heart.

---

**FURTHER STUDY**

Lam. 3:20–32;
Joel 2:12–13;
Micah 7:18

1. What are we to rend?
2. What does God delight in?

---

## Prayer

O Father, it gives me a new awareness of sin when I see how it affects You in the deepest part of Your being. It is an offence not merely against a principle but against You as a Person. Help me never forget this. In Christ's Name I pray. Amen.

# The first move is ours

*"... the Lord says ... 'Break up your unploughed ground and do not sow among thorns ...'" (v.3)*

**For reading & meditation – Jeremiah 4:1–4**

Whenever we move away from our relationship with God either through a sin of commission or a sin of omission, *the only way back is the way of repentance.* But what does it mean to repent? Is it merely a matter of kissing and making up? No. Repentance, as a little boy once put it, is not merely being sorry about sin, but being sorry enough to quit.

The opening words of this chapter reveal God's concern, expressed through Jeremiah, that the repentance of His people should be genuine and lasting. Acts of idolatry and all sinful practices must be given up. The people are told that as a plough breaks up the rocky soil so they must break up the hardness of their hearts in the same way. The seeds of repentance can be sown only in prepared soil. Unless there is a complete breaking with sin, there is little hope of the spiritual life ever flourishing in the way it should.

Many Christians who have been engaged in some sinful practice have excused themselves by saying, "I don't feel convicted about what I am doing. When or if God convicts me, then I will give it up." That is very dangerous. Enough is said in Scripture to show us what is right and what is wrong. Jeremiah reminded the people that they needed to remove the sin that hardened their heart before the good seed of God's Word could take root. If we say to God, "Restore me and then I will give up my sin," the result is a spiritual stalemate. The first move must be ours.

**FURTHER STUDY**

Hosea 10:12–13;
14:2;
Isa. 55:6–7

1. What had Israel depended on?
2. What is the first step to repentance?

## Prayer

Father, I see that I must be willing to remove any heart-hardening sin if Your Word is to take root and grow in my life. Help me to be ever ready to make the first move if and whenever my relationship with You needs to be improved. Amen.

# Are you listening?

*"Hear this, you ... who have eyes but do not see ...
ears but do not hear ..." (v.21)*

**For reading & meditation – Jeremiah 5:18–31**

Jeremiah 4:5 to 6:26 is a vivid, poetic description of the judgment that is to come upon the people because of their refusal to repent. Babylonian armies would come from the north to destroy them. Language is stretched to its limits to describe the terrifying things that will happen to God's people because of their refusal to turn back to Him. The picture is so black that in places it resembles the description of a nuclear holocaust.

Verse 21 reveals the degree of their spiritual deafness and blindness to God's message. There is a saying that "there are none so deaf as those who do not wish to hear, none so blind as those who do not wish to see." How do you feel when you find yourself talking to someone about something important only to realise that they have not heard a single word you have said? You probably feel frustrated and ignored. Imagine how God must have felt as He pleaded with the people to turn from the impending disaster that was coming upon them only to find them tuning Him out.

Our Lord made the same criticism of some of the people of His day: "You will be ever hearing but never understanding; you will be ever seeing but never perceiving" (Matt. 13:14). Nothing can be more spiritually damaging than to tune God out when He is speaking. Those who think that the problem in their spiritual life is that God doesn't speak to them may find that the problem is rather that they are not listening to a God who is always trying to speak.

FURTHER STUDY

Rev. 2:11, 17, 29;
3:6, 22;
Eccl. 5:1;
James 1:19

1. What admonition
is continually
repeated?
2. Why should we go
to the house of God?

## Prayer

O God, can it be that You are speaking to me and I am not listening? Forgive me if this is so. Help me to tune my spiritual ear, and to focus my spiritual perception so that I hear and see all that You want me to hear and see. In Jesus' Name. Amen.

# Healing wounds "lightly"

*"They dress the wound of my people as though it were not serious." (v.14)*

**For reading & meditation – Jeremiah 6:1–15**

One of the great tragedies in Jeremiah's day was the fact that the priests were as insensitive to God's warnings as were the people. Treachery, fraud, and deception were part of their daily lives. Following Jeremiah's burning denunciation of the people's lifestyle one would have hoped that the priests would have gone into mourning and pleaded with God to withhold His judgment. But they did not.

Instead they set about trying to heal the serious rupture between the people and the Almighty with superficial remedies. They dressed the wound of the people "lightly" by saying that all was well when it wasn't. This was about as helpful as a doctor telling a patient with a brain tumour to take a couple of aspirin each day in the hope that it will disappear. The priests adopted the common attitude that if they ignore the problem it would go away. They didn't even know how to blush.

This attitude can be seen in many parts of the Church today. People who are called by God to apply spiritual remedies to serious matters do so in a way that only heals the wound "lightly". Ministers, leaders, counsellors and others who offer spiritual direction do the people of God a disservice when they deal only with symptoms instead of confronting, for example, the issues of sin in a person's life when sin is the root of their problem. Just as a doctor who would suggest treating lung cancer with cough medicine deserves to be struck off the medical register, so Christians who treat the issue of sin lightly deserve no recognition as spiritual leaders.

**FURTHER STUDY**

1 John 3:1–6; 5:17;
Prov. 20:9;
Isa. 53:6

1. How does John define sin?
2. How does Isaiah define sin?

## Prayer

My Father and my God, thank You for reminding me that sin is never removed by denying its existence. Give us leaders who, without going on witch hunts for sin, will fearlessly yet lovingly confront it. In Christ's Name. Amen.

# The past is important

*"Stand at the crossroads and look; ask for the ancient paths ..." (v.16)*

**For reading & meditation – Jeremiah 6:16–30**

Jeremiah is often depicted as the prophet of doom and gloom, but in many of his prophecies there is also a bright gleam of hope. Take today's text for example. There are ancient paths, he says, which people have trodden through the centuries. They are well marked, clearly defined, and all one has to do is to look for and travel along them. They lead to a life that is good and pleasing to God.

What are these paths? Without question Jeremiah is talking about the principles laid down in the written Word of God. He may be referring to the scroll of Deuteronomy which recently had been discovered in a corner of the Temple and given great publicity and prominence by King Josiah (2 Chron. 34). The word given to the people by Jeremiah is a word that needs to be repeated boldly in our churches today. Some are asking whether the Bible is as relevant in modern times as it was in the past.

Occasionally I get letters taking me to task for my strong stand on the authority of Scripture and the standards laid down there. Some tell me my views are so Victorian and that I should come into the twenty-first century. My response is that when we talk about truth and morality we are dealing with the living and timeless God. To live successfully in the present and the future we must listen to the past. And what does the past tell us? That there are ancient paths marked out for us by God. To stray from them is to put our lives in peril.

**FURTHER STUDY**

Psa. 119:33–48, 97–112;
Isa. 28:11–14;
Deut. 26:16–19

1. What was the psalmist's prayer?
2. What was the psalmist's view of God's Word?

## Prayer

Heavenly Father, I am so thankful that You have given me in Your Word some clear directions for making my way through the world. Help me to heed and obey them. In Jesus' Name I pray. Amen.

# Deceptive words

*"But look, you are trusting in deceptive words that are worthless." (v.8)*

**For reading & meditation – Jeremiah 7:1–11**

The entrance to the Temple in Jerusalem was an excellent setting for one of Jeremiah's most powerful sermons. Undoubtedly he had watched many times as the people entered the beautiful courtyards and cried out: "The temple of the Lord! The temple of the Lord, the temple of the Lord." But the prophet saw right through their subterfuge and hypocrisy. The words were nothing more than a religious cliché.

Deep down in their hearts they believed that though God might let the state of Judah fall He would never allow His Temple to be destroyed. They believed wrongly that the presence of the Temple and its rituals in their city would protect them. "You are deceiving yourselves," cries the prophet. "You are in the right place, saying all the right things, but you yourselves are not right. You use the Lord's house as a robber's den – a safe place from which to make your forays into idolatrous and ungodly behaviour. The Temple and its rituals are meaningless unless your behaviour matches your words."

Someone has pointed out that though Christians may not *say*

FURTHER STUDY

2 Tim. 3:1–5;
Isa. 1:13; 29:13;
Matt. 23:23

1. How did God
describe Judah's
gatherings?
2. Why did Jesus
reprove the
Pharisees?

lies in church, they often *sing* them. For example: "I surrender all", "Take my silver and my gold." Do we really mean what we sing? Or do we fool ourselves into thinking that the more religious phrases we use the safer we are spiritually? One person put it like this: "Standing in a church singing a hymn doesn't make us holy any more than standing in a barn and neighing makes us a horse." It's not so much what we say but who we are that's important.

## Prayer

My Father and my God, save me from the kind of subterfuge and hypocrisy that I have read about today. Let there be no dissonance in my spiritual life, but may my behaviour always match my words. In Christ's Name I ask it. Amen.

# "I am sorry!"

*"When men fall down, do they not get up?"*
*(v.4)*

### For reading & meditation – Jeremiah 8:1–21

It is very strange that in our relationship with God we sometimes act in ways that are diametrically opposite to our natural inclinations. When we fall down physically, we immediately try to get up. If we discover that we have lost our way on a journey we immediately try to find the right road. Why is it that when we fall spiritually or move away from a close relationship with God we do not seek to correct it immediately?

In the moral realm we don't like admitting that we have erred. Research has found that of a long list of statements which people found difficult to say, the one they found most difficult was: "I am sorry." There is a moral madness in us that can only be explained by the fact of indwelling sin. As Jeremiah points out we can easily go off in the wrong direction like galloping horses (v.6) or pretend we know better than God (v.8).

If we remain unrepentant then judgment has to be meted out. In Judah's case it came as a failure of the harvest (v.13). God's judgment on our sinfulness may seem harsh but it is prompted more by love than indignation. He loves us as we are, but He loves us too much to let us stay as we are. Permit me to ask you two pointed and personal questions. Are you aware that you might have strayed from the path spiritually? And what are you doing to get back on the right path? The first step to moving in the right direction begins with the words *"I am sorry."*

**FURTHER STUDY**

Luke 15:11–32;
Jer. 3:13;
Prov. 28:13;
1 John 1:9

1. How had the son strayed from the path?
2. What steps did he take to return?

## Prayer

Father, thank You for reminding me that when I have strayed it is not enough just to seek to get back on the right path; I must also admit my failure. Help me acknowledge that true repentance begins when I say, "Sorry." In Jesus' Name. Amen.

# When did you last weep?

*"Oh, that my head were a spring of water and my eyes
a fountain of tears!" (v.1)*

**For reading & meditation – Jeremiah 9:1–26**

Today's verse, together with the last few verses of chapter 9, provide a vivid picture of what went on in Jeremiah's heart as he watched the nation reject God. This sensitive prophet was in tears as he contemplated the plight of his people. He had mixed emotions. He felt intense anger with them concerning their sin, but deep compassion born out of godly concern towards them too. He thought momentarily of leaving them and quitting his task as a prophet (v.2) but as he spelt out once more the judgment that was to fall upon the nation for its rebellious attitude towards God, he knew he was unable to give up. This chapter describes in horrifying detail the anguish that Judah would feel when God allowed the invading armies to take control of the land.

Jeremiah's godly concern for his people leads us to ask, how do we feel about the pitiable state of the Church and the world? Does it drive us to our knees in fervent intercessory prayer? When did we last weep over the condition of both the world and the Church? I confess I have to hang my head in shame as I face those challenging questions. How about you?

**FURTHER STUDY**

Psa. 78:32–39;
Matt. 23:37–39;
Luke 19:41–44;
Psa. 88:13–17

1. What emotion did Jesus display?
2. What was the psalmist's experience of God?

But however ashamed we feel we must not leave it there. We must ask God to forgive our lack of compassion and invite Him to break our hearts for the world He so deeply loves. Godly concern is not something that can be manufactured. It comes only as we are willing to press our hearts against His. And it is the source of true prayer.

## Prayer

O God, help me feel some of the compassion You feel for a world that is lost in sin. Pull my heart into close proximity to Your own, so that I might share Your concerns. In Christ's Name I ask it. Amen.

# We *must* worship

*"No-one is like you, O Lord ..."*
(v.6)

**For reading & meditation – Jeremiah 10:1–16**

Nowhere in Scripture (with the possible exception of Isaiah 44) will you find such a scathing denunciation of idolatry as there is in this chapter. The picture of relying on idols would be laughable if it wasn't so sad.

Why did the people of God in Old Testament times allow themselves to be inveigled into worshipping idols? I think it is because we were designed by our Creator to worship Him. That is not because He is egotistical and likes to be affirmed, but because in the act of worshipping God every part of us is drawn to wholeness. Worship makes it possible for God to enter our lives and to be to us all that He promises to be. But we cannot truly worship God without at the same time obeying Him. And there, as they say, is the rub.

If we are not willing to bow the knee to the true God then we are unable to worship Him, and a part of our soul shuts down, demeaned because it is unexpressed. Idolatry is so appealing. We can express our need to worship without having to make those deep inward changes that the true God demands. Those who do not worship the true God will worship something else, for they *must* worship. The people of Judah worshipped the stars as well as gods of wood and stone. They substituted the unreal for the Real. A little boy was asked to define the word "idol". He said it was "something that doesn't work". He was thinking of the world "idle". But he was not far wrong.

**FURTHER STUDY**

Ex. 20:1–17;
Lev. 26:1;
Deut. 7:25; 11:16;
Isa. 42:8

1. What was God's clear command?
2. What was His declaration and warning?

## Prayer

O God, now that I see more clearly the motive behind idolatry may the hymn-writer's words be my constant theme: "The dearest idol I have known, help me to tear it from thy throne." In Jesus' Name I ask it. Amen.

# Unfaithful in marriage

*"Both the house of Israel and the house of Judah have
broken the covenant I made with their forefathers."* (v.10)

**For reading & meditation – Jeremiah 11:1–17**

It was bad enough that the people of Jeremiah's day had turned
from their Creator to worship idols. An even more serious charge
results: they have broken the covenant that God had made with
them when He brought them out of Egypt. He tells Jeremiah to
remind them of the historic agreement sealed centuries earlier at
Sinai in which God promised to supply all the needs of His chosen
people in return for their undivided worship and obedience.

That covenant was similar to a marriage. God committed
Himself to the nation of Israel in the same way that a man commits
himself to his wife at a wedding. The Almighty refers to His people
as His "beloved" (v.15); with the marital relationship in mind He
condemns them for spiritual adultery. In turning to other gods the
people had become unfaithful. They had broken their marriage
vows to God. Once again the people are told that God must
inevitably punish such behaviour.

Such is the pain that pulses in the heart of God that He instructs
Jeremiah to stop praying for the people and to tell them that He will
not listen to them when *they* pray (v.14). Think
over those staggering words. A time comes when
God must inevitably judge sinful behaviour.
Remember that there is no point in asking God to
bless our lives when we are engaged in wilful sin.
Thankfully He does not wipe us out every time we
err. He is incredibly patient with our frailties. But
He cannot tolerate repeated rebellious sin. The
judgments of God are not unreasonable but they
are inevitable.

**FURTHER STUDY**

Isa. 65:1–7; 30:1;
Ezek. 2:1–5;
1 Sam. 15:23

1. How did God
describe His people?
2. How is
rebelliousness
described?

## Prayer

O God, help me to grasp that I am part of Your Church that is described in
Your Word as "the Bride of Christ". Do whatever is necessary to keep me and
all your people free from idolatry and forever faithful to You. In Christ's Name
I pray. Amen.

# Dealing with doubts

*"You are always righteous, O Lord, when I bring a case before you." (12:1)*

**For reading & meditation – Jeremiah 11:18 –12:4**

Jeremiah must have been greatly shocked when God told him that the people of his own village of Anathoth were planning to kill him. Anathoth, about six kilometres from Jerusalem, was known as a "priestly village" (see Joshua 21:18 and 1 Kings 2:26). Some of the priests who lived there were probably incensed at Jeremiah's continuous indictment of them for their spiritual failures, and shared in plotting his assassination. How does Jeremiah react to the news that his life is in danger?

First, he expresses surprise and astonishment at such a revelation. "I had been as unsuspecting as a lamb or ox on the way to slaughter. I didn't know that they were planning to kill me!" he says (v.19, TLB). Then as the full impact of the news hits him he turns to God and pours out his frightened feelings in passionate prayer. Many have been puzzled by Jeremiah's strong reaction as he changes from being a confident prophet to a man seemingly plagued with doubts. Is he guilty, they have asked, of leading a double life? Was he a hero when standing before a crowd, but a coward in private? I don't believe so. His reaction is that of any normal person in such circumstances. There is nothing wrong in having doubts; it is what we do with those doubts that is important. Doubt is best dealt with in prayer before God, not peddled in public. I deal with my own doubts in the best possible place – before God in prayer. I invite you to take yours to the same place.

**FURTHER STUDY**

Gen. 15:1–8; Judg. 6:17; Matt. 11:2–3; John 11:37; 20:24–25; Acts 12:14–15

1. What is common to all these Bible characters?
2. What is the difference between doubt and unbelief?

## Prayer

Father, I cannot stop doubts entering my heart but I can stop them residing there. Help me to bring my doubts to You, dear Lord, and to leave the place of prayer, as Jeremiah did, with doubts turned into convictions. In Jesus' Name. Amen.

# Struggling well

*"Yet I would speak with you about your justice: Why does the way of the wicked prosper?" (v.1)*

**For reading & meditation – Jeremiah 12:1–4**

Why does Jeremiah seem so rocklike on the outside but so prone to discouragement on the inside? Did he ever arrive at a place in his life where he never had another moment of discouragement? Being a servant of God does not mean that you will never again face and feel discouragement. Some Christians believe that you can be so filled with God's life that discouragement can find no room to lodge in you. But that is unrealistic. Some of the finest saints I have known confess to feeling discouraged at times. They do not indulge themselves in it, but they do admit it. And that's the difference between a realistic and an unrealistic Christian. The realistic Christian says, "I am discouraged and I will bring it to God in heartfelt prayer." The unrealistic Christian says, "God is on the throne, and because of that I can never be discouraged." Being honest with one's feelings is a mark of maturity, not of immaturity.

And did Jeremiah ever come to a place in his life where he never had another moment of discouragement? I do not think so. The first section of his prophecy (chapters 1–20) focuses on his inner sufferings while the second part focuses on his outer sufferings. I believe his struggles continued for most of his life, but he learned to struggle well. That means relying not on our own strength of character but on the strength of God's righteous character, whose justice is real even if it is not always obvious as we struggle against the situations which discourage us.

---

**FURTHER STUDY**

1 Kings 19:1–21;
Job 10:1–2;
Lam. 3:19–26

1. How did Elijah and Job deal with despair?
2. Where does the writer of Lamentations find hope?

---

## Prayer

Father, I see that I shall never be exempt from struggles. So help me I pray, as You helped Jeremiah, *to struggle well.* May Your unfailing grace and power be my constant strength. In Christ's Name I ask it. Amen.

# Running with horses

*"If you have raced with men on foot and they have worn you out, how can you compete with horses?" (v.5)*

**For reading & meditation – Jeremiah 12:1–17**

If God is good, why does He allow evil to flourish? That very modern question was often asked by Old Testament prophets, especially when they faced difficulties. Jeremiah asks it here. Why does God allow miscarriages of justice? Why does He allow the wicked to get away with so much? Jeremiah knew that God's justice will ultimately be seen to be done but he wants to see it *now*.

Have you noticed that God never answers the vexed question of why there are so many apparent miscarriages of justice in His world? Instead He rebukes, redirects or reassures us. Job never got his questions answered but he did get a richer experience of God. The Almighty is not in the business of explaining things but in getting us to trust Him. He deals with us not as a philosopher but as a pastor.

Jeremiah was in danger of lapsing into self-pity; the remedy is not a doctrinal statement but a challenge. God gives him a bracing reply: *If you raced with men on foot and they have worn you out how can you compete with horses?* He turns the focus on Jeremiah himself rather than on his complaint. His problems with the wicked now were nothing compared with the difficulties that he would face in the future. If he can't trust God in the darkness how will he trust Him in a raging storm? What was Jeremiah's response to this stern challenge? His biography from here on leaves us in no doubt. He responded not by argument but by action. He rose to the challenge. *He ran with the horses.*

FURTHER STUDY

Psa. 118:1–9; 71:5;
141:8;
Isa. 12:2

1. What does the psalmist say it is better to do?
2. What decision does Isaiah take?

## Prayer

Father, I see that Your greatest concern is to get me to live by faith – to take You on trust. Help me come to the point at which the absence of explanations makes no difference to my trust and confidence in You. In Jesus' Name. Amen.

# Curious but not convicted

*"For as a belt is bound round a man's waist, so I bound
the whole house of ... Judah to me ..." (v.11)*

**For reading & meditation – Jeremiah 13:1–14**

Actions often speak louder than words. In today's passage Jeremiah is being instructed by God to buy a linen belt, to wear it for a length of time around his waist without washing it, and then to bury it in Perath. "Many days later" he is commanded to dig it up only to discover, as he expected, that it was "ruined and completely useless" (v.7).

Jeremiah used this incident as a parable to point out that, just as the linen belt was ruined by its contact with the earth, so the people would be corrupted by their idolatrous behaviour and thus would be fit no longer to be part of the divine purposes. A linen belt (or loincloth) was an intimate garment and God told Jeremiah to use this incident to challenge the people about the way they covered up their spiritual nakedness with superstitious devotion to pagan deities.

In the second parable Jeremiah is commanded to tell the people: "Every wineskin should be filled with wine", a popular saying of the day. When they gave the usual response, "I agree," Jeremiah is to tell them: "You're getting the wrong impression. I will fill everyone living in this land with helpless bewilderment" (v.13, TLB). In other words, unless you act on what God is saying one day you will stagger like drunkards, spiritually and socially lost. Such words and actions aroused the people's curiosity, but did nothing to change their minds. Persistent sin can so dull and deaden our conscience that no matter what God does we cannot hear Him and see no need to turn back to Him.

**FURTHER STUDY**

1 Tim. 3:1–9; 4:2;
Heb. 10:22;
2 Cor. 1:12;
1 Tim. 1:19

1. What instruction did Paul give Timothy?
2. What was Paul able to say?

## Prayer

O God, the thought that I might become desensitised to Your Spirit's convictions or reproofs concerns me deeply. Save me from such a predicament. Help me put away all my sin. In Jesus' Name. Amen.

# God – an unhurried judge

*"Can the Ethiopian change his skin or the leopard its spots?"* (v.23)

**For reading & meditation – Jeremiah 13:15–27**

Jeremiah used parables to bring God's message, containing clear warnings, home to the people. Here three more spiritual alerts are given. In one (vv.15–17) he describes the people as travellers overtaken by darkness and stumbling in the gathering gloom as they try to make it to their destination. In another (vv.18–19) he calls on the youthful king Jehoiachin and his mother Nehushta (see 2 Kings 24:8) to come off the throne because they were unfit to rule God's people and had ignored God's warnings. The final picture (vv.20–27) is of a flock that must be mourned because its shepherds have failed to look after the sheep entrusted to their care. Evil had so gripped the people that it was now a lifestyle they could not change any more than an Ethiopian could change the colour of his skin or a leopard its spots.

Why were so many warnings given and why did God take so long to pour out judgment? Certainly God seems an unhurried judge in the chapters we have perused so far. Is He not as concerned as He appears to be, or is He more longsuffering than we can imagine?

Obviously it is not because of lack of concern. It is rather as the apostle Peter puts it; He does not want anyone to perish but wants all to come to repentance (2 Peter 3:9). God's unhurried ways might encourage us to think casually about His inevitable judgment on sin. If we do, then we think wrongly. Praise Him for His patience that waited for you, but don't try His patience with persistent sin.

**FURTHER STUDY**

Rom. 9:1–33;
Isa. 48:9;
2 Pet. 2:3–9

1. What question does Paul ask?
2. How does he answer it?

## Prayer

Heavenly Father, help me not to make the mistake of thinking that because Your judgments are slow they are not sure. You will not overlook sin, but You will look over it – to Calvary. May my attitude be one of continuous repentance. In Jesus' Name. Amen.

# God has feelings too

" … 'Let my eyes overflow with tears night and day without
ceasing; for … my people … has suffered …'" (v.17)

**For reading & meditation – Jeremiah 14:1–21**

It is difficult to imagine any suffering worse than that triggered by
drought. Derek Kidner points out that the word translated *drought*
here is in the plural 'indicating a series of such disasters, each one
leaving the survivors less able to face the next'. Following the
graphic picture of the suffering caused by drought (vv.2–6),
Jeremiah is seen rising to the challenge with a powerful prayer of
penitence and intercession (vv.7–9). He uses similar language to
that of many of the other great intercessors of the Old Testament –
Abraham, for example – but his intercession has no effect on the
Almighty.

Jeremiah is told to stop praying as God's mind is already made
up (v.11). A further argument by Jeremiah that the people can
surely be excused because they are the victims of false prophets is
firmly rebutted by the Lord. It was the responsibility of all who lived
in Israel to discern a false prophet. All they had to do was to
evaluate his words in the light of God's written revelation. Jeremiah
is to be commended for his desire to intercede for his people but he
is out of touch with their stubborn commitment
to independence.

**FURTHER STUDY**

Rom. 8:18–27;
2 Cor. 5:4

1. When was the last
time you felt God's
grieving heart?
2. Take time today to
let the Holy Spirit
reveal it to you.

In verse 17 we get a glimpse into God's
personal feelings. The Almighty is heartbroken.
It's sad that so often we are more concerned about
our own anguish than God's. It breaks His heart to
see the waywardness and obstinacy of His people.
How different our lives would be if we could see
that sin is not just a collision with the divine will
but a wound in the divine heart.

## Prayer

O God, help me never to forget that You have feelings too. May I learn the vital
lesson that whenever I sin I do not just break a commandment – I wound Your
loving and sensitive heart. Give me this perspective always. In Jesus' Name.
Amen.

# Spiritual stalemate

*"Even if Moses and Samuel were to stand before me,
my heart would not go out to this people." (15:1)*

**For reading & meditation – Jeremiah 14:22 & 15:1-4**

Having foreseen the terrifying drought that will fall upon unrepentant Israel, Jeremiah is moved to intercede for them. What a powerful prayer it is (14:7-9). Yet again God tells Jeremiah not to pray for the people (v.11). Later the Lord tells him (in our text for today) that even if Moses and Samuel were to stand before Him and plead for the people's well-being He would not listen. Moses and Samuel were two of God's greatest prophets and like Jeremiah they had interceded between God and the people (Ex. 17:11-13; 1 Sam 7:7-9).

Intercession is a vital part of the Christian life but what should one do when God says "Stop praying"? It is important to remember that when Moses and Samuel prayed, the people displayed a readiness to repent. The nation at the time of Jeremiah, however, was stubborn, obstinate and recalcitrant. Jeremiah's intercessions, though sincere and well meaning, did not reflect the true mood of the people. They paid lip service to the faith that had been handed down to them by their predecessors, but their hearts were set on idolatry and pagan practices. Although in previous times God had responded to the voice of a single intercessor, here the situation was different. The people knew that God wanted to bless them and that they could receive that blessing only if they repented. They wanted God to do His part, but they were not prepared to do theirs. Hence, they were locked in spiritual stalemate and could not move forward with God. God's blessings are there to be taken, but they are never to be taken for granted.

FURTHER STUDY

1 Kings 3:10-15;
Ex. 19:5;
Deut. 5:29;
James 1:25

1. What was God's promise to Solomon?
2. What is the key to blessing?

## Prayer

Gracious and loving heavenly Father, help me never to take Your blessings for granted but with the gratitude born of a repentant heart. This I ask in Christ's peerless and precious Name. Amen.

# "My wound is grievous"

*"Why is my pain unending and my wound grievous and incurable?" (v.18)*

### For reading & meditation – Jeremiah 15:1–18

Several times we catch glimpses of Jeremiah at prayer. Sometimes he prays for the people but other prayers are what the commentators call "confessionals" (honest complaints). There are seven of them in the book (8:18–9:3; 11:18–23; 12:1–6; 15:10–12, 15–21; 17:14–18; 18:18–23; 20:7–8). Today's passage includes one of them. In each of the confessionals all his emotions come to the surface as he wrestles with them in the presence of God. His inner life is exposed for all to see.

All his fear, loneliness, hurt and anger are poured out into God's ear. Some people think of prayer as a time of quiet and calm solitude before God, but it can be a time of great personal struggle also. I know you might say, "But such prayers are not right. They show no respect or faith in the Almighty." I have discovered that God will never be against us for honest praying. He would far rather that you identify what is going on within you and that you talk to Him about it than to push it down inside you and pretend you do not feel that way.

FURTHER STUDY

Jeremiah 8:18–9:3;
11:18–23; 12:1–6;
15:10–12, 15–21;
17:14–18; 18:18–23;
20:7–8

1. Read through the
7 "confessionals" of
Jeremiah.
2. Write out your own
"confessional" today.

In God's presence we need pretend about nothing, because God sees and knows us as we really are. And He understands our feelings of hurt and anger; it is not sinful to feel such things, although they may lead us to sin if we don't share them with God. Permit me to ask if you ever experience the feelings Jeremiah talks about here – fear, loneliness, anger and hurt? You do. So pray about them, as Jeremiah did.

## Prayer

Gracious God, I realise that no one alive is a stranger to the feelings I have read about today. Help me whenever I next feel scared, lonely, hurt or angry to do more than just bear it. Help me to pray about it. In Jesus' Name. Amen.

# Renewed and restored

*"If you repent, I will restore you ..."*
*(v.19)*

**For reading & meditation – Jeremiah 15:19–21**

How does God respond to Jeremiah's bold and honest prayer? He says something that at first seems strange and insensitive – *"repent"*. This was one of the key words in Jeremiah's message to the nation. Now God gives him a taste of his own medicine.

This does not mean that God was oblivious to the hurt and pain that Jeremiah was experiencing. God knew full well the anguish that the prophet was going through but He would not let him indulge in it. One commentator suggests that there was quite a lot of self-pity circulating in Jeremiah's heart at this stage, hence he needed this bracing reply. So what was the reason behind God's demand that Jeremiah should repent? It implies that some sin has been committed. Of what sin was the prophet guilty? It was the sin of misplaced dependency. Sin, you see, is subtle as well as obvious. Deep down in his heart the prophet was failing to trust the word that God had given him in the beginning.

Whenever we sin there is *only* one way back to God. And that is through the door of repentance. Admit your misplaced dependency, God is saying. If you repent of it you will be restored. You will stand on your feet once again. God doesn't change, neither does His Word change. But we do. And when doubt and fear cause us temporarily to lose our bearings, if we are willing to admit it and repent of it then God delights to restore us and confirm afresh the work to which He has called us.

**FURTHER STUDY**

Hosea 14:2;
Acts 17:30;
3:11–19

1. What does God command?
2. What follows repentance?

## Prayer

Father, I see that though Your call does not change and Your Word does not change, the relationship between You and me is under constant assault. Help me to talk to You constantly. And I know You will always talk to me. Amen.

# Whose side are you on?

*"Let this people turn to you, but you must not turn to them." (v.19)*

**For reading & meditation – Jeremiah 15:19–21**

I want to consider once more the passage we looked at yesterday. The statement made by the Almighty in today's text is so important that it cries out for comment. Jeremiah was a faithful preacher of righteousness. Whenever he preached he stood firmly on God's side telling the people everything that God told him to say. However, in the prayer recorded earlier in this chapter he seems to have moved from God's side to the side of the people.

Now in one sense that is quite understandable. Many of the Old Testament intercessors, Moses and Abraham for example, identified themselves with the people and interceded for them. But here the situation is quite different. The people are stubborn and obstinate and there is no room to excuse their human fallibility. Because Jeremiah is wavering God confronts him with these direct words: *"You are to influence them, not let them influence you"* (v.19, TLB).

Christians involved in pastoral ministry, such as counsellors, ministers and church workers, can easily find themselves taking the side of the people against God, rather than standing solidly on the side of the Almighty. This is not to say that we must lose our compassion for people, or fail in our responsibility to intercede for them. But where obstinacy and rebellion remain in the heart, no matter what the extenuating circumstances, sin must be identified and God's perspective made clear. Those who minister to others must ask themselves often: whose side am I on? When it comes to a matter of sin there is only one side – God's side.

**FURTHER STUDY**

Psa. 34:8–18;
51:17;
Isa. 66:2

1. What sacrifices are acceptable to God?
2. What does the Lord esteem?

## Prayer

Heavenly Father, help me when I minister to others to be more influenced by You than I am by them. I do not want to lose my compassion but I want it always to be known that it is Your side I am on. In Jesus' Name. Amen.

# No private life

*"You must not marry and have sons or daughters in this place." (v.2)*

**For reading & meditation – Jeremiah 16:1–21**

At first sight it seems rather harsh of God to require Jeremiah to remain celibate all his life. Celibacy was rare in that culture. Having children provided a retirement plan, and was also a way of preserving one's family name indefinitely. Earlier, the animosity of his enemies focused on this when they said: "Let us cut him off from the land of the living, that his name be remembered no more" (11:19). Remember that Jeremiah had already lost his brothers (12:6); now he is allowed no family to replace them. But God demands even more. He is not even to join in the normal community experiences; he is forbidden to weep with those who weep or laugh with those who laugh (vv.5–9).

Why? It could be that God was saving Jeremiah from overwhelming heartbreak because disease and famine would devastate the next generation of children. Or a wife and family might have distracted him from his single-minded ministry.

The chief reason, I believe, was that Jeremiah's personal life was to be an object lesson, an acted parable, about Judah's condition. Compared to the serious spiritual condition into which Israel had fallen, and the devastation that was to come upon them because of that, *the loneliness that came from being without a wife and family was as nothing*. There is no such thing as a private life for those who commit their ways to God. Our time, money and relationships *all* belong to Him. A measure of the depth of our spiritual commitment would be to ask ourselves: what would I not give up if required by God to do so?

FURTHER STUDY

1 Cor. 7:1–40;
Matt. 19:10–12;
Luke 14:33;
18:29–30

1. What was Paul's view?
2. What did Jesus say was a condition of discipleship?

## Prayer

O Father, this is a question I would rather not answer. Help me think this through and evaluate anew the depth and degree of my faith. In Jesus' Name I pray. Amen.

# Keeping Sunday special

*"... keep the Sabbath day holy, as I commanded your forefathers." (v.22)*

**For reading & meditation – Jeremiah 17:19–27**

The theme of this chapter is sin and its consequences. Unless Judah repents she will pay the consequences of her continued rebellion against the Lord. There is a special reference to the Sabbath. Sabbath keeping had always been taken as a sign of loyalty to God ever since it was laid down at Sinai (Ex. 31:12–17). Those who sought to keep it showed signs of spiritual health; those who profaned it showed signs of spiritual ill health. The Sabbath was usually the first thing to be violated when the people began to backslide.

What is your view about keeping the Sabbath that we call Sunday? We can become legalists who see the keeping of the Sabbath as essential to salvation. We can become liberationists who see it as unnecessary and unimportant. I am not comfortable with either of these positions. In Jeremiah's day the people were liberationists; in Christ's day they were legalists.

The true attitude, I believe, is to see it as a gift from God that gives us more freedom than usual to focus on Him, worship Him, and to enjoy fellowship with others who also love and serve Him. Derek Kidner puts it helpfully when he says that the Sabbath should not be flooded with the mundane nor frozen by the forbidden. Whatever the world thinks of the Sabbath the Church should think of it as special. You might find it helpful to list the things you do on a typical Sunday, and then to ask: Is there too much? Could some things be done on Saturday? Does God get the time He deserves from me?

**FURTHER STUDY**

Ex. 20:8; 34:21; 35:2–3; Mark 6:2; John 7:23; 9:14; Matt.12:1–12

1. What does the law say about the Sabbath?
2. What did Jesus say about the Sabbath?

## Prayer

Father, I do not want to become legalistic on the one hand or liberationist on the other. Help me be balanced on this matter and give Your day the honour and respect it deserves. In Jesus' Name I pray. Amen.

# The potter's house

*"... so the potter formed it into another pot, shaping it as seemed best to him." (v.4)*

**For reading & meditation – Jeremiah 18:1–12**

Jeremiah draws an intriguing analogy between what he sees in a potter's house and what God is doing with the people of Judah. The prophet is commanded by God to go into a potter's house to watch him at his work. Jeremiah sees him place a formless lump of clay on his wheel and stands entranced as under the potter's skilful touch a beautiful pot begins to take shape. But suddenly – disaster. There is a flaw in the clay and the vessel becomes misshapen. Now what will the potter do? Toss it aside and begin with a new lump of clay? No. His original intention frustrated, he begins again to shape a new vessel. It is not the one he originally intended, but it is a beautiful one nevertheless.

Jeremiah gets the point. The clay may hinder the purposes of the divine Potter and prevent Him achieving His original intention, but even so He will not discard it. Judgment will fall and the people will experience the full weight of evil but the Almighty will pursue them with infinite patience and persistence.

Though we mess up God's original purposes for our lives by our stubbornness, He nevertheless pursues His purposes with us still. It might not be what He originally wanted. But His skill and power can make something of us beyond what we dare imagine or even deserve. If by your sin or failure you have frustrated God's original purpose but have repented and come back to God, take heart. He may not be able to achieve His original purpose but He can make something beautiful of you still.

FURTHER STUDY

2 Tim. 2:14–21;
Rom. 9:21;
2 Cor. 4:1–7

1. How did Paul describe 2 different kinds of vessels?
2. What does God deposit in clay vessels?

## Prayer

O Father, I am so thankful that You do not toss me aside when I frustrate Your purposes by my sin and failure. You are ready to make me again. My gratitude knows no bounds. Thank You dear Father. Amen.

# A ministers' conference

*"... I will smash this nation and this city just as this potter's jar is smashed ..." (v.11)*

**For reading & meditation – Jeremiah 19:1–15**

Fresh from the insights gained in the potter's house and ready to obey God's instructions Jeremiah arranges a conference of some of the religious leaders of Jerusalem. These men were actively engaged in the Temple worship but they were slow to rebuke iniquity and were nothing less than blind leaders of the blind. The site he chose was a few hundred yards south of the Temple in the valley of Hinnon, also called Topheth. It was the garbage dump for the city. Here child sacrifices had been carried out and were still being done in secret (7:31). What a place for a ministers' conference! Jeremiah knew that no religious community ever rises higher than its leaders, so if his message is to get through then it must be aimed first at those who led the people in worship.

As he speaks to them he holds a clay jug under his arm, and after a blistering rebuke he raises the jug above his head and hurls it at their feet where it shatters into a dozen different pieces. His point? Whereas a spoiled vessel on a potter's wheel could be reshaped, once it had hardened it was beyond reshaping and was fit only for breaking. Judgment is coming, says Jeremiah, and you had better face up to it.

**FURTHER STUDY**

1 Pet. 4:7–19;
Isa. 9:15–16;
1 John 3:7–8

1. Where must judgment begin?
2. What is John's admonition?

Many a modern-day ministers' conference could do with a visit from Jeremiah, especially where leaders have lost their confidence in the Scriptures and close their eyes to sin. And a few jugs being broken in the middle of a service might bring home to many a congregation the inevitable consequences of sin.

## Prayer

Father, desperate situations need desperate measures. Forgive us for the sins of indolence, lethargy and lukewarmness. We need to be shaken up, dear Lord. Send some Jeremiahs into our midst to do just that. In Jesus' Name. Amen.

# What screams the loudest?

*"Sing to the Lord! Give praise to the Lord!"*
*(v.13)*

**For reading & meditation – Jeremiah 20:1–13**

Jeremiah's scathing condemnation of the leaders and his prediction of divine punishment is met with a prompt response from Pashhur, the Temple overseer. The prophet is beaten and put in the stocks. Jeremiah responds to this humiliation by predicting Pashhur's downfall and giving him a nickname *Magor-Missabib* – "terror on every side". This name stuck to Pashhur for the rest of his life and has come down the centuries. In my South Wales village I often heard people say of someone, "He is a real *Magor-Missabib*" – meaning "he is a real pain in the neck".

As a result of the beating and humiliation Jeremiah plunges into the depths of despair. He accuses God of deceiving, failing and of bullying him. He has been discouraged before but has never quite spoken like this. His words sound like high treason. Will the Almighty let him get away with it?

God does not respond. As Jeremiah reflects on the clear call that came to him in his youth and the Word that God gave him to speak, something begins to burn within him. It is the message that God gave him. His hurt and confused feelings scream out within him, but God's Word screams louder. He had allowed God's Word to penetrate his being to such an extent that in the moment of overwhelming test it was the divine Word that cried out the loudest. If we allow God's Word to so live and take root within us, when our hurts and frustrations scream within God's Word will burn in us with His warming love, and we will hear His message above the din.

**FURTHER STUDY**

Isa. 40:1–8;
Psa. 119:89;
Matt. 5:18;
1 Pet. 1:25

1. What was Isaiah's conviction?
2. What did Jesus declare concerning the law?

## Prayer

My Father and my God, let Your Word so penetrate and permeate my being so that when my emotions scream within me Your voice will scream the loudest. I ask this in and through our Lord's precious Name. Amen.

# Swinging emotions

*"Why did I ever come out of the womb to see trouble and sorrow …?" (v.18)*

**For reading & meditation – Jeremiah 20:14–18**

Yesterday we left Jeremiah rejoicing that the Word, which God had given him when he was a youth, still burned within him. His depressed spirit rises in praise and gratitude to God (v.13). But his words of expectation and praise do not last long. Very soon he descends once again into the depths of despair. He wonders why his mother did not abort him when he was in the womb.

I heard one psychiatrist call Jeremiah a "manic depressive", basing his diagnosis on these verses in which Jeremiah swings from the heights of spiritual ecstasy to the depths of pessimism. "If I had been treating him," he said, "I would have recommended Lithium – a remedy often used to treat manic depression." But is Jeremiah suffering a psychological mood swing or is there a spiritual battle going on in his soul? I think it was the latter.

Faith and doubt are locked together within him and he finds it difficult to endure the strain of the tension. How can he at one and the same time claim that God is within like a mighty warrior (v.11) and then in the next breath curse the day he was born (v.14)? And

**FURTHER STUDY**

Psa. 73:1–28;
Ex. 14:13;
Isa. 41:13

*1. Why did the psalmist get discouraged?*
*2. How did he overcome it?*

why did he write it down? Those who have battled with discouragement and despair will understand. Jesus would have understood. In Gethsemane He broke down under the tension, sweating blood and begging to be released from His mission – yet remained willing to obey His Father's wishes. Whatever is going on must not be denied. Tell God honestly how you feel. In His presence no anguish need be stifled or repressed.

## Prayer

O God, I am so thankful for the honest reporting of the Scriptures. You let me see Your servants under all conditions. Help me understand that I can share my negative feelings with You without being rejected. What relief and release this gives me. Amen.

# The new shoot

*"The days are coming ... when I will raise up ... a
righteous Branch ..." (v.5)*

**For reading & meditation – Jeremiah 23:1–8**

The next section of Jeremiah (chapters 21–52) at first might
appear confusing. Many of the chapters follow no clear
chronological order. The events in chapter 21, for example, took
place twenty years after those in chapter 20, and it properly fits with
chapters 32, 34, and 37 to 39. The book of Jeremiah is a collection
of prophecies, not a diary of events, but this will not inhibit our
devotional study of the prophet's life.

In today's passage Jeremiah contrasts the present corrupt kings
and priests with the coming Messiah who is to be a perfect King and
Priest. The only real hope for Judah's future is found in none other
than the Son of God, our Lord Jesus Christ. The prophet is given a
glimpse into the future where he sees that one day someone from
King David's own line will come to reign over Israel with true justice
and power.

"The shoot is that which sprouts from the roots of a fallen tree,"
comments R. K. Harrison. "New life will thus spring forth from the
fallen dynasty." The name given to the future Saviour indicates His
true character – *the Lord Our Righteousness* (v.6).
The "shoot" that will emerge – our Lord Jesus
Christ – will impart to people a righteousness,
which is not earned by works but given through
grace. The high ideals commanded at Sinai which
people felt were utterly beyond them will at last
become realisable through a new covenant sealed
in Christ's blood. Our Lord not only imputes
righteousness to our spiritual account, He also
imparts it to our daily lives.

**FURTHER STUDY**

Isa. 11:1–16; 4:2;
Jer. 33:15–16;
Zech. 3:8; 6:12

1. How is the
"branch" described?
2. How is the fruit
described?

## Prayer

Father, I am so thankful that in Christ the demands of the law are not brought
down to my level, but that through my Saviour's power and grace I am brought
up to their level. I give honour and glory to His wonderful Name. Amen.

# False prophets

*"… My heart is broken within me … because of the
Lord and his holy words." (v.9)*

**For reading & meditation – Jeremiah 23:9–40**

One of the contributing factors to the people of Jeremiah's day
becoming corrupt was the way in which the false prophets
lulled them into a false sense of security. These men had a large and
enthusiastic audience. They were very popular because they told
the people what they wanted to hear.

How can we tell the difference between true and false prophets?
There are at least four evidences. First, a false prophet may appear
to live according to God's design but in fact he does not. Second, he
tampers with God's message, puts a spin on it, and makes it more
palatable. Third, he encourages his listeners (usually subtly) to risk
displeasing God. And fourth, he tends to be arrogant, self-serving
and more interested in pleasing people than in pleasing God. Some
would add a fifth difference – the words of a false prophet would not
be fulfilled (unless coincidentally), whereas the words of a true
prophet would in God's time become fact.

But be careful that you don't write someone off as a false
prophet just because of their over-enthusiasm. I have often
witnessed sincere but misguided Christians who, swept along by
the emotion of the moment, have made
predictions that never came true. Many of them
were later embarrassed and felt deeply ashamed.
They were not false prophets, just over-
enthusiastic believers. A false prophet would feel
no shame or embarrassment. There are more false
prophets in the Church of today than we might
imagine. Thankfully God has given us the Bible –
*a more sure word of prophecy* – by which to test all
other prophecies and teaching. Be sure to use it.

FURTHER STUDY

2 Pet. 1:12–20;
Luke 21:33;
1 Cor. 14:29–32;
1 Thess. 5:20

1. What is our
benchmark for
prophecy?
2. What are we
exhorted to do?

## Prayer

Father, thank You that I have Your own eternal, errorless Word as a judgment
bar to which I can bring all prophecies. Help me to test all things by the Bible
without becoming over-critical of what others say. In Jesus' Name. Amen.

# Thank God for trouble

*"The good [figs] are very good, but the poor ones …
cannot be eaten." (v.3)*

**For reading & meditation – Jeremiah 24:1–10**

This incident took place after Nebuchadnezzar had captured and enslaved Jerusalem. The king of Babylon had sent his crack troops across the desert and marched the cream of Judah's society back to Babylon – the carpenters, the skilled tradesmen, the blacksmiths and so on. You might assume that those who had been taken into captivity were like bad figs, fit only to be thrown away. And that those who remained in Jerusalem were like good figs, worth keeping. But the opposite was true.

In the vision Jeremiah, a true prophet as distinct from the false prophets, shows that appearances can be deceptive. As far as God was concerned the people who were carried away were the good figs, and the ones who remained were the bad figs. This was because the future lay not with those who had remained and who lived under the treacherous regime of Zedekiah and the politicians who manipulated him, but with those who had been carried into captivity in Babylon. The exiles would be so shocked by their change of circumstances that their hearts would respond readily to God's Word, whereas those who remained in Jerusalem would continue to be stubborn and obstinate.

It's a sad fact that sometimes God has to corner us before we admit that His way is best. Trouble is often a blessing in disguise. Where would you and I be now I wonder if God had not loved us enough to chastise us at certain periods in our lives? We would be like bad figs, fit only to be thrown out.

**FURTHER STUDY**

Deut. 8:1–5;
Psa. 94:12;
Prov. 3:12;
John 15:2

1. How does the psalmist describe discipline?
2. What is the end result of discipline?

## Prayer

Thank You, my Father, that You love me enough to discipline me. Your chastisements hurt but they always turn to my good. Hence I can truly say thank You for them. They yield more than they cost. I am so grateful. Amen.

# Twenty-three years!

*"For twenty-three years ... the word of the Lord has
come to me and I have spoken to you ..." (v.3)*

**For reading & meditation – Jeremiah 25:1–14**

We are now at the middle of the book of Jeremiah and the
prophet is at the mid-point of his career. The date is
the fourth year of Jehoiakim's reign – 605 BC. For twenty-three
years Jeremiah has been proclaiming the Word of God faithfully,
calling on the people to repent, but they have not listened. Now
God tells them that they are going to endure a seventy-year captivity
in Babylon as the cup of God's wrath is about to be poured out.

How was it possible for Jeremiah to keep preaching the same
message for twenty-three years while continually being harassed,
ridiculed and rejected? He had times of great discouragement and
came close to giving up – but *he never did*. There is a great contrast
between him and the people of his time. They were vacillating
people whose interests and commitments changed from one day to
another. In John Fowles' book *The Ebony Tower* there is a character
who wanted to climb Everest in a day, but if it took two days he just
wasn't interested. Jeremiah wasn't like that. He lived for God the
only way – one day at a time.

**FURTHER STUDY**

Gal. 6:1–9;
Heb. 12:1;
James 1:12; 5:11

1. What was Paul's
admonishment to the
Galatians?
2. What is the
reward of
perseverance?

The pursuit of excellence requires the ability
and commitment to keep returning to the task
you know God has called you to and never to give
up. It might sound dull and boring doing the
same thing day after day but if God has
commanded it, it is never the *same* thing. Nothing
can be greater than to do whatever God wants us
to do. We will never be bored by it.

## Prayer

O Father, whatever discouragements may come my way grant that I, like
Jeremiah, might never give up. Show me that nothing can be boring when You
are in it. Impress this truth deeply into my spirit I pray. In Jesus' Name. Amen.

# Never give up!

*"... the Lord ... said to me: 'Take from my hand
this cup ...'" (v.15)*

**For reading & meditation – Jeremiah 25:15–38**

Perhaps you are about to quit something God has called you to do. You have been labouring faithfully at the task for many years, but there don't seem to be many positive results. Life is hard and nobody seems to appreciate you.

If Jeremiah was there with you he would probably say, "I know how you feel." For twenty-three years day after day he preached the same message that God had given him – apparently to no avail. But Jeremiah was a sticker. In today's passage, we meet him yet again carrying the message of judgment wherever the Lord sent him. Paul tells us in 1 Corinthians 4:2 "it is required that those who have been given a trust must prove faithful." Note he says *faithful*, not successful.

When God gives us a task He wants us to stick to it no matter what happens. Perseverance is not a popular idea today. But it carries great weight in heaven. When Sir Winston Churchill was an old man he was invited to give a speech to the students graduating from a university. He arrived very late, after the diplomas had been given out. Out of courtesy to the great man the organisers asked him if he would like to say a few concluding words. He rose to his feet, fixed the audience with his gaze and said: "Never give up. Never, *never* give up. Never, never, *never* give up." That was all. He sat down to a standing ovation. Jeremiah says that to us. He knew God never gives out impossible or fruitless tasks, and He never gives up on us.

FURTHER STUDY

Matt. 25:1–46;
1 Cor. 4:2;
1 Pet. 4:10;
1 Tim. 6:20

1. What were the words
of commendation
from the master?
2. What were the words
of condemnation from
the master?

## Prayer

My Father and my God, help me persevere on this pilgrim journey, not thinking about the long road that lies ahead but just the task You have given me for this day. And may I never, never, never give up. In Jesus' Name. Amen.

# Thank God for the laity

*"… I will make this house like Shiloh and this city an object of cursing …"* (v.6)

**For reading & meditation – Jeremiah 26:1–24**

The situation we have read about in this chapter is thought by commentators to be the same as that described by Jeremiah in chapter 7. But here we have more information about the consequences. Imagine someone getting up in the middle of a Sunday morning service in Westminster Abbey and saying: "This great building, beautiful though it may be, will be demolished. God will not hesitate to destroy it no matter how sacred you think it is." Can you picture what a furore such an action would cause? So it is not surprising that after making the statement Jeremiah's life is threatened. In those days to say anything against the Temple was regarded as treason.

Jeremiah is called to appear before the officials and rulers to give account of himself, but so moving is his presentation and defence that many of his hearers come over to his side. Some of the people who were called to judge Jeremiah were laymen but they seemed to know more about Scripture than some of the priests.

I am deeply thankful for the ministry of what is sometimes referred to as the laity: the body of men and women who though untrained at a seminary level delve deeply into the Word of God and are experienced in applying it to their lives in the world. Without such people we would lose a perspective on the Scriptures which the best Bible college in the world may be unable to convey to trainee ministers. Think of lay people whose ministry God has used to bless you, and thank Him for them.

**FURTHER STUDY**

John 5:31–40;
Acts 17:10–12;
Rom. 15:4

1. What indictment did Jesus lay at the feet of His Jewish hearers?
2. What was the characteristic of the Bereans?

## Prayer

O God my Father, I am grateful that You have drawn me, along with millions of other ordinary Christians, to search the Scriptures daily. This builds beneath my feet a solid foundation on which I can stand faithfully for You. Amen.

# Under God's yoke

*"… 'Bow your neck under the yoke of the king
of Babylon …'" (v.12)*

**For reading & meditation – Jeremiah 27:1–22**

Here Jeremiah is instructed by God to make a yoke and to fasten it on his neck with leather thongs "as you would strap a yoke on a plough-ox" (v.2, TLB). Then he was told to send messages to the heads of the surrounding nations, through their ambassadors in Jerusalem, that it was futile to fight against the Babylonian armies, because they would all have to accept the "yoke" of service to Babylon. Jeremiah does as God says and he goes about his daily tasks carrying the yoke illustrating the message that had come to him from God.

There is a phrase in this section that at first is difficult to understand. The Almighty refers to Nebuchadnezzar as "my servant" (v.6). Nebuchadnezzar was one of the most ruthless, despotic and godless men who have ever walked the face of the earth. How could he be described as God's "servant"? Isaiah says something similar of Cyrus, king of the Persians, when he declared that the purposes of the Almighty lay behind all Cyrus's empire-building. It is in this sense that God refers to Nebuchadnezzar as His servant. Without realising it, Nebuchadnezzar was being used to advance the purposes of the Almighty, even though he was a worshipper of idols.

God is not limited to working through His own people. He has the whole world and its peoples in His hand. They are under His yoke. We may find events mysterious, and wonder what God is doing. Jeremiah reminds us that God is doing something, even if we don't understand it.

FURTHER STUDY

Matt. 11:25–30;
Acts 15:10;
2 Cor. 6:14–18

1. What does Jesus
   invite us to do?
2. What does Paul
   warn against?

## Prayer

Gracious Father, thank You that You are a sovereign God and that all peoples are ultimately within Your power. Help me to trust You when events seem inexplicable. In Jesus' Name. Amen.

# Prophet against prophet

*"At this, the prophet Jeremiah went on his way."*
*(v.11)*

**For reading & meditation – Jeremiah 28:1–17**

It is sad when people prefer comforting lies rather than the painful truth. But that is what is happening here. Jeremiah had prophesied that Jerusalem would fall and that it was futile to fight the Babylonians, but Hananiah (a false prophet) stood toe to toe with Jeremiah in the Temple and dismissed his prophecy with these words: "This is what the Lord Almighty, the God of Israel, says: 'I will break the yoke of the king of Babylon. Within two years I will bring back to this place all the articles of the Lord's house that Nebuchadnezzar king of Babylon removed from here … '" (vv.2–3).

Jeremiah's reply shows how secure he was in God. "Amen! May the Lord do so" (v.6). In other words: "It would be wonderful if the disaster could be avoided, but I am afraid it will not be." Jeremiah knew that his prophecies had come from God. So confident was he that when Hananiah broke the symbolic yoke and separated it from Jeremiah's body the prophet simply walked away. He would not enter the debate unless he had a fresh word from the Lord and that did not come immediately (vv.12–14).

**FURTHER STUDY**

Col. 2:1–4;
2 Tim. 2:23;
Titus 3:9–11

1. What was Paul's concern for the Colossians?
2. What was his warning to Timothy and Titus?

How different life would be for many of us if we were secure enough in God to walk away from unnecessary arguments. Jeremiah was not afraid of an argument but he was not drawn into one simply for the sake of it, *even though he knew that he was right!* He felt no need to defend himself; he was content to let time tell who spoke truly. It's an example we should follow.

## Prayer

O Father, give me the courage to present what I believe with conviction. Give me the courage to walk away when that is the right thing to do. And give me the wisdom to know when to do one or the other. In Jesus' Name. Amen.

# Dear exiles, I love you

*"This is what the Lord Almighty ... says to all those
I carried into exile ..." (v.4)*

**For reading & meditation – Jeremiah 29:1–32**

A t this stage in Jeremiah's life, Nebuchadnezzar had taken several
thousand of Jerusalem's key people into captivity. In Babylon
things were vastly different. All that was familiar had gone.
Naturally the exiles were downcast and depressed. Some religious
leaders, sensing the discontent, began to prophesy that soon the
exile would be over and they would return to their land.

Jeremiah, hearing of these false prophecies, saw it as his
responsibility to warn the people against such delusion. So he writes
this letter. They are in captivity, he says, because they have rejected
the Word of God and it will be a long long time before they return
home. Hence it is better to renounce false hope and settle down to
make the best of the situation.

Jeremiah knows that the exile had put the people in a position
where their inner emptiness could be exposed, and now was the
time for them to seek the Lord (v.13). They hadn't done so when
they were in freedom; perhaps now they were in captivity things
would be different. Notice how tenderly He deals with the exiles. He
doesn't say, "Serves you right! Stew there for a
while!" He reassures them of His good plans and
that one day He will restore them (vv.11, 14).
Sometimes God has to upset us in order to set us
up. Are you in "exile" at the moment? Has your
world been turned upside down? Then this is the
time to *seek the Lord*. Search for Him with all your
heart and I promise that you will find Him.
Because He still loves you dearly.

> **FURTHER STUDY**
> 2 Tim. 4:1–5;
> 1 Tim. 1:5–7; 4:2;
> 6:3–4;
> Titus 1:10–16
>
> 1. What charge did
> Paul give Timothy?
> 2. What did he
> exhort Titus to do?

## Prayer

O Father, why is it that sometimes You have to put me on my back before I will
look up into Your face? Once again I want to record my gratitude that You love
me enough to chastise me. Your disciplines develop me. Thank You my Father.
Amen.

# A book of hope

*"… you will be my people, and I will be your God."*
(v.22)

**For reading & meditation – Jeremiah 30:1–24**

Chapters 30 to 33 have been described by commentators as "the book of hope". Jeremiah reaches heights of eloquence that seem at times to surpass even that of the silver-tongued Isaiah. There is good reason; he is looking forward to the restoration of his people from exile. No one reading these chapters can think of Jeremiah simply as a prophet of doom. He is a prophet of hope too.

After the pruning process and the inevitable results of the judgment on a rebellious and obstinate people there is to come a time of restoration and great blessing. God will make a new covenant with them to replace the one they violated. Once they sinned and disobeyed; one day they will repent and obey.

Like Isaiah, Jeremiah associates events in the near future with those in the distant future. The prophecies he makes here have been compared to a range of mountain peaks. From a distance they look as if they are close to one another but actually they are great distances apart. He talks of events as if they will all happen together, but in fact there will be enormous time differences between them.

**FURTHER STUDY**

Jer. 31:1–40;
Matt. 26:28;
Heb. 8:1–13; 12:24

1. What is the key emphasis of this chapter from Jeremiah?
2. What conclusion does the writer of Hebrews come to?

He sees the end of the exile but he also sees the day when Christ will come as King and reign for ever. The verse I have selected for contemplation sums up God's longings since the day He decided to form His human creation: *You will be my people and I will be your God.* Could anything be more beautiful? It applies as much to you and me as it did to Jeremiah's listeners.

## Prayer

O Father, how thrilling it is to see Your longings so beautifully captured in one statement. You long that I might be one of Your family, and I long that You might be my God. Our longings meet together. I am so glad. Amen.

# Invest in the future

*"Jeremiah said, 'The word of the Lord came to me ...'"*
(v.6)

### For reading & meditation – Jeremiah 32:1–15

It's one thing to say you have faith and confidence that God will bring about what He has promised; it's another thing to put that faith into operation. "Putting your money where your mouth is" – exactly what we see Jeremiah doing here.

King Zedekiah, infuriated by Jeremiah's advice to surrender to the Babylonians, has put the prophet in prison. One of Jeremiah's cousins visits him with what seems an insensitive and untimely proposition to sell him a field in Anathoth, then occupied by the invading Babylonians. It was hardly a safe or good investment! But God has already prepared Jeremiah for his cousin's proposition and he clinches the deal immediately by handing over the agreed price of seventeen shekels of silver. To buy land that was occupied by the enemy and take such elaborate care with the title deeds shows a tremendous faith in the future that says "Things might look dark at the moment but God will be true to His Word".

Trust does not come easily. It wasn't easy for Jeremiah publicly to buy the land. But he believed that although God was judging His people, the last word would not be judgment but restoration. Are the promises of God under attack in your life at the moment? Are the enemies of your faith hammering on the door and intimidating you? Does the thing He has promised to do for you look as if it might never happen? Remember God may delay His promises but He will never deny them. Perhaps to act with confidence is the very step of faith God is wanting you to take.

**FURTHER STUDY**

Prov. 3:1–6;
Psa. 37:1–7;
Isa. 50:10

1. What is the psalmist's admonition?
2. Can you make a meaningful acrostic from the word "trust"?

## Prayer

Father, I see that hope is buying into what I believe. Forgive me for doubting so much of what You have told me. I know that none of Your precious promises can fail. Help me put my money where my mouth is. In Jesus' Name. Amen.

# God is merciful

*"Ah, Sovereign Lord ... Nothing is too hard for you."*
(v.17)

**For reading & meditation – Jeremiah 32:16–44**

Jeremiah purchased a field in Anathoth on the prompting of God. And by doing so he gave clear evidence to the people of his belief in and commitment to the continuity of God's promises. But once again his humanity came to the surface and he couldn't help but *feel* somewhat foolish.

How do we deal with negative feelings when they seem to contradict what our minds tell us, namely that we have done the right thing? We bring our whole being, will, thoughts, feelings to God and seek to re-centre them in importunate prayer. Many Bible commentators point out that the prayer of Jeremiah here is a model of how to pray in a difficult or desperate situation. Consider carefully how he prays because you may be called upon to pray such a prayer in the near future. First he focuses on the creative power of God (v.17), then on His faithfulness and justice (v.18). Next he concentrates on God's great redemptive acts (vv.20–22). He concludes by referring to the sins and failing of the past (v.23), the difficulties being experienced in the present (v.24), and the mystery of the future (v.25).

**FURTHER STUDY**

1 John 1:1–10;
Psa. 130:4; 103:3;
Eph. 1:7

*1. What confidence can we have?*
*2. Ask for God's forgiveness today.*

How does God respond to such a prayer? He announces that though judgment is at hand His last word is not judgment, but mercy. God has to judge. He cannot do any other and still remain God. The delight of His heart, however, is to restore, to forgive, and to pour out His blessings on His people. We must hold fast to this. He must judge. But the joy of His heart is to forgive.

## Prayer

Father, I am so grateful that I do not have to wrest mercy from You. You delight to dispense it. Given my repentant heart all heaven bends down to lift and restore me. I am eternally grateful. Amen.

# Turn your face to God

*"Call to me and I will answer you and tell you great
and unsearchable things you do not know." (v.3)*

**For reading & meditation – Jeremiah 33:1–26**

It should not surprise us that God continues to encourage Jeremiah with promises that help him develop a clear picture of how, after a period of judgment, God will restore the fortunes of His people (v.11). It is one of the Almighty's characteristics to hearten His servants in their darkest and most discouraging moments.

The key verse in this chapter is without doubt the one I have selected as our text for today: *"Call to me and I will answer you and tell you great and unsearchable things you do not know."* This is my favourite text in the Old Testament. What a reassuring and encouraging word it is! God is saying that to those who seek His face He will reveal things they could never know by natural means.

Why is it that often when we need help, guidance or encouragement, the last person we call upon is the Lord? Pascal, the great French Christian and philosopher, said: "It ought to be the soul's habit whenever discouraged or in need of guidance to first call out to the Lord before calling out to anyone else." It is not wrong to seek help from others but our first port of call ought to be the Lord.

God can make Himself heard and known without us calling on Him; the whole of the Bible is evidence of that. But what He longs for is a relationship with us. We prefer to talk to a person's face than their back. God does too. Turn your face to Him now, however you feel; perhaps in this chapter there are encouragements for you.

FURTHER STUDY

Psa. 91:1–16;
Isa. 58:9; 65:24;
Zech. 13:9

1. Where did the psalmist choose to dwell?
2. What was the consequence?

## Prayer

O God my Father, forgive me that so often I choose to rely more on human help than I do on Yours. I am grateful for the encouragement I get from my friends but help me make You my first port of call. Amen.

# Permanent or temporary?

*"Recently you repented ... But now you have turned round ..." (vv.15, 16)*

**For reading & meditation – Jeremiah 34:1–21**

Jeremiah is faced with another tough task. He is commanded by God to go and tell King Zedekiah that Jerusalem is about to fall and that he personally will be exiled to Babylon. So Zedekiah, wanting to change God's mind, hits on the idea of encouraging slave owners to give liberty to their slaves as the law required every seven years, in the hope that this might persuade the Lord to turn back the Babylonian armies.

The slave owners respond to Zedekiah's request but not long after they hear that the Egyptian army is on its way to assist them. The intervention appears to be miraculous, and the slave owners, thinking the threat is now over, revoke their earlier decisions and take their slaves back into captivity. This was a breach of faith, and brought from Jeremiah a scathing condemnation.

Let's ask ourselves if we might be guilty of a similar attitude. What do we do when we are in a tight spot? Do we panic and bargain with God, promising that if He delivers us we will be more faithful in prayer, reading the Scriptures and giving to His work?

**FURTHER STUDY**

James 1:1–8;
2 Kings 17:33;
1 Kings 18:21

1. What does double-mindedness produce?
2. What challenge did Elijah put to the people?

Then when the difficulty has passed do we soon forget our promises and go back to living the way we did before? I confess I have done this sometimes and I am sure most of us have done so too. Nothing sharpens up our spiritual lives like a threat to our welfare. But when the threat is over we go right back to living the way we lived before. God looks for permanent heart-changes, not temporary mind-changes.

## Prayer

O God, forgive me that my promises so often are like pie-crusts – pledged under pressure but not kept. I want to be the kind of person You want me to be. Help me dear Lord. In Jesus' Name. Amen.

# Recabite resolve

*"Go to the Recabite family ... and give them wine
to drink." (v.2)*

**For reading & meditation – Jeremiah 35:1–19**

We read in the book of Jeremiah that God uses every means possible to bring home to His people the reality of their spiritual condition. Here we see Jeremiah being commanded by God to invite the Recabite family into one of the side rooms of the Temple and ply them with wine.

The Recabites were a group of nomads who travelled through the land like gypsies performing tasks like sharpening knives, making chariot wheels and straightening bent javelins. They traced their ancestry back over a period of more than 200 years to a man called Jonadab (Jehonadab, a supporter of King Jehu in 2 Kings 10:15,23), the son of Recab, who zealously committed himself and his family to total abstinence. Jonadab's descendants had faithfully followed in his footsteps and were widely known for their refusal to drink alcohol.

Why then would God, through Jeremiah, invite them to break their pledge and to drink wine? God knew that they would not yield to the temptation. He wanted to use this incident to show that here was a group of people committed to the word of a man who lived centuries ago, while Judah's people generally refused to commit themselves to the Word that God was speaking to them now. It must have grieved God to see this group more committed to the keeping of a custom than His own people were to the keeping of the commandments. Is it possible that we, the present people of God, are more loyal to customs than the law of God? It can happen very easily, but we can see it only with difficulty.

FURTHER STUDY

Mark 7:1–8;
Titus 1:16;
Gal. 4:10–11

1. What was Paul's concern for the Galatians?
2. What indictment did Jesus confront the Pharisees with?

## Prayer

O God, show me what customs I am putting before Your commandments, or what laws of the land before the laws of God. Help me to see this, and to remedy it with your grace. In Jesus' Name. Amen.

# God can't be stopped

*"Take another scroll and write on it all the words that were on the first scroll …" (v.28)*

**For reading & meditation – Jeremiah 36:1–32**

God commands Jeremiah to write down all the messages he has been given, and he recruits a scribe named Baruch to help him. Soon after the task is finished the Babylonian armies are reported to be close to the land of Judah. The people of Jerusalem, feeling their lives are under threat, are deeply concerned. A fast is proclaimed but because Jeremiah is out of favour with King Jehoiakim he is not allowed to speak in public. So he appoints Baruch to read to the assembled people the words which had been recorded.

There seems to be no general reaction from the crowd but a man named Micaiah is deeply touched. He speaks to his father Gemariah, a government official, about what he has heard. Gemariah arranges for a second reading for himself and a few other government officials. They too are affected and know that the king must hear these words. But they know too that the king will be incensed by what he hears so they advise Baruch and Jeremiah to hide. When eventually the king hears the scroll being read, he takes a knife, cuts the scroll into pieces and throws it into the fire.

This is the first record of the Word of God being destroyed. God responds by commanding Jeremiah to compile a new scroll. He and Baruch went back to work again. But this time it came out more strongly. It is foolish to think anyone can outmanoeuvre God. He can turn every reverse into a forward direction. The Almighty is never stymied. Remember this incident next time you face opposition or setbacks.

## Prayer

Father, I rest my confidence in Your ability to outmanoeuvre everything that is against You. You turn setbacks into springboards, obstacles into opportunities. I am so grateful that I am Your servant. My trust is in You, Lord. Amen.

# Who should change?

*"... King Zedekiah ... asked ...'Is there any word from the Lord?'"* (v.17)

**For reading & meditation – Jeremiah 37:1–21**

Today's incident is almost twenty years later than yesterday's. The Babylonians have temporarily lifted the blockade against Jerusalem, and King Zedekiah asks Jeremiah to pray that God will turn the situation around. But Jeremiah had already been told to stop praying against defeat (7:16; 14:11). It was a profitless exercise as God's mind was already made up. The prophet informs the king that the siege would be resumed eventually and that Jerusalem, as he had predicted many times, would fall into enemy hands.

When the siege is lifted, Jeremiah tries to leave the city to claim some property that was his by right. But he is seen by one of the sentries, Irijah, who believes he is defecting to the enemy and arrests him. When Jeremiah is brought before the officials they refuse to believe his story and he is severely beaten and thrown into prison. After a long time Zedekiah sends for Jeremiah and enquires of him: "Is there any word from the Lord?" (v.16). Did the king, I wonder, hope that Jeremiah's long incarceration had changed his mind about praying for the deliverance of Israel?

The prophet shows himself to be as faithful as ever to the Word of God and repeats his previous prediction concerning the king's fate. Only then does he plead for better conditions. The king grants his request and moves him to the palace stockade. Zedekiah wanted God to change but he himself didn't want to change. This is typical of human nature. We plead for God to change His mind so that we will not have to change ours. May He forgive our arrogance.

**FURTHER STUDY**

Josh. 23:1–8;
1 Cor. 15:58;
Gal. 5:1;
Phil. 1:27

1. What was Joshua's exhortation to the people?
2. What was a recurring emphasis of the apostle?

## Prayer

O God, forgive me if I seem more concerned about changing Your mind than changing my own. Help me to recognise that no matter what happens or how my life works out, Your purposes are always the best. In Jesus' Name I pray. Amen.

# Standing for justice

*"... these men have acted wickedly in all they have done to Jeremiah the prophet." (v.9)*

**For reading & meditation – Jeremiah 38:1–13**

Some of the officials hear that Jeremiah is telling people to surrender to the Babylonians (v.2) and they demand that the king executes him. The king permits them to arrest Jeremiah and they throw him into an underground storage cistern that is full of mud. As soon as Jeremiah is lowered into it he begins to sink. Clearly he is in imminent danger of dying through either suffocation or exposure.

One of the officials, Ebed-Melech, an African from Ethiopia, hears of Jeremiah's plight and pleads with the king to let him save Jeremiah. The king agrees so Ebed-Melech gets ropes and rags, and with thirty others sets out to rescue Jeremiah. He instructs Jeremiah to put the rags under his armpits so that the ropes would not cut into his flesh, and then they pull him to the surface.

I think it is safe to say that Ebed-Melech feared God more than man. He alone among all the palace officials stood against the murder plot. It is noteworthy that because of this he was spared when Jerusalem fell (39:15–18). How many of us have the courage to speak up when we see injustice being done? Someone has said all that needs to happen for evil to flourish is for good people to do nothing. Do we slink into the shadows or do we stand up for God and for right? Perhaps you can be an Ebed-Melech to someone today. It may increase antagonism towards us, but Jesus promised we will not lose our reward in heaven because we do such things for Him (Matt. 25:34–40).

**FURTHER STUDY**

Acts 5:25–42;
4:19–20;
Job 23:11

1. What stance did the apostles take?
2. What was Job able to say?

## Prayer

O God, make me an Ebed-Melech to someone today. Forgive me that so often bad things flourish around me because I do nothing. Help me stand up for You, and for truth and justice, in our Lord's Name I pray. Amen.

# Zedekiah, the marshmallow

*"King Zedekiah said … 'I am afraid of the Jews who
have gone over to the Babylonians …'"* (v.19)

**For reading & meditation – Jeremiah 38:14–28**

Jeremiah has been rescued from the cistern and is back in the
courtyard of the guard where he is to remain until the fall of
Jerusalem. Once more Zedekiah arranges for a secret rendezvous
with the prophet, this time in the Temple.

His question is the same as before – what is the shape of the
future and what is going to happen to me? Jeremiah is afraid that if
he tells the king once more what God has told him about Zedekiah's
destiny that his life will be in danger. But assured by the king this
will not be so he spells out the frightening alternatives. "If you
surrender," he says, "your life will be spared, and the city will not be
burned down. If you will not surrender, the city will be destroyed
and your life will be in danger." Zedekiah commands Jeremiah not
to divulge their conversation to anyone – on pain of death.

What a spineless and characterless person Zedekiah was. And
how different from Jeremiah. Eugene Peterson describes Zedekiah
as "a marshmallow". Character has been defined as what a person is
like on the inside. Reputation is what other people think of you.
Zedekiah had no stomach for facing reality. He
wanted changes on the outside without being
prepared to change on the inside. Zedekiah was
soft like a marshmallow, and Jeremiah was firm
like a rock. One pursued self-interest; the other
pursued excellence. Every day we face a choice –
living for ourselves and caving in to others'
opinions or living for God and standing firm on
His truth. Which will it be for us today?

**FURTHER STUDY**

1 Tim. 4:1–7;
2:1–2; 6:11;
Titus 2:11–12

1. What was
Timothy to train in?
2. What does God's
grace teach us?

## Prayer

O God, with all my heart I want to live not for myself but for You. But sometimes it's not easy. Give me Your grace to rise to every challenge that faces me
today and to live this and every other day to Your praise and glory. Amen.

# The fall of Jerusalem

*"Take him and look after him; don't harm him but do for him whatever he asks." (v.12)*

**For reading & meditation – Jeremiah 39:1–18**

This chapter is a study in contrasts. Zedekiah, son of King Josiah and last king of Judah, ruled eleven years from 597 to 586 BC. Prior to Zedekiah the kingdom had been ruled by his two older brothers Jehoahaz and Jehoiakim, and by his nephew Coniah (also called Jehoiachin). When Coniah was exiled to Babylon Nebuchadnezzar made twenty-one-year-old Mattaniah the king and changed his name to Zedekiah (2 Kings 24:15–17). Zedekiah rebelled against Nebuchadnezzar who captured him, killed his sons before his eyes, then blinded him and took him to Babylon where later he died.

Note, however, that Jeremiah was treated with respect, even admiration, by the Babylonians. Some commentators suggest that the superstitious Babylonians, who respected magicians and soothsayers, put Jeremiah in this category and treated him as a seer. No doubt they also knew that he had counselled co-operation with Babylon and had predicted a Babylonian victory.

What a difference there is between the fates of Zedekiah and Jeremiah. One was saved by faith; the other was destroyed by fear. One was filled with self-interest, the other with compassion for his people. One was treated with contempt, the other with respect. Note too that Ebed-Melech (who risked his life to save Jeremiah) is blessed by the Lord and protected from the Babylonians. A life of commitment to the Lord can sometimes be tough, but God often has special blessings or compensations for His faithful people. He allows us to be tempted, but He promises also to make a way of escape. He allows us to suffer, but He promises to support us and bring good out of evil.

**FURTHER STUDY**

1 Cor. 10:1–13;
Isa. 30:21; 42:16

*1. Why are the Old Testament accounts recorded for us?*
*2. What is God's promise?*

## Prayer

O Father, I am grateful for those miraculous interventions that are so beautifully timed by You. When my back is against the wall, You have a way of turning the situation around. My hope and trust is in You today, Lord. Amen.

# The choice

*"So Jeremiah ... stayed ... among the people who were
left behind in the land." (v.6)*

**For reading & meditation – Jeremiah 40:1–16**

This is a wonderful moment in Jeremiah's life. It takes place after
the fall of Jerusalem. The city is now in Babylonian hands just as
Jeremiah had predicted; the lies of the false prophets have been
exposed. It is decided to take Jeremiah to Babylon with the other
exiles. Nebuzaradan, the captain of the guard, gives the prophet the
choice of going to Babylon or returning to his native Jerusalem.

This is how the Living Bible paraphrases his remarks: "If you
want to come with me to Babylon, fine; I will see that you are well
cared for. But if you don't want to come, don't. The world is before
you – go where you like" (v.4). What a choice! The prophet can go
to Babylon where he will be given special treatment – no chains,
imprisonment or deprivation. Or he can return to Jerusalem, a city
now in ruins, and be part of the tiny remnant left behind.

Jeremiah is being offered a chance to retire in Babylon. He was
about sixty-five at the time so the offer had its attractions. If anyone
deserved a life of ease with special facilities, it was Jeremiah. But it
didn't take him long to make up his mind. He chose to return to
Jerusalem and live as he had always lived, trusting
God and confident in His purposes. Jeremiah's
choice that day at Rama was typical of how he had
lived all his life. He chose to be where the
Almighty had enshrined His Name – Jerusalem,
the city of God. Comfort or service? The choice
faces us daily, not just at life's big crossroads.

**FURTHER STUDY**

Gen. 13:1–18;
Deut. 30:19;
Prov. 8:10;
Amos 6:1

1. Why do we often
make wrong choices?
2. What does the
flesh prefer?

## Prayer

Father, I face many choices in life and sometimes attractive choices. But no
matter what choices I am faced with help me to always make the choice that is
in line with Yours. In Jesus' Name I pray. Amen.

# Easy way or God's way?

*"They were afraid of them because Ishmael ... had killed Gedaliah ..." (v.18)*

**For reading & meditation – Jeremiah 41:1–18**

Before the Babylonians marched the exiles off to Babylon they had appointed Gedaliah, a life-long friend of Jeremiah, to be the governor of Jerusalem. But not long after his appointment a terrorist outlaw called Ishmael, accompanied by a small group of associates, murdered him and many of the Jewish officials and the Babylonian soldiers. The next day when a large group of people from the surrounding areas approached Jerusalem to worship at the Temple, Ishmael inveigled them inside the city and slaughtered them, throwing their bodies into a huge cistern.

His murderous action was countered by Johanan who organised the people of Mizpah into a formidable band and chased Ishmael and his companions out of the country. Johanan, fearing reprisals from Babylon over the assassination of Gedaliah, decided to move down into Egypt. The question arises, why Egypt? God had clearly told His people that they ought not to align themselves with Egypt (Isa. 30:1–3; Jer. 2:36) yet here a group is bent on settling there.

Egypt represented safety and security – a much more appealing alternative than staying in Jerusalem and depending on God to direct their lives. Jerusalem, with its city reduced to rubble and its economy in ruins, was a hard option. Egypt was an easier one. Many of us when faced with the choice between trusting the invisible God or putting our faith in the things we can see prefer to do the equivalent of living in Egypt. Trusting God is not easy, especially where there is an escape route that leads to more tangible things. But they may prove unable to support us.

**FURTHER STUDY**

Luke 12:13–21;
Job 31:24–28;
Psa. 52:7;
Prov. 18:11

1. What was Jesus' teaching in this parable?
2. What did Job recognise?

## Prayer

My Father and my God, Your Word keeps on finding me out. Yet I would rather be challenged by You than be lulled by the world into a false sense of security. Help me spurn all escape routes and trust only in You. In Jesus' Name. Amen.

# Keep an open mind

*"I have told you today, but you still have not obeyed the
Lord your God ..." (v.21)*

**For reading & meditation – Jeremiah 42:1–22**

You could be forgiven for thinking that Jeremiah's decision to
return to Jerusalem meant that there, in the city of God, he
would end his days. It was not to be. He ended his days in the place
he had told his people not to go to – Egypt. This is how it happened.

When Johanan decided to escape to Egypt he asked Jeremiah to
pray for God's guidance. Jeremiah did so and later passed on God's
response: "Stay here in this land. If you do, I will bless you and no
one will harm you. ... Don't fear the king of Babylon any more, for I
am with you to save you and deliver you from his hand ... O
remnant of Judah, the Lord Almighty, the God of Israel says: If you
insist on going to Egypt, the war and famine you fear will follow
close behind you and you will perish there" (vv.10–16, TLB). But
Johanan spurned the advice given by the Lord and set off for Egypt,
taking Jeremiah and his friend Baruch with him.

It is clear that Johanan, in asking Jeremiah to pray for God's
guidance, had already made his mind up. He didn't want guidance;
he wanted confirmation. It is a problem many of us face in our
prayer lives. We are not truly open to God; we
don't take seriously the possibility that He might
say "No". It is the supreme irony of Jeremiah's life
that he ended his days in Egypt. Doubtless,
although little is recorded about Jeremiah's last
days he would have ended them as he began –
magnificently, honourably, loyally and
courageously.

**FURTHER STUDY**

Psa. 143:1–10; 5:8;
25:5; 27:11

*1. What was the
psalmist's request?
2. Make this your
prayer today.*

## Prayer

Father, can it be that even though I pray for guidance I am more interested in
getting confirmation? Help me dear Father to examine my heart. Help me
when I pray to have a truly open mind. In Jesus' Name. Amen.

# Egypt – no refuge

*"The Lord our God has not sent you to say, 'You must not go to Egypt to settle there.'" (v.2)*

**For reading & meditation – Jeremiah 43:1–13**

When Johanan and his associates asked Jeremiah to pray for God's guidance they really wanted God's confirmation of their own plans. If we are honest, often we are more interested in getting God's approval for our own plans than seeking Him for His. An old Christian told me many years ago: never make any plans unless you are willing to have God change them, and never pray unless you are willing to accept God's answer. They are challenging words.

Johanan and his companions, fearful of staying in Jerusalem and bent on disobeying God, make sure that Jeremiah is with them. Scripture does not say whether Jeremiah and his companion Baruch went willingly. My own guess is that they were pressured, perhaps even forced, to go because Johanan thought that if the prophet was with them then God would spare them and allow none of the things to happen to them that he had predicted.

When Jeremiah arrived in Egypt his first action was to bury some paving stones at the entrance to Pharaoh's palace and announce that Nebuchadnezzar of Babylon would one day set up his throne on the stones that he, Jeremiah, had buried. He did. Nebuchadnezzar actually invaded Egypt in 568–567 BC and overthrew the nation. So much for the great empire on which Johanan and his companions had pledged their hopes. It is an object lesson for us. The things or people we trust may seem strong, but if they are not chosen by God they will let us down. It's sad, but is so often true.

**FURTHER STUDY**

Isa. 2:12–22; 31:1;
Jer. 17:5;
Psa. 118:8–9

1. What is Isaiah's exhortation?
2. What was the conclusion of the psalmist?

## Prayer

O Father, with all my heart I ask You to help me to deepen my confidence and trust in You. Please help me in all that I do today. In Jesus' Name. Amen.

# Jeremiah's last sermon

*"This word came to Jeremiah concerning all the Jews
living in Lower Egypt ..." (v.1)*

**For reading & meditation – Jeremiah 44:1–30**

T he last recorded scene with Jeremiah shows him doing what he
had done for most of his life – preaching God's Word to a
rebellious people. This encounter no doubt took place some months
after their arrival in Egypt. His sermon is a blistering attack on their
refusal to submit to the will and guidance of God, and he reminds
them that their sins had brought destruction on the land. Jeremiah
tells them that they will never return to Judah because they had
gone against God's advice when they travelled to Egypt.

But these people, like the others of their generation, were
unwilling to hear what Jeremiah was saying. Only those who
repented of going to Egypt would escape judgment. One of the great
principles of the Christian life is the further we drift from God, the
more confused our thinking becomes and the more likely we are to
perpetuate our mistakes. Whatever degree of spiritual life the group
who went down to Egypt once had now seemed to be lost. They had
sunk into idolatry, debauchery and pagan worship – the things that
caused all the trouble in the first place. They stubbornly refused to
recognise that the source of their problems was
their departure from God's way.

When we forget a lesson we are in danger of
making the mistake again that the lesson was
meant to counter. Our past is a school of
experience. We live foolishly, even dangerously,
when we fail to let our past mistakes point us in
the direction God wishes us to take now.

**FURTHER STUDY**

Deut. 4:1–9;
6:10–12;
Jer. 3:21

1. What warning is
given to Israel?
2. What is the end
result?

## Prayer

Father, I see that not to learn from my failures is to assure future failure. Just as
I remember the lessons I once learned in school, help me remember also the
lessons I learn in Your school of experience. In Jesus' Name. Amen.

# A boost to Baruch

*"Should you then seek great things for yourself? Seek them not." (v.5)*

**For reading & meditation – Jeremiah 45:1–5**

This, the shortest chapter in Jeremiah's prophecy, is chronologically out of order. It links with the events recorded in chapter 36:1–18. Baruch, you remember, was the scribe who wrote down Jeremiah's words. Clearly the scribe is upset. *The Living Bible* puts it graphically: "You have said, Woe is me ... I am weary of my own sighing and I find no rest." There is little doubt that Baruch is getting his share of opposition for the influence he supposedly has over Jeremiah (v.3). It appears that Baruch had great hopes for himself and his own ministry, but now all those hopes were dashed.

God speaks to him through Jeremiah and reproves him for his negative thinking, but to sustain him he is given a promise of personal survival: "I will protect you wherever you go" (v.5). God is quick to come to the aid of His disconsolate servants and to reassure them of the divine love and compassion. The heart of God's message to Jeremiah is: take your eyes off yourself, and think more of the purposes of God for your life than of making a name for yourself.

When we concentrate more on our own careers or future than on God's purpose for our lives we become ego-centred rather than God-centred. That does not mean it is wrong to think and plan out a career. It means rather that unless God has first claim on our lives then we live superficially no matter how much money we make or how many possessions we own. True greatness in His Kingdom is serving Him and others before ourselves (Luke 22:26–27).

**FURTHER STUDY**

2 Tim. 4:1–8;
Deut. 6:24;
Psa. 31:23; 37:28

1. What was Paul's conviction?
2. Make that your conviction today.

## Prayer

O God, forgive me when I focus in a self-centred way on what I have to give up to serve You. Help me to focus on what I have gained because I know You: real life in this world and eternal life to come. Thank You my Father. Amen.

# A message to the nations

*"This is the word of the Lord that came to Jeremiah the
prophet concerning the nations ..." (v.1)*

**For reading & meditation – Jeremiah 46:1–10**

A superficial reading of the Old Testament may easily lead
someone to conclude that God is interested in just one group of
people – the Jews. But such is not the case. He is the God of the
Jews, but He is also the God of the nations. In fact nearly every Old
Testament prophet has something to say about the nations that lay
outside Israel. Obadiah, for example, focuses on Edom; Jonah and
Nahum direct their message to Nineveh. Jeremiah was called by
God not to be a chaplain to the Jews but a prophet to the nations
(1:5).

Here, Jeremiah's missionary heart is made bare. He had little
opportunity to visit the surrounding nations so in chapters 46–51
we see him preparing oracles or written sermons for ten different
nations: Egypt, Philistia, Moab, Ammon, Edom, Damascus (capital
of Syria), Kedar and Hazor (two nomadic tribes), Elam and Babylon.
His concern for the surrounding nations is a reflection of God's
concern. No one has a greater missionary heart than God. His
primary intention in calling Israel into covenant with Himself was
evangelistic. He wanted them to be a shop window through which
other nations could look in and see the blessings
that come from serving the true and living God.
But as we know, Israel failed to reflect the divine
purposes.

"Biblical religion," says Eugene Peterson, "is
aggressively internationalistic." Our churches
ought not to be cosy places to which we retreat
but centres from which we draw inspiration to
make both individual and corporate evangelistic
forays into the world. Jesus' last words were not
"come", but "go" (Matt. 28:19).

> **FURTHER STUDY**
>
> Matt. 28:16–20;
> Mark 16:14–20;
> Matt. 24:14; Mark
> 13:10; Luke 24:47;
> Acts 1:8
>
> 1. What was a
> constant theme of
> Jesus?
> 2. What did He
> promise His disciples?

## Prayer

Father, help me never to forget that the first two letters of the gospel are GO.
May there be a GO in my faith, and may I share Your heart of evangelistic zeal
I pray. In Jesus' Name. Amen.

# A tale of two cities

*"Babylon's thick wall will be levelled ..."*
*(v.58)*

**For reading & meditation – Jeremiah 51:58–64**

We do not know how Jeremiah got his oracles into the surrounding nations, but we do know he got his message into Babylon. In today's passage we see Jeremiah enlisting the services of Seraiah to take the oracle addressed to Babylon with him as he makes an official diplomatic journey to the city. Jeremiah commissions him to read it and then to take a stone, tie it to the scroll, and throw it into the River Euphrates, announcing: "So will Babylon sink to rise no more" (v.64). Did those words come true? Definitely. Babylon, one of the greatest cities the world has ever known, now lies in ruins. Travellers there say that an eerie atmosphere pervades the place. The city was devastated about seventy years later.

Someone has described the Bible as "a tale of two cities". It centres on Babylon, the symbol of pride and Jerusalem, the symbol of peace. Babylon, built on the site of the original tower of Babel, represents the kind of pride that struts before the Almighty and says: "We can get along without You." Jerusalem, on the other hand,

**FURTHER STUDY**

Psa. 122:1–6;
Isa. 1:26; 66:10;
48:10; 52:1

1. What are we to
pray for?
2. Take a few
moments to do it
today.

represents God-centred worship that says, "We can't get along without You." Only Jerusalem, the city of God, is standing today. Babylon may have gone but its spirit is still with us. However, as we see in the book of Revelation, one day that spirit of pride will be expunged from the earth and the new Jerusalem hold sway. We live today in both cities; our physical life is in Babylon, but our hearts are in Jerusalem. So which one is uppermost in your life?

## Prayer

Father, I see that I can choose my eternal destiny. I choose life. I choose the New Jerusalem, the city of God. All honour and glory be to Your precious Name. Amen.

# A strange ending

*"It was because of the Lord's anger that all this happened to Jerusalem and Judah ..." (v.3)*

**For reading & meditation – Jeremiah 52:1–34**

The book of Jeremiah ends in a slightly unexpected way with the story of the last days of King Zedekiah. The books of Kings and Chronicles both contain these details. Jeremiah has himself referred to the event before (39:1–7). Because of this some have suggested that this chapter happily could have been left out of the Bible. It is without doubt an historical appendix or an editorial edition, but there is no doubt too that God puts it here for a purpose.

The story tells how Zedekiah (who at this point was Nebuchadnezzar's deputy) rebelled against the Babylonian oppression, and how Nebuchadnezzar came to put down the rebellion and lay siege to Jerusalem. The chapter records the removal of the furnishings from the Temple and the execution of some of Jerusalem's leading citizens. It ends with the much later release of Jehoiachin who became a recipient of the king's favour.

I found myself wondering as I came to the end of these meditations: why doesn't the book end as it began with some reference to Jeremiah? I would have liked to have known how and where he died. But then it occurred to me – the book is not so much about Jeremiah as about the word that came to Jeremiah. So this closing chapter is very appropriate, as it shows how events turned out exactly as predicted in God's Word. We can be sure that whatever God says will happen. The divine Word has always been fulfilled, is always fulfilled and will always be fulfilled. Nations come and nations go but God's Word endures forever. Hold firmly to it!

**FURTHER STUDY**

Matt. 24:35;
Psa. 119:89;
Isa. 40:6–8;
1 Pet. 1:13–25

1. What did Jesus declare?
2. What picture did Isaiah give that Peter quotes?

## Prayer

O God, I am thankful that Your Word is truth. It is my joy, my daily bread. I trust that Word, and build my life on it. Help me to know it better and deeper day by day. In Jesus' Name. Amen.

# Average or excellent?

*"Some faced jeers and flogging, while still others were chained and put in prison."* (v.36)

**For reading & meditation – Hebrews 11:32–40**

At the end of our reflections on the prophecy of Jeremiah, what is our conclusion? Surely it must be – when life seems unexciting we must remind ourselves that nothing is more important than doing the work of God. We can opt for the average or we can pursue excellence. Excellence does not always mean the adventurous. It means doing God's work faithfully, industriously and without cutting corners.

Whenever I think of Jeremiah I think of Sir Winston Churchill's picturesque remarks concerning one of the generals who led the Russian armies against Germany in World War II. "He reminded me of a frozen peg hammered into the ground, firm, solid, immovable." We can all choose how we will live – cautiously or courageously. Which one will it be for you? The Word of the Lord came to Jeremiah and despite bouts of discouragement and inward struggles he rose through it all to pursue the task God had given him.

Has the Word of the Lord come to you? Has God spoken into your life and given you clear direction concerning the path He

FURTHER STUDY

Phil. 3:1–21;
Acts 20:24;
Gal. 6:9

1. What one thing
does Paul do?
2. What is his appeal
to the saints at
Philippi?

wants you to go? Then go for it – and never give up. Doing the work of God faithfully is the excellence He looks for. The Word of the Lord is your strength. Give Him praise and honour and glory. Flannery O'Connor, the writer, once said that he had an aunt who thought nothing happened in a story unless somebody got married or shot. Jeremiah doesn't get married and he doesn't get shot. But a lot happened in his story because he gave it all to God.

## Prayer

Father, thank You for all You have taught me through Jeremiah. Now I go out to live faithfully too. In Your strength, may I pursue excellence in all I do. In Jesus' Name. Amen.

# The Care of
# the Soul

# In God's gymnasium

*"... train yourself to be godly."*
(v.7)

**For reading & meditation – 1 Timothy 4:1–16**

To get rid of all flabbiness and to be lean and fit spiritually should be the aim of every disciple of Christ's. "The biggest problem in the contemporary Church," says one writer, "is that Christians regularly report unfit for duty. And a big part of their unfitness results from lack of spiritual exercise."

We keep our physical bodies in trim by exercising. It is a well-known fact that to lose excess weight it is helpful to engage in physical exercise – jogging, weight-lifting – as well as dieting. And just as physical exercises increase the body's fitness and health, so spiritual exercises improve spiritual fitness and vitality. The Authorised Version of the Bible translates the verse before us today in this way: "Exercise thyself rather unto godliness." The word "exercise" in Greek is *gumnazo*, from which our English words "gymnasium" and "gymnastics" are derived.

In this theme, therefore, I am inviting you to join with me in enrolling in God's gymnasium to start a spiritual exercise programme that hopefully will result in us being spiritually fitter than ever before. Clearly, as our text for today makes plain, godliness does not just happen. We have to train ourselves for it. Over a century and a half ago the famous Scottish preacher "Rabbi" Duncan, when encouraging his students to read the works of John Owen, told them to "prepare for the knife". The challenge facing us as we begin this theme is not so much to "prepare for the knife" as to "prepare for a workout". There is no other way to find health for the soul.

| FURTHER STUDY |
| --- |
| 1 Cor. 9:19–27; Gal. 5:7; Phil. 3:14; Heb. 12:1 |
| 1. What does Paul liken the Christian life to? |
| 2. What is his own response? |

## Prayer

O Father, help me rise to this challenge. I want to be fitter than ever this year – fit to carry out Your purposes. May all spiritual flabbiness, all excess spiritual weight be trimmed by exercising my soul. In Jesus' Name. Amen.

# Right acts – wrong motives

*"But by the grace of God I am what I am ..."*
*(v.10)*

### For reading & meditation – 1 Corinthians 15:1–11

Christians are likely to fall into one of two errors over developing godliness: to depend on ecstatic spiritual experiences, or to depend on disciplined effort. Relying solely on either is wrong. Though ecstatic spiritual experiences are to be treasured, it is a mistake to use them as the basis for spiritual growth. Then to regard disciplined self-advancing effort as the secret of becoming a godly person is also an error. It is possible to do right but for the wrong reason.

I have known many Christians who were meticulous in reading two or three chapters of the Bible daily, working through a prayer list, and so on. However, they practised these disciplines not out of gratitude for the grace that saved them but to advance themselves. In other words, they came to depend more on their spiritual exercises for progress in godliness than they did on the grace of God. This is the worst kind of legalism. I think it is safe to say the apostle Paul was one of the most disciplined disciples in history, yet in the text before us today he gave the credit for his spiritual progress not to his disciplined living but to the grace of God: "by the grace of God I am what I am".

**FURTHER STUDY**

Rom. 9:1–16;
Gal. 3:3;
Rom. 11:6;
Titus 3:7

1. What does Paul underline to the Romans?
2. What does Paul chide the Galatians for?

One of the things we must guard against continually is the tendency to place greater emphasis on what we do for God than on what He has done for us. Where is your dependency? The more we learn and understand, the more likely it is that we will depend on our knowledge rather than the grace of God.

## Prayer

Father, although it is right to appreciate what I am taught and then understand, help me not to rely on this, but may I totally depend on You. By grace I was saved, and by grace I am sustained. Thank You my Father. Amen.

# Dependable disciples

*"... do not use your freedom to indulge the sinful nature ..." (v.13)*

**For reading & meditation – Galatians 5:1–15**

Now that we have made it clear that we should depend on Christ, not on ourselves, we are ready to focus on the need for disciplined living. Some Christians shy away from the word "discipline" because it smacks of lack of freedom and harsh rituals. Where there is no discipline there are no dependable disciples. In order to draw our life and strength from God, we must be disciplined. Often "free grace" has been preached in such a way that it has weakened character. Paul warns against this in the passage before us today: "do not use your freedom to indulge the sinful nature". The Galatian converts were in danger of turning liberty into licence. Discipline was needed.

The gift of grace is a blessed privilege but our lives have to be permeated with discipline too. I am fond of the story of the woman who went to a healing service in her Anglican church and was instantly made better. A few days later she said: "Lord, you have healed me of paralysis of the legs. What are You going to do about my overweight?" The answer seemed to come as she opened up her Bible and read: "This kind goeth not out but by prayer and fasting" (Matt. 17:21, AV). Where only dependence could bring results, that was the answer. Where only discipline could bring results, that was the answer.

The effective Christian life is a balanced life. Being dependent means we draw our life from Another; being disciplined means we pay attention to the ways by which we draw from that Other. Dependence plus discipline makes dependable disciples.

**FURTHER STUDY**

Rom. 5:12–20;
6:1–4;
1 Pet. 2:16;
2 Cor. 3:17

1. Define the difference between liberty and licence.
2. What is Paul adamant about?

## Prayer

My Father and my God, You have shown me my need to be dependent on You, and I accept that. You are showing me too my need for discipline. May I also accept that – wholeheartedly. In Jesus' Name. Amen.

# Discipline without direction

*"For those God foreknew he also predestined to be conformed to the likeness of his Son ..."* (v.29)

**For reading & meditation – Romans 8:28–39**

It is hard to be a disciplined person unless one sees the point of discipline. "Discipline without direction," says Donald Whitney, "is drudgery."

A story tells of a schoolgirl doing piano exercises while her friends were playing outside. She found the task tiresome. Suddenly she was visited by an angel who whisked her away to a concert hall. There she watched a young woman playing, holding the audience enthralled by her virtuoso performance. "Who is that amazing pianist?" the young girl asked the angel. "That," came the reply, "is you in a few years' time." From then on, the girl had an entirely different attitude to her daily piano practice.

When it comes to discipline in the Christian life many believers feel that practice is tiresome. But how different when we see the direction in which discipline takes us. Our reading today informs us that we are predestined to be made like Christ – God's grace is working in our lives.

But if we are *predestined* to be conformed to Christ's image, what need is there of discipline? Because it is through discipline that we assent to God's purposes for our lives. Just as Zacchaeus put himself in a position where he could see Jesus, so spiritual discipline puts us in a position where we will receive the grace that flows from the heart of our Saviour. C.H. Spurgeon put it well when he said: "I must take care above all that I cultivate communion with Christ, for though that can never be the basis for my peace ... it will be the channel of it."

**FURTHER STUDY**

2 Cor. 3:1–18;
1 Cor. 15:49;
Phil. 3:21;
2 Pet. 1:3–4

1. What has God's divine power given us?
2. What does the divine nature enable us to do?

## Prayer

O Father, thank You for reminding me again that Your biggest single purpose for my life is to make me like Jesus. I am predestined for this and I will co-operate with You. You will do Your part, help me do mine. Amen.

# Love that "springs"

*"The goal of this command is love, which comes from a
pure heart and a good conscience and a sincere faith."* (v.5)

**For reading & meditation – 1 Timothy 1:1–11**

The Christian way is often referred to as "The Christian
Discipline". Translator James Moffatt worded our text for today:
"… the aim of the Christian discipline is the love that springs from
a pure heart, from a good conscience, and from a sincere faith." We
don't usually connect discipline with spontaneity, but this is what
the apostle Paul seems to be doing here. Discipline produces a love
that "springs", he says.

We are predestined to be conformed to the image of Jesus. Has
there ever been anyone more disciplined and yet more free than
Jesus? Yet He was free because He was disciplined. Society today has
a false idea of freedom. "I am free to do as I *like*," is a comment
frequently heard. But the true Christian says, "I am free to do as I
*ought*." A young student said to his teacher: "Sir, this is supposed to
be a free country. I'm told to study. And I *have* to do it. Where's the
freedom in that?" He was serious – and in serious trouble with
himself. Liberty comes from obedience to law. No law – no liberty.
That is the way life works.

Love can "spring" only as it comes from a
pure heart, a good conscience and a sincere faith.
In other words, from a life that has discipline. Any
supposed freedom that leaves you with an impure
heart, a bad conscience, and an insincere faith
ends not with a love that springs but with a love
that sighs. And a love that sighs soon dies. A
disciplined person has a love that springs – and a
love that sings.

FURTHER STUDY

John 14:15–21;
Matt. 7:24;
James 1:25

1. What did Jesus say
about love and
obedience?
2. How does James
describe the law and
its results?

## Prayer

Father, help me grasp the fact that freedom and discipline are not mutually
exclusive. I am free not to do as I like but to do as I ought. Drive this truth deep
into my spirit I pray. In Christ's Name. Amen.

# God's only published work

*"All Scripture is God-breathed ...useful for teaching, rebuking, correcting and training in righteousness ..."* (v.16)

**For reading & meditation – 2 Timothy 3:12–17**

Godly people are *disciplined* people. Call to mind the names of some of the heroes of Christian history – Augustine, Martin Luther, John Calvin, John Bunyan, John Wesley, George Whitefield, Charles Haddon Spurgeon, George Muller, Billy Graham – and what do you find? All were disciplined people. I have never known a man or woman who evidenced a high degree of spiritual fitness who was not a disciplined person.

• What is one of the first things we must discipline ourselves to do if we are to train ourselves for godliness? It is to have a regular (preferably daily) intake from the Word of God. No spiritual exercise is more important than reading, studying and meditating on the Scriptures. Someone has described this as "The first exercise of the soul." The Bible is God's one and only published work. Other books may draw their inspiration from the Scriptures, but the Bible is the only book that has upon it the stamp of divine infallibility. Would you like to know who God is and what He is like? Do you want to know how to live a life that pleases the Lord? The information essential for answering such questions cannot be found anywhere else.

**FURTHER STUDY**

Psa. 119:33–48;
119:72; 119:97;
119:140

1. What was the psalmist's prayer?
2. What was his promise?

If we are to know God and train ourselves for godliness we must dip into the Word of God frequently. The number of committed Christians who spend time studying the Bible daily, or even regularly, is astonishingly low. If all the Christians who neglect regular reading of the Word of God were to blow the dust off their Bibles simultaneously we would probably experience the greatest dust storm in history.

## Prayer

Father, I already realise the importance of exposing my soul to Your Word regularly, but help me become even more deeply convinced of this. May Your Word be my "necessary food". In Jesus' Name. Amen.

# *Hearing* the Word of God

*"Until I come, devote yourself to the public reading of
Scripture, to preaching and to teaching." (v.14)*

**For reading & meditation – 1 Timothy 4:1–16**

The soul needs to be exercised just as much as the body, and one
of the most important exercises is to absorb the Word of God
daily or at least regularly. In many Christian meetings or services
little or no place is given to the public reading of the Scriptures. I
have been in several churches recently where there was a great deal
of music, singing and worship, but not once were the congregation
asked to remain silent and listen to the reading of the Word of God.
I feel deeply saddened about this omission in some Christian circles.

A verse in Romans 10 says: "faith comes from hearing the
message, and the message is heard through the word of Christ"
(v.17). That does not mean a person can come to faith in Christ only
by *hearing* Scripture for, as history shows, multitudes have come to
know the Lord through reading it for themselves. What Paul is
emphasising is the need to preach and teach God's message, and part
of that commission is to deliver the precise words of Scripture.
Many a time as I have listened to the Bible being read in church I
have picked up something through the reader's emphasis on a
particular word – something I had missed in my
personal reading of the Scriptures.

It is important for God's people to sing, praise
and worship Him but it is also important for them
to hear His Word. We must exercise ourselves to
listen to that Word. But how can we do that if,
when we go to church or a meeting, the Bible is
not read?

**FURTHER STUDY**

Luke 4:14–21;
Matt. 21:42;
Rev. 1:3

1. What example did
   Jesus set?
2. What challenging
   questions did Jesus
   put to His listeners?

## Prayer

O Father, awaken Your Church to the importance of publicly reading Your
Word – the Word that is greater than men's words. Help us give it its rightful
place in our midst. In Christ's Name. Amen.

# Reading the Bible

*"Man does not live on bread alone, but on every word that comes from the mouth of God." (v.4)*

**For reading & meditation – Matthew 4:1–11**

T he daily or regular intake of the Scriptures is not only "the first exercise of the soul"; it is also the broadest. A Gallup Poll conducted some years ago in the USA concluded that no factor is more influential in shaping a person's moral and social behaviour than regular *reading* of the Bible. If you want to become more like Jesus and reflect His character then discipline yourself to read the Scriptures. Some pastors told me recently that they had discovered many people object to emphasis on the need to read the Bible daily on the grounds that it is legalistic. One pastor said: "I dare not use the word 'daily' in reference to Bible reading because if I did it would bring howls of protest."

John Blanchard writes, in *How to Enjoy the Bible*: "Surely we have to be realistic and honest with ourselves to know how regularly we need to turn to the Bible. How often do we face problems, temptations and pressures? *Every day!* How often do we need instruction, guidance and greater encouragement? *Every day!* How often do we need to hear God's voice, feel His touch, know His power? The answer to all these questions is the same: *Every day!*"

But perhaps the great American preacher D.L. Moody put it best when he said: "A man can no more take in a supply of grace for the future than he can eat enough for the next six months or take sufficient air into his lungs at one time to last a week."

**FURTHER STUDY**

Job 23:1–12;
Deut. 8:3;
Psa. 119:103;
Jer. 15:16;
1 Pet. 2:2

1. What was Job able to testify?
2. What was Jeremiah's testimony?

## Prayer

Father, I see I have to draw on your boundless store of grace, some of which comes to me only as I read Your Word, from hour by hour and day by day. I see this but help me live by it. In Christ's Name I pray. Amen.

# "Every day with Jesus"

*"Now the Bereans were of more noble character ... for they ... examined the Scriptures every day ..."* (v.11)

**For reading & meditation – Acts 17:1–15**

Hearing and reading the Word of God are important and effective spiritual exercises. So also is *studying* it. Reading the Bible has been likened to cruising the width of a lake with clear waters while studying the Bible is like slowly crossing the same lake in a glass-bottomed boat. Jerry Bridges expressed it in this way: "Reading gives us breadth; but study gives us depth."

In the passage before us today we find that Paul and Silas, having provoked the Jews at Thessalonica by their effective evangelism, were forced to flee to save their lives. They escaped to Berea, where their message met with a completely different response. The Bereans, we read: "were of more noble character than the Thessalonians, for they ... examined the Scriptures every day to see if what Paul said was true." Willingness to examine the Scriptures is here commended as revealing a noble character.

The daily readings in *Every Day with Jesus* will help prime your spiritual pump at the start of the day, but you will remain spiritually impoverished if you rely solely on these. The more you study the Bible the more you will grow. When the apostle Paul was languishing in prison and anticipating the arrival of his young friend Timothy he said: "When you come, bring the cloak ... especially the parchments" (2 Tim. 4:13). In cold and miserable conditions the apostle asked for two things: something for his body and something for his soul. Paul had witnessed some wonderful events and had touched heaven, but he still wanted to delve into the Word of God until the day he died.

**FURTHER STUDY**

Rom. 15:1–4;
1 Cor. 10:1–13;
Deut. 17:18–19;
John 5:31–40

1. Why does Paul say the Scriptures are given to us?
2. What did Jesus declare of the Scriptures?

## Prayer

O Father, give me the same desire that Paul had, I pray: to delve into Your Word and explore its mysteries and wonders until the day I die. Help me discipline myself to find the necessary time. In Jesus' Name. Amen.

# Read less – meditate more

*"My heart grew hot within me, and as I meditated,
the fire burned …" (v.3)*

**For reading & meditation – Psalm 39:1–13**

No principle of Scripture is more important than that of meditating on what God has written in the Bible. People often ask me how I am able to come up with so many themes in the *Every Day with Jesus* series. Meditation is the answer. The more I meditate on Scripture the more I become conscious of important themes.

One of the tragedies of our day is that meditation is linked more to non-Christian systems of belief than it is with biblical Christianity. I have heard Christians warn: "Meditation has its roots in Eastern mysticism." There is a vast difference between, say, transcendental meditation and biblical meditation. Meditation is deep focused thinking. It involves taking a text, putting it like a sweet on your tongue and holding it there until you have sucked every precious drop of spiritual liquid from it. Only about 1 per cent of Christians engage in this spiritual exercise. How sad. We read the Word, study it – both good spiritual exercises – but we will never get the best out of it until we know how to meditate on it.

The added exercise of meditation acts like bellows on a little flame and transforms it into a blazing fire.

**FURTHER STUDY**

Josh. 1:1–8;
Psa. 1:2; 19:14;
119:148; 143:5

*1. What injunction was given to Joshua?
2. What was the psalmist's request?*

Thomas Watson, a Puritan pastor, said: "Why does the Word of God so often leave us cold, and why don't we have more success in our spiritual life? The reason we come away so cold from reading the Word is because we do not warm ourselves at the fire of meditation." Here's one of the most helpful pieces of advice I can give: read less and meditate more.

## Prayer

Father, I love Your Word. I love to read it daily, but forgive me that I fail to meditate on it enough. Help me to re-establish my priorities so that I give less time to other matters and more to this. In Christ's Name. Amen.

# Regular respiration

*"Then Jesus told his disciples a parable to show them
that they should always pray and not give up." (v.1)*

**For reading & meditation – Luke 18:1–8**

If the hearing, reading, study and meditation of the Word of God combine to form the first spiritual exercise, what is the second? It is *prayer*.

Throughout the history of the Christian Church, people have always given the matter of prayer a high priority. In the Acts of the Apostles we read that the first Christians devoted themselves to (1) the apostles' teaching, (2) the fellowship, (3) the breaking of bread, (4) *prayer* (Acts 2:42). John Wesley stressed the importance of these four spiritual exercises and added to them one more: fasting. In medieval times the Church advocated nine. Richard Foster in his book *Celebration of Discipline* mentions twelve spiritual exercises. In this theme I am focusing on ten. But however many spiritual exercises we undertake, if the reading of Scripture and prayer are not the foremost then we will benefit little from practising the others.

One of the major reasons for lack of godliness is prayerlessness. A tiger's first objective when it attacks another animal is to slit its throat with its sharp claws. When the animal is no longer able to breathe it is finished. Satan, the enemy of our souls, follows this same strategy in his attack on us. If he can stop us breathing spiritually by preventing us from praying, then we become powerless and a plaything in his hands.

Do you long to be a godly person? Fine. But remember, whatever else you do and however many Christian meetings you attend there can be no advance towards godliness unless you give time to prayer.

**FURTHER STUDY**

Matt. 26:36–41;
1 Chron. 16:11;
Luke 18:1–8;
Eph. 6:18

1. What is the antidote to temptation?
2. What did Paul admonish the Ephesians?

## Prayer

Gracious Father, help me to give no place to the devil, especially in this matter of prayer. May I constantly replenish my spiritual life through prayer. In Jesus' Name. Amen.

# God's "VLE"

*"Call to me and I will answer you and tell you great and unsearchable things you do not know." (v.3)*

**For reading & meditation – Jeremiah 33:1–9**

"There is no more certain way of making Christians feel guilty," said Dr Martyn Lloyd-Jones on one occasion, "than by asking them how much time they spend in prayer." God delights in talking to us – our text for today makes that clear. But how eager are we to talk to Him?

I once watched a television programme that reported on the setting up of a large radio receiver in New Mexico, designed to pick up any signals that might come from life-forms in outer space. It has been named the "VLE – Very Large Ear". I thought to myself as I watched: I wonder how many of those scientists realise that a word has already come to us from the heavenly realm – a Word made flesh in the Person of God's Son. But not only has God spoken to us in Christ; He has made it possible for us to speak to Him. One writer commenting on the VLE in New Mexico said: "God too has a VLE – a Very Large Ear." And that ear, I might add, is continually open to us. He hears even the weakest and faintest of cries. I love the way Ethel Romig Fuller puts it in her poem:

**FURTHER STUDY**

Psa. 91:1–16;
Isa. 58:9; 65:24;
John 15:1–8

1. Why are we confident about prayer?
2. What is Jesus teaching in this passage?

*If radio's slim fingers can pluck a melody*
*From night – and toss it over a continent or sea,*
*If songs like crimsoned roses are culled from*
*    thin blue air,*
*Why should mortals wonder if God hears*
*    and answers prayer?*

# Prayer

Father, I do not wonder for I have often gone to my knees feeling defeated and have risen again victorious. I am more grateful than I can say for the privilege of being able to talk to You in prayer. Thank You my Father. Amen.

# Christ *expects* us to pray

*"He said to them, 'When you pray, say: "Father,
hallowed be your name ..."'" (v.2)*

**For reading & meditation – Luke 11:1–13**

The Gospels reveal quite clearly that Jesus thought those who
loved God would want to read His Word and pray. Several times
He asked people questions that went right to the heart of their
understanding of the Scriptures, beginning with the words: "Haven't
you read ...?" He assumed that those who professed to love God
would have read the Scriptures. That same assumption was made in
relation to the matter of prayer. In our text for today our Lord says:
"When you pray ..." Note: not *if* you pray but *when* you pray.

Prayer is not optional. Whether or not we think prayer is a good
idea is irrelevant – Christ *expects* us to pray. We live in an age when
people don't much like being told what to do. When we become
Christians, we submit to Christ's commands, one of which, as we
have seen, is that we should always pray (Luke 18:1). A Christian
who doesn't pray is being insubordinate. Prayerlessness is in effect
reacting to Christ's statement "You should always pray" with the
attitude "I don't care what You say, I am not going to do it." What if
Christ appeared to you right now and said to you: "I expect you to
pray, regularly and often?" How would you
respond? Would you not immediately extend
your prayer time with Him, knowing that He
personally expected and asked that of you? What
He has said in His Word about prayer conveys His
will for you as strongly as if He appeared to you in
your room and spoke to you personally.

| FURTHER STUDY |
| :--- |
| Phil. 4:1–7; |
| 1 Thess. 5:17; |
| 1 Tim. 2:8; |
| Col. 4:2–3 |
| |
| 1. What was Paul's |
| exhortation to the |
| Thessalonians? |
| 2. What was Paul's |
| instruction to the |
| Colossians? |

## Prayer

Gracious Father, help me not to wriggle when I am cornered like this. You
challenge me in order to change me. Help me deepen my prayer life and expand
my times of communion with You. In the Saviour's Name I pray. Amen.

# *Every prayer answered*

*"Before they call I will answer; while they are still speaking I will hear …"* (v.24)

**For reading & meditation – Isaiah 65:17–25**

If prayer is of such prime importance, why do some of us pray so little? One reason is lack of discipline. Prayer is not planned. It is fitted in around other things. Build other things around your prayer time rather than building your prayer time around other things.

For some people another reason may be that they doubt if anything happens as a result of prayer. I have never heard anyone admit this publicly, but I have often heard it mentioned behind the sound-proofed walls of a counselling room – even by those with a long experience of the Christian life. We need to remember that prayer is not like putting money in a slot machine and getting immediate results. Sometimes the results are instant but more commonly they are not. Many times prayer is answered in a way that we human beings cannot see or understand. But God hears and answers *every* prayer. He does so by giving us what we asked for, by saying "No" because what we have requested is not good for us, by giving us something different, or by answering our prayer in a way that is beyond our comprehension.

Yet another reason why we do not pray more is because of self-sufficiency. Many reading these words will have received a fairly good education. As a consequence life seems manageable and prayer is made only when something happens that is far too big to handle. Jesus said: "Apart from me you can do nothing" (John 15:5). Nothing really matters unless He is in it. And if He isn't then it doesn't really matter at all.

**FURTHER STUDY**

2 Chron. 7:1–14;
Jer. 29:13;
James 5:16;
1 John 3:22

1. What precedes prayer?
2. What kind of prayer is effective?

# Prayer

O teach me to pray, for if I fall down here I fall down everywhere – anaemia weakens my whole being. Give me the mind to pray, the will to pray and the love to pray. In Jesus' Name. Amen.

# An important secret

*"… in everything, by prayer and petition, with
thanksgiving, present your requests to God." (v.6)*

**For reading & meditation – Philippians 4:1–9**

If you are feeling discouraged by your disinclination to obey our
Lord's command to pray then let me share with you a way of
overcoming this reluctance. It will take a little discipline, but the
rewards will far outweigh the effort.

The secret is to begin your prayer time with meditation. I
learned this many years ago from the writings of George Muller,
who said that the practise of meditating on Scripture before
beginning his prayer time transformed his relationship with the
Lord. "For the first ten years of my Christian life," he wrote, "my
habit was to wash and dress myself, then turn to prayer." But often
he felt his prayer time was tedious and boring. Then, as he changed
his approach to prayer by first reading the Word of God and
*meditating* on it, he found his heart would leap toward prayer almost
of its own accord. He would speak to God about the things he had
discovered in the Word and never again did he find prayer
wearisome. Those who must have discovered this secret also were
the Puritans who lived in the sixteenth and seventeenth centuries.

Richard Baxter advocated this method, John
Owen (chaplain to Oliver Cromwell) made the
same recommendation, and so did Matthew
Henry, the famous Bible commentator.

Permit me now to lay this challenge before
you: as our Lord expects us to pray, and to pray
often, are you prepared to look at your prayer life
and make a fresh evaluation of it? Our Lord
prayed much. Do you want to be like Him? Then
discipline yourself to be a person of prayer.

FURTHER STUDY
Luke 5:1–16;
Mark 1:35;
6:46–47; Luke
6:12; 9:18

1. What was Jesus'
pattern of prayer?
2. What is your
pattern of prayer?

## Prayer

Gracious Father, I cannot pray as I ought unless Your Spirit inspires me, so that
I may more and more pray according to Your will. I would live a Spirit-inspired
life hence a Spirit-empowered life. In Jesus' Name. Amen.

# "Worth-ship"

*"You are worthy, our Lord and God, to receive glory
and honour and power ..." (v.11)*

**For reading & meditation – Revelation 4:1–11**

Yet another important spiritual exercise is *worship*. Some Bible teachers are hesitant to call worship a discipline as (so they claim) it is not something that can be generated. "Worship is the response of a heart in love with God," says one writer, "which is more spontaneous than calculated, more responsive than predicted." I take a slightly different view.

Worship most certainly is "the response of a heart in love with God", but how does the heart become filled with love for God? Though we do not develop love for God by self-effort we can focus the soul's attention on God, His attributes and character. The more we focus on God the more responsive we become to Him, and thus the more godly. Thus we can train ourselves to be godly by commanding our souls to stand to attention before God, to focus on Him and reflect on His love, His holiness and His glory.

But what really is worship? How can it be understood. And how different is it from prayer and praise? The word "worship", as you might know, comes from the Saxon word "weorthscype" which later became "worthship", now *worship*. So worship is ascribing proper worth to God, exalting Him and regarding Him as being deserving of adoration and honour. Notice how in the passage before us today the twenty-four elders laid their crowns before the throne and cried: "You are *worthy*, our Lord and God, to receive glory and honour and power ..." The soul knows nothing of worship unless it has a deep understanding of the Almighty's intrinsic worth.

**FURTHER STUDY**

1 Chron. 16:8–36;
Psa. 96:8–9;
Rev. 5:6–14

*1. What do you understand by the word "worship"?*
*2. Think of 5 other words that mean "worship".*

## Prayer

O God, my soul was made to worship. This is the purpose for which I was created. Teach me how to worship You with all my heart. In Jesus' Name. Amen.

# In awe of God

*"My ears had heard of you but now my eyes have seen you." (v.5)*

### For reading & meditation – Job 42:1–6

The more we understand how worthy God is the more our souls are filled with awe. Have you noticed how infrequently the word "awe" is used nowadays? A well-known British psychiatrist, Dr Anthony Claire, said: "One of the things that troubles me about this present generation is that it seems to have lost its sense of awe." He was speaking about society in general, but I wonder whether we in the Christian Church have not similarly lost our sense of awe in relation to divine things.

Another psychiatrist, Dr John White, says: "During the past century God has been trivialised, packaged for entertainment, presented as a sort of psychological panacea, a heavenly glue to keep happy families together, a celestial slot machine to respond to our whims, a formula for success, a fund raiser for pseudo-religious enterprises, a slick phrase for bumper stickers, and a sort of holy pie and ice cream. How impoverished this all is, how virtually blasphemous when compared to the experiences recorded in Scripture."

It is probably right to assume that most believers know how to pray and praise, but how often do we stand in awe before God? As is clear from our reading today Job developed a sense of awe as a result of God's dealings with him. Daniel responded similarly. After God had addressed him he said: "I stood up trembling" (Dan. 10:11). Do we ever tremble before God? We will never be able to truly convey to others what God means to us unless we know what it is to stand in awe before Him and tremble at His glory.

**FURTHER STUDY**

Psa. 33:1–8;
Ex. 3:5; 15:1–21;
Psa. 89:7; Dan. 9:4

1. What question did Miriam pose? How did she answer it?
2. How did Daniel describe God?

## Prayer

O God, I ask myself: Am I in awe of You? I love You, praise You, and pray to You, but am I in awe of You? Grant that my familiarity with You will not blunt my need to see You as an awesome God. Amen.

# Worship – God's right

*"For great is the Lord and most worthy of praise;*
*he is to be feared above all gods." (v.25)*

**For reading & meditation – 1 Chronicles 16:7–36**

Bible teachers recognise that worship is easier to describe than define, so my definition is not the last word on the subject: worship is focusing on the greatness, glory and supreme worth of God and responding to Him in adoration.

C.S. Lewis spoke in *Reflections on the Psalms* about his difficulty with the idea that it was God's "right" to be praised. But the more he thought it through the more he came to realise what was meant. Lewis put it: "What do we mean when we say that a picture is 'admirable'? We certainly don't mean that it is admired (that's as may be) for bad work is admired by thousands and good work may be ignored. Nor that it 'deserves' admiration in the sense in which a candidate 'deserves' a high mark from the examiners – i.e. that a human being will have suffered injustice if it is not awarded. The sense in which the picture 'deserves' or 'demands' admiration is rather this; admiration is the correct, adequate, or appropriate, response to it, that, if paid, admiration will not be 'thrown away', and that if we do not admire we shall be stupid, insensible, and great losers, we shall have missed something."

**FURTHER STUDY**

Psa. 99:1–9;
Isa. 6:1–3;
Phil. 2:1–11;
Rev. 4:11

*1. Why is God worthy of worship?*
*2. How can we ascribe to God His true worth?*

All right-minded people respond to beauty with admiration. Just as a glorious sunset evokes a spontaneous response, so the soul cannot encounter the worthiness of God without responding in true worship. If, at this moment, you could catch a glimpse of how worthy God is, how beautiful His character, how glorious His nature, the inevitable consequence would be that you would fall on your face and worship Him.

## Prayer

O Father, help me contemplate Your glory, Your character, Your power and Your might in such a way that I will be humbled and fall in awe before You. This I ask in the Saviour's peerless and precious Name. Amen.

# "In spirit and in truth"

*"For it is we who ... worship by the Spirit of God ..."*
*(v.3)*

### For reading & meditation – Philippians 3:1–11

John, in his vision, recorded in the book of Revelation, saw those around the throne bowing in worship. But you say: "I am not in heaven so such a response cannot be expected of me." It is true you are not in heaven, but it is still possible to focus on God's worth and respond similarly.

God reveals Himself to us in many different ways. Creation is just one of them. Who hasn't been thrilled at some aspect of creation and thought: Only a great and mighty God could have made this? God has made Himself known to us also through the Person of His Son, the Lord Jesus Christ. He came to this earth, lived and died, rose again, and ascended to the Father. Another way in which God reveals Himself to us is through His Word, the Bible. As we read the Scriptures the Holy Spirit opens the eyes of our understanding and what we see of God causes our soul to respond to Him in adoration.

Our Lord said to the woman at the well: "God is spirit, and his worshippers must worship in spirit and in truth" (John 4:24). How do we worship "in spirit and in truth"? We do so when we have the Spirit of God within us and live our lives according to the truth contained in the Scriptures. That is why meditation on God's Word is an essential prerequisite not only for prayer but also for worship. There is a sense in which all acts of obedience are acts of worship, but worship reaches its highest point when God is being contemplated.

**FURTHER STUDY**

Psa. 95:1–11;
Gen. 17:3;
Ex. 34:8;
2 Chron. 20:18;
Matt. 2:11

1. What does the psalmist invite us to do?
2. How did the visitors to Jesus respond?

## Prayer

God my Father, You are teaching me how to pray; teach me also how to worship. Help me contemplate You in such a way that my soul is filled with admiration, with awe, and with worship. In Jesus' Name. Amen.

# Praise and worship

*"Within your temple, O God, we meditate on your unfailing love."* (v.9)

**For reading & meditation – Psalm 48:1–14**

The more we focus on what the Bible has to say about God the greater will be our response in worship. This is why in both public and private worship an appropriate reading from Scripture is an essential prerequisite to divine worship. By "appropriate" I mean a passage that opens up our understanding of who God is, not just what He does. The psalm we have read today is one such example.

Prayer involves talking to God and God talking to you. Praise is thanking God for the things He has done, is doing, and is going to do. Worship is adoring God not so much for what He does but for who He is. Before I worship I focus on some of the attributes of God – such as love, holiness, righteousness, power and grace. And as I meditate the fire burns and my soul soars in adoration of God.

Some Christians think of worship as something they do only on Sundays when they meet with other Christians in church. This is a false view of worship. A.W. Tozer said: "If you will not worship God seven days a week you do not worship Him on one day a week." We cannot expect to enter into worship on the Lord's Day if worship has not flowed from our hearts over the preceding six days. Corporate worship must never be a substitute for individual worship. If we could interview the great saints of the past and ask them to share their experiences with us they would all agree, I am sure, that training ourselves to worship leads to increased godliness.

**FURTHER STUDY**

Psa. 47:1–9;
63:2–5; 134:1–3;
150:1–6;
Eph. 5:19–20

1. List different ways of expressing worship.
2. Are these part of your own expression of worship?

## Prayer

Thank You my Father. I see that worship is different from praise and different from thanksgiving. Help me from this day forward to enter more keenly into the exercise of worship. In Jesus' Name. Amen.

# "Open-doored to God"

*"At daybreak Jesus went out to a solitary place."*
*(v.42)*

**For reading & meditation – Luke 4:38–44**

The next exercise of the soul we shall look at is seeking *solitude*. Extroverts who draw their energy from being with people will find this exercise difficult. However, even if you are an extrovert I would nevertheless urge you to consider its benefits. James Russell Lowell says of solitude:

> *If the chosen soul could never be alone*
> *In deep mid-silence, open-doored to God,*
> *No greatness ever had been dreamed or done;*
> *The nurse of full-grown souls is solitude.*

What does seeking solitude entail? It involves temporarily withdrawing from activity and finding a quiet or private place in order to rest, relax and give oneself to spiritual purposes. It is this giving of oneself to spiritual purposes that differentiates seeking seclusion from having a day out or a brief holiday.

Our Lord often sought solitude. In the passage before us today we find Him involved in a tremendous time of ministry. He healed various kinds of sickness and cast demons out of many people. Crowds flocked to Him for spiritual and physical help. But after all this activity we read: Jesus "went out to a solitary place". At that moment it was more important to discipline Himself to be alone than to continue healing the sick and casting out demons. Involvement with people and ministry to others is important, but so also is solitude. The art is to know which of these is the priority of the moment.

**FURTHER STUDY**

Matt. 14:23; 15:29;
Mark 6:31

1. What discipline had Jesus developed?
2. When did you last spend time in solitude?

## Prayer

Father, it is not always easy to know which should be the priority of the moment. Teach me how to prioritise so that I am engaged in the things that You want me to be engaged in. In Christ's Name I pray. Amen.

# "Islands of solitude"

*"Be silent before the Sovereign Lord, for the day of the Lord is near." (v.7)*

**For reading & meditation – Zephaniah 1:1–13**

"Many of the ills of life," said Blaise Pascal, the seventeenth-century French philosopher, "come from not being able to sit in a room – alone." I wonder what he would say were he alive now. A large section of the population today, especially the young, seem afraid of being alone. They keep up a constant string of words, always have their personal stereos with them, and appear to be more comfortable with noise than with silence.

Jean Fleming, in *Finding Focus in a Whirlwind World* observed: "We live in a noisy busy world. Silence and solitude are not twentieth-century words. They fit the era of Victorian lace, high-button shoes and kerosene lamps better than our age of television, video arcades and joggers wired with earphones. We have become a people with an aversion to quiet and an uneasiness with being alone." Those who do not have what someone has called "islands of solitude" soon become frantic personalities. Kenneth Fearing says of such people:

*And wow they died as wow they lived,*
*Going zoom to the office, and whoosh home to sleep.*

**FURTHER STUDY**

Rev. 7:9–8:1;
Eccl. 3:7;
Hab. 2:20;
Zech. 2:10–13

1. What is part of the worship in heaven?
2. What was Zechariah's injunction to all mankind?

The solitude I am talking about is not taking a break from activities in order to rest and relax but using seclusion for spiritual purposes. Our text for today bids us to "be silent before the Sovereign Lord". That is the reason Jesus found solitude essential. It may be helpful to find a tranquil spot away from noise and other people. But much more is required. We need to be silent before our God.

## Prayer

O God my Father, help me to find an "island of solitude" in the midst of this frantic age in which I live. I see the value of doing so but I need Your guidance in this matter. Help me dear Father. In Jesus' Name. Amen.

# "Not enough silence"

*"And after the fire came a gentle whisper."*
*(v.12)*

**For reading & meditation – 1 Kings 19:9–18**

Those who have practised the exercise of seeking solitude over a number of years talk in terms of hours rather than minutes. One advocate puts it like this: "A day is an ideal time but even half a day can bring rich spiritual rewards. Solitude can be found in a quiet place at home, but wherever possible it is best to get away from home. A different environment can have a dynamic effect on the soul."

So what is the real point of exercising the soul through solitude? The primary purpose is to hear the voice of God more clearly and to equip ourselves to be of better service to others. The Bible fairly bulges with accounts of men and women who had a daily appointment with God yet felt it necessary to find solitude at times in order to hear His voice more clearly. I think of Habbakuk standing at his guard-post, waiting to hear what God would say to him (Hab. 2:1). I think also of Paul making his way into the deserts of Arabia to rethink his theology (Gal. 1:17). Then in the passage before us we see Elijah having a spiritual tête-à-tête with the Almighty and hearing the gentle whisper of His voice.

This is not to say that we have to be alone to hear God's voice. But sometimes we need a time of solitude in order to hear more clearly what God is saying. T.S. Eliot put it thus: "Where shall the world be found, where will the word resound? Not here, there is not enough silence."

FURTHER STUDY

Psa. 46:1–11;
Isa. 30:15;
Job 37:14;
Psa. 4:4

1. When are we best able to know that God is God?
2. What did Elihu exhort Job?

## Prayer

Lord Jesus Christ, if You needed solitude to hear Your Father's voice and discover His will then how much more do I? Help me to add finding time for solitude to my regular spiritual workout. In Jesus' Name. Amen.

# Deepened understanding

*"... Jesus ... said to them, 'Sit here while I go over there and pray.'" (v.36)*

**For reading & meditation – Matthew 26:36–46**

Dietrich Bonhoeffer, in *Life Together*, pointed out that although living in community is important, we often need solitude to serve the community more effectively. He wrote: "Let him who cannot be alone beware of community ... Let him who is not in community beware of being alone ... Each by itself has profound pitfalls and perils. One who wants fellowship without solitude plunges into the void of words and feelings, and one who seeks solitude without fellowship perishes in the abyss of vanity, self-infatuation and despair."

It is in the recreating atmosphere of solitude that we find the resources to be with others more meaningfully. The Puritan Thomas Merton put it equally effectively when he said: "It is in deep solitude that I find the gentleness with which I can truly love my brothers. The more solitary I am the more affection I have for them ... it teaches me to love my brothers for what they are, not what they say."

If we want to be like Jesus – and that is the purpose of every spiritual discipline – then we must get away from people so that we will have more to offer when we are with others. Solitude deepens our understanding of people, increases our compassion, gives us a new freedom from our own concerns and heightens our sensitivity towards others. We are better able to give ourselves to others after giving ourselves to God during times of solitude. If you are saying to yourself now, "This makes sense but I'm too busy," then I would reply that the busier you are the greater your need of solitude.

**FURTHER STUDY**

Gen. 32:1–32;
Psa. 131:2;
Isa. 32:17;
Lam. 3:25–26

1. What was Jacob's experience when he was alone?
2. What was the psalmist able to say?

## Prayer

O Father, You know how busy my life is. I am aware that I am busier than I should be. I need Your help in organising my life so that spiritual exercises take priority over other things. Help me begin today. In Jesus' Name. Amen.

# "Settling down in God"

*"… no hammer, chisel or any other iron tool was heard
at the temple site while it was being built." (v.7)*

**For reading & meditation – 1 Kings 6:1–13**

When Solomon's Temple was being erected, the building blocks were dressed at the quarry so that no tools were heard at the Temple site. We cannot directly compare our souls with the Temple of Solomon but there is a sense in which we – as temples of the Holy Spirit – need to be built up through times of quietness. Plan such times, for if you don't fix dates then they'll be crowded out. No one plans to fail; people fail because they fail to plan. The disciplined person does what needs to be done, when it needs to be done.

All the great men and women of God have been disciplined, including finding time for solitude. I realise that some reading these lines – mothers with families, for example – will find it almost impossible to have an extended period of solitude. My advice is this: do whatever you can. Susannah Wesley, mother of John and Charles Wesley, had a very large family, and although she longed for times when she could be alone with God she found it difficult. When she needed solitude she would pull her apron over her head and "settle down in God" as she put it. This action didn't block out all the noise but it was a sign to her children that she was not to be disturbed.

Remember above all that the purpose of finding solitude is to train the soul for godliness, not to enjoy a break from normal duties. "Nothing great was ever done by anyone," said Francis Schaeffer, "in science, literature, or religion, who did not enjoy and know how to use solitude."

**FURTHER STUDY**

Isa. 30:15–18;
Psa. 116:7;
Matt. 11:29

1. What did the Lord say to the children of Israel?
2. What did Jesus promise?

## Prayer

Father, I must find times when I can "settle down in God". Circumstances may be difficult but I can do something. Help me to have the will for then I know You will help me find the way. Thank You, Father. Amen.

# "Planned neglect"

*"Be very careful, then, how you live ... making the
most of every opportunity ..." (vv.15–16)*

**For reading & meditation – Ephesians 5:1–17**

Another important spiritual exercise in which all Christians
should participate is *stewardship*. My dictionary defines a
steward as "a person who is entrusted with the possessions or
interests of another". Spell the word "another" with a capital "A" –
"Another" – and you have a good definition of Christian
stewardship. All the great theologians of the past have seen
stewardship in terms of three things: time, treasure and talents. No
one can have a soul that is fit and healthy unless it is being exercised
in the proper deployment of all three.

Take the first – *time*. Once, after I had spoken on "Time
Management", a man said: "We have had our insides sandpapered
today." All of us need to be thoroughly sandpapered by the
sandpaper of discipline to make us burnished and fit.

Malcolm Muggeridge, the famous broadcaster and wit, was once
asked what was the first requirement for success. He replied: "A
waste-basket." When pressed to explain what he meant he said:
"Life depends on elimination as well as upon assimilation. One has
to learn what does not contribute – and throw it away." I thank God

**FURTHER STUDY**

Matt. 25:14–30;
1 Cor. 4:1–7;
1 Tim. 6:20;
2 Tim. 1:14;
1 Pet. 4:10

1. What was Jesus
teaching in this
parable?
2. What was Paul's
charge to Timothy?

for my waste-basket. It relieves me every day of
things that would be a serious waste of my time.
People often ask me: "How have you been able to
write *Every Day with Jesus* for over thirty years and
do all the other things you do?" I usually answer:
"By planned neglect." Certain marginal matters
(not family responsibilities) have to be
deliberately neglected in order to focus on the
task in hand. Sometimes the good has to be
sacrificed on the altar of the best.

## Prayer

O Father, help me say "No" to lesser things in order to be free to say "Yes" to
the greater things. And may I understand also that my capacity to say "No"
determines my capacity to say "Yes". In Jesus' Name. Amen.

# The test of time

*"Teach us to number our days aright, that we may gain a heart of wisdom." (v.12)*

**For reading & meditation – Psalm 90:1–17**

Charles Hummel's little pamphlet, *The Tyranny of the Urgent*, has influenced me greatly. In it he pointed out that until we know the difference between the urgent and the important we will never become good stewards of our time. Our lives are often ruled by the urgent because we have never taken the time to put things in their proper order of priority. The man who influenced the world most – our Lord Jesus Christ – was a man with a leisured heart. He was never hurried, never flurried and never worried. But He always had time for the things that mattered.

If I asked you: "What do you propose to do at 5 p.m. yesterday?" what would you say? Probably: "Selwyn, are you mad? Yesterday has come and gone." But what if I were to ask: "What do you intend to do at 5 p.m. tomorrow?" Ah, that's different. The choice can still be made. Time past is time gone, over which we have no control; time to come is time concerning which we must search ourselves because we cannot escape the responsibility of deciding how we will spend it. The use of time subjects us to a test, trying us as silver refined in a furnace.

Will your life be ruled by the important or by the urgent? You can decide. A boy late for school prayed: "Lord, help me be there on time." He ran out of his house but stumbled and fell. "Lord," he said, "I asked You to help me, not push me." Don't let life push you; you will stumble if you do. Discipline your time.

FURTHER STUDY

Psa. 90:1–12;
Eccl. 12:1;
1 Cor. 7:29–31;
Col. 4:5

1. What was the psalmist's request?
2. What was Paul's admonition to the Colossians?

## Prayer

O God, give me the same disciplined, poised life that Jesus had. He never hurried, but always had time for the necessities of the day. Help me manage my time so that I have time for the things that matter. Amen.

# God owns – we owe

*"The earth is the Lord's, and everything in it."*
(v.26)

**For reading & meditation – 1 Corinthians 10:23–33**

Now we think about what we should do with our treasure. I use the word "treasure" not in the usual sense of accumulated wealth but in connection with those things we regard as valuable – possessions, savings, and so on.

When I first became a believer (in my mid-teens) I used to resent people taking up a collection every time I went to church. Once I asked my pastor: "Can't we be followers of Christ without having to give Him access to our money?" I will never forget his reply: "You can't be a follower of Christ unless He has access to everything you have, including your money." At the time I thought the terms were harsh, but I soon came to see that accepting the Bible's guidance on the use of our money is crucial to our growth in godliness. And this is the reason why: the way we use our money is an indication of who we are, how we see our priorities, and what is really in our hearts.

The use of our time (as we saw) is a mark of our spiritual maturity. The same is true of the way we use our money. The first thing we must do is to establish in our minds the fact that God is the owner of everything; we are owers. This means we are managers, or stewards, of what God has given us. The house or apartment you live in is God's property. The car you drive, the clothes you wear, the food you eat – all belong to God. Viewing life in this way can change your entire perspective.

**FURTHER STUDY**

2 Cor. 9:1–15;
Mark 12:41–44;
Deut. 16:17;
Mal. 3:8–10;
2 Cor. 8:12

1. What kind of giver does God love?
2. What was Jesus' teaching to His disciples?

## Prayer

O God my Father, help me walk through every day realising I am not the proprietor but a steward of the resources You have put into my hands. Give me a biblical mindset on this issue I pray. In Christ's Name. Amen.

# Steps to stewardship

*"If anyone asks you, 'Why are you doing this?' tell him,
'The Lord needs it …'" (v.3)*

**For reading & meditation – Mark 11:1–11**

What steps do we need to take to train ourselves to be godly with regard to our possessions? First, settle the issue once and for all: you own nothing. Everything you have is a trust. You must give an account of everything you possess to God. You are not free to manage your belongings as you like, but as *He* likes. Second, acknowledge His ownership by giving one tenth of all earnings. Tithing should be seen as a minimum. God may then guide you to give out of the remaining nine-tenths. Be open to that.

Third, limit your spending to needs, not luxuries disguised as needs. Necessities contribute to life; luxuries choke. If you eat beyond your needs you overload the system and your body puts on useless fat – surplus baggage which you have to carry around. It is the same with money and material things. If you have more than you need invest some of it in people. Give to those who are less fortunate than you. But when you give to others make sure your money will be used wisely.

Fourth, make your will under God's guidance. You have a responsibility to leave something to your family, but consider also leaving something as an investment to be used for the kingdom's purposes. Suppose the owners of the colt we read about in the passage today had said: "You can't have our colt. We need it more than your Master." For the rest of their days they would have had regrets. After they had let Jesus have it, it came back to them – the most famous colt in history.

> **FURTHER STUDY**
>
> Matt. 19:16–24;
> 1 Cor. 16:1–3;
> Matt. 6:3; 10:8
>
> 1. How could the young man deposit treasure in heaven?
> 2. What did Paul admonish the Corinthians to do?

## Prayer

O Father, You have opened the doors of life to me. Help me to open the doors of my heart to others. You have entrusted me with things; I want to be worthy of that trust and use them wisely for You. Amen.

# Saved to serve

*"But I am among you as one who serves."*
(v.27)

**For reading & meditation – Luke 22:7–38**

We consider now the stewardship of our talents. Some limit the use of the word "talent" to the skills with which we are born. When we become Christians, they say, then God adds to our natural abilities certain spiritual gifts, which are specifically designed to be used for the building up and extension of His Church. However, I am using the word "talents" here to cover all our God-given abilities, whether they are seen as natural or supernatural.

Whatever your abilities, *they are given for the purpose of serving others*. In the Bible God's people are referred to not only as His children but as His *servants* also. Recall how Paul starts his letters to the Romans, the Philippians, and his friend Titus: "Paul, a *servant* …" Every Christian is a servant of God, and servants *work*. Paul describes his service to God: "To this end I labour, struggling with all his [God's] energy, which so powerfully works in me" (Col. 1:29). Notice he "struggled" but it was "with all his energy, which so powerfully works in me". God supplies us with the power needed to work for Him.

**FURTHER STUDY**

Mark 10:35–45;
Rom. 12:1–8;
Eph. 6:7;
John 13:14

1. How did Jesus say greatness is achieved?
2. How are we to serve?

Donald G. Bloesch in his book *The Crisis of Piety* says: "The spiritual disciplines are not to be seen as a pretext for separation and isolation from the world … not the renunciation of the world but service in the world." We are saved to serve – and if we are not serving then quite simply we are not in training to be godly. God asks for our time, our treasure and our talents to be put to *His* use.

## Prayer

Lord Jesus Christ, I see what I have always seen, but now see even more clearly – being a Christian is a serious business. It demands my all. But then You gave Your all for me. Help me never to forget that. Amen.

# "You've gotta serve"

*"… he poured water into a basin and began to wash his disciples' feet …" (v.5)*

**For reading & meditation – John 13:1–17**

Service can sometimes be hard – that is why it must be seen as a discipline. Otherwise we will serve occasionally or do only those things which please or satisfy us. If the latter then service becomes *self*-service.

But why should serving be seen as a spiritual discipline? And does it mean that every time we serve we should be doing it in order to become more godly? In his book *The Spirit of the Disciplines* Dallas Willard says: "Not every act that *may* be done as a discipline *needs* to be done as a discipline. I will often be able to serve another simply as an act of love … without regard to how it may enhance my abilities to follow Christ. There certainly is nothing wrong with that and it may, incidentally, strengthen me spiritually as well. But I may also serve another to train myself away from arrogance, possessiveness, envy, resentment or covetousness. In that case my service is undertaken as a discipline for the spiritual life."

Serving others, it must be said, is not an option for Christians. Every one of us is expected to serve. Can you imagine an angel refusing to serve? It is almost unthinkable. But of course, some did, and it was an unwillingness to serve that turned angels into devils. Christians who sit on the sidelines watching others serve and excusing themselves on the grounds that they do not have enough time, show by their very actions that they have little idea of what true godliness is. Remember the old song, *You've gotta serve somebody?* You have. You either serve or sag.

FURTHER STUDY

James 2:14–26;
Matt. 5:16;
1 Tim. 6:18;
Gal. 6:2–10

1. How does James equate deeds with discipline?
2. What are we to be rich in?

## Prayer

Gracious Father, help me never to forget that my soul is in training for godliness. And serving others is part of that training. I want my soul to thrive. Help me to be at my very best for You. In Jesus' Name. Amen.

# Inflow – outflow

*"Jesus ... said, 'Go home to your family and tell them
how much the Lord has done for you ...'"* (v.19)

### For reading & meditation – Mark 5:1–20

A nother important discipline is sharing our faith with others.
Some of the disciplines we are looking at in this theme relate to
inflow; this one is concerned with outflow. There can be no outflow
without an inflow, and the inflow will come to a complete halt if
there is no outflow. To describe sharing as a discipline may sound
strange, but if we do not discipline ourselves to do so we may never
do so at all. We should discipline ourselves to share by deed and
word what we have found as we have prayed and read the Word.

Many fail to do this. They are earnest and regular in the way
they take in, but not as disciplined in the way they give out.
Sometimes, when they are in the mood, they will share the Lord
with others, but this seems to depend more on feelings than choice.
A number of Christians have told me that they consider they are
living in obedience to the Lord regarding the other disciplines, but
not one person has ever said they are as obedient in sharing with
others as they should be. Time and time again I have heard older
Christians comment: "My greatest regret in life is that I have missed
so many opportunities to share Christ with
others," or, "If I could relive my life I think I
would be more faithful in sharing my faith with
others."

Training the soul to be godly requires that we
discipline ourselves to share Christ with others –
when appropriate – even though we may not be in
an evangelistic frame of mind.

**FURTHER STUDY**

2 Tim. 1:1–8;
Rom. 1:16;
1 Pet. 3:15

*1. What was Paul's
admonition to
Timothy?
2. What was his own
testimony?*

## Prayer

O God, forgive me that I miss so many opportunities to share my faith. Help
me discipline myself in this regard, but grant me wisdom so that I don't pester
people and so discredit the faith. In Jesus' Name. Amen.

# Ready and alert

*"Always be prepared to give an answer to everyone …
for the hope that you have …" (v.15)*

**For reading & meditation – 1 Peter 3:8–22**

George Barna, a Christian researcher, says that seven out of ten Christians who share their faith with others come away feeling they have failed. Fear of failure is one of the chief reasons why people fail to share their faith. When we fear something we avoid it. Unless we have a disciplined approach to sharing our faith with others it simply will not get done.

In my youth I was encouraged to share Christ with someone every day, and to be alert to every opportunity. At the age of eighteen I was drafted into the mines to do a two-year period of National Service. The mining industry was more in need of help than the Armed Forces so I found myself, much against my will, working in a coal mine. One morning, deep underground, I turned to the young man next to me and though I did not feel in an evangelistic mood asked him if he had ever thought seriously about where he would spend eternity. He said he hadn't, and that led to an interesting few minutes at the end of which he accepted Christ. This conversation took place during an official break, of course; it would be wrong to evangelise when paid to do something else. An hour later this young man lay dead – killed by a large stone that fell from the roof and literally flattened him. Were it not for *disciplined sharing* I might have missed the opportunity to prepare him for eternity. Honesty compels me to admit, however, that over the years I have missed more opportunities than I have taken.

**FURTHER STUDY**

John 15:18–27;
Isa. 43:10;
Acts 1:8; 5:20

1. What did Jesus say was a "must" for His disciples?
2. What did He assure them of?

## Prayer

O God, forgive us for the fact that so often we are oblivious to those moments of opportunity when it would be appropriate to share our faith with others. Help us be more disciplined in this direction. For Jesus' sake. Amen.

# Witness for the defence

*"… and you will be my witnesses in Jerusalem, and in all Judea and Samaria, and to the ends of the earth." (v.8)*

### For reading & meditation – Acts 1:1–11

Our text for today tells us that Christ's followers are His witnesses. One preacher described being a witness like this: "Jesus is on trial again before the world, and every one of His disciples is called on as a defence witness. Suppose we refuse to say a word on His behalf. Then by our silence we join the prosecution for He said: 'He who is not with me is against me.' Or suppose when called we talk about ourselves and our achievements instead of talking about Him. Or suppose we mumble and apologise and contradict ourselves. We let Him down – and badly. And in the process we let ourselves down" (paraphrased).

A verse in Revelation says: "They overcame … by the blood of the Lamb and by the word of their testimony" (12:11). They overcame by what *Christ* did for them – the blood of the Lamb – and by what *they* did – the word of their testimony. One commentator says of this verse: "If the word of our testimony is silent then the blood of the Lamb is silenced and does not speak on our behalf. We cut ourselves off from His cross if we do not take up ours, we cancel its power for ourselves unless we pass on its power to others." This seems to go beyond what is stated in Revelation, but it had a great impact on me. Some words written by a very old Christian spring into my mind as I write: "No heart is pure that is not passionate, no virtue safe that is not enthusiastic, no life Christian that is not Christianising."

---

**FURTHER STUDY**

Acts 8:26–39;
16:11–15;
2 Tim. 4:5

1. How did Philip respond to the eunuch's question?
2. What was Paul's directive to Timothy?

## Prayer

O God, help me to be Your witness. Over the radio and television I constantly hear the voice of materialism persuasively promoting temporal things. Help me to witness more clearly to You, the Eternal Reality. Amen.

# Receptivity and response

*"Land that drinks in the rain ... and that produces a
crop ... receives the blessing of God." (v.7)*

**For reading & meditation – Hebrews 6:1–12**

"To know Jesus and to help others know Him, as Saviour and
Lord" sums up the Christian faith. These two matters constitute
the heartbeats of the gospel: intake and outflow, receptivity and
response. And if both processes are not in operation the Christian
heart ceases to beat.

Our text features the two actions so vital to Christian living –
taking and giving. Land which absorbs the rain then produces a
crop useful to those for whom it is farmed. This type of land receives
a blessing from God. But if it only received and never gave – what
would happen to it? Then it would be cursed. In 2 Corinthians we
read the words: "he who supplies seed to the sower" (9:10). Note
the words again: "he who supplies seed to the sower." What would
happen if the sower didn't use the seed? Most likely he would not
get any more.

Not long ago I heard about a husband and wife planning what
they described as an "amicable divorce". Their nine-year-old
daughter had become a Christian, and as they all met to discuss the
details the little girl bowed her head and prayed:
"Dear God, You have made such a change in me
since I came to know You. Help my mother and
father to change also." The father and mother
looked at each other and as the tears came into
their eyes they bowed their heads and received
Christ into their lives. The impulse in that little
girl's heart to share Jesus is in every one of His
followers. It's sad that so often we stifle it.

FURTHER STUDY

Matt. 13:1–13;
John 15:16;
Rom. 7:4;
Col. 1:10

1. What is at the
heart of this parable?
2. What seeds have
you sown lately?

## Prayer

O God, who could look into Your face and not want to share? The impulse is
there in every one of us, just as it was in the heart of that little girl. Inherently I
am an evangelist. Help me not to choke the impulse. Amen.

# "Say so"

*"Let the redeemed of the Lord say this – those he redeemed from the hand of the foe ..." (v.2)*

**For reading & meditation – Psalm 107:1-16**

What if the psalmist had urged: "Let the redeemed of the Lord keep their mouths shut"? You and I might then have never heard the truth of the gospel. However, because we have tasted of the Lord we must share our good news. Psychology advocates a similar form of behaviour: "You must be the sharing, communicative type to be healthy." If we keep things to ourselves we become self-focused and thus unhealthy.

In the first chapter of John there are three finds: Andrew finds Peter, Jesus finds Philip and Philip finds Nathanael. The gospel is a gospel of finding, not keeping. Did you know that most of the people whose healing is recorded in the Gospels were brought to Jesus by another person?

One woman found it very difficult to share anything about her faith with others until she received this suggestion: "Ask those you know well about their problems so that you can bring them to the Lord in prayer." She put this advice into practice and the results were astonishing. People were so moved by her expression of concern they opened up to her in a way they had never done before. She led five of her friends to Christ in the first month. Yet the secret was not so much the actual method but the passion which motivated her. Some could follow this example and get nowhere because they would be more interested in just gaining a convert than in being a blessing to them. "I do all this for the sake of the gospel," said Paul, "that I may share its blessings" (1 Cor. 9:23).

**FURTHER STUDY**

Prov. 11:21-30;
Dan. 12:3;
John 1:41-42;
James 5:20;
Isa. 62:1

1. How do we display wisdom?
2. What are we to remember?

## Prayer

O God, You have given me the greatest work in the world – that of bringing others to You. Here and now I dedicate myself to that task. Help me to be faithful and discipline myself to carry it out. In Jesus' Name. Amen.

# "In simplicity sublime"

*"Jesus replied, 'Foxes have holes ... but the Son of Man has nowhere to lay his head.'" (v.20)*

**For reading & meditation – Matthew 8:14–27**

The next spiritual exercise is the discipline of adopting simplicity. An early task assigned to me by my pastor after my conversion was to study the life of Jesus as portrayed in the four Gospels. The thing that came home to me time and time again was the astonishing simplicity of His lifestyle. The poet Tennyson when writing about a close friend said: "He was rich in common sense; in simplicity sublime." Surely no one has ever demonstrated the sublimity of simplicity as did Jesus. His entrance into this world was simple. He was born in a humble cattle shed. He spent His life in a little village called Nazareth not as a king (which He was) but as a carpenter. When He started to preach His words were direct and straightforward. Sometimes His parables stretched people's imagination but His language was the language of simple men. His way of life, too, was simple and uncomplicated, in contrast to that of the Pharisees who were bound by all kinds of regulations. "Beauty," it has been said, "is an absence of superfluities." If that is so then none has been more beautiful than our Lord Jesus Christ. In Him there was no superfluity or pretence, no useless verbiage, no quibbling or prevaricating.

I say without fear of being corrected that if we are to train ourselves to be godly then imitating Jesus in this respect must be one of our spiritual exercises too. We must train ourselves in the art of simplicity. We must discipline ourselves to be like Jesus and be "rich in common sense; in simplicity sublime".

**FURTHER STUDY**

2 Cor. 11:1–15;
Phil. 3:1–16;
Matt. 16:24–26;
Luke 14:33

1. What was Paul's fear for the Corinthians?
2. What was the pursuit of Paul's life?

## Prayer

Simple but sublime Saviour, rid me of all complexity and artifice that I might be direct and as self-verifying as You were when You were on this earth. For Your own dear Name's sake. Amen.

# "It's all too simple"

*"... unless you change and become like little children,
you will never enter the kingdom of heaven." (v.3)*

**For reading & meditation – Matthew 18:1–9**

Many Christians are being drawn towards a simpler lifestyle. Is this a tug of the Holy Spirit, I wonder? Can it be that in a sophisticated age such as this the Spirit of God is prodding His people to show the world that life can be lived to the full and still be simple?

When I heard the comment: "The Christian life is the way of complete simplicity", I thought: "If that is true, why have we made it so complicated?" The writer of Ecclesiastes said: "God made man simple; man's complex problems are of his own devising" (7:29, Jerusalem Bible). In days gone by the Quakers sang a song the sentiment of which will, I think, be shared by many Christians today:

*It's a gift to be simple, it's a gift to be free,
It's a gift to come down where we ought to be,
And when we see ourselves in a way that's right,
We live in a valley of love and delight.*

**FURTHER STUDY**

Matt. 11:25–26;
Mark 10:15;
Luke 18:16–17;
Psa. 116:1–6

*1. Why did Jesus give praise to the Father?
2. Who does the Lord protect?*

One great difference between the Christian faith and every other religion is its simplicity. To find God, says Scripture (as in our text for today), you have to move away from all that is complicated to what is simple. And what can be more simple than a child opening up its hand to receive a gift? Some people stumble over this very simplicity and reject the Christian message. A doctor of philosophy I tried to lead to Christ said, "It's all too simple." How sad.

## Prayer

O God my Father, I am attracted to the idea of a simpler, less complicated lifestyle. Help me strip myself of all those things that make my life so complex, and move towards a simpler lifestyle. In Jesus' Name. Amen.

# "Ouch, stop squeezing!"

*"Do not conform any longer to the pattern of this world,
but be transformed by the renewing of your mind …" (v.2)*

**For reading & meditation – Romans 12:1–8**

J.B. Phillips made what I consider one of the best translations of
this verse: "Don't let the world around you squeeze you into its
own mould, but let God re-mould your minds from within, so that
you may prove in practice that the plan of God for you is good,
meets all his demands and moves towards the goal of true maturity."
What sort of shape is contemporary culture in? One feature is what
Richard Foster calls "an insane attachment to things". Arthur G.
Gish, in *Beyond the Rat Race*, puts it even more powerfully: "We crave
things we neither need nor enjoy … we buy things we do not want
to impress people we do not like." Advertisers set out to make us
feel ashamed if we do not wear the latest fashions, drive the most
up-to-date car, or eat at the priciest restaurants.

"Society is psychotic." This is the pronouncement of a
commentator on worldly affairs. A psychotic is someone who is out
of touch with reality, who lives in a world of illusion – and that, I am
afraid, is the realm in which many of our secular friends and
colleagues seem to be living. Today's heroes are people who go from
poor to rich rather than those who give up their
riches to become voluntarily poor. Covetousness
is termed ambition, hoarding is regarded as
prudent, and greed is defined as being
industrious.

Until we understand the thinking of our sick
society we will not be able to see how we are
being squeezed into the world's mould – how
much of the spirit of mammon we have absorbed.

FURTHER STUDY

Matt. 6:19–24;
Luke 16:1–15;
21:34;
Col. 3:1–2;
Titus 2:12

1. What does God's
grace teach us?
2. Where are we to
set our affection?

## Prayer

Father, I must pause again to ask myself: Am I allowing the world to squeeze
me into its own mould? Help me face this question today and do whatever is
necessary to resist the spirit of the world. In Christ's Name. Amen.

# Steps to simplicity

*"But seek first his kingdom and his righteousness, and
all these things will be given to you as well." (v.33)*

**For reading & meditation – Matthew 6:25–33**

"The majority of Christians," says a contemporary writer, "have never seriously wrestled with the problem of simplicity, conveniently ignoring Jesus' many words on the subject." In my opinion he hits the nail on the head. To discipline ourselves to live more simply is demanding because it strikes at the very heart of our desire to have an affluent lifestyle. We must be on our guard against legalism, of course, for it is possible to have an outward form of simplicity without the inner reality. Simplicity begins on the inside and works itself out.

Some suggestions as you seek to discipline yourself to adopt a simpler lifestyle: (1) *Seek first the interests of the kingdom.* Let nothing come before your concern for the kingdom of God, including the desire for greater simplicity. When the kingdom is your first priority then it will be much easier to evaluate what needs to be kept and what needs to go. (2) *Examine your life to see if complicated motives are producing anomalies in your attitudes and acts.* Mixed motives produce complications. Are you at war with yourself? Purify your motives inside and your conduct too will be right.

**FURTHER STUDY**

Eccl. 2:1–26;
Psa. 39:6; 127:2;
1 Cor. 4:5

1. What is the conclusion of the writer of Ecclesiastes?
2. What does God expose?

(3) *Resist all attempts to persuade you to buy things for their status rather than their usefulness.* An outspoken friend of mine told me he stayed in the home of a couple where there were ten rooms. "Why do you need ten rooms for just two people?" he asked. "It *feels* good," was the reply – an emotional response to a rational question. Beware of feelings that override your common sense.

## Prayer

O God, I am grateful that You love me enough to confront me. You awaken me to the reality of my situation but so often I am unwilling to do anything about it. Help me I pray. In Jesus' Name. Amen.

# "De-accumulate"

*"But I have stilled and quietened my soul; like a
weaned child with its mother …" (v.2)*

**For reading & meditation – Psalm 131:1–3**

More suggestions towards simplicity: (4) *Be alert to the possibility
of becoming addicted to things.* If there are things you find you
cannot do without and they are not necessities – alcohol, television,
new fashions – then be ruthless with yourself and give them up. You
must be a slave only to Christ.

(5) *Cultivate a way of thinking that says not "What can I keep for
myself?" but "What can I give away?"* Take a look in your wardrobe.
Can you see anything there in good condition which you rarely use?
Give it to someone who is in need. The big word in the area of
simplicity, says Richard Foster, is "De-accumulate". When we hoard
things we don't need we complicate our lives. They have to be
stored, sorted – and dusted! (6) *Refuse to be taken in by slick
advertising.* Develop a more critical attitude to what is pushed at you
by the media. A sense of responsibility to the environment would
lead us to reject half of the gadgets available today. And whatever
you do, adopt a healthy scepticism to the phrase "Buy now – pay
later".

(7) *Cut out all affectation in speech and act.* Go
over your life and decide that everything you
do and say will be true. Abandon such ploys
as talking for effect and using weasel words.
Live honestly before everyone. Decide to
be fundamentally simple and you will be
fundamentally sound. Then you will be able to
say: "I have stilled and quietened my soul; like a
weaned child" – weaned it from all that is
complicated. Sublime.

**FURTHER STUDY**

Luke 12:13–21;
James 4:13–17;
Prov. 19:21; 10:22

1. What did Jesus say
we are to watch
out for?
2. What kind of
wealth doesn't have
trouble attached
to it?

## Prayer

Gracious Father, I pray again: make me a more simple person – simple but not
simplistic. Speak the word and release me from the terrible bondage to things. I
would be like Jesus – uncomplicated. Help me my Father. Amen.

# Fallacies about fasting

*"When you fast, do not look sombre as the hypocrites do …" (v.16)*

**For reading & meditation – Matthew 6:16–24**

We now consider a discipline which has fallen into disrepute in modern times – fasting. Most of us, if we are honest, are more interested in feasting than in fasting. Why then should something given such a high priority in Scripture be regarded with suspicion by so many Christians today?

One reason is a fear of becoming legalistic. The Church has suffered greatly from legalism in the past – engaging in what appeared to be spiritual practices but lacking inward power. No one wants to return to the days when people wore black to church, carried black Bibles, and entered the house of God looking as if their faces would make a good frontispiece for the book of Lamentations. But to say that fasting can draw us back to legalism is to misunderstand Scripture.

Further reasons why fasting is viewed with suspicion are that the propaganda of our consumer society encourages us to satisfy every appetite every day of our lives, and the subject is not proclaimed from modern-day pulpits. In some churches you can go for years without ever hearing a sermon on the subject of fasting.

FURTHER STUDY

Ex. 34:1–35;
Luke 4:1–15;
Joel 2:12

1. What was the result of Moses' period of fasting?
2. What was the result of Jesus' period of fasting?

To overlook fasting and ignore its biblical significance is to deprive ourselves of an exercise of the soul that was taught and practised by our Lord, taken up by His disciples, and has been part of the life of the Church throughout its history. Now let me say at once that some people should not fast for medical reasons, but their numbers will be comparatively small. The discipline of fasting does wonders for the soul. Put it to the test and see.

## Prayer

Lord Jesus Christ, help me realise that You never ask me to do something You did not do Yourself. But I confess this is a challenge that I do not find easy. Help me consider it, and practise it. In Jesus' Name. Amen.

# A cutting question

*"How can the guests of the bridegroom mourn while he is with them?" (v.15)*

**For reading & meditation – Matthew 9:9–17**

This passage is used by some to argue that followers of Jesus should not fast. Our Lord is enjoying a meal with Matthew the tax collector and some of his friends. A group of Pharisees hear of this, and question His disciples: "Why does your teacher eat with tax collectors and 'sinners'?"

The disciples of John appear to have been similarly perplexed. Like John they were ascetics – men who were single-minded, who ate coarse, simple food and frequently engaged in long, rigorous fasts. These men had given themselves to promoting John's teaching, calling men and women to repentance, baptising them in water and advocating fasting. They knew too that part of John's ministry was to point men and women to Jesus; how could they do that when He seemed to be more interested in feasting than in fasting? Thus they thrust this question at Jesus: "How is it that we and the Pharisees fast, but your disciples do not fast?"

Jesus responds by pointing out that guests at a wedding do not mourn or abstain from food during the festivities. It was His way of saying: "The kingdom of heaven is like a wedding feast and I am here to introduce it. My disciples are filled with joy, therefore it would not be appropriate while the Bridegroom is present for them to fast." Our Lord was giving here not only an intimation of His death but also of His Messiahship. However, He added: "When the bridegroom will be taken from them; then they will fast" (v.15). Well, the Bridegroom *has* been taken away. But how many of His disciples fast?

**FURTHER STUDY**

Acts 13:1–3;
Psa. 35:13;
Jonah 3:1–5

1. What happened when the Early Church were praying and fasting?
2. When was the last time you fasted?

## Prayer

Father, I think the answer has to be, comparatively few. I am committed to You but I see there are some things to which I need to be more deeply committed. Teach me more, dear Lord. And help me. In Jesus' Name. Amen.

# A futile fast

*"While they were worshipping the Lord and fasting,
the Holy Spirit said ..." (v.2)*

**For reading & meditation – Acts 13:1–12**

Consider with me today what fasting is *not*. Fasting is not going on a diet. People often cut down their food intake to improve their health or lose weight. This may be commendable but it is not biblical fasting. Nor is fasting going without food in order to manipulate others. Mahatma Gandhi often started a fast to force people to reconsider their decisions. He would state that he would fast to his death unless those in power adopted different strategies. Indeed, his periods of fasting were highly successful in bringing about changes in the political system of his day. However, the fasting spoken of in Scripture is always for a spiritual, not a political or selfish purpose.

The first time I fasted was a few months after my conversion to Christ. I had overheard several older Christians saying that fasting was commanded in the Bible and should be practised from time to time by every Christian. I decided to enter into a three-day fast to see what it was like. It was one of the hardest, most miserable experiences of my life. All that happened was that I got hungrier and hungrier, and after thirty-six hours I broke my fast. Sometime later I realised I had been fasting for the sake of it, not for the Lord's sake. I had no God-given purpose in fasting. My abstinence was not so much fasting as an experiment in not eating. And without the intention of discovering God in a greater way fasting can be a miserable experience. So remember, although fasting is an important spiritual exercise, the motivation is of crucial importance.

FURTHER STUDY

Acts 27:13–38;
1 Kings 19:7–21;
Ezra 10:6;
Dan. 10:3

1. Is this an account of fasting in Acts 27?
2. Were Elijah, Ezra and Daniel fasting?

## Prayer

Father, fasting is so clearly included in Your Word that there is no escaping it. The Early Church practised it, and so have saints down the centuries. But I am still struggling. Help me, dear Father. In Jesus' Name. Amen.

# The purpose of fasting

*"There … I proclaimed a fast … that we might humble our-selves before …God and ask him for a safe journey …" (v.21)*

**For reading & meditation – Ezra 8:15–23**

Many reasons for fasting are given in Scripture. One is to add power to our prayer lives. John Calvin advised this: "Whenever men are to pray to God concerning any great matter, it would be expedient to appoint fasting along with prayer." Ezra followed this pattern. The exiles needed a safe passage to Jerusalem so, according to Ezra: "We fasted and petitioned our God about this, and *he answered our prayer*" (v.23).

A second reason is to discover God's guidance. One passage that illustrates this principle is found in Judges chapter 20. Some members of the tribe of Benjamin had committed a terrible sin, which led to the other eleven tribes going to war against the Benjamites. But though the eleven tribes outnumbered the tribe of Benjamin by fifteen to one they lost the battle. The next day the eleven tribes fought and lost again. Only after they had fasted and prayed did the Lord make His will plain and grant success (vv.26–28). However, remember this: fasting does not guarantee that guidance will certainly be given but it certainly makes us more receptive to the One who guides.

A third reason is to deepen the expression of an act of repentance. The Old Testament is replete with instances of fasting accompanying repentance. Joel 2:12 is just one verse that records God urging His people to show their sincerity by fasting. One way to make sure that repentance is heartfelt is to reinforce the prayer of repentance with a short period of fasting. I have known many whose lives have been transformed in this way.

**FURTHER STUDY**

Joel 1:1–14;
1 Sam. 7:6;
Acts 9:1–19

1. How did Joel link barrenness and fasting?
2. How was fasting linked to Paul's conversion experience?

## Prayer

Lord Jesus, tender and skilful Invader of my soul, You keep bringing me back to reality. By Your Holy Spirit and through Your Word You teach me Your way. Now help me walk in it. In Jesus' Name. Amen.

# A day for decisions

*"Today, if you hear his voice, do not harden your hearts …"* (v.15)

**For reading & meditation – Hebrews 3:1–15**

Biblical fasting must always have a spiritual purpose. There can be little doubt that God rewards fasting undertaken for a spiritual reason with great blessing. For instance, I know churches that have experienced tremendous blessing after a corporate fast. "Fasting," says one writer, "hoists the sails of the soul in hopes of experiencing the gracious wind of God's Spirit. It adds a unique dimension to one's spiritual life and helps the soul grow more Christlike."

Now I realise that my writings of the past few days on this theme of fasting may have made some people feel guilty, and that they might therefore decide to fast simply to rid themselves of those feelings of guilt. Examine your heart on this issue. I would like to feel that you are drawn to fasting for the right reasons, not the wrong ones. Think the matter through carefully. Fasting is commanded by God and is clearly taught in Scripture. If you make the decision to fast occasionally that does not mean you must start today. Pray and ask God to guide you. All you need to say is: "Lord, I recognise this truth and I am willing to follow Your leading." God will guide you as to the right times, the appropriate times. Read a good book on the theme of fasting before you begin. And keep in mind the caution I gave earlier: if you are suffering from a medical condition that precludes you from fasting then *don't do it*. God understands. Focus on the other spiritual exercises and the Lord will count your willingness to fast as the deed done.

**FURTHER STUDY**

Neh. 1:1–11;
Judg. 20:17–28;
Acts 14:23

1. How did Nehemiah respond to Jerusalem's devastation?
2. What did Paul and Barnabas do with prayer and fasting?

## Prayer

My Father and my God, I see this is a day for decision. I yield to You. Give me the insight I need and the wisdom I need to draw from fasting the benefits it can bring to my soul. In Jesus' Name. Amen.

# "Good for the soul"

*"Then I acknowledged my sin to you and did not cover up my iniquity ..." (v.5)*

**For reading & meditation – Psalm 32:1–11**

The next spiritual exercise we examine is that of confession and forgiveness. Confession is owning up to God and others about the wrongs we have done, and forgiveness is being willing to wipe the slate clean regarding any who have wronged us.

An old saying goes: "Confession is good for the soul." It is. Here modern psychology agrees with the teaching of Jesus. C.H. Barbour says in *Sin and the New Psychology*: "When the conscience acting in the capacity of an observer condemns the ego for wrong actions and the feeling of guilt results there are three possible modes of conduct open to the conscious mind. The consciousness may do nothing whatever about it, allowing the emotion full play; it may repress the feeling, or it may rid itself of the depressing sensation by means of spiritual catharsis [cleansing] through confession."

The first two methods are obviously unsatisfactory. To find oneself in the wrong and do nothing about it is to live with a self one cannot respect. Repression is just as bad. When we drive guilt into the subconscious and shut the door we do not get rid of it. There it festers and sets up an irritation. Time and again people in a counselling room have said to me: "I am ill at ease and I don't know why." More often than not I have found that the cause was some unconfessed sin. When the sin was identified, exposed to the light of Christ and resolved through confession, joy returned to the soul. There is simply no other way out. All other routes lead to an incipient hell.

> **FURTHER STUDY**
>
> 1 Cor. 8:1–7;
> Rom. 2:15;
> Acts 24:16;
> 1 Tim. 1:5;
> Heb. 9:14
>
> 1. What happens to a weak conscience?
> 2. What did Paul strive for?

## Prayer

Lord Jesus Christ, You have come to me at supreme cost. You knock with pierced hands at the door of my heart. Help me to rid my soul of all corrosive guilt through the exercise of confession. In Jesus' Name. Amen.

# To whom do we confess?

*"Cleanse me with hyssop, and I shall be clean; wash me, and I shall be whiter than snow."* (v.7)

**For reading & meditation – Psalm 51:1–19**

If we are to get rid of guilt, to whom do we confess? Obviously it is to the one or ones we have wronged.

All wrongs must, of course, be confessed to God. The awful thing about sin, as I have said before, is not only that it breaks God's law but that it breaks His heart. We must tell Him we are sorry about that, naming the transgression so that we are clear about what we are confessing. Have no fear as to how to approach God for access to God has been made easy through Jesus. Our Lord's awful purity made sinners feel condemned, yet His purity was not forbidding but forgiving. If you dare to expose your heart to His heart you will find not merely relief but release. And you must find that, for with guilt in your system your soul will turn sour. Then if we have wronged others we must make confession to them too. Confession must be always as wide as the circle of offence.

In the psalm before us today David confesses his sin against Bathsheba and Uriah, but look what he says in verse 4: "Against you, you only, have I sinned." Is he saying he has not sinned against Bathsheba and Uriah? No. He is recognising that all sin is first and foremost a sin against God, and He is the first one from whom forgiveness must be sought. One final point: confession must be wholehearted, without anything held back. Just one matter held back spoils it all – and cancels the rest.

**FURTHER STUDY**

1 John 1:1–10;
Ezra 10:11;
Prov. 28:13;
Ezek. 18:21

1. What does God show to the penitent?
2. What needs to follow on from confession?

## Prayer

Lord Jesus Christ, Your knife cuts deep. I wince and yet I know that what You say is true. Help me to be ready to confess all sin and have done with it. I don't just want to be better, I want to be whole. In Jesus' Name. Amen.

# "I can't forgive"

*"But if you do not forgive men their sins, your Father
will not forgive your sins." (v.15)*

**For reading & meditation – Matthew 6:1–15**

What should we do when others have wronged us? We should
forgive. But you protest: "I can't forgive." Then I say very
quietly, tenderly, but also solemnly: if you won't forgive you can
never be forgiven. Listen again to Jesus' words: "If you do not
forgive men their sins, your Father will not forgive your sins." By
refusing others forgiveness you are breaking down the bridge over
which you yourself must pass, namely that of forgiveness.

Having heard our Lord's solemn words surely you are convinced
of the need to forgive, but perhaps you are saying to yourself: "I can
forgive but I can't forget." Well, take those words and apply them to
the Lord's Prayer. Repeat it like this: "Father, forgive me as I forgive
others. I forgive that other person but I won't forget what they have
done to me. I will keep it in mind and never let it slip from my
memory. Now, dear Lord, forgive me in the same way. Forgive me
but don't forget my sins. And when I do something wrong remind
me of it repeatedly." Do you see how absurd it is? How glad we
should be that God does not forgive like that. He removes the record
of our sin from His book of remembrance.

Since God forgives you, you can forgive
others. But if you exclude others from your
forgiveness then you shut yourself off from God's
forgiveness. Oh, the wonder of God's forgiveness.
When we see how much we have been forgiven
that in itself should be enough to send us out
filled with joy to forgive others.

**FURTHER STUDY**

Mark 11:20–25;
Luke 17:1–4;
Eph. 4:32;
Col. 3:13

1. What was Jesus'
teaching in these
passages?
2. What did Paul
urge?

## Prayer

O God, perhaps the reason I find it difficult to forgive is because I haven't
really seen how much I have been forgiven. I open myself to a new
understanding of that today. In Jesus' Name. Amen.

# "What's eating you?"

*"… forgive whatever grievances you may have against one another. Forgive as the Lord forgave you." (v.13)*

**For reading & meditation – Colossians 3:1–17**

I once read of an experiment in which a tube was put into a man's stomach to test its contents, according to the various states of his mind. When he was in a good humour the digestive processes were normal, but when he was angry or resentful digestion stopped completely. Only when he returned to being good-humoured would he start to digest food again.

At one time I had to consult a doctor over indigestion. He asked: "What sort of frame of mind are you in when you eat?" Astonished, I said: "What has that got to do with it?" He replied: "It's got everything to do with it. It's not so much what you eat but what's eating you. If you aren't in a good state of mind you had better lay off eating until you are." He was right. I realised my indigestion was caused by a harboured resentment. I forgave the person I was resentful towards and my digestive tract gave me no further trouble. The stomach was made for goodwill, not ill will. Goodwill sets it up and ill will upsets it!

The same is true of the soul. It was not designed to harbour resentments, and when we force it to do so it rebels. Nothing can be more important to the soul's health than making sure the exercise of forgiveness is carried out regularly. Flush all bitterness out of your soul as you would flush a toxic substance out of your body. Say to yourself today: "My soul is too great to be the enemy of anyone."

**FURTHER STUDY**

Heb. 12:14–17;
Rom. 8:22–23;
James 3:13–16;
Eph. 4:31

1. What are we to make every effort to do?
2. What happens when we miss the grace of God?

## Prayer

O God, I would have a soul that is fit and healthy – a soul free of guilt. Help me to constantly practise forgiveness. For how can I be forgiven if I do not forgive? Once again help me in this matter. In Jesus' Name. Amen.

# "The way of the Master"

*"Be kind and compassionate ... forgiving each other,
just as in Christ God forgave you." (v.32)*

**For reading & meditation – Ephesians 4:17–32**

During World War II, when Japan was determined to wipe
out Christianity, a test was devised. A cross was laid on the
ground and when one suspected of being a Christian was brought
before the tribunal he or she was told to walk upon the cross. Those
who refused were killed and those who did were freed. I saw one of
those crosses when I was in South Korea. It had on it a faint
reproduction of the face of Christ – a face that had almost been
worn away by the many who had stepped on it. Would it be going
too far, I wonder, to suggest that when we refuse to forgive we
trample on the cross? Let me put it another way: when we refuse
to forgive we bring pain to the heart of our Lord. When nailed to
a cross the Master prayed: "Father, forgive them, for they do not
know what they are doing" (Luke 23:34). As an old hymn puts it: "It
is the way the Master went, should not the servant tread it still?"
When Tokichi Ishii, a Japanese renegade, was awaiting the death
sentence in a Japanese prison he was given a New Testament and
came on those words in Luke. They moved him deeply and brought
about his conversion.

What greater joy can there be than having a
soul free of guilt? Confession and forgiveness are
the way to achieve that. But there must be no half-
confessions, no partial forgiveness. Both must be
full and frank and free.

**FURTHER STUDY**

Psa. 38:1–12;
32:1–5; 40:12; 51:3

*1. What did the
psalmist say about
his guilt?*
*2. What was David's
ultimate testimony?*

## Prayer

Lord Jesus Christ, my Saviour and my God, You hung on a cross and were
tortured in every nerve yet You prayed for Your enemies: "Father, forgive them."
Help me this day to forgive those who have wronged me in lesser ways. Amen.

# "Keep on keeping on"

*"... let us run with perseverance the race marked
out for us." (v.1)*

**For reading & meditation – Hebrews 12:1–17**

We reach now the last spiritual exercise – *perseverance*. The dictionary defines it: "the steadfast pursuit of an aim; constant persistence". My one-time pastor used to end every service by pronouncing the benediction, adding: "Keep on keeping on." This phrase has come back to me time and again when I have been tempted to give up on something I knew I should be doing.

Many people begin each new year by making good resolutions. How many fall by the way? So often we take up good things but don't carry them through. Our lives are strewn with the wreckage of good beginnings which became poor endings. When I watched a recording of the London marathon race I was intrigued to see how a camera frequently focused on a man who looked as if he wouldn't make the first mile. But he kept on and on, and although he reached the finishing point long after the winners, he did at least *finish*. A large number dropped out but he carried on doggedly. The crowd at the finishing line gave him as much applause as they did the winner.

In 1 Corinthians 16:9 Paul says: "I will stay on at Ephesus ... a great door for effective work has opened to me ... [but] there are many who oppose me." Our reaction might have been: "I am quitting. A great door for effective work has opened but there are too many who oppose me." An old song goes: "It's not how you start but how you finish." You have started well, now decide to finish it well.

**FURTHER STUDY**

Josh. 23:1–8;
Job 11:14–15;
1 Cor. 15:58;
Gal. 5:1; Phil. 1:27

*1. What was Joshua's
instruction to Israel?
2. What did Paul
exhort the Corinthians
and Galatians and
Philippians?*

## Prayer

Father, help me to keep on keeping on. However many of these exercises of the soul I have begun, help me to keep on with them. I don't want to begin well but finish badly. I want to start and end well. In Jesus' Name. Amen.

# The *Helper*

*"So be careful to do what the Lord your God has commanded you ..." (v.32)*

**For reading & meditation – Deuteronomy 5:22–33**

Dr Martyn Lloyd-Jones in *Studies on the Sermon on the Mount* says: "We must discipline our lives but we must do so all the year round ... not merely at stated periods." If the soul is to be trained in godliness then there must be no let-up. Physical training experts tell us that many begin an exercise programme thinking that a daily work-out in a gym over a period of a month or so will set them up for years. This is a fallacy of course, for exercise must be regular if it is do any good. It is the same with the soul.

I like the way James Moffatt translated our text: "You must not swerve to the right or to the left, but always follow the straight road of life which the Eternal God has laid down for you that you may live." Some might say: "But I'm the spontaneous type who finds it difficult to develop disciplined habits." If you are a Christian then the Holy Spirit dwells within you to make you like Christ. You may not be a disciplined or persistent person, but the Holy Spirit is.

"He who began a good work in you will carry it on to completion until the day of Christ Jesus" (Phil. 1:6). The Holy Spirit's task is to produce within you the desire to train yourself to be godly. Your task is to co-operate with the Spirit. He will help you persevere. One translation refers to the Holy Spirit as the *Helper*. He helps by providing the power. All you have to do is to provide the willingness.

FURTHER STUDY

Heb. 13:1–6;
Psa. 40:17;
Isa. 41:10; 50:9

1. What can we say with confidence?
2. What was Isaiah's testimony?

## Prayer

Father, how can I ever cease to thank You for the help You provide for me through the Holy Spirit? Strengthen my will so that I become even more willing. In Jesus' Name I pray. Amen.

# Last but not least

*"But the fruit of the Spirit is love, joy, peace …
gentleness and self-control." (vv.22–23)*

**For reading & meditation – Galatians 5:16–26**

Many find they need the Holy Spirit as the Helper most in the matter of perseverance.

Earlier I referred to the fact that people often wonder how I have been able to write *Every Day with Jesus* for over thirty-five years. They comment: "You must be a very disciplined person." Actually my temperament is by nature more spontaneous than disciplined. As a child I hated anything that required discipline. One of my school reports even criticised me for being "lacking in self-discipline". It was the Holy Spirit who turned me into a disciplined person. All the credit goes to Him alone. Left to myself I would have forsaken the path of discipline many a time, but the Holy Spirit preserved me by pouring into my soul the grace I needed to persevere in the work to which He had called me.

Self-control, as our text for today tells us, is a fruit of the Spirit. Notice it comes last on Paul's list, though that does not mean it is least in importance. I make the point because many systems, ancient and modern, would put self-control first. Confucius thought that self-control is what produces the "superior person". Hinduism teaches that breath- and thought-control will produce the "realised person". Stoicism, through will-control, tries to produce the "imperturbable person". The Christian message is that the Holy Spirit's direction produces a self-controlled person. But note: we do not gain the Holy Spirit through self-control; we gain self-control through the Holy Spirit. We begin with love – love for Christ and love for others – and end up with self-control.

**FURTHER STUDY**

Rom. 6:1–12;
Prov. 16:32;
2 Pet. 1:1–9;
Titus 2:2

1. What was Paul's exhortation to the Romans?
2. When does Peter say we are short-sighted?

## Prayer

Father, some have so much self-control that they appear rigid, tense and nervous. I want the self-control that stems from the Holy Spirit's control – the kind that is supernaturally natural. In Jesus' Name. Amen.

# Together

*"The one who calls you is faithful …"*
(v.24)

**For reading & meditation – 1 Thessalonians 5:12–28**

Timothy Jones, in an article in *Christianity Today*, tells how he discovered the Holy Spirit's role in helping him develop a disciplined prayer life. He knew it was not just a matter of resolving to pray more, so he began to pray *about praying*. He expressed to God his frustrated longings, his jaded sense of caution about trying again to develop a regular prayer life, his failure in discipline. As he prayed he found that … well, let him tell you himself.

"I was drawn into the presence of One who had, far more than I did, the power to keep me close. I found my focus subtly shifting away from my efforts to God's; from rigour to grace, from rigidity to relationship. I soon realised that this was happening regularly. I was praying much more. I became less worried about the mechanics and methods and in turn I was more motivated. And God so cares for us that I realised anew … he himself helps us pray. I must admit I can't explain how it is that the Holy Spirit prompts us and produces in us the desire to persevere in things. All I know is – he does."

Our text reminds us that God is faithful in keeping us. Oh how grateful we should be for this. He will always be faithful to His children and will help them persevere to the end. Our task, I say once again, is to yield ourselves to Him, to make sure that our hearts are not hardened and that we stay alert and responsive to His promptings. We will make it – together.

**FURTHER STUDY**

Rom. 8:9–27;
John 14:17;
1 Cor. 3:16;
1 John 2:27

1. What is the "obligation" Paul talks about?
2. How does Paul say the Spirit helps us?

## Prayer

Father, thank You for this thrilling truth that perseverance does not involve just my effort or just Your effort. It is the combination of the two. I give myself to You and You give Yourself to me. I am eternally grateful. Amen.

# The Christian struggle

*"For physical training is of some value, but godliness
has value for all things ..."* (v.8)

**For reading & meditation – 1 Timothy 4:1–16**

Have you ever heard anyone say: "I thought the Christian life would be a bed of roses. I never realised it would be such a struggle"? Over the years I have heard this, or a similar statement, hundreds of times. Such thinking results from wrong teaching – teaching that raises false hopes in people. On occasions I have heard preachers say something to this effect: "Give your heart to Jesus Christ and life will forever be plain sailing." It simply is not true. Storms and high seas are as much the lot of Christians as they are of non-Christians. Giving our hearts to Christ means that He is with us in life's storms, not that storms will never buffet us. All Christians struggle from time to time – but we have the help of God in those struggles.

Let me pick out a phrase in the passage we are considering and draw it to your attention: "and for this we labour and strive" (v.10). Doesn't all this talk about struggling, labouring and striving sound more like a theology of works than of grace? Do I seem to be emphasising human effort to the exclusion of divine provision?

**FURTHER STUDY**

Phil. 2:12–18;
Job 17:9;
Gal. 6:9;
Acts 20:24

1. What were the Philippians to continue to do?
2. What was Paul's only desire?

Then let me attempt to clarify further what I said earlier: progress in Christian growth is made through a combination of God's effort and our effort. Do you remember our meditation on Colossians 1:29: "I labour, struggling with all his energy, which so powerfully works in me"? This is important New Testament teaching. Those who teach "Let go and let God" are giving only half the truth. The other half is "we labour and strive".

## Prayer

Father, though at times I am called to struggle, I know that You are with me in the striving. The struggle is not my struggle but our struggle. This makes all the difference. Thank You my Father. Amen.

# "Practice makes perfect"

*"Whoever loves discipline loves knowledge ..."*
*(v.1)*

**For reading & meditation – Proverbs 12:1–15**

D o you want to be a godly person? The path that leads to godliness is the practice of spiritual disciplines. Some people always look for short cuts and, while that may be acceptable as regards some aspects of living, it is not so in relation to the care of the souls.

John Guest, an American writer, related the story of a farmer who went to collect eggs from his chicken shed. On his way he noticed that the yard pump was leaking so he stopped to fix it. After that he saw that a pitchfork needed a new handle so he went back to his storehouse and got one. When he had finished fitting the new handle he noticed something else needed doing ... and so on. It was late morning by the time he finally got to collect the eggs. Does the farmer's morning remind you of your own spiritual life? Is it sporadic and spontaneous rather than directed? Most certainly we should not deride spontaneity, but spontaneity without discipline won't get us very far.

I have often been told: "You play the piano beautifully." This is because I am good at improvising a few melodies which usually impress those who know little about piano playing. Those who are accomplished pianists, however, realise when they hear me play that my playing is the result of spontaneity rather than disciplined practice. When I was young I would not give myself to the discipline of practising the scales and other fundamental exercises. Some people's spiritual lives are like that. They impress others with their spontaneity but deep down they lack discipline.

FURTHER STUDY
James 5:11;
Heb. 12:7;
James 1:12;
Rev. 3:11

1. Who are
considered blessed?
2. What did the angel
say to the church at
Philadelphia?

## Prayer

Heavenly Father, although I do not want to lose my spontaneity I pray that You will help me undergird it by sound self-discipline. Help me maintain this balance all the days of my life. In Jesus' Name. Amen.

# In training for eternity

*"… according to his eternal purpose which he accomplished in Christ Jesus our Lord." (v.11)*

**For reading & meditation – Ephesians 3:1–13**

"The future of the world," said Dr E. Stanley Jones, "is in the hands of disciplined people." I think he meant that the undisciplined waste their energies on themselves and their own entanglements. E. Stanley Jones added: "The future of the world is in the hands of people who are disciplined to the highest ends." Often our disciplines are geared to ends which are good but which are not the highest. Modern life is compartmentalised, specialised and it lacks *total* meaning. For instance, "Much of science," according to one writer, "is abstracted knowledge – it abstracts knowledge about specific things, but fails to deal with the sum total of reality and its meaning. Hence science can never exert a total discipline."

Psychoanalysis, a therapy many people put their faith in, pulls people to pieces, but often it cannot restore them, at least not on a higher level. "My psychoanalyst analysed my problem, but he couldn't put me together again," said a brilliant but deeply disturbed woman. Just as the spokes of a wheel hang loose without a hub so do the powers of life unless they are fastened to the central hub – the Lord Jesus Christ. He and He alone gives total meaning to life. This is why we must keep God and eternity in view while practising spiritual disciplines.

**FURTHER STUDY**

Prov. 6:1–11; 13:4;
24:30–31;
Eccl. 10:18

1. What illustration is given of industriousness?
2. Whose desires are satisfied?

The great revivalist Jonathan Edwards used to pray: "Oh God, stamp eternity on my eyeballs." Imagine the difference it would make if we saw everything from the viewpoint of God and eternity. To view discipline as simply relating to time is short-sighted. We are in training for eternity.

## Prayer

Father, what a thrill it is to know that the blessings that come from spiritual gymnastics extend beyond time into eternity. "Stamp eternity on my eyeballs." In Jesus' Name I pray. Amen.

# "Great gain"

*"But godliness with contentment is great gain."*
*(v.6)*

### For reading & meditation – 1 Timothy 6:1–10

Today we conclude our meditations on the theme of caring for the soul, but hopefully for many this is not the end, but the end of the beginning. From here a new vista opens up – a vista which includes not only time but also eternity. We have looked at ten of what theologians call "the classic disciplines": (1) regular reading of the Scriptures, (2) prayer, (3) worship, (4) seeking solitude, (5) stewardship, (6) sharing the faith, (7) simplicity, (8) fasting, (9) confession and forgiveness and (10) perseverance. Some Christians, as we said at the beginning, would add more to this list – keeping a spiritual journal, submission, and so on – but in my view the ten we have looked at comprise the irreducible minimum. They are, to borrow a phrase, "the Himalayas of the spirit". Miss out on one of these and the soul will not remain healthy and fit.

Development of the soul does not just happen. The soul has to be trained to be godly. Richard Foster, in *Celebration of Discipline*, said: "Superficiality is the curse of our age. The desperate need today is not for a greater number of intelligent people, but deep people." The way to God, we know, is through Christ, and the way to godliness is through the spiritual disciplines. Are you willing to commit yourself to ongoing training for godliness? Does being godly mean as much to you as getting a gold medal means to an Olympic contestant?

Let me give the last word to Vance Havner, a blunt and direct country preacher from the United States: "The alternative to discipline is disaster."

FURTHER STUDY
1 Tim. 6:1–8;
Deut. 4:40;
Eccl. 8:12;
Isa. 3:10;
Titus 3:8

1. What was Paul's perspective of godliness?
2. What will we enjoy the fruit of?

## Prayer

O God, nothing repels me more than the thought that I might experience spiritual disaster. By Your grace I will give myself to training my soul for godliness. My resistance is gone. Now onward for ever. Amen.

# The
# All-Sufficient
# Christ

# Shut up – to write

*"Paul, an apostle of Christ Jesus by the will of God ..."*
*(v.1)*

### For reading & meditation – Colossians 1:1

Paul's letter to the Colossians is one of Paul's finest, written or dictated by him during his imprisonment in Rome in AD 62. Colosse was one of three towns in the Lycus valley, the other two being Hierapolis and Laodicea. We have no record of Paul having visited Colosse personally, and it is most likely that it was Epaphras who had brought the gospel to the area.

The letter seems to have been prompted by Paul's discovery that the Colossian Christians were experiencing a threat to their faith, described by Bishop Handley Moule as "error that cast a cloud over the glory of the Lord Jesus Christ, dethroning Him and emptying Him of His divinity, thus making Him one of a multitude of mediators ... instead of the *only* mediator". The apostle, always ready to defend the Saviour he loved, writes to show that Christ is first and foremost in everything. Believers are rooted in Him, alive in Him, hidden in Him, complete in Him, and so are equipped to make Christ first in every area of their lives.

Paul begins his letter by laying down his credentials: "an apostle of Christ Jesus by the will of God". It might seem sad that an apostle should be shut up in prison. Although circumstances prevent him from travelling, his spirit is free to reach out through his pen and bless the world. Had he not been imprisoned we might never have had his New Testament letters. From prison his influence extended to the ends of the earth and throughout the ages. He was shut up to write – immortally.

> **FURTHER STUDY**
>
> 1 Tim. 4:14;
> 2 Tim. 1:6;
> Matt. 25:14–30
>
> 1. What gift or gifts do you have? Are you neglecting it/them?
> 2. Read the parable carefully – especially if you only have one.

## Prayer

O Father, help me understand that to a Christian there is no bondage but sin. Physical restrictions may hinder me bodily but my spirit is always free to soar. Circumstances do not have the last word in my life – You do. Amen.

# "Grace and peace"

*"To the holy and faithful brothers in Christ at Colosse:*
*Grace and peace to you from God our Father." (v.2)*

**Reading & meditation – Colossians 1:2**

"When Paul wrote his letters to the churches of the New Testament," says Dr William Barclay, "he wrote in exactly and precisely the way ordinary everyday people wrote ordinary everyday letters in the ancient world." First there is a greeting, then a word of thanksgiving, next the special contents, finally a closing greeting and, in some instances, an autographic conclusion.

Paul greets the Colossian Christians with an endearing phrase: "holy and faithful brothers in Christ". The faith of the Colossian Christians may have been under attack, but there is nothing to suggest that they had *succumbed* to error. Certainly there is nothing that comes anywhere near the strong words addressed to the Galatians who had embraced false ideas concerning the faith. I doubt whether Paul would have called the Colossian believers "stalwart followers of Christ" (as Eugene Peterson words verse 2 in *The Message*) if they had been moved from their true spiritual centre in Christ.

He continues: "Grace and peace to you *from God our Father."* Can grace and peace come from sources other than the Father? Of course. Insurance companies talk about periods of "grace"; politicians talk about negotiating "peace" between warring countries or troubled groups. But what a difference between the grace and peace which comes from human hearts and the grace and peace which comes from the heart of the Father. One is temporal, the other eternal; one limited, the other unlimited. The best of men and women are only men and women at best. But what comes from God is always perfect. *Perfect* peace, *perfect* grace.

**FURTHER STUDY**

Eph. 2:8;
John 14:27

1. What is achieved by God's gift of grace?
2. What should result from God's gift of peace?

## Prayer

Father, when You are the source of the peace and grace that flow into my life then I need never be impoverished. Your heart is always open to give; may my heart be always open to receive. In Jesus' Name. Amen.

# Scripture's Siamese twins

*"We always thank God ... because we have heard of your faith ... and of the love you have ..."* (vv.3–4)

**For reading & meditation – Colossians 1:3–4**

How encouraging for the Colossians to know they were remembered in Paul's prayers. He had heard good things about them from Epaphras and, whenever he prayed for them, he gave thanks to God for their faith in Christ and their love for all the saints.

These words link together two important qualities: faith and love. The New Testament often joins these two together; sometimes they are even called "Scripture's Siamese twins". If you are to have love for others you must first of all have faith in God. Pagan psychology teaches that love for other people is an integral part of good emotional health, but it has nothing to say on the need for a relationship with God. Without a vertical relationship with God, however, love for others can soon run out of energy.

An African government agency once invested in a building programme designed to improve the lifestyle of a tribe living in grass huts on a hillside. To replace these, they built in brick at the foot of the hill, but the tribespeople felt uncomfortable in their new houses and, after just a few days, decided to move back into their old huts. An exasperated official said to the missionaries who lived among them: "These ungrateful people need a lot of loving. I'm afraid the best we can do is to lift them; we leave it to you to love them." Love that is not linked to God soon runs out of impetus. Only when we have faith in God can we go on loving the unlovely and the unresponsive. No faith in God, no love like God's.

> **FURTHER STUDY**
>
> Gen. 15:6;
> James 2:14–24
>
> 1. What is the consequence of faith?
> 2. How do we prove we have faith in God?

## Prayer

O God my Father, teach me the secret of faith and love, the alternate beats of the Christian heart. My faith draws love from You, and my love expresses that faith in love to everybody. Thank You Father. Amen.

# A spring in our step

*"... the faith and love that spring from the hope that is stored up for you in heaven ..." (v.5)*

**For reading & meditation – Colossians 1:5a**

Where do faith and love come from? Paul tells us that they come from the *hope* that is stored up for us in heaven. The Christian experience is characterised by hope as much as by faith and love. The concept of hope was something the ancients repudiated, regarding it as dubious and uncertain. But Christian hope is as certain (if not more certain) as tomorrow's dawn. It is the assurance that whatever we enjoy of God's presence and blessings here will be multiplied in heaven. Some think of heaven as the place where the finishing touches will be added to what we have received on earth. But we are promised much more than that. Heaven is the *beginning* of things beyond the power of our imagination to conceive.

How powerfully does the prospect of heaven influence your daily walk with Christ? We must be careful, of course, that we do not become so heavenly minded that we are no earthly good. However, we ought to live in the light of heaven's coming glory. What we have here "in Christ" is just a foretaste of what is to come.

**FURTHER STUDY**

Gal. 5:5;
Rom. 8:19–25

*1. What do we hope for, and how do we hope for it?*
*2. What is the hope in which we are saved?*

Some of our present spiritual experiences may seem like heaven, but really they are just a little bit of heaven to go to heaven in.

Note too that hope is not a consequence of faith and love but its origin. Faith and love *spring* from hope. When we hold before us the sure and certain hope of our accommodation in heaven then out of that hope spring faith and love. They don't just saunter into our lives – they *spring*!

## Prayer

O God, there is so much emphasis on the "now" that I am apt to forget the truth of what I have been reading about today. Help me keep heaven ever before me. Then I know faith and love will "spring". Amen.

# "That's the truth"

*"All over the world this gospel is bearing fruit
and growing ..." (v.6)*

**For reading & meditation – Colossians 1:5b–6**

T he reason Paul tells the Colossians they had heard the true
gospel was to hold up before them a standard by which all other
gospels could be evaluated. If there were those in the Colossian
church who were casting doubt on the completeness of the
Christian message as delivered to them by Epaphras, they would
through this letter have noted Paul's reassurance that what they had
learned through him was the word of truth.

How we need to lay hold on what Francis Schaeffer described as
"true truth". What is "true truth"? It is the truth contained in the
gospel of Jesus Christ. It is the final truth. Nothing can be added to
it, nor subtracted from it. It is the truth, the whole truth and
nothing but the truth. Some young intellectuals say: "Well, that may
be true for you, but I have a different truth." The truth of the gospel,
however, is not relative (one thing for me and another thing for
you); it is absolute and therefore universal – the same truth for all.

Paul reinforces this point by telling the Colossians that the
gospel they had received was the same gospel that was being
received all over the then known world – and was
bearing fruit. The gospel of Christ does not need
to be "enriched" with new ideas; it is well able to
sprout and bring forth life of itself. The gospel is
"the grace of God in truth". God's mercy, not our
merit, was the magnet that drew Him from above.
That's the truth. Nothing must be added to it and
nothing must be taken away.

FURTHER STUDY

John 17:17;
Gal. 1:6–12

1. Where is true
truth to be found?
2. Take seriously to
heart what Paul
wrote to the
Galatians.

## Prayer

Father, how grateful I am for the simplicity of the gospel. I can add nothing to it
to make it more effective, and if I take anything away it becomes ineffective. May
I never be moved from its simplicity. Amen.

# High praise indeed

*"You learned it from Epaphras, our dear fellow-servant,
who is a faithful minister of Christ ..." (v.7)*

**For reading & meditation – Colossians 1:7–8**

The Bible, among other things, is a book of biographies. Some are short, as is that of Epaphras, the leader of the church at Colosse. Though there is another reference to Epaphras in this letter, we have enough information here to put together a picture of him: "our dear fellow-servant, who is a faithful minister". This is high praise indeed.

The worth of praise is always determined by the one giving the praise. Who praised Epaphras? Paul, the great apostle. It has been said that the final test of an individual's work is not only to ask "What has he or she done?" but also: "Could other people work with him or her?" Epaphras was a good colleague – Paul called him a "fellow-servant". Yet in addition he was a "faithful minister". He wasn't merely loyal to his fellow workers in the ministry; he was devoted to the needs of his flock.

In emphasising the point Paul continues: "who also told us of your love in the Spirit". Epaphras would have been well aware of the faults of the Colossian Christians, but he was not obsessed by them. He was ready to notice and commend the virtues of his people. It still remains a wonderful compliment to say with truth of a particular person: "You never heard him say an unkind word against anyone." No greater eulogy, I believe, could be given of any of us at our passing than that we were good colleagues, faithful in our work and service for Christ, and swift to see and ready to speak of the good in others.

FURTHER STUDY

1 Cor. 3:5–8;
Acts 9:36–39

1. What is the secret of successful co-operation?
2. Will your death generate the same reactions as Dorcas's did?

## Prayer

O God, may I so live before You that at my passing people may also say of me that I was easy to work with, devoted to Jesus Christ, and saw the good in others more quickly than the bad. In Jesus' Name. Amen.

# There's more

*"… we have not stopped praying for you and asking God to fill you with the knowledge of his will …" (v.9)*

**For reading & meditation – Colossians 1:9–10**

The apostle Paul was not only a great preacher; he was also a great pray–er. Many times when writing his letters he paused to break out in extempore prayer. And his prayers were not rambling petitions but always bore down on particular matters. Those who seem to have great prowess in prayer, though they are careful to worship and adore God, don't indulge themselves in flowery phrases. Instead they quickly get down to details. Watch how Paul does this in the verses before us.

After telling the Colossian Christians that he had prayed ceaselessly for them since the day he had heard about them, he first asks God to fill them with knowledge of His will through all spiritual wisdom and understanding. Notice the word "fill". It suggests that however much the Colossian Christians had received from the Lord, there was still room for more. You see, no one can ever rest and say: "I am now *completely* Christian." For the definition of a Christian grows the more we see of Christ and the more we know of Him. Rabindranath Tagore, the Indian poet, said "The eternal cry is – more." Whatever the Colossians knew of God, there was much more to know and much more to discover.

Also significant is the phrase "bearing fruit in every good work". Paul prayed that the life of God might flow through the Colossian Christians and produce substantial spiritual fruit: not fruitless suckers but fruit that the Master can enjoy – on the lowest branches the low-hanging fruit of humility and on the highest branches the knowledge of God.

**FURTHER STUDY**

1 Cor. 3:1–2;
John 16:12–15

1. What do we lose by not being ready to receive?
2. What is the condition for receiving more?

## Prayer

O God, the days of my life go by at tremendous speed, but You are still pouring, and there is always room in my heart for more. And the more of You I receive the more of You I want. I love You Father. Amen.

# You'll get through

*"... being strengthened with all power ... so that you
may have great endurance and patience ..." (v.11)*

**For reading & meditation – Colossians 1:11–12**

One contemporary Christian buzz word is "power". People say: "We need more power to witness, more power to work miracles, more power to make the world sit up and take notice." I agree. My personal burden and prayer for many decades now has been to see the power of God moving mightily on masses of people in true revival. There's nothing wrong with asking God to demonstrate His power to save, heal and deliver; it's a legitimate prayer concern. But what Paul has in mind as he prays for power to be seen in the lives of the Colossian Christians is power to joyfully endure all trials and come through them with thanksgiving.

The world in which you live and work is one where you need a full supply of God's power if you are to continue steadfastly and persevere despite opposition, setbacks and frustrations. Paul, when writing to the Corinthians, said that through endurance the servants of God commend themselves (see 2 Corinthians 6:4). Today many of you have to go out and contend with fierce antagonism, bitter disappointment, rejection from friends or family, a marriage failure, loss of friendship, a financial reversal or something similar. But listen carefully to me: *you will get through.* And the reason you will get through is because God's power is at work in your life. You may be shaken but you will not be shattered, knocked down but not knocked out. What is more, you will come through the experience with thanksgiving. You will be thankful because through your difficulties you will be brought closer to God Himself.

**FURTHER STUDY**

Zech. 4:6;
Acts 1:8

1. How does God work?
2. What happens when God exercises His power?

## Prayer

My Father and my God, You do not promise to keep me from difficulties, but You do promise me that You will bring me through. On that I can rely. And that is enough. Thank You Father. Amen.

# Gone! Gone!

> "... the Father ... has qualified you to share in the
> inheritance of the saints ..." (v.12)

**For reading & meditation – Colossians 1:12–14**

Exactly where Paul's prayer for the Colossians finishes we can't be sure. Probably it ends with the phrase "joyfully giving thanks to the Father" (v.12a) because what he talks about next were things the Colossians possessed already: a share in the inheritance of the saints, deliverance from the kingdom of darkness, a place in the Kingdom of the Son, redemption, and the forgiveness of sins. They did not need to seek these; the blessings were already theirs.

All the conditions necessary for becoming an heir of God and a joint heir with Christ had been met by their acceptance of Christ, and they were now full members of God's new society. But more: they had been "rescued ... from the dominion of darkness and brought ... into the kingdom of the Son he loves." We must never forget that salvation is a rescue mission – a deliverance. We don't climb out of the darkness; we are delivered from it. That's why the Son gets all the glory, for the glory always goes to the One who saves, not to the one who is saved.

Then: "in whom we have redemption, the forgiveness of sins". The Christian faith begins here. We need redemption from our sins and forgiveness for our sins. Both are provided in Jesus Christ. I know of nothing more wonderful than redemption and forgiveness. The slate is wiped clean. Once I ask for forgiveness from Christ then I am, as far as God is concerned, a person without a past history. I am just like a newborn baby; I have a future but no past. How amazing.

| FURTHER STUDY |
| --- |
| Isa. 9:2; 1 Pet. 2:9 |
| 1. What picture does Isaiah use to describe redemption? 2. What are you because of God's forgiveness? |

## Prayer

O Father, forgive me if the wonder of redemption and forgiveness does not hit my soul with the force and power it ought. Help me open my heart to the thrilling fact that all my sins are gone. Gone! Hallelujah!

# The right way for everything

*"He is the image of the invisible God, the firstborn over all creation." (v.15)*

**For reading & meditation – Colossians 1:15–16**

Paul now plunges into the main purpose for his letter – to remind the Colossian Christians of the supremacy and sufficiency of Christ. He knows that once they grasp this, it will be more than enough to protect them from error. Jesus is the image of the invisible God, he tells them. Christ takes the place of idols in their lives. Idols misrepresent God – Jesus represents Him.

He goes on to say that "He is the firstborn over all creation." This does not mean, as the Jehovah Witnesses (and others) claim, that Christ is the first created Being. It is ridiculous to say that of the One who is the image of the invisible God, for the word "image" means *exact* representation.

But pause to consider these amazing words: "all things were created by him and for him." The Church, generally speaking, has never taken these words seriously. But if everything is created *by* Him and *for* Him then creation is designed to work His way. When it does it works effectively; when it follows some other way it works towards its ruin. The way of Christ is written not only into the texts of Scripture but into the texture of the whole of creation. If we are created by Him and for Him then He is inescapable. You cannot escape Christ, for His stamp is upon the whole of His creation. Like the watermark in paper, Christ is written into the structure of our beings. This means that the Christian way is the right way to do everything. The non-Christian way is the wrong way to do everything. *Everything.*

**FURTHER STUDY**

Rom. 7:18–25a;
1 Cor. 15:20–28

1. How was Paul rescued from wrong living?
2. What will happen when all Christ's enemies are subdued?

## Prayer

Father, I look around and see that the world is finding out how not to live. And finding out painfully – through inner conflicts, guilt and fears. Oh why don't people turn to You? Father, I am so thankful I know You. Amen.

# Christ – a centripetal force

*"He is before all things, and in him all things
hold together."* (v.17)

**For reading & meditation – Colossians 1:17–18**

These words clinch everything: "in him all things hold together."
We could also say: "Out of Him all things fly apart – they go to
pieces." One commentator puts it like this: "Everything in Him
[Jesus] is centripetal; everything outside of Him is centrifugal."
Everything in Christ is bound together in perfect harmony, not
simply by power but by love. In this very same epistle we find the
words: "And over all these virtues put on love, which binds them all
together in perfect unity" (Col. 3:14). A man who was disinherited
by his family because he became a Christian rose to become a
leading figure in society, and sought to relate to his family even
though they were reluctant to have anything to do with him. Slowly
his love for them won through. He held the family together because
he was held together within – by being in Christ. One day, a nuclear
scientist shut himself in his office for hours and refused to take any
calls because the fact hit him as never before that what held all
creation together was not a force but a Person – Christ.

On one occasion our Lord said: "He who is not with me is
against me, and he who does not gather with me
scatters" (Matt. 12:30). Everything outside of
Christ scatters. Get among any group of
Christians, talk about Christ and you are together.
Talk about our "church customs" and you are
apart. Let this simple but solemn truth grip your
soul with new force today: in Him all things hold
together, out of Him all things fly apart.

**FURTHER STUDY**

John 1:3;
Rev. 1:12–18

1. *Ponder John's
words for an
explanation of
Colossians 1:17.*
2. *Use the verses
from Revelation for
an expansion of
Colossians 1:18.*

## Prayer

O Father, I am so grateful that Your Son is my centre and my circumference. In
Him I am held together, never to fly apart. Let this truth be more than something I hold; may it be something that holds me. In Jesus' Name. Amen.

# "The Order of the Resurrection"

*"And he is the head of the body, the church ..."*
*(v.18)*

**For reading & meditation – Colossians 1:18**

Colossians and Ephesians have similar themes, looked at from different perspectives. Ephesians portrays the Church of Christ, whereas Colossians depicts the Christ of the Church. Ephesians focuses on the Body; Colossians focuses on the Head. In today's verse Paul shows that Christ is not only the Head of creation; He is also the Head of the Church. The formation of the Church is undoubtedly the greatest project God has ever undertaken. An outstanding Welsh preacher, Tom Rees, described it as "The Divine Masterpiece". Nothing in heaven or earth can ever eclipse it. And just as Christ's being Lord of creation reveals His pre-eminence so does His position as Head of the Church.

Those of us who count ourselves as part of Christ's Body, the Church, should remember, as Dick Lucas points out, that: "If a body does not hold fast to its head it can hardly hope to survive!" The Head will never lose contact with the Body, but often the Body loses contact with the Head. When the Church fails to hold fast to its Head it soon loses direction. We cannot say Christ's pre-eminence is being acknowledged in the Church if the Church refuses to go in the direction that the Head desires.

**FURTHER STUDY**

Rom. 14:9;
Eph. 1:9b–23;
Heb. 2:5–8

*1. What does Romans teach us about Christ's resurrection?*
*2. How can we reconcile the verses from Ephesians and Hebrews?*

When Paul says Christ "is the beginning and the firstborn from among the dead" he is referring to our Lord's resurrection, which marked the beginning of a new order – what might be called "The Order of the Resurrection". Others who were physically raised from the dead were raised only to die again. Those who die in Christ will be raised *never* to die again.

## Prayer

Father, how glad I am that I belong to "The Order of the Resurrection". I can think of nothing surer and more secure. All honour and glory be to Your matchless Name. Amen.

# Christ – the pleasure of God

*"For God was pleased to have all his fulness dwell
in him ..." (v.19)*

**For reading & meditation – Colossians 1:19–20**

This passage is bursting with meaning. Paul has moved from
thinking of Christ as the originator of creation to Him being the
Head of the Church and the procurer of our redemption. In case
some might think that God's relationship to Christ when He was
here on earth was different from the relationship they experienced
in eternity, Paul tells us that "God was *pleased* to have all his fulness
dwell in him."

"God dwells in every Christian," said E. Stanley Jones, "but He
dwells sufferingly. We give Him a great deal of pain. He stays, but
not without some degree of travail." The one Person in whom God
dwells without any pain is Jesus. One commentator put it: "God is
at home in Jesus", and "The attempt to impose divine qualities upon
the framework of human nature has always resulted in a
monstrosity – always except in the case of Jesus." Others have
attempted to make themselves divine; Jesus' divinity was part of His
very nature. In Him the supernatural was natural. All His virtues
were balanced by opposite virtues. Considering the sinless life of
Jesus it is no surprise to find that at the River
Jordan God opened the heavens above Him and
said: "This is my Son, whom I love; with him I am
well pleased" (Matt. 3:17). No wonder, for He is
such a wonderful Son

Paul also reminds us that Jesus is the centre of
reconciliation for everything, and that through
the cross peace will be established in every corner
of the universe. He restores to the universe the
principle of harmony which sin so brutally
disturbed.

**FURTHER STUDY**

Isa. 53:10a;
2 Cor. 5:17–21

1. What did God's
pleasure cost Jesus?
2. What does
reconciliation entail?

## Prayer

Father, how I long that by dwelling in Your Son I too might become a centre of
reconciliation. Through Christ's work in me may I bring peace and harmony to
my world today. Amen.

# Three life positions

*"Once you were alienated from God and were enemies
in your minds ..." (v.21)*

**For reading & meditation – Colossians 1:21–23**

These verses have been described as one of the most beautiful sections of the New Testament, comparable with many of the statements in Ephesians 2. Paul reminds the Colossians of what Christ has done. We should never tire of hearing it, for the central dynamic of the Christian life is not what we do for Christ but what He has done for us. Dick Lucas analyses these verses: what you once were, where you now stand, and how you must go on.

What were we? "Enemies," says Paul. Many are unwilling to apply this term to themselves in their unconverted state. They say: "I was never at enmity with God, just apathetic to Him." But dig deep into every human heart and you find not just apathy towards God but antagonism. Embedded like splintered glass in every soul is a basic hatred of God. We don't like the idea of God telling us what to do and act rebelliously. Yet where are we now through grace? Reconciled. The enmity is over and peace has come to our hearts. We stand in God's presence "holy ... without blemish and free from accusation".

FURTHER STUDY

Gal. 3:2–5;
Matt. 13:13

1. What is the result
of believing?
2. What is a
condition for being
saved?

And how do we go on? We are to "continue in [the] faith, established and firm, not moved from the hope held out in the gospel" (v.23). If we are to continue in the faith then we must remain content with the gospel that brought us to Christ and not try to change it. Those who seek to add or take away from the gospel do not continue in the faith; they contaminate it.

## Prayer

Father, grant that I might never move from the gospel that challenged me and changed me. May my song ever be: "On Christ the solid Rock I stand, all other ground is sinking sand." In Jesus' Name I pray. Amen.

# The continuing cross

*"… I fill up in my flesh what is still lacking in regard
to Christ's afflictions …"* (v.24)

**For reading & meditation – Colossians 1:24**

When Paul says he must fill up in his flesh "what is still lacking
in regard to Christ's afflictions" is he suggesting there was
some deficiency in Christ's atonement? No. Christ had suffered on
the cross for the sins of the world and now Paul "filled up Christ's
afflictions by experiencing the added sufferings necessary to carry
this good news to a lost world" (NIV Study Bible).

J.B. Phillips gives an interesting translation of this verse: "I am
suffering on behalf of you who have heard the gospel, yet I am far
from sorry about it. Indeed, I am glad, because it gives me a chance
to complete in my own sufferings something of the untold pains
which Christ suffers on behalf of his body, the Church." We make
much of the sufferings of Christ on the cross – and rightly so – but
what about the continuous suffering He undergoes from those who
bear His Name yet do such ugly things? Sometimes members of
His body quarrel over seemingly insignificant things. Paul had
strong words to say to such immaturity when he reproves the
Corinthians for dividing over personalities (see 1 Cor. 3:1–3). Such
fragmentation in His body causes the Head of the
Church to suffer again.

Paul, in this verse, is saying something like
this: "Daily I enter into the crucifixion of Jesus,
take my share of His sufferings, and bleed with
Him and for Him. I am in Christ therefore I
participate in His sufferings for the Church." Next
time you have a cross to bear because of some
people in the Church remember Christ has a cross
to bear for all the people in the Church.

FURTHER STUDY

2 Tim. 3:12;
Matt. 26:37–39;
Mark 10:38–39

1. What is the cost of
living a godly life in
Christ?
2. What light does
Matthew throw on
the verses in Mark?

## Prayer

O Father, I accept that because I am in Christ I am involved in His sufferings
also. Help me to regard this as a real privilege, and not a problem, as a blessing,
not a burden. In Jesus' Name. Amen.

# Saying goodbye to a text

*"I have become its servant by the commission God gave me to present to you the word of God in its fulness ..." (v.25)*

**For reading & meditation – Colossians 1:25**

What constitutes a God-given ministry? Today's verse gives the answer: *having the heart of a servant*. There are many definitions of servanthood but the one I prefer is: "becoming excited about making other people successful". True servanthood will always involve a desire to make the Word of God fully known and Christians fully mature ... and being excited about that fact.

Paul says: "I ...present to you the word of God in its fulness." How do we make known the Word of God in its fulness? One way is by following closely the principles of exposition. A crying need of the contemporary Church, generally speaking, is for verse-by-verse exposition of the Scriptures. There is a tendency to devise clever talks on current events, which may commence with a text from the Bible but make no further reference to it. One man said to me recently: "Our pastor always begins with a text from the Bible ... then immediately says goodbye to it." Though there is a place for topical preaching, if a church does not have a regular system of presenting to its people a verse-by-verse exposition of the Scriptures then the Word of God will not be fully known.

**FURTHER STUDY**

Luke 24:27;
Acts 17:11

1. What is the standard for measuring the Church's proclamation?
2. What distinguished the Bereans from the Thessalonians?

You will have heard the following statement many times before I am sure: "A text taken out of its context quickly becomes a pretext." No one can know Christ better without knowing the Scriptures better, and there is no better way of knowing the Scriptures than by doing as we are doing now – going through them verse by verse.

## Prayer

Father, I see that only through systematic study of Your Word can it be fully understood, and only through the Word can Christ be fully known. Help all your servants handle the Word of God well – myself included. Amen.

# A Christ not in us ...

*"... the glorious riches of this mystery, which is Christ
in you, the hope of glory." (v.27)*

**For reading & meditation – Colossians 1:26–27**

A true servant of God seeks to make the Word of God fully known and Christians fully mature. Paul claims that he has been commissioned for this task, and clearly he did his work well. He based his work on this great truth: "Christ in you, the hope of glory". Paul refers to it as a mystery which though kept hidden for generations had now been made known. "The mystery ... now disclosed" refers, of course, to the fact that Christ indwells Gentiles as well as Jews and welcomes them into His Church on equal terms with Israel – a revelation that first came through the apostle Paul (see Ephesians 3:2–6).

There are many who hold to the fact that Christ is for them, but they have no experience of Christ being in them. They may be ready to assert with the rest of us that we have an advocate with the Father, Jesus Christ, the Righteous One (1 John 2:1), but they do not know Him as a power within them. Paul is saying the secret of maturity is having Christ within, thinking, willing and feeling in the heart of His consenting servant.

"Christ *in* you, the hope of glory." What a phrase. But is it only a hope – a possibility? The word "hope" in Scripture means a sure and certain expectation with no shadow of doubt. To have Christ near to us is not enough. He must be *in* us, subduing the deep selfishness of our nature, ridding us of our moral rottenness. And as William Law said: "A Christ not in us is ... a Christ not ours."

**FURTHER STUDY**

John 15:4–5;
Gal. 2:20

1. What proves you are in Christ?
2. What does Christ living in you entail?

## Prayer

O Father, what a thought: Christ is not just near to me or around me but living in me, His conquering life overcoming my inward death. How wonderful. All honour and glory be to Your precious Name. Amen.

# Beyond "small talk"

*"We proclaim him, admonishing and teaching everyone
with all wisdom ..." (v.28)*

**For reading & meditation – Colossians 1:28**

The word "everyone", which appears twice in this verse, suggests that Paul was thinking here of his personal relationships with believers. Paul had no time for what some people call "the Church within the Church" – those Christians who are more committed than others and more ready to respond to deeper truths. Maturity is not for a spiritual elite – it is for everyone.

How did Paul go about the task of helping people become mature? By "admonishing and teaching everyone with all wisdom". To admonish individuals is to correct them, to teach is to educate – to lead people into deeper truths and a richer understanding of the things of God. Does this mean that in all our conversations with fellow Christians we ought to be seeking to correct and teach each other? Of course not. I am sure Paul enjoyed "small talk" in the same way that we do, but I am sure also that when an occasion arose in which he saw a need to correct, encourage, or exhort, he would immediately seek to do so. Paul concentrated on the goal of bringing others to maturity, and I can imagine him asking at appropriate times questions such as these of his fellow believers: How is your prayer life going? What's your relationship with the Lord like? Are you having any struggles that you might want me to pray about, or help you with? How different relationships would be in the Body of Christ if, when talking with our Christian brothers and sisters, we would be as interested in their spiritual health as we are in their physical health.

**FURTHER STUDY**

Eph. 5:19, 21

1. What does the first verse teach about giving encouragement?
2. What helps when we need grace in receiving admonition?

## Prayer

Heavenly Father, I know that to be mature in Christ is to be mature indeed. Help me become excited about making others spiritually successful. I yield my all to be mature and to help others become mature. In Jesus' Name. Amen.

# "Mightily enkindled"

*"To this end I labour, struggling with all his energy, which so powerfully works in me." (v.29)*

**For reading & meditation – Colossians 1:29**

The Amplified Version expresses this verse: "For this I labour, striving with all the superhuman energy which He so mightily enkindles and works within me." Paul's labour did not depend on human energy but the power that came from Christ. He lived by all the energy that Christ mightily enkindled and generated within him. He put into his ministry all the energy he could muster and found that as he did, Christ added His energy also.

I have often heard my friend Dr Larry Crabb talk to counsellors about this verse. He asks them: How often when you interact with people in counselling are you aware of an energy flowing through you that doesn't come from you but from Christ? When he invites a show of hands in response, few are raised. Permit me to ask you a similar question now: How aware are you when you go about your service for Jesus Christ (and I am not just talking about counselling) of an energy flowing through you and out of you that is superhuman? If you were to ask that question of me I would say: "Much too infrequently".

Paul, however, threw his heart and soul into everything he did and found the energy of Christ matching his every effort. When he said "I labour" he was using a term (*kopiao* in the Greek) which signifies labouring to the point of weariness. He poured out what was poured in, not with reservation but with *all* the energy that Christ generated within him. Far too often our experience begins and ends in these words: "To this end I labour, struggling."

**FURTHER STUDY**

Eph. 3:16, 17b–19

1. What are the source and the course of Christ's power?
2. What results from being rooted and established in love?

## Prayer

O God, forgive me that so much of my life can be expressed in those words: "I labour … struggling." Help me experience the energy of Christ working in me and through me. In His Name I pray. Amen.

# One heart and one mind

*"My purpose is that they may be encouraged in heart
and united in love ..." (v.2)*

**For reading & meditation – Colossians 2:1–2**

Here Paul really opens up his heart to the Colossians and also the believers in Laodicea, to whom his letter would be read (see 4:16). He speaks of his great concern that a serious error was circulating among them. The apostle longs that they may "be encouraged in heart and united in love". The Amplified Bible has: "that your hearts may be encouraged as they are knit together in love". Nothing is more encouraging to believers than knowing their hearts are united in love. However, the opposite is also true.

The wise apostle is aware that lasting unity depends on truth as well as love. The believers at Colosse must be of one mind as well as one heart; hence his concern that they may have the full riches of understanding in order to know the mystery of God, namely Christ. The "errorists" in Colosse believed that revelation could be received outside of the Saviour, but here Paul lays down the thought that all essential truth is found *in* Christ, and they need not look any further than Him for spiritual understanding.

Just as in New Testament times, so today errorists are creeping into the Church – men and women who claim to have insight and revelation beyond that which Scripture unfolds. The unity of believers is at risk when the people of God are not of one mind on the things that are essential. A common mind about the truths of the Bible and the supremacy of Christ is the only possible basis for Christian unity. If there is no common mind there can be no common heart.

**FURTHER STUDY**

John 17:21;
Eph. 4:3

1. Why did Jesus want all believers to be one?
2. How must the unity of the Spirit be kept?

## Prayer

O Father, help Your children everywhere to have not only a common heart but also a common mind. And help us, too, not to sacrifice truth in the interests of unity. In Jesus' Name we pray. Amen.

# An exciting treasure hunt

*"... in whom are hidden all the treasures of wisdom
and knowledge." (v.3)*

**For reading & meditation – Colossians 2:3**

There is enough truth in these glowing words to feed our minds and hearts for a whole year. The point Paul has been making is that no essential truths are withheld from anyone who belongs to Christ. "*All* the treasures of wisdom and knowledge" are hidden in Him. But it is hidden truth. Our Lord conceals as well as reveals. You know and you don't know. But what you don't see spurs you on to continuous discovery.

This perpetual discovery has become the most thrilling thing in my life. Every day I feel there is some new surprise to be found up ahead. Daily (with few exceptions) I come to the Bible, and there are times when I am beside myself with excitement as I see something I had never seen before. Christians who go from week to week without ever opening up their Bibles and focusing on some aspect of God's message to them must live dull lives. I fail to understand how they can exist without delving into the treasures of wisdom and knowledge that are found in Christ and revealed to us in the Scriptures.

"This unfolding revelation of Christ," says one writer, "puts a surprise around every corner, makes life pop with novelty and discovery, makes life well worth the living." The Christian life is dynamic, not static. The more you know, the more you know you don't know, and what you know sets you on fire to know more. The more we know of Christ the more we want to know, and this discovery will go on forever. We will never go beyond Him. Never.

FURTHER STUDY

Isa. 45:3;
Rom. 11:33–36

*1. What is God's
purpose in revealing
hidden treasure?
2. Turn Paul's words
into a direct hymn of
praise to God.*

## Prayer

O Father, I am so glad that what I know of You and Your Son impels me to find out more and more. I am on the most exciting treasure hunt in the world – set to discover the treasures hidden in Christ. Amen.

# "In good order"

*"I tell you this so that no-one may deceive you by
fine-sounding arguments."* (v.4)

**For reading & meditation – Colossians 2:4–5**

The reason Paul told the believers at Colosse and Laodicea that all the treasures of wisdom and knowledge are embedded in the mystery of Christ and nowhere else is because, as Eugene Peterson puts it in *The Message*, he didn't "want anyone leading them off on some wild-goose chase after other so-called mysteries or secrets". They must not allow themselves to be deceived.

The very first sin, you remember, took place because Eve allowed herself to be deceived. Had she checked Satan's words against the Word that had been given her by God, and held to that, then she would not have succumbed to the first temptation. There are many persuasive speakers in today's Church, and all Christians would do well to check everything they hear or read against the infallible Scriptures for the truthfulness of its content.

Though error was threatening the churches at Colosse and Laodicea it is obvious from Paul's next words that things were not all that bad. "I ... delight to see how orderly you are and how firm your faith in Christ is." They were standing firm in an orderly and unbroken fashion. These two go together – orderliness and a firm faith in Christ. It works the other way also: where there is no firmness of faith in Christ there is no order; instead there is disorder. Firmness of faith in Christ and good order are root and fruit. Loss of faith in Christ and disorder are also root and fruit. In Him we are in good order; out of Him we are in dis-order.

FURTHER STUDY

1 Tim. 6:3–5;
1 Thess. 3:7–9

*1. What is often the
motive behind false
teaching?
2. What are the
results of standing
firm in the Lord?*

## Prayer

My Father and my God, I am so thankful that life holds together at the centre when we are firmly fixed in Your Son. We stay in good order when we are under Your orders. Amen.

# Give, take, build

"... just as you received Christ Jesus as Lord, continue
to live in him, rooted and built up in him ..." (vv.6–7)

**For reading & meditation – Colossians 2:6–7**

These two verses sum up the entire epistle. No better definition of the Christian life could be given than: "as you received Christ Jesus as Lord, continue to live in him". These two requirements – receiving and continuing – ought to be made clear to every new Christian. And those who have been on the Way some time need to be reminded of them also. Receiving Christ is only the beginning. The foundation is there to be built on.

We received Christ by surrender and receptivity. We give to Him and take from Him – relationship reduced to its simplest terms. Our giving involves giving ourselves. When He has that, He has all. And part of the purpose of giving is so that we may receive. God asks that we give our all in order that He may give His all. Paul says: "As you received Christ Jesus as *Lord*", not merely Example or Teacher. And you cannot really call Him Saviour unless you call Him Lord. He saves those He owns – no others.

When we continue to give ourselves to Him then we are rooted in Him, built up in Him, and our lives overflow with thankfulness.

Rooted in Christ we grow in Him. We hardly bury a seed to see the last of it. Established in Him we are built up in Him. And the final test is how thankful you are. If you do not give thanks regularly for the fact that you are favoured of God then you ought to question whether you are indeed a Christian.

**FURTHER STUDY**

James 1:4–8;
Eph. 4:13–15

1. What are the conditions for receiving from God?
2. How does Paul define Christian maturity?

## Prayer

Dear Father, I would give, give, give, take, take, take, build, build, build. Let all I take from You fit me to give more. I would be the best person I can be. And above all, thank You for saving me. In Jesus' Name. Amen.

# Godless philosophies

*"See to it that no-one takes you captive through hollow and deceptive philosophy …" (v.8)*

**For reading & meditation – Colossians 2:8**

Paul now challenges the Colossians with a clear warning: don't go near to false teachers – those who mix truth with error, and spout deceptive philosophies; they will take you captive. J.B. Phillips words Paul's cautionary message: "Be careful that nobody spoils your faith through intellectualism or high-sounding nonsense. Such stuff is at best founded on men's ideas of the nature of the world and disregards Christ!"

Philosophy is described by the dictionary as "seeking after wisdom or knowledge, especially that which deals with ultimate reality". Yet any philosophy that is not built on God's revelation in Scripture leads nowhere. Philosophical reasoning and theories may sound fascinating but they contain no real answers to the mysteries of the universe. The truth is found only in Christ. "Any philosophy that leaves out God," said someone, "is like a blind man in a dark room looking for a black cat that isn't there."

It is likely that when Paul used the words "hollow and deceptive philosophies" he had in mind the particular error of the Gnostics who based their reasoning on human theories rather than on Christ.

**FURTHER STUDY**

1 Tim. 1:3–7;
1 Cor. 1:18–25

1. What results from teaching false doctrines?
2. Make Paul's summary of genuine Christian philosophy your own.

Gnosticism purported to offer mature Christians a more excellent way whereby they could outgrow the simplicities of the teaching they received from the apostles and move on through secret knowledge, combined with their faith in Christ, to deeper and more enlightening things. This was nonsense, of course, but many fell for it in the days of the early Church. If something is not Christocentric it will end up being eccentric – off centre. Our Lord is the *truth*, as well as the way and the life.

## Prayer

Gracious and loving heavenly Father, how glad I am that my faith has come to rest not in a combination of Christ and secret knowledge, but in Him and in Him alone. Protect my soul from entertaining error, dear Lord. Amen.

# "Music vaster than before"

*"For in Christ all the fulness of the Deity lives in
bodily form ..." (v.9)*

**For reading & meditation – Colossians 2:9**

The false teaching brought forth the amazing statement: "For in Christ all the fulness of the Deity lives *in bodily form*." God came into matter at the Incarnation and made it the vehicle of divine revelation. Nothing could be more important for our existence on earth, environed as we are with matter. The material is not alien; it is an ally.

The spiritual world manifests itself through the material, in material form and material relationships. "... a body you prepared for me ... I have come to do your will, O God" (Heb. 10:5, 7). God's will for Christ was to be done in and through a body. The Gnostics taught that matter was evil. Hindus believe matter is illusion. Christians, however, say matter is God-made ("God saw that it was good" – Gen. 1:9) and can be used to good purposes. The Kingdom of God, remember, is to come on *earth*.

In case some might claim God came into matter temporarily and partially, Paul says that "all the fulness of the Deity lives in bodily form". There is nothing in God that isn't in Jesus – at least in character and essence. Jesus is God accommodated to human form, not for a short time, but now and always. Christ's body was taken up into Deity and will probably bear the marks of the nail prints through all eternity. His humanity is not something He takes off like a wrap. Christ is both human and divine – forever. In our Lord body and spirit were reconciled, and because of that, as one poet put it: "There beats out music vaster than before."

FURTHER STUDY

Phil. 2:9–11;
Heb. 2:14–18

1. What was the consequence of Christ's self-humbling?
2. Why was Jesus made like His brothers in every way?

## Prayer

O Lord Jesus Christ, the meeting place of God and man, matter and spirit, and the reconciling place of all, grant that I may witness to the Word who became flesh. In Jesus' Name I ask it. Amen.

# "Fulness of life in Him"

*"… and you have been given fulness in Christ, who is the head over every power and authority." (v.10)*

**For reading & meditation – Colossians 2:10**

The Gnostics had bypassed the Incarnation saying it was beneath God's dignity to touch matter, let alone enter into it. Instead they taught you could attain fulness of life by knowing God directly. In reality, however, we come to fulness of life in Jesus Christ or we do not come to it at all. E. Stanley Jones said: "Apart from Jesus we know little or nothing about God, and what we do know is often wrong." Jesus said: "I am the way and the truth *and the life*" (John 14:6). He is life, and apart from life we cannot and do not come to fulness of life.

Nowadays some Christians, in order to accommodate other religions, take Christ and someone else: Christ and Mohammed, Christ and Buddha, Christ and Jung. They do this, they say, in the interests of universality. But by adding to Him they reduce universality, for He is universal. To be in Him is to be in everything that is of reality in the universe.

But there's more: the believer also shares His victory – He is Head over every power. We need fear no longer the prince of darkness or any other authority. Christ is the One who is in control of everything and everyone. Dick Lucas says that this verse unfolds two themes: the fact that because we have the fulness of God's presence with us here then we have all we can have this side of heaven; and with regard to heaven's victory over powers and principalities we share with Christ all that He has won. To this I say a hearty "Amen".

**FURTHER STUDY**

John 14:7–11;
Eph. 1:9–13

1. What is the condition for knowing God?
2. Is the fulness of life described by Paul a reality for you?

## Prayer

O God, help me to make this my affirmation: fulness of life is in Christ; emptiness of life outside of Him. This is my verdict. May I live by it every day of my life. In Jesus' Name. Amen.

# Complete in Him

*"In him you were also circumcised, in the putting off of the sinful nature ..." (v.11)*

**For reading & meditation – Colossians 2:11–12**

It is unlikely that these verses are intended to combat the same error that had caused controversy in the Galatian churches, namely that Gentiles should be circumcised just like Jews. What is more probable is that the false teachers were urging on the Christians the idea that they needed to combine their faith in Christ not just with secret knowledge but with man-made regulations such as circumcision.

It may have been also that Gnostics were persuading the Colossian and Laodicean believers to accept the idea that circumcision was an act of dedication and consecration, a second initiation subsequent to baptism. Paul is saying circumcision is unnecessary because they already possess a purification of which Christ is the source. At conversion, he explains, there takes place a circumcision not done by hands – that of sins being forgiven and cleansing from unrighteousness.

"You were buried with Christ in baptism," he continues. They had already died with Christ so now it followed that as He was raised from the dead so they too were raised with Him. We need not add to what Christ has already done. God can do nothing greater for us than He has done in Christ.

Paul, in the previous verse, made the point that Christians are complete in Christ. Here he adds that we are only complete in Christ when we acknowledge His completeness. "It takes a complete Christ," said D.L. Moody, "to make a complete Christian." It's no good saying Christ is complete then trying to add something to Him. He is either complete or incomplete. Period.

FURTHER STUDY
Rom. 6:3–4;
Heb. 7:24–28

1. What is baptism intended to lead on to?
2. What are the grounds for our confidence in Christ?

## Prayer

O Father, I see the importance of trusting only in You and in the atoning merits of Your Son. I need nothing for my salvation other than my trust in Him. Thank You my Father. Amen.

# Our cancelled IOUs

*"He forgave us all our sins, having cancelled the written code ... nailing it to the cross." (vv.13–14)*

**For reading & meditation – Colossians 2:13–14**

God cannot do for us anything greater than that which He has already done in Christ. When we were dead in our sins His Spirit moved into our lives, cut into our sinful nature, and now continually seeks to render inoperative the energy of sin. Does that mean it is *not* possible to sin again? No, but God has made us alive with Christ, and when His life pulses through our soul then freedom from sin *is* possible. Paul now launches into a graphic description of salvation. God has not only made us alive with Christ but He has cancelled the written code that was against us, nailing it to His cross. What beautiful word pictures.

"Written code" means a handwritten note. It is the Greek term for an IOU with certain penalties being required if payment is not made. The word "cancelled" in the Greek (*exaleipho*) means to wipe off. This is what Christ has done with our sins. The blood of Christ has sponged off the written code that condemned us. It is as if it had never been.

Paul uses one more word picture: "he took it away, nailing it to the cross". In ancient times the record of a paid debt would sometimes be nailed to a public notice board so that everyone could see the matter was settled. Our Lord has taken the debt we owed and nailed it to the most public place in the universe – the cross. When Christ cried "It is finished" He meant the work of our redemption was complete. The cancelled note hangs on the cross for all to see.

**FURTHER STUDY**

Matt. 18:23–35;
John 8:10–11

1. What obligation goes with cancelled IOUs?
2. What is required of those who have been forgiven?

## Prayer

Father, when the hosts of hell try to tell me that my sins are not forgiven I shall point them to the cross and show them the cancelled note, placarded there for all to see. I am eternally grateful. Amen.

# Stripped of sham authority

*"And having disarmed the powers and authorities, he made a public spectacle of them ..." (v.15)*

**For reading & meditation – Colossians 2:15**

This is exciting stuff. To feel the impact of Paul's words I quote two different translations of this text: first, J.B. Phillips: "And then, having drawn the sting of all the powers ranged against us, he exposed them, shattered, empty and defeated, in his final glorious triumphant act!" Now, Eugene Peterson: "He stripped all the spiritual tyrants in the universe of their sham authority at the cross and marched them naked through the streets" (*The Message*).

Doubtless the picture Paul had in mind was the triumphal procession that customarily took place after a great conquest in Roman times. Hundreds of weary prisoners of war would be tied to chariots and dragged through the streets so that everyone could witness their shame. For the citizens who belonged to the conquering army it was a wonderful sight, but a sad experience for those who had been conquered.

What a striking illustration this is of the conquest that our Lord achieved for us at Calvary. Just as the Roman citizens could see that they had nothing to fear from the once proud soldiers now being paraded before them, so we no longer need to fear Satan and his minions who tried to end the life and ministry of Jesus at the cross. If Satan and his forces have any power over us it is only because we let them. They attempt to masquerade as conquerors but it is all a sham. They have been ignominiously defeated. Satan thought he would have a great victory at the cross but the tables have been turned. It is Christ's victory the cross proclaims. And how!

**FURTHER STUDY**

Rom. 8:31–39;
Eph. 6:10–13

1. Turn the plural pronouns in the Romans verses into singular ones.
2. What enemies are ranged against us as Christians?

## Prayer

O Father, I see that Christ's victory on the cross is my victory too. He won it by fighting; I enter into it by just trusting. It sounds too good to be true. But also too good not to be true. Amen.

# Shadow-lands

*"Therefore do not let anyone judge you by what you eat or drink, or with regard to a religious festival …"* (v.16)

**For reading & meditation – Colossians 2:16–17**

Paul now encourages the Colossian believers to celebrate Christ's victory for them in a life free from unnecessary rituals and ceremonies. Clearly an attempt was being made in the church at Colosse to persuade the believers to be concerned about such matters as diets and keeping religious festivals. This erroneous approach was calculated to make people believe that Christ's sacrifice and presence in the life of the believer were not enough to achieve holiness; other matters such as rituals and ceremonies were essential. Paul will have none of this, of course, and dismisses the idea in no uncertain terms. This is how Eugene Peterson paraphrases the opening statement of verse 16: "So don't put up with anyone pressuring you in details of diet, worship services or holy days." Strong words – and words most definitely needed if they were to maintain their life of freedom in Christ and assert that He was all that mattered to them.

Paul goes on to say: "These are a shadow of the things that were to come; the reality, however, is found in Christ." The shadow-land referred to here is the law found in the Old Testament. The rituals it prescribed were to be kept, but they were just *shadows* of what was to come. Their true value lay not in what they were but what they pointed to. Christ is the fulfilment of all that the Old Testament prefigured, and in Him is found all spiritual reality. Those who depend on rituals and ceremonies for their salvation are living in the shadows. Christ is all that is needed. All.

**FURTHER STUDY**

Rom. 14:1–23;
Heb. 10:11–14

1. How do the verses in Romans differ from today's reading?
2. What is the effect of the sacrifice Jesus made?

## Prayer

Father, how glad I am that I am in Christ and that He is in me. What need have I of standing in the shadows when I can stand in the sunshine of Your love as shown to me in Christ? Amen.

# Pride must die ...

*"Do not let anyone who delights in false humility and the
worship of angels disqualify you for the prize." (v.18)*

**For reading & meditation – Colossians 2:18**

J.B. Phillips translates another warning from Paul to the Colossian
believers: "Don't let any man cheat you of your joy in Christ by
persuading you to make yourselves 'humble' and fall down and
worship angels. Such a man, inflated by an unspiritual imagination,
is pushing his way into matters he knows nothing about, and in his
cleverness forgetting the Head."

Some commentators believe that one aspect of the error
threatening the church at Colosse was the insistence on the
veneration of angels, to seek mediators in addition to Christ. If so, it
was Gnosticism in another guise. Paul has no intention of allowing
the false teachers to rob those who are "in Christ" of their prize, and
sets about characterising the individuals concerned: "Such a person
goes into great detail about what he has seen [in visions], and his
unspiritual mind puffs him up with idle notions." Here is the root of
the trouble: those advocating the worship of angels were puffed up
with pride. They claimed to have inside knowledge but really they
had found a "spiritual" way (so called) of drawing attention to
themselves and a new device for inflating their
self-importance.

When counselling Christians with strange
ideas about the faith I have found that often the
underlying motivation is to be different. Having
little sense of identity, and as aligning themselves
with others is not enough of a boost for them,
they go in the other direction. Thus they are
*different*. The root of all this is, as Paul discerned,
pride. William Law put it well: "Pride must die in
us or Christ cannot live in us."

**FURTHER STUDY**

Heb. 1:1–14;
3 John 9–11

1. Why has God set
Jesus above His
companions?
2. What damage can
pride do in a church?

## Prayer

Father, help me to remember that it was pride that turned an angel into a devil
and brought havoc to this fair universe. May I be so secure in You that I will find
my identity in that, not in being different. In Jesus' Name. Amen.

# Keep connected

*"He has lost connection with the Head, from whom the whole body ... grows ..."* (v.19)

**For reading & meditation – Colossians 2:19**

Paul says the type of person causing trouble in the Colossian church had lost connection with the Head. Apparently they were still Christians, but had not held fast to Christ, the Head of the Church.

A similar situation, you remember, occurred when a group of Christians in the church in Pergamum followed the erroneous teachings of Balaam and the Nicolaitans (see Revelation 2:12–17). Apparently they were still members of the congregation. The reason why Christ called them to repentance was because it is impossible to remain true to Christ and at the same time toy with the error that robs Him of His supremacy and sufficiency.

Paul shows us in this verse – perhaps more clearly than anywhere else in the New Testament – that when we drift away from Christ then we drift away from each other. Show me a church where the members have lost connection with the Head and I will show you a church whose members have lost connection with each other. That church may have exciting social activities, a wonderful musical programme and clever debates, but if its members are not united with Christ then it no longer functions as a church; it becomes a club. What contributes to the spiritual life and health of a church is the Head. Its ministers, teachers, musicians, all have a place, of course, but as Paul explains: "the whole body ... grows as God causes it to grow." This is an astonishing statement. Growth comes not from people but from God. Aggressive methods and strong appeals can add numbers to a church, but only God can make a church *grow*.

**FURTHER STUDY**

Psa. 34:8;
1 Pet. 2:2–3;
Heb. 3:12–14

1. What must follow on from tasting that the Lord is good?
2. What results from holding firmly till the end?

## Prayer

Father, save me from thinking that because a church increases in numbers it is growing. I see that growth comes only when we, Your people, are connected to the Head. Help us stay connected, dear Father. Amen.

# Rules versus relationships

*"Since you died with Christ to the basic principles of this world, why ... do you submit to its rules ...?"* (v.20)

**For reading & meditation – Colossians 2:20–22**

These verses imply that some Colossian converts had already succumbed to false teaching. If so, how can we reconcile this with Paul's commendation of their faith in chapter 1? I think the answer must be that a small number were in danger of being swayed by this error, and it is to those he now issues his warning. Paul is at his most trenchant. Why do you live, he asks, as if you still belonged to this world? Why do you submit to its rules? He is equating the theories of the errorists with the religion of the world.

The world cannot do without religion because humanity, having been made in God's image, has an inbuilt desire to worship. Since it rejects Christ as the only way to God it has to find the elements of its religious structure elsewhere. Satan, the prince of this world, delights in providing people with a religion that satisfies their need to worship but does not ask them to bow the knee to Christ. One commentator says: "The closer in language [Satan's] religion can be to the truth, while yet being different, the better this wily prince is pleased." Rules such as "Do not eat this" are elements of the world's religion and will one day pass away.

Since you died with Christ, says Paul, you are no longer governed by rules, but by your relationship with Him. You are saved not by what You do but by what Christ has done. God has put the Church in the world, but we must make sure that the world does not get into the Church.

FURTHER STUDY
Mark 7:1–23;
John 15:18–21

1. Does Mark 7:8 make you feel uncomfortable?
2. What does relationship with Jesus entail?

## Prayer

Father, You have taken me from the world and put me into Your Church. Help me not only tell others where and to whom I belong but to show them by my every action, my every attitude. Amen.

# The problem of the self

> *"Such regulations ... have an appearance of wisdom, with their self-imposed worship, their false humility ..."* (v.23)

**For reading & meditation – Colossians 2:23**

I wonder how the small group at Colosse who were caught up propagating error responded to Paul's sharp condemnation of their theories. They had persuasive arguments, lived lives of self-discipline, and showed great commitment to what they believed, but the motivation behind it all was worldly pride. On the surface it looked as if these people had a high degree of wisdom but, says Paul, it was merely the appearance of wisdom. Their self-imposed worship, their false humility and their harsh treatment of the body made no impression on him. He saw these things as just ways of showing off, of making themselves look important.

We must pause for a moment to make clear what is meant by "self-imposed worship". J.B. Phillips translates this phrase as "self-inspired efforts at worship". The people Paul is denouncing worshipped God not in the way He wants to be worshipped, but in the way they *thought* He should be worshipped. Referring again to Phillips' translation, he renders the NIV phrases "false humility" as "their policy of self-humbling", and "their harsh treatment of the body" as "their studied neglect of the body". These graphic phrases take us to the very heart of their motivation – they were using spiritual thoughts and ideas as a means to pander to their self-centredness and pride.

I am of the opinion that self-centredness lies at the root of most of our spiritual problems. If we could eliminate self-centredness from the human heart we would have very few difficulties. Of that I am sure. And self-centredness is never more deadly than when it is dressed up in a spiritual garb.

**FURTHER STUDY**

John 4:23–24;
1 John 4:7–12

1. Why must we worship in spirit and in truth?
2. How can we combat self-centredness?

## Prayer

Gracious and loving heavenly Father, help me not to use my faith in the service of self-centredness and egotism. Help me to have a faith that works by love, and nothing but love. In Jesus' Name. Amen.

# Our chief business

*"Since ... you have been raised with Christ, set your
hearts on things above ..." (v.1)*

**For reading & meditation – Colossians 3:1**

Paul's purpose in this letter (as we have repeatedly seen) is to show that Christ is pre-eminent – first and foremost in everything – and that the life of every Christian should reflect that priority. Eugene Peterson paraphrases Paul's words: "So if you're serious about living this new resurrection life with Christ, *act* like it. Pursue the things over which Christ presides." Because we are rooted in Him, alive in Him, hidden in Him, and complete in Him then we must live for Him.

*Living for Him* is the theme that Paul embarks upon as he begins this third chapter, and the way in which he delineates that theme is in terms of *relationships*. First, our relationship with Christ, second, relationships in the local church, third, relationships with the family, fourth, relationship to one's daily work, and fifth, relationships with unbelievers. It has been said that "The chief business of every Christian is to maintain his relationship with Christ." If this relationship is not kept intact then it is impossible for other relationships to succeed.

The injunction to set our hearts on things above, where Christ sits, is based on the fact that we have been raised with Him. Think what that means: we have been granted a relationship with Christ, who is at God's right hand. This relationship we are to pursue by holding fast to Christ, who is the centre and source of all our joy. A Christian is someone who in a sense lives in two places at once: in their earthly place of residence and in Christ. We have to ask ourselves: Where are we most at home?

## Prayer

Father, in coming to Jesus I have come home. Now help me be at home in Him – even more at home than I am in my own home. In Your Son's Name I pray. Amen.

# At home in the heavenlies

*"For you died, and your life is now hidden with Christ in God." (v.3)*

**For reading & meditation – Colossians 3:2–3**

Our relationship with Christ shapes every other relationship. So important is this truth that Paul continues with his theme in the second verse. He is saying: "Look up and see what is going on around Christ. That's where the action is. See things from His perspective" (Eugene Peterson, *The Message*).

It has been said that the Christian faith, unlike some other world religions, has no geographical centre. Judaism focuses on Jerusalem and Islam on Mecca. The Christian faith, however, focuses on heaven, where Christ is seated at the right hand of God. Without being "other worldly" and ignoring our responsibilities here on earth, we seek the things that are beyond the earth. We have died in Christ and now we enjoy a new life – hidden with Christ in God. Why "hidden"? Well, the union that exists between Christ and His people is hidden from the eyes of the men and women of this world. Though they see us going about our tasks they are unaware that the strength by which we live and the power by which we practise our faith is drawn from another world. But believers can only enjoy and draw upon this life as they daily reach up through the avenue of prayer and avail themselves of the resources that are hidden with Christ in God.

**FURTHER STUDY**

Heb. 13:14;
11:13–16

1. Why do Christians have a different view of life from unbelievers?
2. Of whom is God not ashamed to be called their God?

Another believer once asked a wise old Christian: "Where do you live?" With a twinkle in his eye he passed on his business card to the enquirer and said: "This is where my residence is, but if you really want to know where I live – I live *in Christ*."

## Prayer

O God my Father, forgive me if my energy is drawn more from the resources that are below than those that are above. Help me to be at home in the heavenlies. In Jesus' Name. Amen.

# What a day that will be!

*"When Christ , who is your life, appears, then you also
will appear with him in glory." (v.4)*

**For reading & meditation – Colossians 3:4**

The day will dawn when Christ, whom we worship but do not see, will be revealed to the world in all His glory. A paraphrase of this verse might read: "When Christ, your real life, shows Himself physically and visibly once again in the world, you, who are His people, will be as glorious as He." What a day that will be!

As a boy in my native Wales I went to the local pithead to listen to the miners sing as they came up to the surface after their day's work. As the cage brought them up to the pit top they would sing a song that has ineffaceably imprinted itself on my memory:

*Oh that will be, glory for me,
Glory for me, glory for me,
When by His grace I shall look on His face,
That will be glory, be glory for me.*

Although usually just a handful of Christians would start up the chorus, everyone else would join in. Welshmen, as you probably know, love to sing. Often tears would flow down their faces as they sang, leaving white stains on their coal-blackened countenances. Now, whenever I come to this verse in Colossians, my mind goes back to that song and those childhood memories.

When Christ returns it will not just be that His glory is manifested; it will be glory for me also. And for you, if you belong to Him.

**FURTHER STUDY**

1 Thess. 4:16–18;
Matt. 13:36–43

1. How should believers react to thinking of the Day of the Lord?
2. What will happen to believers on the day?

## Prayer

Father, the promise that I will be with You in glory is what keeps me going. What a day it will be. Even so, come Lord Jesus. Amen.

# An idol factory

*"Put to death, therefore, whatever belongs to your earthly nature ..." (v.5)*

**For reading & meditation – Colossians 3:5–6**

Having exhorted his readers to *set* their hearts on the things that are above, Paul invites them to search their hearts. The thrust of his argument is irresistible: if Christ is your life then that means putting to death all things connected with the way of death – sexual immorality, impurity, lust, evil desires and greed. Setting our hearts on the things that are above, and searching our hearts for those things that hinder Christ's life from flowing through us, go together.

Some Christians are against all forms of self-examination, believing it to be a negative approach to life. Concentrate on Christ, they advise, and sinful things will drop away of their own accord. But the phrase "put to death" suggests that something has to be done *by us* to rid us of the evils that reside in our hearts – utilising the power, of course, that comes from Jesus Christ.

Even though we are Christians and have been saved from sin, that does not mean (as we saw) that the roots of sin have been dislodged from our hearts and will never trouble us again. A number believe we can have such an experience of God that sin is completely eradicated and we reach a state of what they describe as "sinless perfection". I do not share that view myself. I know that my heart – even after several decades of divine working – has the possibility of becoming an idol factory. That's why, in addition to setting my affections on things above, I must also search my heart. The one follows on from the other.

**FURTHER STUDY**

Jer. 17:9;
Psa. 139:23–24

1. If you think you can be perfect, reflect on Jeremiah 17:9.
2. If you cannot trust your self-examination, pray Psalm 139:23–24.

## Prayer

Father, I come to You today and ask for Your divine illumination as I search my heart. I want no idolatry within me, no worship of other things. And whatever I find there, help me not to put it to sleep but put it to death. Amen.

# "I'm in for it now"

*"Because of these, the wrath of God is coming."*
(v.6)

**For reading & meditation – Colossians 3:6–7**

It has been said that Paul's imperatives are always supported by incentives. He gave us in verse 4 the incentive of Christ's appearing, and he now attaches to his imperative another inducement, that "the holy anger of God falls upon those who refuse to obey him" ( J.B. Phillips).

The apostle is talking here about those who continue in sin. Those who sin and immediately cry out in repentance are at once forgiven and restored. What is more, providing they are open to God, they will receive the empowerment they need to go on and not sin in that way again. But for those who continue in sin things are quite different. The NIV Study Bible says in its commentary on this text: "God is unalterably opposed to sin and will invariably make sure that it is justly punished." But when? The text is not talking about the judgment that comes at the end of time, but the judgment that God metes out while we are in this body.

Let's face it, often God does not seem in a hurry to judge. How many times have believers committed sin, not repented, and said to themselves: "Uh! That was a terrible thing I did. I'm in for it now"? But seemingly nothing has happened. The truth is that God's judgments are often silent – something dies within us when we continue in sin. We become less of a person. Our creativity shrivels up, our zest for life is eroded by guilt, our ability to stand stress is reduced. The worst thing about sin is to be the one who has sinned.

**FURTHER STUDY**

2 Sam. 12:13–19;
Acts 13:6–12

1. David was forgiven, but what did he still suffer?
2. What words imply Elymas' judgment was remedial?

## Prayer

O Father, help me to understand that Your judgments are not retributive but remedial. You search me in order to save me. Drive this point deep into my spirit. In Jesus' Name. Amen.

# "Life is decision"

*"But now you must rid yourselves of ... anger, rage, malice, slander ..."* (v.8)

**For reading & meditation – Colossians 3:7–10**

Paul considers Christian relationships in the Church. This list of sins is not just plucked out of the air, for every sin mentioned here – anger, rage, malice, slander, filthy language and lying – has the potential to destroy relationships. What an ugly bunch of words!

These things are understandable before our conversion, says Paul, but they ought not to be practised by those who belong to Jesus Christ. Indeed, he tells us in verse 8 to rid ourselves of these non-Christian practices. I know many Christians who react by saying: "Easier said than done." So how do we get rid of anger, rage, malice, slander, filthy language and lying? We stop ourselves having anything to do with them.

Let me expand on that last statement because to some it might sound like exhortation without explanation. "Life," said one philosopher, "is decision." We can decide to be angry or not angry, to lie or not, to use filthy language or not to use it. It is foolish to believe that these just flow out of us of their own accord.

**FURTHER STUDY**

Eph. 4:22–24;
Luke 11:24–26

1. How are we to put off the old self and put on the new?
2. What does Luke say about the dangers of half decisions?

Prior to angry or inappropriate words coming from your mouth you have a moment of choice – to stop them or let them come out. The moment of choice may only be a second – even a split second – but it is there nevertheless. If our lives are under the rule of Christ then it follows that our decisions will come under His rule as well. So it is just a question of will-power. You have to decide: "I will no longer do this." You supply the willingness – He will supply the power.

## Prayer

Father, I decide now to have done with the old life. I am going to strip off the filthy set of ill-fitting clothes and put them in the fire. Instead I'm going to have a new wardrobe – custom-made by Christ. Amen.

# Is a lie justifiable?

*"Do not lie to each other, since you have taken off your
old self with its practices" (v.9)*

**For reading & meditation – Colossians 3:9**

Paul focuses now on the issue of lying. A friend of mine says that
the ultimate test of a person's character is: will that person lie?
How easy it is to lie – even for those who are committed Christians.
Most believers would strive hard not to tell an outright lie, but what
about twisting a meaning to gain a point, misquoting something
someone has said if the misquotation gains an end, exaggerating to
make an impression, or lack of the complete truth? Is there any
difference between telling an outright lie and being loose with the
truth? Some would say there is no difference at all – and I agree.
What lies at the basis of a looseness with the truth? Is it not the fact
that sometimes we persuade ourselves a lie is justifiable?

A group of non-Christian students was asked whether a lie is
ever justifiable. There were five different responses: (1) Yes – in
business. (2) Yes – in politics. (3) Yes – to save a life. (4) Yes – in
war. (5) Yes – when done on behalf of a great cause. The ability to
lie, however, is not an asset but a liability. Paul's command is quite
clear. "Don't do it", he said, "lying is a mark of the old self. Now you
are in Christ you must be different." A preacher
by the name of Dr Speer said Christians must get
hold of two principles: first, God cannot lie;
second, He will not delegate to us the task of lying
for Him. Truth is inviolable. A God who cannot
lie wants followers who will uphold His
principles, not desecrate them.

FURTHER STUDY
John 8:44;
Eph. 4:15, 25

1. Where do lies
come from?
2. How should
Christians speak?

## Prayer

My Father and my God, help me to have truth in the inward parts. Make me
from this moment a transparent person with nothing covered, nothing which I
must conceal from others. In Jesus' Name. Amen.

# "Christians never lie"

*"Do not lie to each other, since you have taken off your old self with its practices" (v.9)*

**For reading & meditation – Colossians 3:9**

Eugene Peterson in *The Message* paraphrases Paul's words: "Don't lie to one another, You're done with that life." The contrast could not be more clear; lies are part of the old life, truth is part of the new. If lies are still in us then we have one foot in the old life. Think of the early Christians standing before tribunals their lives hanging in the balance. A lie would save them from death. They refused. They could die, but they could not lie.

One day a Hindu doctor in India noticed that while relief money was being handed out to a long line of people the man responsible for passing on the rupees occasionally missed out about one in ten and pocketed the money for himself. As the doctor watched, two women he knew passed down the line but were hurried along by the man and given no money. The doctor intervened: "Why did you not give those two women who just passed you the money they were entitled to?" The man insisted that he had given them the money. The doctor asked the women: "Did you receive any money?" "No", they said, whereupon the doctor rebuked the man: "Give them what is due to them right away. Don't you know these women are Christians? And Christians never lie."

**FURTHER STUDY**

John 14:6;
Matt. 5:37

1. Who is our example in truthfulness?
2. Should we embellish the truth?

The words "Christians never lie" may not always be true of us, but they ought to be. When Christians lie they are not being true to their faith. If lies are still in us then we are still in the old life.

## Prayer

O God, You relentlessly pursue my soul. You have put your finger on an important issue. Help me not to dodge it. Make me a truthful person, in word and in deed. For Jesus' sake. Amen.

# The Designer's label

*"... and have put on the new self, which is being renewed
in knowledge in the image of its Creator" (v.10)*

**For reading & meditation – Colossians 3:10**

"You're done with the old life. It's like a filthy set of ill-fitting
clothes you've stripped off and put in the fire. Now you're
dressed in a new wardrobe. Every item of your new way of life is
custom-made by the Creator with his label on it" (*The Message*).
Having been made in God's image, we were not designed to live lives
of unrighteousness. We were built for truth, not dishonesty;
forgiveness, not lingering bitterness or anger; wholesome words,
not crude or malicious ones. I am astonished at the number of
Christians nowadays who when things go wrong think nothing of
using four-letter words.

A well-known British politician who professes to be a Christian
was the subject of a documentary which showed him being
confronted by a problem. His first reaction was to use a swear word.
The television crew reacted in amazement and the interviewer said:
"Did you notice the reaction of the crew? They were horrified that
you should use such language." His response was: "I may be a
Christian but I am not a saint."

Whether he saw himself as a saint or not, that
is what Paul said Christians are called to be: "To
all in Rome who are loved by God and called to be
saints" (Rom. 1:7) Anger, rage, malice, and filthy
language are ill-fitting clothes for those who are
truly Christ's. We have a new wardrobe with the
Designer's label stamped clearly on it. It's time we
ditched the old clothing and put on the clean
custom-made garments available to us through
Christ's redemptive work on the cross.

FURTHER STUDY

Isa. 64:6;
Rom. 12:2;
Eph. 4:22–23

1. How does Isaiah
describe human
righteousness?
2. What are the
characteristics of
the new self?

## Prayer

Father, forgive me if I prefer the old, ill-fitting garments to the custom-made,
designer-label apparel vouchsafed to me through Your Son's great sacrifice on
Calvary. Forgive me and change me. I give myself afresh to You for that purpose.
In Jesus' Name. Amen.

# The charter of equality

*"Here there is no Greek or Jew … but Christ is all,
and is in all." (v.11)*

**For reading & meditation – Colossians 3:11**

Paul, having spoken of the Christian's relationship to Christ (3:1–4) is at this point well into his portrayal of the relationship of Christ to His Church (3:9–17). The verse before us today is one of the most important in Scripture, depicting our life in Christ and our relationship to one another in the Church. In an age seeking equality of opportunity for all, this is *the* charter of equality. Nothing today can compare with it. Listen: "Here [in the new nature of those who form Christ's Church] there is no Greek or Jew [no racial distinction], circumcised and uncircumcised [no religious distinction], barbarian, Scythian [people known for their brutality], slave or free [no social, economic or cultural distinction]." Galatians 3:28 adds: "There is neither … male nor female [no sexual distinction]." The words "Here there is no Greek or Jew" could be translated: "Here there *cannot* be any Greek or Jew." That sweeps the field. There just cannot be any distinctions in Christ. If you hold to distinctions then you cannot be in Christ. You are governed by something else. The equality in Christ's Church is not artificial – it is real.

**FURTHER STUDY**

Matt. 20:1–16;
1 Cor. 12:4–6

*1. Is Jesus' story about justice or generosity?*
*2. What is the basis of the equality underlying our differences?*

Then notice also the phrase "Christ is all, and is in all." What it means is this: Christ is all that matters. If Christ becomes all in all to us we cannot remain the people we were. What is more, everyone else becomes all in all also. Why is the Church so slow in showing the world what a classless, raceless society is like? I am afraid there can only be one answer: Christ is not all in all.

## Prayer

O Father, You inspired Your servant Paul to sweep the decks of all artificiality and snobbery but we, Your people, have been so slow to accept this. Forgive us, dear Lord, and help us fulfil Your purposes. Amen.

# "Overalls or evening dress"

*"Therefore, as God's chosen people, holy and dearly loved, clothe yourselves with compassion ..." (v.12)*

**For reading & meditation – Colossians 3:12–14**

Paul here takes the characteristic descriptions of Israel and applies them to the Church: "God's chosen people, holy and dearly loved." He urges on the Colossian Christians the qualities that ancient Israel came to recognise in God's dealing with them: "compassion, kindness, humility, gentleness and patience". There is neither time nor space to identify the Old Testament texts relating to this, but they are there. God chose the people of Israel because He wanted them to be His "shop window", through which the Gentile nations could look in and see the blessings that come to those who serve the Lord.

Israel, as we know, failed miserably in this respect, but it is Paul's hope and prayer that the church at Colosse – part of the new Israel of God – would treat others as God in Christ treated them. How could this happen? First, by being considerate to each other – despite all provocation – and by forgiving each other. "Forgive as the Lord forgave you" (v.13). This is how the Lord acts towards you, Paul is saying, so it is only right that you follow suit.

Verse 14 is one of my most favourite texts: "And over all these virtues put on love, which binds them all together in perfect unity." "Love," it has been said, "is a colour that can be worn with anything – overalls or evening dress." Or think of it as a kind of a topcoat, if you like, an overgarment that covers all other virtues. It brings harmony to all disharmonies. Love is the garment the world sees. All other virtues are undergarments.

**FURTHER STUDY**

1 Pet. 2:12;
Luke 6:27–36

1. What is the reason for good "shop-window" standards?
2. Ask for God's help to love as Jesus taught us to.

## Prayer

Father, help me to remember that virtues can become vices when love is not present, and that love makes all other virtues blend in unity. And may I not just remember this but live by it. In Jesus' Name. Amen.

# Every church a haven?

*"Let the peace of Christ rule in your hearts ... And be thankful." (v.15)*

**For reading & meditation – Colossians 3:15**

Perhaps no other verse in the New Testament has been wrested from its context as much as this one has been. Some say it means: if you don't have a troubled spirit then it indicates that you are walking in the perfect will of God. But there are Christians whose consciences are so calloused that they are almost insensitive to the pleadings of the Spirit.

Others use the verse to teach that when you wish to know the will of God, the options that gives you the most peace is the one you should choose. There is some sense in that, but that is not what the text is indicating. Paul is telling us here that when we are under the rule of Christ the inevitable result is that we experience peace in our relationships. Listen to these words again: "... since as *members of one body* you were called to peace". Every Christian congregation ought to be a haven of peace. It is sad that many are not. I heard one preacher say, when likening the Church to Noah's Ark, that "If it wasn't for the storm on the outside we wouldn't be able to stand the strain on the inside".

**FURTHER STUDY**

1 Cor. 1:10;
Matt. 18:19–20

1. What is Paul's reason for appealing for agreement?
2. Who is present when believers meet together?

Isn't it a bit unrealistic, though, to expect Christians with different views, different backgrounds and different temperaments to live harmoniously with one another? Some might think so. But Paul wouldn't share that view. When Christ rules in the hearts of believers then peace will rule in that community of believers. Nothing could be simpler yet nothing, it seems, is more difficult.

## Prayer

Gracious Father, our life strategy is all wrong and thus things don't work out right. We become tangled up because we do not take Your way. Help us see that for peace to rule we must come under Your rule. Amen.

# Gratitude for grace

*"Let the word of Christ dwell in you richly as you
teach and admonish one another ..." (v.16)*

**For reading & meditation – Colossians 3:16**

It is interesting to examine many of the 3:16s of the New
Testament. Doubtless you are familiar with John 3:16, but 1 John
3:16 is not a verse that Christians like to memorise. The verse before
us today is one of the New Testament's most beautiful 3:16s. We are
instructed to let the Word of Christ dwell in us richly. The word
"dwell" here (*enoikeo*) has the meaning of permanent residence, of
being at home. Eugene Peterson paraphrases it: "Let the word of
Christ have the run of the house." Give it plenty of room in your
lives.

How wonderful it is when Christians allow the Word of God to
be at home in their hearts, when they draw their spiritual
sustenance from the Word of God and not from other things,
however exciting. This is not to say that we cannot enjoy spiritual
experiences, but we are not to let them divert us from attention to
the Word. The Word of God must control all the ministries of the
local church. It is to dwell in us richly as we teach, admonish,
counsel, and so on.

It is the Word of God, also, that must guide us
as we sing. Some like to differentiate between
psalms, hymns and spiritual songs, and they may
be right. However, what Paul has in mind here is
not so much the different types of praise and
worship, but the content. All the songs we sing in
church should be consistent with the Word of
God – that's his point. A gospel of good news
must be echoed by songs of gratitude – gratitude
for grace.

FURTHER STUDY
Luke 1:46–55,
68–79;
1 Cor. 14:15

1. What reasons
underlie the songs in
Luke?
2. What does Paul
teach about balance
in worship?

## Prayer

O God, save us from being so carried away by the melody of what we sing that
we overlook its meaning and content. You have saved us by grace; help us reflect
that in the worship we offer to You. Amen.

# "The Jesus Christ man"

*"And whatever you do, whether in word or deed, do it all in the name of the Lord Jesus ..."* (v.17)

**For reading & meditation – Colossians 3:17**

Paul stresses that we must do everything in the Name of the Lord Jesus. He has emphasised the receptive side of being in Christ, but that must work itself out in activity. We are to do as well as receive and be. Being can only be manifested by doing, and the doing has a definite characteristic: you do everything in the Name of the Lord Jesus. You are to do everything as representing Him, you are to do it in His Name, in His stead, and in His Spirit.

Dr E. Stanley Jones told of riding his bicycle along a country road in India and hearing a young boy who was a cowherd call out to another: "The Jesus Christ man is going along." He said that when he heard those words he felt like getting off his bicycle and dropping to his knees in prayer that he might not be unfaithful to the village boys' estimation of him – as a "Jesus Christ man".

We are all to be Jesus Christ people – to do everything in His Name. It has been said: "We are the only Bible some people will read." This does not mean we live out our lives in fear that we might say or do something that misrepresents Him. We are to be controlled by a spirit of thankfulness: "… giving thanks to God the Father through him". Those who go about with an attitude of thanksgiving to God for all His benefits soon come to appreciate what He does. The more we focus on how good God is, the more we are set free from fear.

FURTHER STUDY

2 Tim. 2:19;
Eph. 5:20

1. What must confessors of the Name do?
2. What must we always do in the Name?

## Prayer

Dear Father, I want to represent You today just as Christ represented You. Grant that my words and my deeds shall be the clear instruments of Your glory. When I speak may it be You speaking. In Jesus' Name. Amen.

# A word to wives

*"Wives, submit to your husbands, as is fitting
in the Lord." (v.18)*

**For reading & meditation – Colossians 3:18**

Paul now takes up the theme of the Christian's relationship to the
family. He has a word for each member of the family: for wives it
is *submit*, for husbands it is *love* and *understand*, for children it is *obey*.
Many Christians, conditioned by a secular society, approach these
words of Paul somewhat warily and see them as belonging more to
the culture of the first-century Christians than to the contemporary
Christian Church. Let's understand what Paul is teaching here
before we attempt to apply it to the present day.

First, he addresses wives, exhorting them to submit to their
husbands. What does it mean for a Christian wife to submit? Is it
doing everything her husband demands of her? I do not believe so.
What if a husband asks his wife to engage with him in some sinful
practice? Is she to obey? Of course not. Submission is a *disposition* to
defer in everything that is right. It is not to be seen as servility. A
woman who practises biblical submission will have a strong positive
desire to support her husband as he fulfils his role in the family.
Some reject Paul's teaching here on the ground that it contradicts
what he says in Galatians 3:28 where the equality
of male and female is celebrated. Equality and
submission (they say) cannot co-exist in a
relationship. But they can. Christ is equal with
God but yet is in submission to Him.

Before a woman can submit to her husband
she must first be submitted to God. Without
submission to God submission to one's husband
does not constitute a spiritual exercise.

FURTHER STUDY

Titus 2:3–5;
1 Pet. 3:1–4

1. What reason
underlies Paul's
practical words to
wives?
2. What can a wife's
submission achieve?

## Prayer

O God, we live in a day when culture shouts at us in ways that contradict the
teaching of Your Word. Help us in the clash between Christ and culture to take
Your way. For Jesus' sake. Amen.

# Love is ...

*"Husbands, love your wives and do not be harsh with them." (v.19)*

**For reading & meditation – Colossians 3:19**

A well-known Christian feminist says: "Many husbands don't deserve a wife who shows a submissive spirit; they mistake it for weakness and exploit it to their advantage." Well, Paul has a word for such husbands: "Love your wives and do not be harsh with them." It's interesting that here Paul is *commanding* love as if he knows that one of the easiest things in the world is for a husband to say to his wife, "I love you," but then fail to demonstrate that love in a practical way. A woman told me once: "My husband's parting words to me when he goes off to work are, 'I love you,' but then I go to the bathroom, find his shaving kit all over the place, the bathroom sink filthy, and towels strewn all over the floor. If he really loved me then he would clean up after himself." I agree. Love is not just something you say, love is something you do.

And here's a further test of love. "Do not be harsh with them." J.B. Phillips has here: "Husbands, be sure you give your wives much love and sympathy; don't let bitterness or resentment spoil your marriage." Men, generally speaking, are much more prone to bitterness and resentment than women. Take this scenario: a woman fails to come up to her husband's expectations of her as a submissive wife, so he turns on her harshly and says: "The Word of God says you must submit." In that action he has violated the law of love. It's not his wife's problem he needs to be concerned about, but his own.

**FURTHER STUDY**

Eph. 5:25–28;
1 Pet. 3:7

1. How should husbands love their wives?
2. Why should husbands treat their wives with respect?

## Prayer

O God, strengthen my spirit as I follow a way of life that is governed by Your Word and not by the moods and whims of culture. May I embrace Your way whether others live by it or not. In Jesus' Name. Amen.

# How to serve the Lord

*"Children, obey your parents in everything, for this pleases the Lord." (v.20)*

**For reading & meditation – Colossians 3:20**

Many commentators on Colossians have expressed the wish that Paul would have dealt more deeply with the subject of relationships in the home. Paul, however, is stating basic principles. Now he comes to talk to the children – who have reached the age of understanding – and tells them that they too must come under the rule of Christ.

Once a family with a son aged twelve came to me. Although the boy had committed himself to Jesus Christ he was being somewhat rebellious towards his parents. He obviously loved the Lord, and as we talked about his Christian faith and what he wanted to do with his life, he told me that he would like to serve Christ in the field of Christian journalism. I asked him if he would be interested in knowing how he could express his desire to serve the Lord Jesus *at the present moment* – and he nodded his head vigorously. I read him our text for today in J.B. Phillips' translation: "As for you children, your duty is to obey your parents, for at your age this is one of the best things you can do to show your love for the Lord." He got the point. We prayed together and his parents told me later that the transformation in him was remarkable. He is now working for the Lord in a distant country, not as a journalist but as a preacher of the gospel.

Disobedience to parents is one of the frightening features of this present age. I see little hope for the families of the future unless they come under the rule of Christ.

**FURTHER STUDY**

Eph. 6:1–3;
Matt. 18:2–6, 10

1. Why does Paul say: "Children, obey your parents"?
2. Do you value children as Jesus did?

## Prayer

Father, forgive us that we ask for light and guidance in running our families and yet sometimes balk at the directions You give us. Help us see that we either heed the helm or heed the rocks. In Jesus' Name. Amen.

# Problem fathers?

*"Fathers, do not embitter your children, or they will become discouraged." (v.21)*

**For reading & meditation – Colossians 3:21**

There are two sides to every relationship, and in the text before us now Paul, as always, shows that not all the rights are on one side and all the duties on the other. Fathers too have a responsibility to their children – not to "over-correct [them], or they will grow up feeling inferior and frustrated" (J.B. Phillips).

Why aren't mothers included in this instruction? It is my conviction, based on years of experience in counselling, that generally fathers tend to be harsher with their children than mothers. A Christian psychiatrist says: "Behind most problem children you will find a problem father." He was speaking hyperbolically, of course, for we all know children with the most loving parents who have come from the most wonderful homes and yet have turned out delinquent. I think, however, that statistics will support the statement that fathers tend to come down more heavily on their children than mothers.

Hear what Paul says once again: "Fathers, do not embitter your children, or they will become discouraged." Coming down hard on children crushes their sensitive spirits. It is no good a father lamenting the fact that his child is not as strong and self-reliant as he himself is if he uses his strength to squash and undermine the child's fragile ego rather than develop it. Endless criticism, harsh punishments, unrealistic expectations, will have their effect in the long run. Many a child who is timid, fearful and plagued with deep feelings of inferiority and guilt has got that way not so much by nature as by nurture. Christ's rule applies as much to fathers as to anyone.

**FURTHER STUDY**

Num. 14:18;
Ezek. 18:2;
Luke 15:11–32

1. If you are a parent, be aware of your extended responsibilities.
2. How did Jesus think parents should treat problem children?

## Prayer

O Father, our slowness in heeding the principles of Your Word is written in the devastation, frustration and breakdown of our family life. Give us another chance and help us to learn the ways of Your Word. In Jesus' Name. Amen.

# Free – on the inside

*"Slaves, obey your earthly masters in everything … with sincerity of heart and reverence for the Lord." (v.22)*

**For reading & meditation – Colossians 3:22–24**

Paul now discusses a Christian's relationship to work. Paul's instruction to slaves to obey their masters has recently brought him much criticism. For example: "I cannot help feel a tinge of disappointment that Paul did not use his influence to call for social change as it related to the distressing subject of slavery." And: "His instruction that slaves obey their masters puts them on the level of childhood for ever."

In the early days of my Christian life I tended to view Paul's instructions here as helping to fasten the yoke of bondage more firmly than ever on those who were bound in servility. However, I soon came to see that Paul was writing, not to leaders of society, but to the Church. If Paul had told slaves to revolt it would have hindered the gospel rather than helped it. The truths he presented in his letters did eventually lead to the abolition of slavery, albeit many centuries later. Being unable to deal with the situation horizontally, Paul focuses on dealing with it vertically. He exhorts those who find themselves in slavery to concentrate on the fact that they are working for the Lord and not for men. This change of perspective, Paul believed, would enable them to find inner freedom. Pagan slaves might obey out of fear of their master, but the Christian slave is to obey for a different reason: to do it out of reverence for the Lord. Paul was unable to set the slaves of his day free on the outside, but he certainly showed them how to be free on the inside.

**FURTHER STUDY**

John 8:31–32, 36;
Eph. 6:5–8;
Titus 2:9–10

1. What is the secret of inner freedom?
2. What 2 reasons underlie Paul's advice to slaves/employees?

## Prayer

Father, help me learn the lesson that even when I cannot change the outer climate, I can change the inner climate. I am so thankful. Amen.

# A heated talking point

*"Masters, provide your slaves with what is right and fair, because ... you also have a Master in heaven." (4:1)*

**For reading & meditation – Colossians 3:25–4:1**

It is difficult to read the last verse of chapter 3 without feeling that Paul had in mind not only Christian slaves but their Christian masters also. Once again (4:1) Paul presents the other side of an issue. Who was the greater wrongdoer, the slave who held back part of his efforts, or the master who held back a proper reward and consideration because it was not in keeping with the culture? It must have been a new thought for slave masters that they should show consideration towards slaves, and I can imagine it becoming a heated talking point in the slave markets. Did you notice how often the word "Lord" (or "Master") is mentioned in the verses to do with slavery? Five times. "Lift up your eyes and see the Lord as your Master," he says to the slaves. And to the slave masters he says the same: "Don't forget for a minute that you too serve a Master – God in heaven" (Eugene Peterson, *The Message*). Just as Christ showed fairness in the way He dealt with the slave masters, so they in turn are to show fairness in the way they deal with their slaves.

Now that we have surveyed Paul's teaching on the subject of slavery (albeit briefly), do you agree that Paul was doing the right thing in deciding not to call for the abolition of slavery? He laid down, nevertheless, some basic principles which eventually led men such as William Wilberforce to crusade to set men, women and children free. The weapons Paul forged hundreds of years ago helped bring that victory.

**FURTHER STUDY**

John 13:13–17;
Philemon 1–25

1. What follows on from calling Jesus "Lord"?
2. What does Philemon teach about subordinate/superior relationships?

## Prayer

Father, I see that to have mastery in life I must bow my knee to the Master. Your ways, and Your ways alone, are the ways of mastery. Help me follow them in all of life's difficult situations. In Jesus' Name. Amen.

# First talk to God

*"Devote yourselves to prayer, being watchful and
thankful." (v.2)*

**For reading & meditation – Colossians 4:2–4**

Paul now focuses on the Christian's relationship to outsiders –
those not part of the family of God. These verses might seem at
first glance to contain a random list of admonitions, but really they
are tightly constructed to show us how to relate to those we know
who are outside Christ.

He begins by pointing out that before we talk to others about
God we ought to talk to God about others. Evangelism is best
undertaken in a spirit of prayer – by praying for people before
talking to people. Paul asks for the prayers of the Colossian
Christians that, even though he is in prison, God will grant him
many opportunities to preach the gospel. "Pray that every time I
open my mouth," he says, "I'll be able to make Christ plain as day to
them" (Eugene Peterson, *The Message*). There is a God-dependence
here that is touching. Paul does not rely on his gift of apostleship, or
his previous experience of planting new churches; he knows that
without prayer his efforts will bear little fruit.

I am sometimes astonished by training courses on evangelism,
noticing how little emphasis is placed on the need
for personal, powerful intercessory prayer.
Evangelistic techniques, methods, systems and
procedures all have their place. However, they are
but the ashes upon a rusty altar if they do not
come out of a heart that is given to prayer. Notice
that when Paul talks about prayer he also adds
this: "being watchful and thankful". Prayer needs
to be coupled with praise, just as praise needs to
be coupled with prayer. The one fuels the other.

**FURTHER STUDY**

Acts 13:1–5;
Phil. 1:3–4

*1. What 3 things
preceded evangelism
in Cyprus?
2. What did Paul
always combine with
his prayers?*

## Prayer

Father, drive this truth deep within my spirit – that before I talk to people about
You, I must talk to You about people. Help me be more than just a hearer in
this issue; help me be a doer. In Jesus' Name. Amen.

# "The right to say 'No'"

*"Be wise in the way you act towards outsiders ..."*
*(v.5)*

**For reading & meditation – Colossians 4:5–6**

Eugene Peterson's rugged paraphrase of these verses is: "Use your head as you live and work among outsiders. Don't miss a trick. Make the most of every opportunity. Be gracious in your speech. The goal is to bring out the best in others in a conversation, not to put them down, not cut them out."

Many are not wise in the way they share their faith. They are insensitive and intrusive. A dear old Christian wrote in the flyleaf of my Bible: "To win some be winsome." When Paul talks about our conversations being "always full of grace, seasoned with salt, so that you may know how to answer everyone" he is not thinking of memorising systematically prepared theological arguments so that we can give biblical answers to questions that may be asked of us. No, he is thinking not so much about *what* we say but *how* we say it.

How many times have you been closeted with a salesman who by his slick sales techniques has intimidated you and you have bought something just to get rid of him? Evangelism should never be a "hard sell". We should take advantage of every opportunity to share Christ, even offer Him, but we must always respect the right of the person to whom we are witnessing to say "No". There was an occasion when Jesus talked to a rich ruler who turned away from His words (Luke 18:18–25). Did Jesus run after him, and try to press him into making a decision? No, He let him go because He respected his right to say "No".

**FURTHER STUDY**

Acts 17:22–31;
1 Pet. 3:15–16

1. How did Paul practise what he preached?
2. Take Peter's preaching to heart, especially his first 9 words!

## Prayer

Father, forgive me if I put people off by insensitivity and aggressiveness. You respect my right to say "No"; help me respect that right in others. In Jesus' Name. Amen.

# Paul – a people-person

*"Tychicus … a dear brother, a faithful minister and
fellow-servant in the Lord." (v.7)*

**For reading & meditation – Colossians 4:7–9**

Paul was a true people-person. He did not just remember names;
he cared deeply for those whom he counted as his friends. Paul
was greatly loved because he loved greatly. This final section of his
epistle is rich in personal messages and greetings. Paul wants his
friends to realise something of his tremendous concern for them.

He begins with Onesimus and Tychicus. Onesimus was a
runaway slave who had almost certainly robbed his master, then
escaped, met Paul and accepted Christ. He is the subject of the letter
to Philemon in which Paul urges the slave-owner to welcome
Onesimus back as a brother in the Lord because he had been so
helpful to the apostle.

Tychicus was a companion of Paul, representing him on a
number of different occasions. He is described as "a dear brother, a
faithful minister and fellow-servant in the Lord". Most significantly,
Tychicus was "a faithful minister". He had a call and was faithful to
that call and that gave him drive and direction. But he did not allow
this single-mindedness to prevent him being a dear brother and a
fellow servant. Some Christian workers are
faithful servants but not very "dear", and not
good "fellow servants" either. This is particularly
true of the strong, devoted, driven types. They are
extremely busy and absorbed in fulfilling their
mission, but no one would ever refer to them as
"dear". And they are so taken up with their own
ministry that they cannot work with others.
Tychicus was a well-rounded person, faithful in
his ministry, a dear brother and a fellow worker.

FURTHER STUDY
Phil. 4:4–8;
Luke 22:39–44

1. To be "well-
rounded", check
yourself against
Paul's prescription.
2. What might
submerging your will
cost you?

## Prayer

Father, I too would be a well-rounded person. Help me submerge my will and
affection in a larger Will and Affection, for it is only then that I can expect to
attain wholeness and roundedness. In Jesus' Name. Amen.

# More names on the list

*"Epaphras ... is always wrestling in prayer for you ..."*
*(v.12)*

**For reading & meditation – Colossians 4:10–13**

Paul adds four more names to his greetings list: Aristarchus, Mark, Justus and Epaphras. Aristarchus was a Macedonian who accompanied Paul on some of his missionary travels and was seized during the riot in Ephesus (Acts 19:29). Paul refers to him here as "my fellow-prisoner", so obviously Aristarchus was with Paul in prison, possibly voluntarily.

Paul and Barnabas had a violent quarrel over Mark, and the apostle appeared to have little confidence in the young man who seemed so ready to run at the first hint of trouble (see Acts 15:36–40). Now, about twelve years later, the wound has been healed and Mark is clearly one of Paul's fellow workers. Elsewhere he is described by Paul as "helpful to me in my ministry" (2 Tim. 4:11). There is no other record of Justus.

We met Epaphras earlier. Paul now adds one more quality to the list: "He is always wrestling in prayer for you." The foundations of this man's character were set deep in the soil of prayer. The phrase "wrestling in prayer" suggests that his prayers were largely intercessory. What an insight Paul must have gained into the character of Epaphras during their time together in Rome as he listened to him pray for the church back at Colosse. There is no doubt in my mind that the secret of Epaphras's spiritual success lay in his prayer life. He was great in soul because he prayed much and because he prayed with the unselfishness which marked all he did. Earnest and persistent prayer was the secret of his sanctity. That secret is available to us all.

**FURTHER STUDY**

Gen. 32:24–28;
1 Thess. 1:2–3

1. What do the Genesis verses teach about real intercession?
2. What 3 graces does Paul link with much praying?

## Prayer

Father, I always need a prod to pray. Forgive me if I do not commune regularly with You. Prayer moments are the only real moments. Help me to see prayer as not just a luxury, but a necessity. In Jesus' Name. Amen.

# Final greetings

*"After this letter has been read to you, see that it is also read in the church of the Laodiceans ..." (v.16)*

**For reading & meditation – Colossians 4:14–16**

Paul ends his greetings with the names of Luke and Demas. Luke often accompanied Paul on his travels and was with him in Rome during his imprisonment. Demas was also a companion of Paul but sadly later deserted him because of his love for this world.

Paul then gives more general greetings – to the brothers at Laodicea, and to Nympha and the church in her house. For the most part the early Church met in homes (see Rom. 16:5; 1 Cor. 16:19; Philemon 2 and Acts 12:12).

Paul asks that his letter be read in the Laodicean church as well, and the Colossians in turn were to read the letter from Laodicea. Obviously Paul also wanted the Laodicean believers to be aware of possible threats to their faith. This exchange of letters shows the importance of reading all we can. The more of Scripture we absorb the stronger our defences against false teaching will be.

The reference to the letter from Laodicea, however, is somewhat puzzling. Perhaps the Laodiceans were to lend the Colossians a letter that Paul had originally written to them. Not all Paul's letters were included in the canon of Scripture. Many think the letter referred to here was Paul's letter to the Ephesians, which was making its rounds as a circular. In the early Church, letters were read aloud to the assembled congregation. Imagine, therefore, what a thrill it must have been for those Christians to receive a letter from the apostle Paul. Little did they realise that what they were reading then would be read by the whole world close on two thousand years later.

| FURTHER STUDY |
| --- |
| Luke 9:62; John 6:66–69 |
| 1. If you are tempted to go with Demas, ponder the words in Luke. |
| 2. In any case, think hard about Peter's words in John. |

## Prayer

Father, may I be diligent in my reading of Scripture. I am living in days when there are just as many threats to my faith as in the days of the Colossians. Help me learn all I can so that I may be the best I can be. Amen.

# Say "No" to the marginal

*"Tell Archippus: 'See to it that you complete the work you have received in the Lord.'"* (v.17)

**For reading & meditation – Colossians 4:17**

There is a slight suggestion here that Archippus did not find it easy to follow through on things. Paul describes him as a "fellow-soldier" in Philemon 2, but here he seems to draw attention to a matter that Archippus needed to work on. J.B. Phillips translated the verse this way: "God ordained you to your work – see that you don't fail him."

I wonder, was Archippus the kind of man who allowed himself to be so absorbed in the marginal that he had little drive left for the central issues of his life? I have met many servants of Christ like that. They have been called to minister to people – to lead them to Christ, develop them, and help them on to maturity – yet have ended up doing everything but that. Paul said on one occasion, you remember, "But one thing I do" (Phil. 3:13), not "These forty things I dabble in." Those who focus on what they are supposed to be doing leave a mark; those who don't leave a blur.

The temptation to do the easier things and not to follow through on issues plagues us all. Paul's words – "See to it that you complete the work you have received in the Lord"

**FURTHER STUDY**

Luke 14:28–30;
10:38–42

1. What is the effect of leaving things unfinished?
2. What is the reward for saying "No" to the marginal?

– strike home to every one of us I am sure. Notice the words: *you have received in the Lord.* Everybody *in the Lord* is in service for the Lord. It means being involved in the Lord's plans for us. Let no unimportant weeds choke the fine wheat of the kingdom. Say "No" to the marginal so that you can say "Yes" to the central.

## Prayer

Lord Jesus Christ, You fulfilled Your Father's purposes in everything that You had to do. Help me, too, fulfil the ministry You have chosen for me. Amen.

# Closing words

*"I, Paul, write this greeting in my own hand.
Remember my chains. Grace be with you." (v.18)*

**For reading & meditation – Colossians 4:18**

These are Paul's last words to the Christians at Colosse. It was his custom to dictate his letters and then pen a few greetings in his own hand at the end. His signature was the guarantee that the letter had come from him.

Paul's closing words are as rich and as beautiful as any of the others in this highly personal letter: "Remember my chains. Grace be with you." This was a plea to the Colossians to remember him as he remained incarcerated in prison. His chains have gone, his words have not. They come to our hearts with as much force as they did to those to whom they were directly addressed.

I wonder what we would say if we found ourselves in a similar position – locked up in a jail because of our passion for the gospel. Probably this: "I am in chains. Ask God to give me grace." But listen again to Paul's words: "I am in chains. Grace be with you." I believe one of the greatest evidences of spiritual maturity is the desire, when under deep personal pressure or pain, to reach out and give to others. Paul was such a man. In the midst of overwhelming difficulties his final thought is for others.

So ends an important letter, one in which he has encouraged us to see Christ as all-sufficient and all-supreme – "all" and "in all" (3:11). As we end our time reflecting on the words of the great apostle Paul let me ask this highly personal question: We are all in all to Christ. But is He all in all to us?

**FURTHER STUDY**

John 19:25–27;
20:28

1. Meditate on Jesus' thought for others, even in utmost agony.
2. If Christ is all in all to you make Thomas' words your own today.

## Prayer

O Father, I offer myself to You again today and pray that just as Your Son is the centre of all things in Your universe so may He be the centre of all things in my universe. In Christ's precious Name I pray. Amen.

# Index

**EVERY DAY WITH JESUS – ONE YEAR DEVOTIONAL**
Bread for the Journey

Published 2002 by CWR, Waverley Abbey House, Waverley Lane, Farnham, Surrey, GU9 8EP, UK. Registered Charity No. 294387. Registered limited company No. 1990308. Reprinted 2005 and 2007.

Features previously published editions of *Every Day with Jesus* as follows: The More Excellent Way, 1988, The Wondrous Cross, 1996, The Treasures of Darkness, 1990, The Pursuit of Excellence, 1996, The Care of the Soul, 1997, The All-Sufficient Christ, 1998.

Revised edition in this format 2002 © CWR

Further Study sections compiled by Trevor J. Partridge except The All-Sufficient Christ compiled by David Gurney

Unless otherwise indicated, all Scripture references are from the Holy Bible, *New International Version* (NIV) Copyright © 1973, 1978, 1984 by the International Bible Society.

Concept development, editing, design and production by CWR

Typesetting by Start

Cover photograph by Pictor

Printed in Finland by WS Bookwell

ISBN-13: 978-1-85345-224-6
ISBN-10: 1-85345-224-6

# National Distributors

**UK: (and countries not listed below)**
CWR, Waverley Abbey House, Waverley Lane, Farnham, Surrey GU9 8EP.
Tel: (01252) 784700  Outside UK (+44) 1252 784700

**AUSTRALIA:** CMC Australasia, PO Box 519, Belmont, Victoria 3216.
Tel: (03) 5241 3288  Fax: (03) 5241 3290

**CANADA:** Cook Communications Ministries, PO Box 98, 55 Woodslee Avenue, Paris, Ontario N3L 3E5.
Tel: 1800 263 2664

**GHANA:** Challenge Enterprises of Ghana, PO Box 5723, Accra.
Tel: (021) 222437/223249  Fax: (021) 226227

**HONG KONG:** Cross Communications Ltd, 1/F, 562A Nathan Road, Kowloon.
Tel: 2780 1188  Fax: 2770 6229

**INDIA:** Crystal Communications, 10-3-18/4/1, East Marredpalli, Secunderabad – 500026,
Andhra Pradesh.
Tel/Fax: (040) 27737145

**KENYA:** Keswick Books and Gifts Ltd, PO Box 10242, Nairobi.
Tel: (02) 331692/226047  Fax: (02) 728557

**MALAYSIA:** Salvation Book Centre (M) Sdn Bhd, 23 Jalan SS 2/64, 47300 Petaling Jaya, Selangor.
Tel: (03) 78766411/78766797  Fax: (03) 78757066/78756360

**NEW ZEALAND:** CMC Australasia, PO Box 303298, North Harbour, Auckland 0751.
Tel: 0800 449 408  Fax: 0800 449 049

**NIGERIA:** FBFM, Helen Baugh House, 96 St Finbarr's College Road, Akoka, Lagos.
Tel: (01) 7747429/4700218/825775/827264

**PHILIPPINES:** OMF Literature Inc, 776 Boni Avenue, Mandaluyong City.
Tel: (02) 531 2183  Fax: (02) 531 1960

**SOUTH AFRICA:** Struik Christian Books, 80 MacKenzie Street, PO Box 1144, Cape Town 8000.
Tel: (021) 462 4360  Fax: (021) 461 3612

**SRI LANKA:** Christombu Publications (Pvt) Ltd., Bartleet House, 65 Braybrooke Place,
Colombo 2. Tel: (9411) 2421073/2447665

**TANZANIA:** CLC Christian Book Centre, PO Box 1384, Mkwepu Street, Dar es Salaam.
Tel/Fax: (022) 2119439

**USA:** Cook Communications Ministries, PO Box 98, 55 Woodslee Avenue, Paris, Ontario N3L 3E5,
Canada. Tel: 1800 263 2664

**ZIMBABWE:** Word of Life Books (Pvt) Ltd, Christian Media Centre, 8 Aberdeen Road, Avondale,
PO Box A480 Avondale, Harare.
Tel: (04) 333355 or 091301188

**For email addresses, visit the CWR website: www.cwr.org.uk**

**CWR is a registered charity – Number 294387**

**CWR is a limited company registered in England – Registration Number 1990308**

# Every Day with Jesus

With nearly a million readers an issue worldwide, this bestselling daily Bible reading tool offers practical help with life's challenges and insight into the deeper truths of Scripture. It is designed to challenge, inspire, comfort and encourage readers in their spiritual walk as they study six topics in depth each year.

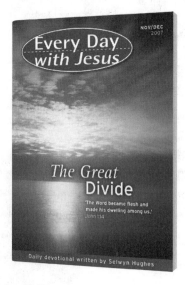

Price: £2.25 each

**UK Annual Subscription:** £12.50 (for six issues)

Also available in large print format and by daily email

**Email Subscription:** £12.50 per year

## Walking in His Ways

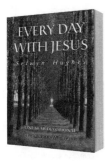

Changing Times – Unchanging Truth, God's Last Word, The Surprises of God, Bringing the Bible to Life, The Peak of the Epistles, The Grand Design – Meditations on the Book of Revelation

ISBN: 978-1-85345-314-4
Price: £6.99

## Treasure for the Heart

The Songs of Ascent, The Divine Eagle, The Lord's Prayer, The Armour of God, Hinds' Feet on High Places, Your Father and My Father

ISBN: 978-1-85345-151-5
Price: £6.99

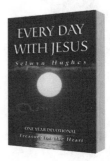